RELIGIOUS RADICALIZATION AND SECURITIZATION IN CANADA AND BEYOND

After the terrorist attacks of 9/11, attacks in London and Madrid, and the arrest of the "Toronto 18," Canadians have changed how they think about terrorism and security. As governments respond to the potential threat of home-grown radicalism, many observers have become concerned about the impact of those security measures on the minority groups whose lives are "securitized."

In *Religious Radicalization and Securitization in Canada and Beyond*, Paul Bramadat and Lorne Dawson bring together contributors from a wide range of academic disciplines to examine the challenges created by both religious radicalism and the state's and society's response to it. This collection takes a critical look at what is known about religious radicalization, how minorities are affected by radicalization from within and securitization from without, and how the public, media, and government are attempting to cope with the dangers of both radicalization and securitization.

This collection is an ideal guide to the ongoing debates on how best to respond to radicalization without sacrificing the commitments to multiculturalism and social justice that many Canadians hold dear.

PAUL BRAMADAT is the Director of the Centre for Studies in Religion and Society and an associate professor in the Department of History and the Religious Studies Program at the University of Victoria.

LORNE DAWSON is a professor and Chair of the Department of Sociology and Legal Studies at the University of Waterloo.

Religious Radicalization and Securitization in Canada and Beyond

EDITED BY PAUL BRAMADAT
AND LORNE DAWSON

UNIVERSITY OF TORONTO PRESS
Toronto Buffalo London

© University of Toronto Press 2014
Toronto Buffalo London
www.utppublishing.com
Printed in the U.S.A.

Reprinted 2016

ISBN 978-1-4426-4631-5 (cloth)
ISBN 978-1-4426-1436-9 (paper)

Printed on acid-free, 100% post-consumer recycled paper.

Library and Archives Canada Cataloguing in Publication

Religious radicalization and securitization in Canada and beyond / edited by
Paul Bramadat and Lorne Dawson.

Includes bibliographical references and index.
ISBN 978-1-4426-4631-5 (bound). – ISBN 978-1-4426-1436-9 (pbk.)

1. Religion and politics – Canada. 2. Religion and sociology – Canada.
3. Internal security – Canada. 4. Canada – Religion. 5. Religion and politics.
6. Religion and sociology. 7. Internal security I. Bramadat, Paul, 1967–,
editor II. Dawson, Lorne L., editor

BL65.P7R445 2014   322'.10971   C2014-902345-6

University of Toronto Press acknowledges the financial assistance to its
publishing program of the Canada Council for the Arts and the Ontario Arts
Council, an agency of the Government of Ontario.

Canada Council   Conseil des Arts
for the Arts   du Canada

ONTARIO ARTS COUNCIL
CONSEIL DES ARTS DE L'ONTARIO
an Ontario government agency
un organisme du gouvernement de l'Ontario

University of Toronto Press acknowledges the financial support of the
Government of Canada through the Canada Book Fund for its publishing
activities.

This book is dedicated to the academics and government policymakers working to keep Canada safe from the threat of terrorism without sacrificing the religious and cultural diversity, freedom, and mutual respect that distinguish Canadian society.

Contents

Securitization and Canadian Ethno-religious Minorities

Public Discourse and Religious Radicalization

Figures and Tables

Figures

Tables

Acknowledgments

This book is the fruition of a unique collaboration between scholars and policy analysts from a wide range of disciplines. Anthropologists, political scientists, sociologists, and scholars trained in religious studies, Islamic studies, and cultural studies engaged in a two-year-long conversation about the complex relationship between religion, radicalization, and securitization. The full research team met in Victoria twice. We met first to discuss our overarching questions and concerns, the kinds of contributions we each might make to the debates raging within and outside of the academy about religion and radicalization. Then, a year later we met again to discuss and critique the chapters we had all written in the intervening months. Before, during, and after these meetings, many of us met at conferences and workshops, as well as socially.

It is extremely challenging to manage a project with colleagues from diverse disciplinary backgrounds, provinces, countries, and political and intellectual schools of thought and with varied writing styles. The fact that the process worked so well is a testament to both the soundness of the research model (pioneered by the Centre for Studies in Religion and Society for the past two decades) and the collegiality of all of the project members and supporters.

We would like to thank, first, Public Safety Canada and Defence Research and Development Canada (DRDC) for their generous support. Brett Kubicek at Public Safety and Ahmad Korchid at DRDC were indefatigable advocates of our free-ranging research process and offered brilliant and balanced insights that greatly enriched the conversations we had over the last two years.

Second, Leslie Kenny and Rina Langford-Kimmett at the Centre for Studies in Religion and Society at the University of Victoria expertly organized our face-to-face meetings in Victoria and ensured that the co-editors and authors stayed on schedule and in communication throughout the writing and revising processes.

Third, Doug Hildebrand at the University of Toronto Press saw the value of both this book's topic and the interdisciplinary approach we adopted and was an enthusiastic and much appreciated supporter throughout the peer review process.

Fourth, our families – Karen Palmer, Max Bramadat, and Pauline Dawson – encouraged us throughout the project and served as sounding boards for some of the ideas we present here.

Finally, the book's authors agreed to participate in a somewhat atypical writing process in which we not only each offered a critical evaluation of all chapters but also cultivated a conversation among ourselves within the pages of the book so that it reads not like a series of disconnected essays but rather as an account of a healthy and vigorous intellectual exchange among experts.

It is no small feat that as we reach the end of this project, we can say that we have answered some questions, clarified some issues that remain unresolved, and, above all, enhanced the community of colleagues within the academy and government interested in addressing the complex intersection of religion, radicalization, and securitization in Canada and beyond. More work remains to be done – of course – but our hope is that this book contributes something to the broader conversations that have just begun.

Paul Bramadat
Centre for Studies in Religion and Society,
University of Victoria
Victoria, British Columbia

Lorne Dawson
Sociology and Legal Studies,
University of Waterloo
Waterloo, Ontario

22 July 2013

RELIGIOUS RADICALIZATION AND SECURITIZATION IN CANADA AND BEYOND

1 The Public, the Political, and the Possible: Religion and Radicalization in Canada and Beyond

PAUL BRAMADAT

For over a century before the events of 11 September 2001, scholars worked to elucidate the subtle ways religion should be factored into any comprehensive analysis of social change. By now, the wisdom of this foundational research seems quite clear when the changes in question are obviously related to religion (as in the rise of the Christian right in American politics). However, the centrality of religious ideas and institutions is also increasingly evident when the domain in question appears to be entirely "secular" (as in changes in immigration policies and municipal zoning restrictions). Nonetheless, I suspect it is usually the case that inasmuch as most scholars and laypeople concern themselves with religion in the public arena at all, they are usually worried about the way a particular religion might threaten public safety and political order. Those who are less concerned about threats posed by specific religions are likely to be concerned about Western states bringing their security apparatus to bear on minorities and thus allegedly abrogating their often much-vaunted commitments to human rights, liberalism, and multiculturalism.

In this book, a team of scholars addresses a closely related pair of concerns articulated by academics, policymakers, and those in the general public in Canada and elsewhere.[1] As the title of the book suggests, we are interested, on the one hand, in *securitization*, the way the state and society frame the individuals and groups drawn to radical religious subcultures. On the other hand, we are interested in violent forms of *religious radicalization*, the processes by which individuals and groups with a wide range of motivations come to embrace religious feelings, beliefs, and practices that put them very severely at odds with their society and (often) family members. Although there are a great many books on radicalization, this book's focus is mainly, but not exclusively, on the Canadian situation, which makes it unprecedented. I suspect the emphasis here on the global and local – the "glocal" – forces involved in almost every form of extremism in the West will be of great interest to academic and non-academic readers. Moreover, a distinctive feature of this project is the way it uses a rigorously interdisciplinary approach to understanding the dialectical relationship between radicalization and securitization. All chapters have been subjected not just to the scrutiny of external readers and the editors but also to a thorough face-to-face critical review process in which disciplinary boundaries were compromised and expanded to strengthen each chapter and the book as a whole. One of the objectives of this book is to provide people working in the field – as scholars, activists, and representatives of state security agencies – with a richer account of the various issues at stake in the radicalization-securitization dialectic. Such an analysis will be of inestimable benefit for anyone seeking to engage religious and ethnic communities in dialogue about these complex processes. In an effort to inform and improve the kinds of discussions that might occur in the future, Lorne Dawson and I have assembled a group of scholars and security analysts to address the connections that do, and those that are thought to, exist between religion, radicalization, and securitization. In this chapter I would like to propose ways we might effectively orient ourselves to the issues of radicalization and securitization. Before I offer four general observations that might guide research and policy related to religious radicalization and securitization, I should address three key questions that might already have occurred to readers.

What Do We Mean by Radical, Radicalization, Security, and Securitization?

For some, the terms "radical" and "radicalization" are – like "freedom," "love," or "culture" – so ubiquitous that they are impossible to use with much precision and are certainly inappropriate core concepts for serious academic research (Sedgwick 2010). Indeed, the term "radical" may be used to validate *or* invalidate an idea, movement, or person. After all, on the one hand, ideas and individuals once called radical have a much valued place in the historical development of Western societies – without social movements such as abolitionism, feminism, liberalism, and democracy, our societies would be unrecognizable.[2] Even in contemporary society, radicals and mavericks are often the heroes, the people who resist structural violence, ecological destruction, an invading force, or a heartless regime: think of the man who stood in front of the tanks at Tiananmen Square, the Dalai Lama, Burmese leader Aung San Suu Kyi, Greenpeace activists, HIV/AIDS activist Stephen Lewis, and former Canadian politician Tommy Douglas. These figures and movements are radical in the literal sense that they seek or sought to uncover the fundamental sources of a problem (the etymology of the term is the Latin word *radicalis*, referring to the root). Virtually all religions could be considered radical in this sense as well, since they typically grow out of and promote a view of the world (and often the hereafter) closely linked to transcendent, supernatural, metaphysical, or at the very least highly unconventional ethics and states of being that are meant to challenge traditional and received notions of the good, the true, and the beautiful.

Of course, the term is often deployed pejoratively too, to refer to someone who or a movement that has adopted an adversarial and often hostile approach to the dominant society.[3] Here the term "radical" suggests a person who has abandoned hope that she or he can live comfortably within the status quo and has in the process abandoned conventional notions of reason and moderation in favour of some sort of schismatic or even apocalyptic world view oriented to a violent upending of the dominant society: think of Jim Jones, the Unabomber, Timothy McVeigh, Osama bin Laden.

Although these comments on the wide range of uses of the word "radical" might seem to be merely academic in the narrow sense, my objective here is to underline why the concept is defined quite differently depending on the frame of reference one has adopted or into which one has been socialized. Our analyses begin with the awareness that to other members of the movements in question the actively violent individuals that concern us are often viewed as martyrs, heroes, visionaries, and radicals in the positive sense. From their own radical perspective, it only makes sense to view a particular society as rapacious and its members as guilty by association. The rest of "us" are the ones deemed to be lost, intransigent, or hopelessly naive about the "cosmic battle" (Juergensmeyer 2003) in which "we" are waging a war against all that is godly.

While our main concern is violently radical religious groups and the broader subcultures in which they are embedded, we are also interested in radicalization, the process by which a person might make a transition from being merely alienated from or irritated by the dominant culture to being enraged by and violently disposed towards that culture. Although there is a vast literature on the meanings and histories of these key terms, for the sake of clarity the authors of this book adopt Anja Dalgaard-Nielsen's succinct definitions of "radical," "radicalization," and "violent radicalization" (2010, 798):

> [A] radical is understood as a person harboring a deep-felt desire for fundamental sociopolitical changes and radicalization is understood as a growing readiness to pursue and support far-reaching changes in society that conflict with, or pose a direct threat to, the existing order ... [and] violent radicalization [is] a process in which radical ideas are accompanied by the development of a willingness to directly support or engage in violent acts.

As several authors in this book demonstrate, scholars have so far failed to identify a predictable psychosocial trajectory to explain why some movements or individuals undergo this process and the vast majority do not (Dalgaard-Nielsen 2010; Dawson 2010); moreover, the study of de-radicalization is so new (Ashour 2009; Bjørgo and Horgan 2009) that it is also difficult to anticipate what kinds of efforts might delegitimize violent radicalism. Since there is a demonstrable lacuna in what we know about radicalization processes, we have tried to pay close attention to changes over time in the particularities of the individuals, religious communities, and political facts on the ground.

With the end of the Soviet Union, the meaning of the term "security" underwent a significant development in many Western liberal democracies. Whereas the term was once synonymous with national security, after the fall of the Berlin Wall we witnessed an increased focus on individual and communal security. Under the leadership of Lloyd Axworthy, Canada's Foreign Affairs Minister from 1996 to 2000, human security and the "responsibility to protect" became the buzzwords for foreign policy (Axworthy 2003; Hampson, Hillmer, and Molot 2001).

However, a decade of liberal triumphalism and the possibilities of more humanitarian-centred foreign policies arguably came to an abrupt halt with the events of 9/11 (Rosenberg 2005). Many people became troubled by the implications of advances in transportation and communication technologies, all of which would enable terrorist networks to operate beyond the control or even awareness of the state. Moreover, some argued that the signature features of Western states – our openness, multiculturalism, high immigration rate, and liberal democratic rights laws and policies – were also our Achilles heel, making us especially vulnerable to attack (Homer-Dixon 2002). In an effort to respond to some of these anxieties, very soon after the dust had settled in Manhattan in 2001 there emerged in North America a new and far more integrated constellation of policies which tended to blur the distinction between external (foreign) and internal (domestic) security regimes (Cesari 2005; Hocking 2003; McNeil 2005; Paye 2006; Toope 2002). Most significant among these anti-terrorism initiatives were the American Patriot Act (2001), the Homeland Security Act (2002), the Patriot Improvement and Reauthorization Act (2005), and Canada's Anti-Terrorism Act (2001).

In general, these policies accorded greater powers of investigation and detention for law enforcement agencies, which were deemed to be necessary to respond to vulnerabilities and prevent terrorist acts.[4] Alongside or as part of these anti-terrorism laws and policies, states created new or bolstered old immigration and asylum laws to allow them to deport or prevent the entry of individuals considered to be security threats. In some cases (e.g., Germany and the United Kingdom), these laws were contained within anti-terrorism legislation, and in others (e.g., Italy, France, Spain) they were enacted separately (Cesari 2005, 43). The American Patriot Act includes new stricter immigration provisions whereas in Canada, the Immigration and Refugee Protection Act not only included new measures, such as fewer appeal opportunities for refugees and front-end screening for all claimants, but also reaffirmed existing measures, such as the inadmissibility of permanent residents if they are deemed to be a danger to the security of Canada and the use of security certificates, which allows the deportation of foreign nationals and immigrants on national security grounds and – should such individuals refuse to return to their countries of origin because of the likelihood of torture – their indefinite detainment (Crocker et al. 2007).[5] The primacy of national security is apparent in the Canada First Defence Strategy, a 20-year plan to rebuild the Canadian Forces, which points out that the "peace dividend" brought about by the end of the Cold War was "relatively short-lived" and that "Canadians live in a world characterized by volatility and unpredictability," with threats ranging from proliferation of advanced weapons to the "pernicious influence of Islamist militants" (Canada, Department of National Defence 2008, 6).

In this book, the term "securitization" refers to the growing emphasis on national security understood both narrowly (e.g., increased border controls for particular states) and broadly (e.g., increased international cooperation in the "war on terror" and the pursuit of groups such as al-Qaeda). The term as we use it refers not just to the ways particular issues become so politicized that they seem almost to require draconian policy changes and not just to the ways public discourse shifts dramatically and often quickly, but also to the ways specific ethnic and religious groups become the targets of broad social stigma and suspicion, surveillance, and often harassment (Buzan, Wæver, and de Wilde 1998). Although politicians such as former US president George Bush, former British prime minister Tony Blair, former Canadian prime minister Jean Chretien, and leaders of various religious communities acted swiftly and, it seemed, virtually in unison to distinguish between the perpetrators of 9/11 and Islam as such, the backlash has had a lasting effect on Muslims in the West (Cesari 2005, 2010; cf. Seljak 2007).[6] It is interesting, if also somewhat unfortunate, to note that with regard to the backlash, progressive commentators and policymakers in Canada have tended to focus on the question of whether such incidents reflect racial, national, and ethnic profiling in our society.[7] While the critique of such forms of profiling as such is relatively recent, at the root of the debate is a disagreement about the role that visible physical differences ought to play in the way people in positions of power treat minorities. This overarching concern with discrimination and diversity has certainly been a part of the broader public and political debate for several decades, and thus the academic and public conversations around race and racism have become increasingly sophisticated over the years. However, when religion and religious discrimination are addressed, they are addressed superficially or they are conflated uncritically with race and racism.

This treatment reflects a general anxiety about how one ought to analyse politically charged religious phenomena. Indeed, for some colleagues and activists on the left wing of the political spectrum it is offensive even to see the words religion and radicalization in the same sentence, much less in the title of a book. This concern is hardly unfounded. After all, following 9/11, there were vitriolic media and public attacks on Islam as a religion and on Muslims (and those mistaken for Muslims) as individuals. These attacks reflect not just troubling levels of anti-Islamic sentiment in our societies, but also the highly "racialized" nature of post-9/11 (and, for that matter, pre-9/11) anti-Islamic discourse.

The popular conflation of Islam, qua religion, with the largely non-European racial and ethnic backgrounds of Muslims in the West has complicated matters tremendously; a similar complexity is associated with the hazy lines between Sikhism and Punjabi ethnicity.[8] The tendency to blur these distinctions is not the product of nefarious Western bigots but the consequence of the geographical origins and historical spread of Islam and Sikhism themselves. Because the vast majority of the Muslims and Sikhs in the world and the West are non-European and non-white, these conflated identities, legacies, and political projects create a number of complications: Is Islamophobia distinct from racism? Indeed, is Islamophobia an actual phobia (such as claustrophobia), or is it merely a rigid (but considered) posture of rejection? Do critics of Islam or Sikhism distinguish, in their own minds, between the religious and the ethnic, racial, cultural, or national characteristics of these communities? Do these minority religious communities make such distinctions among themselves, or make them clearly enough for outsiders to appreciate? Is it an accident that the traditions – Islam and Sikhism – that often attract the surveillance of the public, politicians, scholars, and security services are mainly the traditions of non-white people? Is it sensible for our society to continue to focus on these traditions and overlook forms of lethal radicalization in other ethnoreligious traditions (e.g., Christian white supremacists)? Regardless of the answers one might offer to these questions, it is clear that those asked to address these matters ought to resist the simple conflation of race, ethnicity, and religion.

Of course, by focusing most of our attention on Islam, the authors of this book run the risk of unintentionally replicating the narrow and often prejudicial nature of the post-9/11 debate on security and radicalization. A similarly legitimate concern might be raised regarding the impression created by the prevalence of non-European and non-white ethnic groups in these chapters. In the initial discussions among the research team, these two issues received a great deal of attention. In the end there was general consensus that the chapter topics reflect fairly accurately the religious and ethnic groups that draw the attention of policymakers, security officials, journalists, and members of the general public. Whether or not these communities ought to be subjected to such scrutiny is a separate matter; the fact is that they are, and as such the groups, and the attention, merit our critical analysis. As well, in fact our focus is not exclusively on Islam; Indo-Canadian Sikhs, American and Canadian fundamentalist Christians, Japanese Buddhists, and Sri Lankan Buddhists and Hindus are also included in our analysis.

There is an additional feature of our shared political reality that also creates certain implicit obstacles to even-handed analysis. As an ideology, "secularism" has become so normalized among so many in the West that it is a virtually invisible part of the way many of us think. Secularism – defined here as the ideological claim that the processes of secularization unfolding in the West represent morally positive and likely irrevocable progress in human development – has left an indelible mark on intellectual discourse not just about radicalization and security but also about human rights, women's rights, individualism, and so forth.[9]

We are in some sense all prisoners of the well-established secularist discourse on religion in general and religious radicalization in particular. Moreover, one of the great challenges posed by the dominance of this perspective is the fact that a great many people know very little about the basic religious forces involved in the forms of radicalization that have drawn our attention and reshaped many national and international security and migration policies since 2001. It is as if a whole generation or two of intellectual, cultural, and political leaders woke up on 12 September and started to have a conversation about a topic – radical forms of religion – that many of them had been convinced to stop thinking about decades before. As a result, security scholars and practitioners who would never engage in serious deliberations about a weapons system, military campaign, or coup d'état without being thoroughly familiar with the ideas, languages, and groups involved often find themselves operating in an intellectual vacuum when it comes to the religious groups and movements they are addressing (Etzioni 2007).

Why Is Religion So Important Now?

This is not the place to comment in depth on the altered and (usually) diminished influence of religion in Western societies over the past century (see Bramadat and Koenig 2009; Taylor 2007). It is important nonetheless to observe that these complex changes – which are usually discussed in terms of "secularization" – not only have quite diverse origins, expressions, and effects but are subject as well to sometimes dramatic reversals resulting in increased power and prestige for particular religions (Berger, Davie, and Fokas 2008; Bramadat 2000; Casanova 1994). Particularly relevant to our topic is the fact that just when it has become more and more possible to live one's entire life outside of what sociologist Peter Berger once called a traditional "sacred canopy" (1967; cf. Taylor 2007), it is also becoming more and more possible for individuals and groups to identify with larger and often "fundamentalist" religious movements that are no longer rooted in one's own region.

Nonetheless, even though the changes occurring within contemporary religion in the West should make us cautious about simple explanations, we can posit three interpretations for the return of religion to the public debates about security. First, religion has re-entered public discourse because unidirectional versions of the secularization hypothesis have begun to break down after approximately twenty years of research have demonstrated the continued – albeit often quite transformed – salience and dynamism of religion (even) in the West and certainly elsewhere (Swatos 1999). Simply put, both academic research and even a passing familiarity with international affairs in the last 40 years demonstrate that some of the grand expectations of often antireligious secularization theorists were wishful thinking (certainly this is the case for those interested in the world outside of Western Europe and parts of North America). This new prominence of religion in public debates reflects the failure of a certain simple form of secularization as a hypothesis; or at least it reflects the vulnerability of public institutions rooted in this hypothesis (cf. Dark 2000; Toft 2011).

Second, the religions at the centre of these debates in the West are no longer primarily Christianity and Judaism (Bramadat and Koenig 2009) but rather religions about which a great many people in Western societies are uninformed and for which our system of laws and policies may not offer very effective guidance.[10] In Canada for example, the suite of federal and provincial policies and laws designed to manage religious diversity were designed mostly to manage tensions between Protestants and Catholics (and simultaneously, of course, English and French Canadians) (Bramadat and Seljak 2013; Milot 2009). Many of the contemporary controversies regarding religion (most notably, those related to Islam, Sikhism, and fundamentalist Mormonism) exist largely because the Canadian institutional structure is not designed to respond to non-Christian (or minority Christian) practices and claims (B. Berger 2007; Moon 2008); this de facto ethnocentrism has greatly increased the interest in the political and public consciousness in "managing" minority religious communities in a rather ad hoc manner, even though these three "problem" minority communities represent a very small group of people, given that only roughly 4–6 per cent of Canadians in total belong to one of these communities.[11]

Third, and most important for the purpose of this book, the events of and after 11 September 2001 have increased the level and changed the type of securitization experienced by many religious and ethnic minorities (Cesari 2005, 2010). This securitization has increased the profile of certain conservative cohorts within relatively new and internally heterogeneous religions in the Canadian public sphere well out of proportion to their actual numbers in society. For example, in the last few years a relatively small number of fully veiled Muslim women in Quebec have become lightning rods for broader anxieties about feminism and multiculturalism, whereas many of these concerns around women's equality, sexuality, and the inclusion of ethnic minorities have existed for many decades. While Canada has adopted legislative measures and anti-discrimination programs to address racism, sexism, and heterosexism,[12] many critics were concerned that after 9/11, religion – especially Islam – came to be understood not only as a merely one identity marker among others (such as race and ethnicity) but as the central non-negotiable marker and also, more troubling, as a risk factor for extremism (Zine 2012). The nearly fetishistic emphasis on a person's religious identity – as though this feature of their identity must dominate all others – reflects a distortion of what scholars of religion have been arguing for decades. In the social scientific study of religion, it has for some time now been fairly unproblematic to assert that one's religious identity is one part of the necessarily shifting ground of one's identity, alongside one's gender, national, class, ethnic, and racial identities (Levitt 2007, 91; cf. Cesari 2005). One of the problems associated with a state's or the society's almost voyeuristic fixation on a person's religious identity is the likelihood that the person and his co-religionists may thereafter feel *compelled* to identify more rigidly and defensively with this feature of their identities. The other dimension of securitization (or political "othering" as some anthropologists might say) that we must note is that this kind of attention is far more commonly experienced by Muslims and Sikhs than by Christians.

Why Islam?

The fact that the 19 hijackers on 9/11 – like the militants involved in the attacks on London (2005), Madrid (2004), Mumbai (2008), and Kuta, Indonesia (2002) – were deeply embedded in a particular form of Islam solidified in the minds of some policymakers and members of the Western public the notion that there is something inherent in Islam that makes it a threat to the West. Of course, this perspective has a history. According to Jocelyne Cesari, "it is striking how the idea of Islam as an international 'risk factor,' current since the 1980s, is bolstered by centuries-old representations of Islam ... [F]ixed ideas of Islam as an inherently violent and fanatical religion are continually re-invoked and readjusted to fit changes in international and domestic situations" (2005, 39; cf. Blom, Bucaille, and Martinez 2007; Etzioni 2007; Huntington 1996; Rashidi 2004). Cesari contends that there is a "convergence of European and American political discourse" (2005, 38) that has resulted not only in the targeting of Muslims in the West but also in the legitimation of deeply held anti-Islamic public claims that were, particularly in Europe, once mainly the purview of far-right-wing elements in the society (2005, 45; Milot 2009; Shadid 2006). In the United States, Samuel Huntington's provocative "clash of civilizations" hypothesis (1996) continues to resonate today in the work of David Kilcullen, one of the primary architects of US counter-insurgency strategy and senior adviser in the wars in Iraq and Afghanistan. In "Countering Global Insurgency," Kilcullen argues that the war on terror is, in actuality, a "defensive war" (2004, 1) against a movement of diffuse Islamic groups seeking to "re-make the world order with the Muslim world in a dominant position" (4). Moreover, a similar concern was expressed by Canada's Prime Minister Stephen Harper in an interview with the Canadian Broadcasting Corporation in September 2011, just a few days before the tenth anniversary of the 9/11 attacks. Commenting on the current threat environment, Harper observed that "the major threat is still Islamicism [sic]."[13]

Clearly, the focus on Islam has not gone unnoticed by many in civil society and in government. In particular, Canada's Anti-Terrorism Act has been criticized by both scholars and activists as a far-reaching measure that could lead to the erosion of basic rights and freedoms. In a brief to the House of Commons, the International Civil Liberties Monitoring Group argues that the Anti-Terrorism Act was passed "without adequate and serious consideration" to existing legislation or human rights frameworks, including the Canadian Charter of Rights and Freedoms, and could lead to racial profiling and the infringement of individual rights and freedoms (ICLMG 2005). Clearly, laws and policies perceived as cynical, draconian, or targeted at particular religious or ethnic minorities may contribute to a climate of mistrust that might – at least in theory – confirm or even inflame the fears and anxieties of subgroups within religious communities that are already inclined to see themselves as being under siege.

One might argue that the fundamental issue at stake in these debates is actually the place of religion as such in modern liberal democracies (Bramadat and Koenig 2009; Turner 2011), or perhaps even the need for Western societies to identify (and pursue) some kind of post–Cold War enemy. Nevertheless, quite aside from whether or not Islam deserves to be at the centre of the global debates on security, as I mentioned earlier, it is certainly the case that for many Europeans and North Americans, it is.[14] As such, we need to grapple with that fact in as honest and critical a manner possible.

The preceding pages addressed some of the key questions one encounters when one enters this political and intellectual domain. Now I would like to provide an account of four general guidelines that would be useful for readers to consider as they read this book or reflect on the wide range of issues we seek to engage. Following these guidelines, I will outline the core contributions of each chapter.

First, as I observed above, it is helpful to see radicalization and securitization as dialectically related. The particular factors that might lead a person, subgroup, or family to espouse a violent, radicalized form of a particular religion ought to be analysed against the backdrop of the broad national and international political discourses that exist vis-à-vis that tradition. As well, and as Amiraux explains in her chapter, playgrounds, restaurants, schools, and shops are also crucial micro-political discursive contexts in which these broader forces are expressed and negotiated. In formal political and micro-political contexts we see a dynamic relationship between the religious actor's perceptions of the state and the state's perceptions of the nature of the threat. The objective of one's analysis should not be only to determine the validity of the state's focus on a given individual or community, nor only to evaluate the veracity of the individual's or community's complaints about the state. In addition, we need to elucidate the ways in which each actor (state, individual, subculture) frames its "other" as hostile, irredeemable, and uncivilized and why, after such a framing, often very particular courses of action are seen as necessary (Blom, Bucaille, and Martinez 2007).

Although in Canada as in other Western states it is not difficult to discern examples of securitization in the political and public arenas, there is, nonetheless, some reason to be optimistic about the abilities of the state to balance its dual commitments to protect the dignity and autonomy of religious minorities and to protect the broader population from violence. In the years after 9/11, for example, Canada's security agencies were at the forefront of instituting community outreach to Muslim communities, both to allay fears of targeting and to prevent a backlash.[15] Indeed, when Canada's own home-grown terrorist plot was thwarted in the summer of 2006 with the arrest of 18 alleged terrorists in Southern Ontario, the public learned that the Royal Canadian Mounted Police

(RCMP) and Canadian Security Intelligence Service (CSIS) had spoken with local imams and even the parents of some of the young suspects before arrests were made. Whether the proactive stance expressed in this outreach movement will be sufficient to quell suspicions that some Canadian Muslims might have about their state remains to be seen. Nevertheless, the fact that the state made these efforts at all reflects an acknowledgment that community perceptions are closely related to the way security personnel conduct their investigations.

Second, it is often the case that religion is framed merely as a "multiplier" in conflicts that are not actually "about" religion. When faced with violent political acts articulated "in the name of" a particular religion, a great many journalists, politicians, and representatives of the religion in the spotlight tacitly agree to articulate the same core argument: that [insert religion here] is the religion of peace but has regrettably been "hijacked" by a minuscule number of despicable people whose real motives are actually economic, political, or perhaps simply idiosyncratically pathological (and thus, presumably, not subject to critical social analysis).

For example, in August 2011, a member of the Nigerian Islamist group Boko Haram detonated a suicide bomb, killing approximately 20 people[16] at a UN compound in Abuja. In the *Globe and Mail* story on this event, journalist Geoffrey York concluded his article with the following sentences: "Analysts say the rise of Boko Haram is more than a religious phenomenon. It has capitalized on widespread anger at government corruption, poverty and unemployment." In a profile of the same group on the Al Jazeera English website, the unnamed author is more definitive: "Analysts have also said that at the heart of the recurring tension is dire poverty and political manoeuvring – not religion."[17] Although neither York nor the Al Jazeera author elaborates on their understandings of the difference between religious and other motivations, I suspect that the distinctions they make would puzzle the members of Boko Haram (the name means roughly "Western education is a sin"). One of the few general defining features of fundamentalists (Bramadat 2000) may be the sense that the whole world is God's world, so to speak, and all discrete events are merely instances in an essentially religious narrative. As such, I would anticipate that the members of Boko Haram would find it odd to hear these writers distinguish between their group's core "religious" mandate and identity on the one hand and their deep feelings of abhorrence about endemic poverty, unemployment, and government corruption on the other hand.[18]

I am not suggesting that political, economic, and other material forces do not influence the violent radicals we discuss in this book. Rather, I am simply reminding readers that the insistence that one can distinguish tidily between one's religious as opposed to one's political, economic, and social commitments and motivations is indicative of a very particular cultural and historical trend. The dominant Western approach to religions, and to religious people, presupposes that under the right (read: liberal, democratic, and affluent) social and economic circumstances, what Bruce Lincoln (2006, 59; cf. Bramadat 2009) calls the "minimalist" vision of religion's role is the one that *all* people would embrace. As such, many people in the West imagine religious "maximalists" – for whom religion is the supreme context in which all human life occurs and has meaning – to be people whose natural minimalist approaches to religion are stifled by some traumatic event such as poverty, corruption, the death of a child, or a military invasion (cf. Bramadat 2000; Juergensmeyer 2003; Lincoln 2006; Venhaus 2010).

This extrication of "religion" from everyday life – especially from *religiously experienced and articulated* feelings of despair and rage that emerge for some when everyday life is patently unjust – will lead to extremely inappropriate policies and practices. To grapple meaningfully with radicalization requires one to work very hard to enter into the intellectual world of individuals and communities with often fundamentally different values, customs, and assumptions (cf. al-Rasheed and Shterin 2009). This is not a simple matter. After all, it is relatively easy for scholars, policymakers, and others in the West to imagine what it is like to walk around the streets of Toronto, Amsterdam, London, Paris, or Tokyo and feel that they are, to some degree, outsiders in such places. Such a feeling can be thrilling and edifying, and it is precisely what attracts many of us to travel. However, it is nearly impossible for many of us to comprehend how a resident of these cities could walk around these places and feel that their neighbours are actively at war with them and with all that is good in the universe. And yet, as Mark Juergensmeyer (2003) reminds us, the deeply felt sense of being engaged in an epic battle with the forces of evil is one of the common sentiments among those Christians, Sikhs, and others committed to or sympathetic with violent radicalization.

It is important for people who feel entirely at home, or at most only moderately alien, in modern Western liberal (and increasingly or ostensibly secular) democracies to take seriously the many ways these societies come to feel – and are made to feel – natural, even inevitable, to their members. For many of the individuals who have inspired this book, however, the relative ease of life in many liberal democracies is in fact the net result of a long and sinister history of colonialism, subjugation, debauchery, and humiliation. Many of us in stable democracies find it nearly impossible, even ludicrous, to imagine ourselves as deeply deluded about the moral value or direction of our lives, not to mention to conceive of the societies in which we live as part of an evil global juggernaut, but until we can comprehend these perspectives, the world views of violent radicals will remain a great mystery. As Lorne Dawson suggests, "We need to imaginatively step beyond our contemporary secular prejudices and recognize the consequences of living a life fundamentally rooted in a faith in providence, in the active role of the supernatural in this world" (2010, 14).

Third, a small handful of attacks have occurred in Europe and North America in the last decade, but as other authors in this book discuss, many more have been prevented by the post-9/11 surveillance measures as well as the internal policing and de-radicalization projects (Ashour 2009) undertaken by religious – especially Muslim – communities themselves. The question of whether the changes in the security regime represent justifiable limits on the rights and freedoms of Canadians and others remains the subject of considerable debate, of course, and this is not the place to elaborate on these discussions (cf. Roach 2003).

What is worth critical scrutiny, however, is the individual many people have in mind when they imagine violent religious radicals. Research on radicalization seems to call into question the widespread assumption that perpetrators would necessarily be members of an uneducated and materially deprived underclass of orthodox believers or that they would necessarily be "lured" into involvement by a charismatic ringleader. As Dawson argues (2010; cf. Blom, Bucaille, and Martinez 2007; Hammond Schbley 2006; Kirby 2007; Venhaus 2010), the profiles we have of religious radicals do include some individuals who fit this description, but it is far from apparent that they represent the majority or some kind of general character type. Indeed, sometimes those who get involved in such activities are only recently religious, often very well educated, well travelled, and well integrated into the Western societies they eventually come to despise.

As mentioned earlier, there are so many entry points to religious radicalization it confounds any precise profiling endeavour. The good news, however, is that an inquiry into the features of Canadian society that might enrage or alienate various kinds of religious individuals might help us to actualize more fully our liberal democratic principles, thwart violence, and comprehend more critically the dialectical relationship between individuals and their state/society. Such critical self-reflection need not be motivated by the collective guilt of people in the West. In fact, seeing our society through the eyes of people who see it as inherently hostile and wicked may be an expression of a deeper diversity – only possible in the multicultural West, some might argue – that would not exclude religious claims from the public arena. Again, one does not need to think radicalized visions of Western societies are accurate or fair, just that there is value in observing the coherence of the accounts.

Fourth, virtually every scholar and security analyst writing about radicalized religious groups today underlines the importance of the Internet in both the development of radicalized perspectives and the potential state responses to them. Many commentators have observed that as a result of the Internet, groups (not just extremist groups but also the dominant moderate groups, NGOs and others) no longer have a single national, cultural, or even spatial mooring; the threat (real and perceived) from violent radicalism is now decentralized in the extreme, and the near anonymity of the Web allows people to experiment with new identities, form new bonds of solidarity, and develop unconventional political perspectives (Bunt 2003; Egerton and Wilner 2009; Kirby 2007; Kohlmann 2006; Ryan 2007; Sageman 2004; Smith 2009; Weimann 2004).

How, though, do we conceive of the Internet? Much more than a tool by which people communicate or a single imaginary place one might imaginatively visit, for many of the recently radicalized individuals for whom we have comprehensive profiles, it is a primary habitus, a complete and encompassing experience-mapping and experience-embodying world. For many current and would-be violent radicals, the Web is the preferred means and site of relating to others and of constructing identities unconstrained by either local conditions (which might indeed be favourable to members of their own immediate religious community) or global conditions (which are usually imagined as hostile and humiliating).

Scholars of Islam now speak of the emergence of the global ummah, an imagined community that galvanizes many Muslims in the West by inscribing them in a worldwide community of solidarity (Roy 2004; Volpi 2007). This global ummah is almost entirely dependent on Internet and satellite communication technologies; in this community, national borders are relatively insignificant, religious identification becomes the crucial mode of identity, and pain suffered by one's putative brothers and sisters thousands of kilometres away is experienced as acutely as if the pain was inflicted on one's own immediate family and community members. Mary Habeck (2006, 173) has argued that "the single best recruiting tool that the jihadists possess [is] the Palestinian-Israeli conflict." It matters little if the Canadian individuals know any Palestinians personally, or whether they themselves are actually disadvantaged (see chapter 10 by Keeble in this volume). What propels them is an identification with the powerful transnational narrative of the oppression of their Palestinian co-religionists. As Volpi (2007, 468) points out,

> Like nationalism before it, the discourse about the "Ummah" produces the kind of imagined community that groups and individuals can refer to in order to change their relation to politics and violence in any part of the world. Within this conceptual (and spiritual) landscape, an individual living in the UK can, like the 7/7 suicide bombers, decide that it is meaningful and appropriate to use random violence against the British population as a means of influencing the foreign policy of their government, thereby "helping" other members of the "Ummah" somewhere else in the world – on that occasion in Iraq.

The de-spatialized ubiquity of the Internet fundamentally changes the way we might understand religious radicalization. The classical models of psychological development (Freud, Piaget, and beyond) generally presuppose that whatever tumultuous biological or subconscious transitions one would need to go through as one matures, all people would work through these changes in the context of a particular culture rooted in specific geographical, social, material, and political conditions. The habitus, the alternative world in which some people – and certainly radicalized religious people – live large portions of their lives, however, is not geographically specific and yet is its own kind of total culture.

Some commentators (Gasser and Palfrey 2008) would describe the Internet generation as "digital natives," that is, people who were born (mostly since the 1980s) into cultures closely identified with the pervasive presence of digital technologies. Their parents and certainly the vast majority of scholars and security officials are, by contrast, "digital immigrants," or people who struggle to come to terms with the sea change that has taken place. The point is that those of us who are digital immigrants (or those who are, as I am, betwixt and between natives and immigrants) would be well advised to pay attention to the profound implications of this generational distinction, since it has arguably weakened the power of families, neighbourhoods, and ethnic and religious groups to mollify opinions and feelings or to correct, re-socialize, or "de-radicalize" people. The fissure between these conventional socialization contexts and the kind of radicalization made possible by the Internet is evident whenever mainstream members of these communities express shock that their own children, friends, and co-workers appear to have been planning to express their anger through mass violence. "We had no idea," they usually say. "They were always such nice boys" (Bramadat 2011). However, these individuals often live not just in different *ways* but in different and Internet-mediated *worlds* than their parents and grandparents and a great many of their co-religionists.

Of course the Internet also gives those within traditional educational settings such as high schools, as well as those in the security establishment, a new and powerful platform from which to encourage youth to reflect critically on the militant ideological narratives they are likely to encounter online.[19] Even more significantly, this new virtual sphere of communications, or sphere of being, also provides security personnel with a powerful new arena for surveillance. So just as the Web has had a massive effect on the way we think of ourselves and the communities we form, as a site of surveillance it has also made it challenging for people to communicate among themselves, create modes of identity, or plot mass murders entirely in private. Emerging from this fact, of course, is the ongoing debate about both how much state or private surveillance of radicalized individuals is acceptable in a liberal democratic society and what we might consider to be the consequences (for individuals, groups, or the whole society) of different levels of surveillance (Maras 2010). Here again we see the dialectic of radicalization and securitization, where security officials may temper the latter in order not to foment the former.

Introduction to the Chapters

Authors examine particular dimensions of these issues in their own ways – some are more theoretically oriented, some are more empirically or ethnographically oriented, some offer policy analysis, and others offer political commentary. The book is divided into three sections. The first set of chapters explores key theoretical and empirical issues related to the study of religion and radicalization; the second set focuses on the securitization of ethno-religious minorities; and the third section examines the way radicalization and securitization appear in and are shaped by public discourse. In the concluding chapter Dawson and I draw out some of the key insights from this book and articulate a series of theoretical and empirical questions raised here that are most in need of academic and political attention.

In the second chapter, using the case of Aum Shinrikyō – a new religious movement in Japan responsible for the infamous Tokyo subway attack in 1995 – as his key case study example, Ian Reader argues that spiritual development, righteousness born of religious convictions, and the twin concepts of a "sacred mission" and "cosmic struggle" are all genuine motivations behind the real phenomenon of "religious violence." Reader compares the Aum Shinrikyō movement with religiously radicalized groups in the United States, Britain, and India to demonstrate the flaws in the common scholarly and popular argument that religious violence is a contradiction in terms. The reality of religiously motivated violence does not invalidate other motivations (economic, political, ideological, etc.), but it is an important factor in identifying and assessing patterns of public violence. In chapter 3, Lorne Dawson analyses the case of the Toronto 18 to determine whether religion is a causal factor in Canadian home-grown terrorism. He situates the Toronto 18 within two broad types of terrorism: domestic, or home-grown, terrorism and global "jihadi" terrorism. In both types, social networks appear to be one of the most significant means by which radicalism is spread. In addition, research of both home-grown and global jihadi terrorism demonstrates a marked increase in the devotion of individuals just prior to the turn to radicalism, but it is unclear why this is the case. Dawson examines some of the key methodological obstacles that preclude empirical certainty and warns against discounting the role of religious rhetoric and ideology in the turn of these mostly young men to radical violence. In the fourth chapter, Valérie Amiraux and Javiera Araya-Moreno examine radicalization as a micro-phenomenon that occurs in the course of ordinary interactions within pluralistic societies. In contrast to the other chapters in this volume that offer case studies and event-based analyses, this chapter examines the practical root of radicalization: particular episodes of miscommunication that inevitably occur in pluralistic societies and that are in some respects the hallmark of such societies. Amiraux and Araya-Moreno use the example of the 2009 minaret ban in Switzerland to illustrate the ways miscommunications in quotidian interactions can breed polarized discourse between religious minorities and the dominant society and thus can increase both radicalization (of the minorities) and securitization (from the majority population). The authors discuss the problems associated with post facto examinations of particular eruptions of radicalization and promote instead an ethnographic approach that will allow scholars and policymakers to better understand the ordinary experiences from which radicalization emerges and to which securitization is often the response. In the fifth chapter and the final one in this section, Peter Beyer analyses the results of a study of 35 university-aged Muslim males and compares his findings with five conventionally understood factors of radicalization. Beyer concludes that these men – who reflect in many ways the broader Muslim population in Canada – displayed few to none of the factors typically found in religious radicals. Any enmity the young men exhibited towards Canadian society pertained to the exclusion of religion in the public sphere – not Islam, in particular, but all religious discourse. While they generally favoured overt religiosity, they rejected the politicization of religion. The most significant practical implication of Beyer's chapter is that according to his study, a person's level of religiosity appears to bear no relation to that person's radical tendencies; in fact, the sample suggests that religion serves as an immunizing force rather than an inculcating factor in radicalization.

The next section addresses the securitization of ethno-religious minorities. Chapter 6, by Uzma Jamil, highlights the dynamic relationship between security regimes and religious communities by investigating how South Asian Muslim communities in Montreal have responded to and are affected by the "war on terror." Jamil uses two community-based research studies to highlight the divergent responses to the war on terror exhibited by middle- and working-class Pakistani and Bangladeshi families in two residential neighbourhoods of Montreal. In these case studies, the perception of marginalization from the broader society was more acute in the less privileged cohort. Moreover, these groups employed different coping strategies in response to discrimination and different approaches to explaining the war on terror to their children. Jamil found that the effects of the war on terror have had an uneven impact on these communities and suggests that the degree of impact may be correlated with other socio-economic factors that contribute to the positioning of these two Muslim communities within the majority society. In the seventh chapter, Doris Jakobsh addresses potential factors contributing to violence or radicalization among Canadian Sikhs. Jakobsh highlights the potentially adverse effects of sweeping depictions of the Sikh tradition as inherently violent and masculinist. Many of these stereotypes are the result of misunderstandings that hold atypical events like the 1985 Air India bombings as representative of general culture. In fact, Sikhs in particular are subject to misidentification and conflation with other religious groups (specifically, orthodox Muslims) by the broader populace because of outward manifestations of faith such as the turban or beard worn by Khalsa Sikhs. These kinds of misconceptions can validate narratives within the Sikh community that may feed into an existing need to "fight for faith and nation." Jakobsh also addresses cultural challenges posed from within the Sikh community, including family and gurdwara politics, nationalism, issues of honour, and gender roles. In chapter 8, Amarnath Amarasingam addresses the complex relationship between Tamil nationalism and religiosity and the role of religion within Tamil political militancy in Sri Lanka and abroad. Amarasingam engages the history of religion in Tamil political and social movements and introduces significant security issues that have arisen as a result of globalization, including the ways nationalist and terrorist movements such as the Liberation Tigers of Tamil Eelam (a nationalist terrorist group based in Sri Lanka) use global connectedness to propagate their national cause to an international network of supporters. The chapter also documents the impact globalization has on the formation of individuals' ethnic and religious identities. Amarasingam suggests that it is crucial for scholars and policymakers to reflect on how broader shifts in Canadian religion and culture influence Tamil religiosity. In particular, he contends that the shift among many relatively young Canadians towards a decentralized form of spirituality rooted in an emerging universal "Golden Rule" religion may serve to mitigate radicalization among the young Tamils.

In the final section of the book, our authors turn their attention to the way religion, radicalization, and securitization are framed and influenced by public discourse. In the ninth chapter, Joyce Smith discusses the dialectical relationship between radicalization and securitization with a special focus on the role of news media in circulating discourses about security. Smith's analysis provides insights into the processes through which narratives on the "security beat" are conceived of and propagated as well as how such narratives are received by religious and non-religious consumers. Smith notes a dearth of knowledgeable reporters working on this topic, a problem that adversely affects the dissemination of information pertaining to security in Canada and results in reporting that is frequently uninformed, static, or biased. Further research is needed to discover if and how news media influences radicalization processes. On the one hand, biased reporting may inflame radical tendencies; on the other hand, the age cohort most likely to undergo radicalization is the same cohort that is least likely to read traditional newspapers. In chapter 10, Edna Keeble reflects on her three-year tenure as a member of the Cross-Cultural Roundtable on Security, from its inception in 2005 to the fulfilment of her term in 2008. She highlights a number of issues from the Roundtable that reflect broader problems in Canada's radicalization-securitization dynamic. First, the Roundtable – like the government that created it – is often regarded with mistrust by some outsiders, yet within government it has been lauded as a successful outreach program for mitigating radicalization. In addition, the Roundtable itself operates on the paradigm of privatized religiosity – a quite limiting normative assumption implicit in most political discourse. The chapter provides a unique insight into the ways state-supported advisory committees and outreach programs function when dealing with complex social and religious issues. In the eleventh chapter, Sean Norton and Afzal Upal discuss the role of "narratives" in the war on terror. Narratives, they argue, are not merely discursive constructions meant to assert particular truth claims but also identity-constituting social phenomena. As such, the conventional practice of combating violent ideologies such as "al-Qaedaism" with carefully constructed "counter-narratives" presupposes a false dichotomy between true narratives (e.g., liberal democratic ideals of freedom and democracy) and false ones (e.g., militant values espoused by terrorists, etc.). By countering one narrative with another, and by focusing exclusively on the falsity of the claims made by hostile narrators, we miss an opportunity to reflect on the internal consistency and "root causes" of the religious movements whose identities are concomitant with such stories.

Conclusion

As a number of authors in this book suggest, radicalization – religious or otherwise – is hardly a new phenomenon; nor is it unprecedented for the state to respond firmly to these phenomena. Nonetheless, as we imagine the shape the West will take in the next several decades, the failure to understand the subtle relationship between religious radicalization and state and social securitization will have major rami-fications. One the one hand, if policymakers and scholars *under-react* to the religious component of security threats in Canada or abroad, we face the daunting prospect of failing to prevent the development and expression of violent or antisocial religious groups determined to wreak havoc on our society. It would be extremely naive to assume such groups do not exist, at least incipiently, in Canada; indeed, our col-leagues in Canadian security institutions confirm that they are aware of a few hundred radicalized individuals in Canada inclined to justify violence in religious terms. On the other hand, if we *overreact* to the religious content of security challenges, we might well create deadly problems where previously only complex ones existed. Here it is instructive to consider the European context, where radical Islam is still virtually the exclusive focus of scholars and policymakers, even after "home-grown" right-wing nativist extremist Anders Breivik bombed a government building in Oslo (killing eight) and then murdered 69 of Norway's Labour Party youth in July 2011. On the issues at stake in the European context, Talal Asad comments, "If Europe cannot be articulated in terms of complex space and complex time that allow for multiple ways of life (and not merely multiple identities) to flourish, it may be fated to be no more than the common market of an impe-rial civilization, always anxious about (Muslim) exiles within its gates and (Muslim) barbarians beyond" (2003, 180). The same prospect faces Canadian and American policymakers and scholars if, like the Euro-peans in Asad's comment, we cannot come to terms with the place of religion in the security concerns embedded in our society.

NOTES

1 This chapter echoes a short magazine article I wrote in 2011 entitled "They Were Always Such Nice Boys: Religion, Radicalization and Securitiza-tion in Canada and Beyond," published in *Our Diverse Cities*. I would like to thank Edna Keeble (Saint Mary's University) and Matthew Lauder (Defence Research and Development Canada) for their collaboration on an earlier unpublished manuscript in which some of these general concerns were initially examined.

2 See the positive use of the term in characterizations of Marx (McBride 2003); Saul Alinsky (Alinsky 1971); and feminism (Rhodes 2005).

3 See, for example, Berman (2009); Burke (2004); Inbar and Frisch (2008).

4 The US Patriot Act (2001) enhanced domestic security (including the introduction of policies to permit use of the military in response to certain emergencies), surveillance capabilities, border protection, intelligence collection, and investigation capabilities (including the authorization of roving wiretaps). The US Patriot Improvement and Reauthorization Act (2005) increased penalties for those involved in terrorist financing, improved protection for mass transportation, and introduced some anti-drug measures. The Homeland Security Act (2002) established the Department of Homeland Security, which brought more than a dozen agencies with intelligence and enforcement functions under a single departmental administration. In fact, even before 9/11, the US administration sought to increase the reach of its security interests. The Anti-Terrorism Act, which was introduced in 1996 in response to three incidents (i.e., the World Trade Center Bombing, Oklahoma City bombing, and the sarin gas attack on the Tokyo subway system), also strengthened border protection capabilities and prison sentences (Purpura 2007). Like its US equivalents, the Canadian Anti-Terrorism Act (2001) defined terrorism, provided the mechanism to designate entities as terrorist groups, and enhanced investigation capabilities as well as penalties for terrorism-related offences. The act also introduced stronger laws against hate crimes and propaganda, as well as streamlining the Canadian Human Rights Act. See www.justice.gc.ca/eng/new-nouv/nr-cp/2001/doc-27787.html.

5 In Canada, security certificates have been in existence since 1979, and a total of 27 persons have been subject to certificate proceeding since 1991. Recently, several sections of the security certificate have been found to be in violation of the Charter of Rights and Freedoms.

6 Following 9/11, incidents of hate and race-based discriminatory behaviour in Canada increased dramatically. Hate-motivated acts targeting the Muslim community included vandalism to mosques in Oshawa, Waterloo, London, St. Catharines, Burlington, Mississauga, and Guelph. Other incidents included an attack on a young person of Middle Eastern descent in Ottawa and an attack on a Middle Eastern doctor in Montreal. From 11 September 2001 through 15 November 2001, the Canadian Council on American-Islamic Relations received a total of 110 reports of hate-motivated crime, including 12 attacks on mosques, across Canada (Lauder 2001). In an analysis of anti-Muslim retaliatory violence following 9/11, Barbara Perry (2003) notes that "visitors, immigrants, and US citizens of Middle Eastern descent bore the brunt of the violent backlash," pointing out that, by 11 October 2001, the FBI were investigating 145 hate crimes thought to be related to the terrorist attacks. Perry further notes

that, though most of the incidents were "motivated by anger and outrage at the 9/11 terrorist attacks, [they are] also informed by a broader culture that supports anti-Muslim, anti-Arab and anti-Middle East sentiments and activities."

7 A report published by the Canadian Race Relations Foundation noted that an analysis of crime data reveals "significant disparities" in the ways in which law enforcement treats people of racialized communities and that a "growing incidence" of racial profiling of those of Muslim or Arab background has been noted since 9/11 (Henry and Tator 2005). In response, James Judd, then director of the Canadian Security Intelligence Service, stated that racial profiling is "fundamentally stupid," further noting that the agency cannot afford to alienate entire communities (Tibbetts 2006).

8 The overlap between Indian ethnicity and Hinduism has created similar problems, although it is arguably the case that conflations involving Sikhism and Islam feature more prominently in the imaginations of policymakers and security analysts.

9 We shall set aside the fact that secularism as an ideological stance often envisions a future very much in keeping with the class and intellectual interests of the elite cohort that propounds its universality; and we shall also bracket both the stubborn resilience of conservative forms of Christianity in the West and the impressive strength of traditional Islam and Christianity in the developing world.

10 See the Pew Forum's 2010 US Religious Knowledge Survey: http://www.pewforum.org/2010/09/28/u-s-religious-knowledge-survey/.

11 See the most recent census: http://www12.statcan.ca/english/census01/products/analytic/companion/rel/canada.cfm. Most statisticians estimate that members of non-Christian religions compose approximately 6–8 per cent of the overall Canadian population, a figure that will increase to 10 per cent by 2017.

12 The Canadian Multiculturalism Act (assented to in 1988 but launched as a policy in 1971) and the Charter of Rights and Freedoms (1982) are the best-known formal statements related to inclusion and diversity. However, the sentiments and logic articulated in these policies are found in many other federal and provincial laws and policies.

13 See http://www.cbc.ca/news/politics/harper-says-islamicism-biggest-threat-to-canada-1.1048280.

14 See the European Monitoring Centre on Racism and Xenophobia report entitled "Muslims in the European Union: Discrimination and Islamophobia," available at http://fra.europa.eu/sites/default/files/fra_uploads/156-Manifestations_EN.pdf. See also the Pew Research

Center's "American Muslims: Middle Class and Mostly Mainstream," available at http://pewresearch.org/files/old-assets/pdf/muslim-americans.pdf, and the Pew Forum study, "Prospects for Inter-Religious Understanding: Will Views Towards Muslims and Islam Follow Historical Trends?" available at http://www.pewforum.org/2006/03/22/prospects-for-inter-religious-understanding/.

15 Introduced in 2005, and in direct response to the 7 July bombings in London (UK), the National Security Youth Outreach Program is a component of the RCMP's Bias-Free Policing Strategy. The objectives of the program are to learn more about how young people perceive national security issues and to prevent youth radicalization leading to violence. See http://www.rcmp-grc.gc.ca/nsci-ecsn/youth-jeune-outreach-extension-eng.htm.

16 Eighteen died that day and dozens others were seriously injured, so precise numbers are difficult to determine at the time of this writing.

17 See http://www.aljazeera.com/news/africa/2010/12/20101231154 25609851.html.

18 After all, many would say that the most liberal Protestant denomination in Canada – the United Church of Canada – also began not just as a religious movement but also as the result of their abhorrence of injustice and poverty (among other issues); church members, of course, would not likely have drawn a definite line between their religious and political motivations.

19 The Royal Canadian Mounted Police have been especially active in this regard. See http://www.rcmp-grc.gc.ca/nsci-ecsn/rad/rad-eng.htm. See also http://mediasmarts.ca/.

REFERENCES

Alinsky, Saul. 1971. *Rules for Radicals: A Pragmatic Primer for Realistic Radicals.* New York: Random House.

Asad, Talal. 2003. *Formations of the Secular: Christianity, Islam, and Modernity.* Stanford, CA: Stanford University Press.

Ashour, Omar. 2009. *The De-radicalization of Jihadists: Transforming Armed Islamist Movements.* New York: Routledge.

Axworthy, Lloyd. 2003. *Navigating a New World: Canada's Global Future.* Toronto: Alfred A. Knopf.

Bartlett, Jamie, and Jonathan Birdwell. 2010. *From Suspects to Citizens: Preventing Violent Extremism in a Big Society.* London: Demos. http://www.demos.co.uk/files/From_Suspects_to_Citizens_-_web.pdf?1279732377.

Berger, Benjamin. 2007. "Law's Religion: Rendering Culture." *Osgoode Hall Law Journal* 45 (2): 277–314.

Berger, Peter. 1967. *The Sacred Canopy: Elements of a Sociological Theory of Religion*. New York: Anchor.

Berger, Peter, Grace Davie, and Effie Fokas, eds. 2008. *Religious America, Secular Europe? A Theme and Variations*. Aldershot, Hampshire: Ashgate.

Berman, Eli. 2009. *Radical, Religious and Violent: The New Economics of Terrorism*. Boston: MIT Press.

Bjørgo, Tore, and John Horgan, eds. 2009. *Leaving Terrorism Behind: Individual and Collective Disengagement*. Oxon: Routledge.

Blom, Amélie, Laetitia Bucaille, and Luis Martinez, eds. 2007. *The Enigma of Islamist Violence*. New York: Columbia University Press.

Bramadat, Paul. 2000. *The Church on the World's Turf: An Evangelical Christian Group at a Secular University*. New York: Oxford University Press.

– 2009. "Religious Diversity and International Migration: National and Global Dimensions." In *International Migration and the Governance of Religious Diversity*, ed. Paul Bramadat and Matthias Koenig, 1–28. Montreal and Kingston: McGill-Queen's University Press.

– 2011. "They Were Always Such Nice Boys: Religion, Radicalization and Securitization in Canada and Beyond." *Our Diverse Cities* 8: 5–58.

Bramadat, Paul, and Matthias Koenig, eds. 2009. *International Migration and the Governance of Religious Diversity*. Montreal and Kingston: McGill-Queen's University Press.

Bramadat, Paul, and David Seljak. 2013. "Between Secularism and Postsecularism: A Canadian Interregnum." In *Secular States and Religious Diversity*, ed. Andre Laliberte and Bruce Berman, 97–119. Vancouver: UBC Press.

Bunt, Gary. 2003. *Islam in the Digital Age: E-jihad, Online Fatwas and Cyber Islamic Environments*. London: Pluto Press.

Burke, Jason. 2004. *Al-Qaeda: The True Story of Radical Islam*. New York: I.B. Taurus.

Buzan, Barry, Ole Wæver, and Jaap de Wilde, eds. 1998. *Security: A New Framework for Analysis*. Boulder, CO: Lynne Rienner Publishers.

Canada, Department of National Defence. 2008. *Canada First Defence Strategy*. http://www.forces.gc.ca/en/about/canada-first-defence-strategy-summary. page.

Casanova, José. 1994. *Public Religion in the Modern World*. Chicago: University of Chicago Press.

Cesari, Jocelyne. 2005. "Islam, Secularism and Multiculturalism after 9/11: A Transatlantic Comparison." In *European Muslims and the Secular State*, ed. Jocelyne Cesari and Sean McLoughlin, 39–51. Aldershot, Hampshire: Ashgate.

– 2010. "Securitization of Islam in Europe." In *Muslims in the West after 9/11: Religion, Politics and Law*, ed. Jocelyne Cesari, 9–27. London: Routledge.

Crocker, D., A. Dobrowolsky, E. Keeble, C.C. Moncayo, and E. Tastsoglou. 2007. *Security and Immigration: Changes and Challenges: Immigrant and Ethnic Communities in Atlantic Canada, Presumed Guilty?* Ottawa: Status of Women Canada and Canadian Heritage.

Dalgaard-Nielsen, Anja. 2010. "Violent Radicalization in Europe: What We Know and What We Do Not Know." *Terrorism and Political Violence* 33: 797–814.

Dark, Ken R., ed. 2000. *Religion and International Relations*. New York: St. Martin's Press.

Dawson, Lorne. 2010. "The Study of New Religious Movements and the Radicalization of Home-grown Terrorists: Opening a Dialogue." *Terrorism and Political Violence* 22: 1–21.

Egerton, Frazer, and Alexandre Wilner. 2009. *Militant Jihadism in Canada: Prosecuting the War of Ideas*. canada.metropolis.net/pdfs/militant_jihad ism_in_canada_e.pdf.

Etzioni, Amitai. 2007. *Security First: For a Muscular, Moral Foreign Policy*. New Haven, CT: Yale University Press.

Gabor, Thomas. 2004. *The Views of Canadian Scholars on the Impact of the Anti-Terrorism Act*. Ottawa: University of Ottawa Press. http://www.justice. gc.ca/eng/rp-pr/cj-jp/antiter/rr05_1/rr05_1.pdf.

Gasser, Urs, and John Palfrey. 2008. *Born Digital: Understanding the First Generation of Digital Natives*. Philadelphia: Basic Books.

Habeck, Mary. 2006. *Knowing the Enemy: Jihadist Ideology and the War on Terror*. New Haven, CT: Yale University Press.

Hammond Schbley, Ayla. 2006. "Toward a Common Profile of Religious Terrorism: Some Psychosocial Determinants of Christian and Islamic Terrorists." *Police Practice and Research* 7: 275–92.

Hampson, Fen Osler, Norman Hillmer, and Maureen Appel Molot, eds. 2001. *Canada Among Nations 2001: The Axworthy Legacy*. Don Mills, ON: Oxford University Press.

Henry, Frances, and Carol Tator. 2005. *Racial Profiling in Toronto: Discourses of Domination, Mediation, and Opposition*. Report published by the Canadian Race Relations Foundation, Toronto, Ontario. http://www.crr.ca/divers-files/en/pub/rep/ePubRepRacProTor.pdf.

Hocking, Jenny. 2003. "Counter-terrorism and Criminalisation of Politics: Australia's New Security Powers of Detention, Proscription and Control." *Australian Journal of Politics and History* 49: 355–71.

Homer-Dixon, Thomas. 2002. "The Rise of Complex Terrorism." *Foreign Policy*, January/February: 52–63.

Huntington, Samuel. 1996. *The Clash of Civilizations and the Remaking of World Order*. New York: Simon and Schuster.

Inbar, Efraim, and Hillel Frisch, eds. 2008. *Radical Islam and International Security: Challenges and Responses*. London: Routledge.

International Civil Liberties Monitoring Group (ICLMG). 2005. *Submission Concerning the Review of the Anti-Terrorism Act*. Submitted to the House of Commons Subcommittee on Public Safety and National Security of the Standing Committee on Justice, Human Rights, Public Safety and Emergency Preparedness. http://www.interpares.ca/en/publications/pdf/ICLMG_Brief_on_C-36.pdf.

Juergensmeyer, Mark. 2003. *Terror in the Mind of God: The Global Rise of Religious Violence*. Rev. ed. Berkeley: University of California Press.

Keeble, Edna. 2005. "Immigration, Civil Liberties, and National/Homeland Security." *International Journal* 60 (Spring): 359–72.

Kilcullen, David. 2004. "Countering Global Insurgency." *Small Wars Journal*, November 30. http://smallwarsjournal.com/documents/kilcullen.pdf.

Kirby, Aidan. 2007. "The London Bombers as 'Self-Starters': A Case Study on Indigenous Radicalization and the Emergence of Autonomous Cliques." *Studies in Conflict & Terrorism* 30 (5): 415–28.

Kohlmann, Evan. 2006. "The Real On-line Terrorist Threat." *Foreign Affairs*, September/October.

Lauder, Matthew. 2001. "False Perceptions of an Inclusive Society: A Century of Racism and Hate in Canada." *Canadian Content*. http://media.learn.uci.edu/cat/media/W03/99012/m_lauder.doc.

Levitt, Peggy. 2007. *God Needs No Passport: Immigrants and the Changing American Religious Landscape*. New York: The New Press.

Lincoln, Bruce. 2006. *Holy Terrors: Thinking about Religion after September 11*. 2nd ed. Chicago: University of Chicago Press.

MacMillan, Margaret. 2002. *Paris 1919: Six Months That Changed the World*. New York: Random House.

Maras, Marie-Helen. 2010. "How to Catch a Terrorist: Is Mass Surveillance the Answer?" *Journal of Applied Security Research* 5 (1): 20–41.

McBride, William. 2003. "The Economic and Philosophical Manuscripts of 1844: Radical Criticism and a Humanistic Vision." In *The Classics of Western Philosophy*, ed. Jorge J.A. Gracia et al., 383–8. Oxford: Blackwell.

McNeil, Christopher B. 2005. "Shifts in Policy and Power: Calculating the Consequences of Increased Prosecutorial Power and Reduced Judicial Authority in Post-September 11 America." *Widener Law Journal* 15: 109–33.

Milot, Micheline. 2009. "Modus Co-Vivendi: Religious Diversity in Canada."
In *International Migration and the Governance of Religious Diversity*, ed. Paul
Bramadat and Matthias Koenig, 105–30. Montreal and Kingston: McGill-
Queen's University Press.

Moon, Richard, ed. 2008. *Law and Religious Pluralism in Canada*. Vancouver:
UBC Press.

Paye, Jean-Claude. 2006. "From the State of Emergency to the Permanent State
of Exception." *Telos* 136 (Fall): 154–66.

Perry, Barbara. 2003. "Anti-Muslim Retaliatory Violence following the 9/11
Terrorist Attacks." In *Hate and Bias Crime: A Reader*, ed. Barbara Perry,
183–201. New York: Routledge.

Purpura, Philip. 2007. *Terrorism and Homeland Security: An Introduction with Applications*. Boston: Butterworth-Heinemann Homeland Security Series.

al-Rasheed, Madawi, and Marat Shterin, eds. 2009. *Dying for Faith: Religiously
Motivated Violence in the Contemporary World*. London: I.B. Tauris.

Rashidi, Khalid. 2004. *Resurrecting Empire: Western Footprints and America's
Perilous Path in the Middle East*. Boston: Beacon.

Rhodes, Jacqueline. 2005. *Radical Feminism, Writing and Critical Agency: From
Manifesto to Modem*. Albany, NY: SUNY Press.

Roach, Kent. 2003. *September 11: Consequences for Canada*. Montreal and Kingston: McGill-Queen's University Press.

Rosenberg, Julian. 2005. "Globalization Theory: A Post Mortem." *International
Politics* 42: 2–74.

Roy, Olivier. 2004. *Globalized Islam: The Search for a New Ummah*. New York:
Columbia University Press.

Ryan, Johnny. 2007. "The Four P-Words of Militant Islamist Radicalization and
Recruitment: Persecution, Precedent, Piety and Perseverance." *Studies in
Conflict & Terrorism* 30: 985–1011.

Sageman, Marc. 2004. *Understanding Terrorist Networks*. Philadelphia: University of Pennsylvania Press.

Sedgwick, Mark. 2010. "The Concept of Radicalization as a Source of Confu-
sion." *Terrorism and Political Violence* 22: 479–94.

Seljak, David. 2007. *Religion and Multiculturalism in Canada: The Challenge of
Religious Intolerance and Discrimination, Final Report*. Ottawa, ON: Multi-
culturalism and Human Rights Program at the Department of Canadian
Heritage, 31 March.

Shadid, Wasif A. 2006. "Public Debates over Islam and the Awareness of Muslim Identity in the Netherlands." *European Education* 38 (Summer): 10–22.

Smith, Angus. 2009. *Radicalization: A Guide for the Perplexed*. www.rcmp-grc.
gc.ca/pubs/nsci-ecrsn/radical-eng.htm.

Swatos, William, ed. 1999. *Sociology of Religion: A Quarterly Review*. Special Issue: "The Secularization Debate" 60 (3).

Taylor, Charles. 2007. *A Secular Age*. Cambridge, MA: Harvard University Press.

Tibbetts, Janice. 2006. "CSIS Boss Calls Racial Profiling 'Fundamentally Stupid.'" *CanWest News Service*, 16 August.

Tirman, John, ed. 2004. *The Maze of Fear: Security and Migration after 9/11*. New York: The New Press.

Toft, Monica Duffy. 2011. *God's Century: Resurgent Religion and Global Politics*. New York: W.W. Norton and Co.

Toope, Stephen J. 2002. "Fallout from 9–11: Will a Security Culture Undermine Human Rights?" *Saskatchewan Law Review* 65: 281–98.

Turner, Brian S. 2011. *Religion and Modern Society: Citizenship, Secularization and the State*. Cambridge: Cambridge University Press.

Venhaus, John M. 2010. "Why Youth Join Al-Qaeda." *United States Institute of Peace Special Report* 236 (May). http://www.usip.org/sites/default/files/resources/SR236Venhaus.pdf.

Volpi, Frederic. 2007. "Constructing the 'Ummah' in European Security: Between Exit, Voice and Loyalty." *Government and Opposition* 42: 451–70.

Weimann, Gabriel. 2004. *WWW.Terror.Net: How Modern Terrorism Uses the Internet*. Washington, DC: United States Institute of Peace. http://www.usip.org/publications/wwwterrornet-how-modern-terrorism-uses-internet (accessed 2 November 2012).

York, Geoffrey. 2011. "Boko Haram Claims Responsibility for Nigeria Blast: Massive Car Bomb Kills at Least 18 at UN Compound; Anti-Western Islamist Group Seems to Be Signalling Its Link to Al-Qaeda." *The Globe and Mail*, 27 August.

Zine, Jasmin. 2012. "Unsettling the Nation: Gender, Race, and Muslim Cultural Politics in Canada." In *Islam in the Hinterlands: Muslim Cultural Politics in Canada*, ed. Jasmin Zine, 41–60. Vancouver: UBC Press.

2 Beating a Path to Salvation: Themes in the Reality of Religious Violence

IAN READER

Introduction

In November 1989, Nakagawa Tomomasa,[1] a young doctor and recent recruit to Aum Shinrikyō, was asked by the movement's founder, guru, and "sacred master,"[2] Asahara Shōkō, to take part in a "salvation mission" (*kyūsai katsudō*) to kill Sakamoto Tsutsumi, a lawyer who was spearheading anti-Aum campaigns on behalf of the families of young people who had joined the movement. Despite having taken the Hippocratic oath to preserve life, Nakagawa stated that Asahara's request made him feel not shocked but proud and elated. It showed he had reached a spiritual level and a state of detachment (*seimutonjaku*) that transcended the boundaries of conventional morality and allowed him to take the lives of others in order to advance Aum's spiritual mission of world salvation (Reader 2000, 150–1). Thus Nakagawa went with a group of similarly "exalted" Aum devotees to Sakamoto's house, where they killed the lawyer (whom Asahara has called an enemy of the truth) and his family – a deed that only became clearly linked to Aum after police investigations in the aftermath of the movement's 20 March 1995 attack on the Tokyo subway.

How was Nakagawa able to abandon the principle that underpinned his profession, going so far as to commit murder while viewing it as a sacred deed that enhanced rather than diminished his spiritual and moral standing? This is a difficult question that addresses powerfully the links between religion and violence and why people who see themselves as motivated by their religious convictions may engage in horrific acts that, for many observers, appear to be antithetical to the core values normally associated with their religion. Aum's leaders, however, saw an indelible connection between their religious beliefs and practices and their manufacture and use of weapons, and that is why I describe the Aum affair as a case of "religious violence" (Reader 2000, 28–31) – violence that was conditioned and framed by the religious orientations of the perpetrators and that could only have come about because of the religious milieu and modes of thought and practice within which they lived and operated.

The Problems of "Religion" and "Religious Violence"

As Bramadat argues in his chapter in this book, when the perpetrators of public acts of violence claim or appear to have some form of religious orientation it is a common public, political, and even academic response to deny that the acts have anything to do with religion. The tendency of liberal democracies to see religion as innately "good" (an issue of relevance in Japan, for example, where laws granting religions legal protections and tax concessions also assume that religions operate for the public good; see Mullins 2001, 72–3) has often been augmented by a concern to distance specific traditions from associations with violence. In Japan, for example, Aum came to be portrayed as a "cult" (*karuto*, a highly pejorative term in Japanese, implying fanaticism, irrational beliefs, and the manipulation of followers by leaders) rather than as a "religion" (Reader 2001). After events such as 9/11, there were frequent attempts by political leaders to draw lines between such atrocities and religion. For example, leaders such as George Bush and Tony Blair swiftly repudiated any connection between Islam and the attacks, proclaiming Islam to be a religion of peace and denouncing the attackers as abusing the name of Islam. Perhaps the politicians wished to ensure that good relations were maintained with their Middle Eastern allies and to indicate that any actions taken in response to such atrocities were not intended as attacks on Islam. Political leaders were also likely to have been motivated by a desire to reassure and calm their own populations while preventing backlashes against their own Muslim minority communities.[3]

It is not only politicians who have engaged in this distancing process; there has been a tendency in some academic circles to do something similar, for example by projecting religion as somehow a pure entity that only becomes violent if or when it is corrupted or "misused" – for example, by people adopting literal readings of texts – at which point it may "become evil" and cease to be "authentic religion" (e.g., Kimball 2002, 41, 46, 72).[4] Another recent scholarly tendency has been to distance religion from violence by arguing that the term "religion" itself is too problematic and too ill-defined to be of value and to claim that the concept of "religious violence" is little but a myth. This is the view espoused by William Cavanaugh, who argues that there is no way one can separate "religious" from "secular" violence, a distinction he portrays as "unhelpful, misleading, and mystifying" (2009, 8). Cavanaugh's argument is grounded in critiques of the concept of "religion," which he presents as something that has been created within a Western framework of reference and imposed, as if it were a transhistorical reality, on the rest of the world. While there are, according to Cavanaugh and others (e.g., McCutcheon 1997), multiple reasons for what they consider to be this transhistorical imposition of a Western model, the one that concerns us here is Cavanaugh's assertion that this imposition serves, in the context of contemporary global politics and the articulation of Western power and visions of social order, to draw an explicit causal link between religion and violence. Cavanaugh (2009) argues that this "myth" of religious violence serves to represent religion in a particularly problematic light – one that justifies its exclusion from the public and political sphere (3) and that serves to deflect attention from and even help legitimate other forms of violence (209). Cavanaugh portrays depictions of religious violence as framed within a Western-centric discourse which in effect portrays the religion of "others" as fanatical and uncontrolled (2009, 17) while depicting the violence of nation states such as the United States as reasonable and necessary to control the violence of others who are driven by religious fanaticism. His basic argument is that notions such as differentiations between the religious and the secular, and religion and politics, are modern Western inventions that serve to create a mythic image of the superiority of Western secularism over non-secular (and hence, within this perception) irrational others. Cavanaugh claims that such differentiations serve to legitimate Western modes of force and violence, depicting them as rational, necessary, and aimed at creating peace and stability by removing dangerous destabilizing forces in other parts of the world, such as Iraq. He further argues that many of the characteristics attributed to "religion" are as readily seen in nationalism (e.g., 2009, 23), and he argues that nationalism also provides striking motivations for acts of violence, citing, for example, how the notion of serving one's country militarily, and being prepared to die for it, is a commonly held notion and is even taken for granted (e.g., 2009, 122).

Richard King (2007) offers similar views, by examining the amounts of money spent by secular nation states on military equipment and by providing data on the extent to which secular agencies such as nation states, often fired by political ideology, have participated in wars, violence, and mass killing. Like Cavanaugh, he portrays the notion of "religion" as a Western construct grounded in a secularist discourse that imposes a universal, Westernized notion on the rest of the world. For King, dispensing with the validity of the term "religion" enables us to get at what he claims is a deeper problem – the problem of violence in general, which he attributes to the blanket category of "ideology." In denying the validity and applicability of the term "religion" Cavanaugh and King both seek to refute the very notion of "religious violence" as a category of analysis.[5]

This is not the forum for an extended discussion of such claims, save to note that several scholars who specialize in the study of religion in Japan have argued that the claim that conceptual frameworks relating to the notion of religion did not exist in other parts of the world until the modern era, when Western concepts were imposed, is questionable (Reader 2004a; Pye 1994, 2002; Shimazono 2004; Kramer 2013).[6] Yet Cavanaugh cites Japan as an example to support his claims about the problematic nature of the term "religion" outside of the West, and he appears to support Fitzgerald's (2000) argument that the term "ritual" should be used instead of religion in the Japanese context while discounting belief as a possible motive or contributing element to what occurs in Japan. In this view all rituals have the same purpose in these non-Western contexts, namely the social fulfilment of obligations and the upholding of social order (Cavanaugh 2009, 97). Unfortunately, Cavanaugh does not examine the corpus of Japanese scholastic work that shows quite clearly that concepts such as belief and faith play a significant role in the construction of Japanese religious traditions and that they cannot simply be lumped together as aiming at the fulfilment of social obligations.[7] As studies of Aum, for example, indicate and as my earlier citation of Nakagawa's views suggests, belief can be a very potent force in Japan, one that for Aum's adherents as for members of many other religions there serves as a means of differentiation and as a rallying call for the reorienting and reshaping, rather than the mere reinforcement, of the social order.

Asserting that categories such as "religion" and "religious violence" are invalid per se might be a suitable way of avoiding talking about the issues involved, but as with Bush, Blair, Kimball, and other apologists of religion, in effect it simply exonerates the religious from any connection with violence and its production. By denying the concept of religious violence, Cavanaugh and King engage in an idealization of religion just as much as politicians who talk of "religions of peace" or scholars who speak of "authentic religion." Such idealization, however, fails to confront the cogent realities embedded in Nakagawa's statement cited earlier, in which he makes direct links between issues of spiritual development, a sense of righteousness underpinned by religious convictions, and the premeditated perpetration of acts of extreme violence.

Of course the motivations behind a given act of violence may matter little to the victims, and other ideologies and ways of thinking can also give rise to violence. The parallels between nationalism and religion that Cavanaugh draws are in many ways quite compelling, and the points he makes about how nationalist images (e.g., the nation and the flag) may often be imbued in state discourse with an aura of sanctity to help justify wars and violence that are manifestations of the self-interests of the nation state are apt. His claims certainly serve as a good argument against the excesses of nationalist discourse that have underpinned American foreign policy over the years and as a critique of attempts by Western powers to rationalize their state violence while condemning the violence of others as irrational through labelling it "religious" (2009, 3–4).

Yet I find the rejection of the category of "religious violence" to be as problematic as King and Cavanaugh's blanket denial of the category of "religion." The alternative to categorizing violence (e.g., with terms such as politically motivated violence or religious violence) is to adopt a simple one-size-fits-all category of violence (as with King's focus on a blanket category of "ideology"), but this means that one is unable to analyse or identify specific causes or particular factors that might be of relevance in understanding how and why particular cases of violence occur. It might serve the political point of showing or suggesting that, for example, the politically driven acts of a state that carries out raids aimed at killing an enemy (as with the US assassination of Osama bin Laden) may be morally little different from the deeds of Aum or a self-proclaimed Mormon prophet whose case will be discussed later and who claimed to have been divinely inspired to kill wavering disciples. Yet it also makes cases such as Nakagawa's and others discussed later more difficult to fathom, and it removes the possibility of producing textured analyses that might better identify underlying patterns, themes, and motivations for violence in particular contexts. Cavanaugh has argued that scholars of religion have shown an "inability to find a convincing way to separate religious violence from secular violence" (2009, 8), but I would question this claim. In the cases that follow I identify a number of distinctive factors associated with the reasons provided by a variety of actors from a variety of religious faiths to explain why they have committed acts of murder and violence. In each of them, faith in various doctrines central to their religion, aligned with beliefs that their acts are closely connected to elevating themselves in spiritual terms, frame their actions as missions to activate an absolute transcendent truth. There is little or no apparent consideration of issues of temporal power and status or matters of political expediency or practicality. Rather, the primary focus is on a mystical notion of a world to come. Such themes serve to demarcate the realms of the religious, and to reject their reality would be to preclude us from understanding why devotees in groups such as Aum acted as they did.

If we are to avoid the problems of the one-size-fits-all use of "ideology" as an explanation for violence, we need to consider more nuanced ways of considering violence, including whether one can use descriptors such as "religious" to describe particular incidents and manifestations of violence. My view is that to reject such descriptors as "myths" grounded in Western-centric colonial impositions on the rest of the world, and as means of reinforcing the supposed superiority of Western social orders upon other cultures, is a retrograde step that shuts off useful analytical categories that the participants in acts of violence might readily accept as appropriate and fitting.

Using a category such as religiously motivated violence does not mean disregarding other motivations for violence such as nationalism, racial hatred, or territorial expansion; nor would the category of religious violence suggest that it is a more pernicious threat than other forms of violence.[8] Nor would the use of this category suggest that other motivating factors in violence are any less, or more, obnoxious or severe. Violence by government regimes fired by political ideologies aimed at creating new politically oriented societies – as with the case of the Khmer Rouge in Cambodia (Hinton 2005) or the Hutu militias seeking to purge Rwanda of its Tutsi population so as to bring about Hutu monopoly of Rwanda's land and resources (Gourevitch 1998) – can put the atrocities of Aum far into the shade. Likewise, as many have pointed out, the deaths in the "war on terror" have far exceeded the deaths caused by the attacks of 11 September 2001.

The issue at stake is not which is worse or more obnoxious but rather why certain acts of violence occur and why, and in what contexts, people who are devout in their faith might turn to violence. The key question is why generally sane people can, for example, see killing as part of their mission as a member of a religious group – and why professionally trained doctors such as Nakagawa (and also Hayashi Ikuo, one of the Aum subway attackers who was also a doctor) could cast aside their professional ethics in the pursuit of what they saw as a higher, religious calling.

Of course, I may have a different perspective than Cavanaugh and King, both of whom examine these issues in the abstract without, it appears, having conducted fieldwork or direct research into specific case studies. My entrée into this field came about through a very practical engagement with the topic. As someone who worked on religious issues related to contemporary Japan, when the Aum affair erupted I found myself, unsurprisingly, needing to find out more about the group that was behind it. I knew that Aum was legally registered as a religious movement in Japan, that it had campaigned hard to achieve this legal recognition in the late 1980s,[9] and that it emphasized this self-perception as a religious movement in its publications. As I gathered and read materials relating to the movement – notably the dozens of books the movement had published, plus copies of Asahara's sermons and training manuals for high-level disciples – and as I interviewed devotees in the years after the attack, it became increasingly difficult for me to make the sorts of category separations that Cavanaugh and King find viable, to accept that the idea of "religious violence" was a myth constructed by those with political axes to grind, or to think that "ideology" alone was a sufficient term to encapsulate what followers of Aum such as Asahara and his disciples were saying and doing. Indeed, it was also impossible to give much credence to the assumption that Cavanaugh appeared to make about Japan in general in thinking that a term such as "ritual" and a notion such as reinforcing social obligation and order could help explain such a phenomenon.[10]

In my interviews with devotees and in reading through Asahara's sermons and Aum publications it became clear that people in Aum saw their activities as framed by concepts of religion (Japanese: shūkyō – a term with a long history, etymology, and set of meanings; see Shimazono 2004). Senior Aum members, who have since produced reflections on and accounts of their engagement with Aum and its crimes, have emphasized the religious motivations and orientations that were central to what they did and why they did it. Thus, for example, Hayakawa Kiyohide, one of Asahara's senior disciples who played a significant role in arms acquisition and preparing for what he and other disciples believed would be a sacred war between good and evil, emphasized that the Aum affair arose out of Asahara's "religious motivations," *shūkyōteki dōki* (Hayakawa and Kawamura 2005, 216). No matter what critics such as Cavanaugh might feel about such matters, those who took part in such activities in Aum found no difficulty in seeing what they were doing as "religious" and in using it as a descriptor conditioning the nature of their deeds. Such comments tell us that, rather than simply dismissing "religion" and its adjectival form "religious" as ideological constructions imposed on others as a way of enhancing Western agendas and thus removing them from our possible conceptual frames of analysis, we should pay more attention to those who actually have been involved in acts of violence and who readily understand and interpret them as religious (in the common sense of actions associated with notions of belief, spiritual advancement, and interactions with spiritual entities beyond the human realm that give them a moral purpose).

Nakagawa, following the teachings of the man he called his guru and spiritual master and seeing himself as a sacred warrior taking part in a "sacred mission," was involved in many of Aum's crimes not *in spite of* regarding himself as an ardent religious practitioner but *because of* this identification. Such perceptions also had great significance for the ways in which Aum carried out its attacks and the ways it perceived its deeds. Aum devotees did not see their violence as "indiscriminate" nor their victims as "innocent"; they were part of a world that had gone astray, opposed the truth, and needed to be purified and punished for its sins so that a new dawn could occur. Violence was a necessary part of the spiritual purification process; it was not indiscriminate and those affected by the violence were thus not innocent. This way of thinking and acting permeated Aum and its teachings – as it did other groups that have similarly made religiously motivated mass attacks, such as those in New York in 2001. These are themes that, I argue here, one needs to comprehend in order to make sense of the subway attack and other acts of public violence perpetrated by people claiming to be inspired in religious terms. This will not only help us unravel some of the complex links between religion and violence but will also enable us to see that attempts to dissociate religion from violence, or to argue that religion is only "good" or that "religious violence" is a myth, are unhelpful.

Aum, Spiritualization, and Punishment

The Aum case is one of the most dramatic and widely analysed examples of a religious group that has become violent, and since a sizeable literature now exists on how and why this occurred (Shimazono 1997; Lifton 1999; Reader 1996, 2000; Shimada 2000), I need not go into detail here save to say that a recurrent theme in such studies is that Aum's religious orientations and nature were crucial. Its apocalyptic vision of the world heading for catastrophe, with a final war between good and evil to purify the world, and its belief that it had a mission of world transformation, in which it was destined to fight this sacred war, were critical elements in this process. So, too, was its belief that those living outside of the "truth" (i.e., those who had failed to acknowledge Aum's righteousness and Asahara's standing as the sacred leader of the world) were damned and that their main hope of salvation was to have their negative karma purified through the intervention of an advanced spiritual practitioner. This doctrinal belief (known in Aum as *poa*) meant that it was a duty for sacred warriors to "intervene" in the lives of others so as to save them from building up further bad karma in this world. Besides liberating them from negative karma that would jeopardize future rebirths, the very fact that an advanced practitioner liberated them would involve a merit transfer that would improve their chances in the next rebirth. This belief justified the killing of others in Aum's view; as such, anyone outside the movement was a legitimate target.

To attain the spiritual status necessary to do this, Aum's disciples had to perform austerities; like many religious groups, Aum believed that ascetic practice was an essential element in the path to purification, salvation, and enlightenment. Those who failed to follow this path were doomed to fall into the Buddhist hells at death. Disciples who were reluctant to engage in the harsh austerities considered necessary for salvation had to be, for their own good, forced to do them. In Asahara's view a guru who failed to push his disciples in this way was not acting with the compassion that was the hallmark of a true spiritual leader; the truly compassionate guru was one who, if necessary, used violence to make his disciples do the spiritual practices that would save them (Asahara n.d., 67; Shimazono 1997, 56–7). Such coercion, which had its legitimating roots in numerous Buddhist stories of spiritual masters training their disciples (see below), provided the first stimulus to violence in Aum and transformed it into a sacred activity (Reader

2000, 137–8). Disciples who performed austerities believed they were liberating themselves from the bonds of this world and were no longer bound by the morality of a corrupt world that was heading for apocalyptic disaster. As an Aum disciple commented to Robert Lifton, "[I]f you have ultimate truth, anything can be justified, everything permitted" (1999, 112–3). A mark of those who had "ultimate truth" was their ability to enter a state of detachment (*seimutonjaku*) in which whatever deeds they did could not affect them spiritually; being detached (a concept Aum drew from Buddhism) meant not being affected by one's deeds in the phenomenal world, and thus being able to kill in this way was a demonstration of spiritual transcendence (Asahara 1991, 51–2; Reader 2000, 80–2). From an Aum perspective, then, Nakagawa's elation at being selected for his sacred mission was quite understandable, as was his readiness to abandon the principles of his medical profession (principles Aum believed were grounded in the conventional morality of a corrupt world facing apocalypse) and engage in murders sanctioned by his spiritual teacher and by the principles and teachings of the religion he followed.

Lifton has stated that Asahara "ransacked" the world's religious traditions for his teachings (1999, 271) – and it is fair to say that Aum (like many Japanese new religions) was eclectic in nature. Yet it is not really the case that Asahara and his disciples ransacked other traditions for teachings that legitimated violence so much as they found that what they were thinking, in terms of their belief that violence and killing were legitimate courses of action, was also widely emphasized in other traditions. They read widely and quickly realized what Mark Juergensmeyer (2000) has demonstrated, that the world's religions are suffused with images of violence and conflict, usually articulated in terms of cosmic wars of good against evil. Thus, Asahara and his disciples, already convinced that the world was heading for an apocalyptic catastrophe, encountered and drew on images of final conflict and war in the Bible[11] and in the images of destruction epitomized by the Hindu deity Shiva.[12] What they found within these traditions reiterated what they knew from their studies of Buddhism, both in its prophecies of cosmic wars[13] and in its stories of killing as a compassionate and spiritually enhancing act when done in order to save someone from greater karmic misfortunes. Thus in the Buddhist Upayakausalya Sutra, the bodhisattva named "Great Compassion" realizes that a man he meets is destined to murder 500 people. The bodhisattva kills the man, thus preserving the lives of 500 future victims while saving the potential murderer from acquiring immeasurable bad karma and endless suffering in hell; the bodhisattva recognizes that although this is a compassionate deed, he will need to accept the negative karma for it and suffer as a consequence (Gethin 2007, 70). Aum drew its teachings about transcending good and evil and going beyond conventional morality from the Vajrayana Buddhist tradition that was influential in Japan (Asahara n.d., 21), and this Buddhist tradition provided numerous stories about how, in order to further the spiritual development of their disciples, it was appropriate for gurus to use force if necessary. Asahara was especially influenced by the story of the famed Tibetan Buddhist master Marpa, who treated his disciple Milarepa harshly, pushing him to the limits of endurance. This was the impetus needed to allow Milarepa to break through the spiritual barriers that had prevented his enlightenment; Milarepa became, as a result, a leading spiritual teacher, and the deeds of his master that, on the surface, appeared cruel were in reality deeply compassionate (Asahara n.d., 63–7). Violence when carried out by a master or advanced practitioner was a compassionate spiritual act; as such, Asahara and his disciples saw themselves as rightfully able to kill and purify the world of spiritual pollutions. Indeed, it was their sacred mission to do so.

Zen, Violence, and Bodily Mutilation

The inherent violence in the guru-disciple relationship evident in the story of Marpa and Milarepa and of Asahara and his disciples is a recurrent theme in East Asian Buddhism. As Stuart Chandler has observed in his study of the modern Taiwanese Buddhist movement Foguangshan, its leader, Master Xingyun, could be kind and compassionate to his disciples, but he could also be a "stern authoritative taskmaster" who scolded, rebuked, and even struck them in public if need be (Chandler 2004, 36). The Zen tradition that has been highly influential in Japan, contributing much to the Japanese traditions of asceticism and meditation that influenced Aum, also provides numerous examples of this "compassionate cruelty" and many stories about the mortification of the body in the pursuit of higher spiritual states (Reader 2009). The use of physical violence – notably the use of the *kyōsaku* or "waking stick" to strike meditating monks while they are seated in zazen (seated meditation) in order to help them achieve a sudden awakening – permeates the tradition. In the meditation hall, a senior monk walks around during periods of meditation, and if a practitioner appears to be losing focus, poor in posture, or dozing off, it is common for the monk to strike the practitioner with the "waking stick." This is portrayed as an act of compassion and is ritually framed; the person to be hit bows in supplication beforehand and then again afterwards to acknowledge and thank the monk for the blows. Stories of practitioners being "awakened" by such blows abound, while other acts of violence are equally vaunted as examples of how deeds normally seen as wrong may, in the context of spiritual striving and practice, be highly valued. Thus the Chinese Rinzai tradition tells of disciples who attained spiritual awakening when struck by their masters, whose blows, albeit severe and painful, were delivered "mercifully" (Suzuki 1975, 306–7).

Perhaps the most famous Japanese example of how Zen elevated acts of violence into spiritually enhancing deeds is that of the Rinzai Zen Buddhist master Hakuin Ekaku (1686–1769). In his account of his awakening Hakuin emphasizes the violence vented on him by his Zen teacher, who struck him repeatedly with a stick and pushed him off a veranda; such blows drove Hakuin onwards in his search for enlightenment, which finally came as he stood before a house during the traditional monastic begging round. The elderly female occupant wanted him to go away, but he failed to take note, so she struck him with a broom; the blow was the spark needed to bring about his final breakthrough into the realms of enlightenment (Suzuki 1975, 339–40; Stevens 1993, 66–9). In such accounts violence is highly beneficial, a critical element in stripping away the delusions that, according to Zen, cloud the mind and prevent one seeing the true nature of reality; as such, D.T. Suzuki has written, Zen masters may legitimately use methods that appear to be inhumane to break through the barriers that humans surround themselves with (Suzuki 1975, 341).

Violence is not just externally directed; the Zen tradition contains many stories in which bodily mutilation is used to demonstrate the importance of casting aside the physical world to bring spiritual advancement. The story of how Hui-ko (the second Zen patriarch in China) cut off his right arm in order to show Bodhidharma (the first patriarch in China, who had previously rejected him as a disciple) how sincere was his pursuit of the truth is one of the most revered of such stories, as is that of Bodhidharma cutting off his own eyelids so as not to waste time sleeping and thereby to spend more time in meditation. By sacrificing their eyelids and arm respectively, Bodhidharma was able to keep meditating and attain enlightenment, and Hui-ko was able to acquire Bodhidharma's teaching, as a result of which he became enlightened and was able to pass on the tradition to later disciples. Via such stories the Zen tradition inculcated a message that sacrifice (including bodily mutilation) could be legitimate in the pursuit of higher spiritual goals; the physical realm was merely a state through which this higher goal was achieved, and if mutilating one's own body or beating that of a disciple could help in that goal, then they were not simply acts of necessity but acts imbued with sacred force. As such, the body was something to be purified, beaten, and if necessary subjugated and cast off as an impediment to higher spiritual goals.

Violence and Spiritual Attainment in Ananda Marga

It is not just in Buddhist contexts that one finds this link among asceticism, the body, enlightenment, and violence in the Asian religious traditions. In India, for example, similar themes can be seen in the activities of Ananda Marga, which emerged out of the Hindu religious milieu and was founded by Prabhat Ranjan Sarkar (1920–90), an Indian guru known to his disciples as Anandamurti. Claims of violence and of murder have been levelled at Ananda Marga in the past, and in 1972, after six bodies – all former Ananda Marga disciples – were found buried in the vicinity of Ananda Marga's headquarters at Ranchi in India, Sarkar was charged and found guilty of murder, although on appeal he was later acquitted. Although the exact circumstances of these deaths have never been clearly determined, there is clear evidence that the movement had a violent dimension, especially while Sarkar was alive. Ananda Marga's teachings indicated that violence was closely related to the movement's concepts and practices of spiritual advancement and that it could be legitimately used against anyone who impeded the movement. As Helen Crovetto has commented, Sarkar believed that "the spiritual evolution of the individual and society was tied to the use of force," while his writings present doctrinal justifications for violence to this end (Crovetto 2008, 27). Sarkar also spoke of the need for perpetual cosmic war in which those seeking spiritual advancement needed to engage in a constant struggle against evil. Evil was identified as anything that impeded the spiritual development of others – a notion that meant that anyone who hindered Ananda Marga was a legitimate target who could be rightfully killed if necessary (Crovetto 2008, 37–41). One can see numerous parallels here to the ways that Asahara legitimated Aum's violence; indeed, in a similar vein to Asahara, Sarkar referred to his followers as "spiritual soldiers" (Crovetto 2008, 42).

As such, violence "was an integral part of the group's internal dynamics" and closely aligned to Ananda Marga's philosophy, concepts of asceticism, spiritual practice, and advancement within the movement (Voix 2008, 4). These, in turn, as Raphaël Voix emphasizes, were embedded within the wider context of Hindu ascetic culture, in which violent acts committed by divine beings who are incarnate on earth for the purpose of preserving the cosmic order (a perception held about Sarkar/ Anandamurti in Ananda Marga) are not considered to be violent, and in which it is permissible for such spiritually advanced beings to take the lives of others if they deem it necessary for the sake of the wider cosmic order (Voix 2008, 6). Ananda Marga emphasized that the world was an arena of struggle between two contradictory forces, ignorance and knowledge – a struggle in which it was fighting on behalf of the latter so as to overcome the former. In such a struggle any acts taken to confront ignorance and sin were legitimate (Voix 2008, 6–7).

In this context, the movement developed a hierarchic structure grounded in personal ascetic attainment and regulated by violence that was viewed as important to maintain spiritual discipline within the movement and ensure that disciples were obedient (Voix 2008, 9). In order to uphold this system Anandamurti, as guru, could – indeed was expected to – use violence to encourage disciples in their fight against ignorance. While he could be kind and gentle towards them, he also needed to be harsh when required and could beat them severely to improve their discipline and to punish any sins they committed. Austerities and beatings were seen as appropriate means to punish members for breaking the stringent rules designed to aid them in achieving spiritual transcendence. Beatings were a form of spiritual practice and were accepted as such by disciples who viewed them as a means of self-transformation and of saving themselves from numerous future rebirths while bringing liberation closer to hand (Voix 2008, 9–13). Indeed, the closer one got to the level of the guru, "the more the disciple experienced the guru's violence as a tool to accelerate personal evolution" (Voix 2008, 18).

In this process, disciples saw their guru as "capable of everything"; he could perform any deed legitimately, even acts of violence, in order to assist them in their spiritual struggle. Indeed, although Sarkar/ Anandamurti was found not guilty of the murders of the six ex-followers mentioned earlier, it is evident that at least some of his disciples thought he had been involved in these deaths and was justified in so doing. One, for instance, informed Voix that the guru was entitled to kill those – such as the aforementioned ex-disciples – who posed a threat to the cosmic order (2008, 16).

Displaying the Right to Prophecy: Two Mormon Cases

There are clearly parallels between Ananda Marga and Aum in their acceptance of violence as a legitimate and compassionate means of helping the individual attain spiritual advancement, in claiming the right of the guru to use violence as a way of eradicating sin (and hence punishing and killing those who act against the movement), and in viewing the world as an arena of cosmic struggle in which those deemed to be on the side of truth and knowledge are seen as spiritual warriors. The notion that committing acts of violence may be viewed as a marker of sacred status, and that such status frees one from the need to conform to conventional moral positions, is not one limited to Asian religious movements centred on gurus and on master-disciple relationships. As Norman Cohn (1970) has shown, such ideas were central to the activities of the Christian millennial movements that wreaked havoc across northern Europe in the Middle Ages in their quest to realize the "world to come" while purging the corrupt world of those who stood in their way. Those who engaged in this millennial fervour saw themselves as an elite of "amoral supermen" who were free of sin; as such, they could act with impunity and kill those whom they believed were hindering the onset of the Kingdom of God on earth (1970, 148). Their murders were thus righteous, mystical deeds designed to purify the world from evil.

Mormonism has given rise to such ideas as well, especially in its fringe traditions of self-proclaimed prophets, many of whom have envisaged themselves as being involved in a conflict between the forces of good and evil. The cases of two secessionist Mormon groups whose prophetic leaders committed murders that they claimed were products of their righteousness and holy missions are salient here. Both occurred in the United States in the 1980s, and both were motivated by concepts of blood atonement and the lines of the Book of Mormon that state "Behold the Lord slayeth the wicked to bring forth his righteous purposes" (Earley 1998, 137; Krakauer 2004, 167). The leaders of these groups believed that they had been commanded by God to kill others – a deed that would thereby demonstrate their own sanctity. As Jon Krakauer (2004) has shown, the brothers Ron and Dan Lafferty created a small breakaway group based around their visions of Mormonism, their reading of its scriptures, and their beliefs that they had been chosen by God to fulfil his mission. Buoyed by the belief that God's law superseded temporal law and that doing things that were morally wrong in the human world was permissible if it advanced God's law, they believed that they were receiving messages from God to kill the wife of one of their brothers, and her baby daughter, because she refused to accept the stringent rules they sought to impose on their extended family. The killings were, in their eyes, legitimated by the concept of blood atonement – a belief that developed in Mormonism in the mid-nineteenth century and taught that some sinners were beyond the redemption of Christ and could only achieve atonement through the shedding of their own blood (Krakauer 2004, 205–6). For the Lafferty brothers, the only way to save the "errant" wife was to make her atone with her own blood, and this they did; by killing her they thereby demonstrated their direct connection to God – a connection that enabled them to transcend the laws of the land and that illustrated their own righteousness.

Another self-proclaimed prophet, Jeffrey Lundgren, similarly saw killing others as a manifestation of his own spiritual power. Lundgren was – like many others discussed thus far – infused with apocalyptic fervour in which he and his followers would become soldiers in the army of Christ, who would return to bring about the end of the present world (Earley 1998, 264–70). His victims were five members of the Avery family, who were part of Lundgren's breakaway Mormon group but whom he suspected of lacking faith. Dennis Avery, the head of the household, appeared to doubt whether Lundgren was truly a prophet; because of this, Lundgren decided Avery and his family were damned, and he had them killed. Lundgren was fired by his belief in the notion of blood atonement and the aforementioned statement from the Book of Mormon in which the "Lord slayeth the wicked to bring forth his righteous purposes"; he believed he had been charged with the mission of "cleansing the vineyard" by destroying God's enemies (Earley 1998, 222–3). The killing of the Averys, in other words, was part of Lundgren's mission. It "showed" that Avery was a sinner who had to be punished for his misdeeds and atone for them with his and his family's lives, and that Lundgren had the spiritual power to carry this punishment out. Lundgren and the Raffertys were criminally responsible and were later found guilty of the murders they committed, as indeed have Asahara and several of his disciples. Their deeds come under criminal law, and the defence that one is following some higher spiritual purpose cannot rightly be considered by the courts as a legal defence. However, this should not stop us from understanding the extent to which a sense of religious mission and purpose provided the stimulus for such deeds; without these, however misguided they might appear to outsiders, and without texts and scriptures to help support them, one has to ask whether Lundgren, the Raffertys, or other self-proclaimed prophets, gurus, or messiahs would have been able to find the resources, motivations, or simple impetus to carry out the crimes they did.

A British "Soldier of God"

The same is true of the next case I wish to consider. While all the examples discussed thus far have involved groups sharing religious teachings, leaders, and senses of mission, one should not think that claims of divine inspiration or of acting as a "soldier" in a sacred mission need only occur in group contexts. Individuals may also see themselves in a similar light and engage alone in acts of terror and violence that they perceive as divinely or spiritually impelled or sanctioned, and for these people a turn to violence is conditioned by their religious orientations. This was the case with the perpetrator of a series of nail-bomb attacks in London in April 1999; the three areas hit were Brixton, the focal point of the British Caribbean community; Brick Lane, a major centre of the Bangladeshi (Muslim) community; and the Admiral Duncan, a Soho pub at the heart of London's gay community. The bombs killed three people (all in the Admiral Duncan) and maimed many others. Police analysts quickly recognized that the perpetrator was probably racist and homophobic and probably had some connections to extreme rightist groups in the United Kingdom, and they soon identified the person concerned – a young, rather inarticulate man named David Copeland, who had been a fringe member of extreme right-wing groups such as the British Nationalist Party and Combat 18. Yet as they investigated him, it became clear that Copeland – who acted alone – had moved from voicing politically extreme views to carrying out acts of violence after encountering various forms of Christian extremism and becoming fired with the idea of a sacred mission. In particular he had come across – through Internet searches – the Christian Identity movement and was inspired by the ideas of a white Christian nation at the sites run by groups such as the Kingdom Identity and Aryan Nations. Their deeply racist and homophobic ideas were backed by biblical citations that portrayed the Aryan race as God's chosen people, and these convinced Copeland that there was a God-driven, religious dimension to his racist political views. From such online sources Copeland learned about, acquired, and read *The Turner Diaries*, the extremist novel widely seen by Christian millennial extremists as a "bible" setting out a vision of the Christian Identity future; he also found out about the activities of Timothy McVeigh, another *Turner Diaries* aficionado with links to Christian Identity who carried out the 1995 Oklahoma City bombing. So fired up was Copeland by these Christian sites, ideas, and visions that fellow right-wing political extremists complained that he was "going on and on" about the Bible and shied away from him (McLagan and Lowes 2003, 46–51, esp. 48).

Copeland came to see himself not as a political extremist but "as one of God's soldiers, enacting a battle prophesied in the Old Testament" (McLagan and Lowes 2003, xix) and "on a mission from God" (50). After he was arrested, he emphasized the importance of his religious convictions repeatedly in police statements and in interviews with psychiatrists who examined him. He wrote, "I am David Copeland and I am a profit [*sic*] sent by God, to show Gods chosen people what must be done to save us from Damnation" (McLagan and Lowes 2003, 218).[14] Since one of the key issues at his trial was whether he was competent to plead,[15] he was examined by several psychiatrists and a number of reports were compiled on him, all of which indicated the strength of his religious visions and their centrality to his turn to violence and terror. One might note that it is normal legal procedure in the United Kingdom to assess whether someone is fit to stand trial, especially in cases where a number of serious crimes have been committed. It may also be surmised that, when someone evokes motives or inspirations beyond the human realm for one's activities, this tends to cause the authorities to look more closely at the mental state of the accused. It may appear ironic, in a country in which the monarch is head of a state church and some religious leaders sit as of constitutional right in the upper chamber of the legislature, and in which religious adherence is thus seen as highly normative, for the legal system to doubt the sanity of someone who claims religious inspiration for their deeds. However, in UK legal terms, culpability is linked to the question of whether the person concerned was fully autonomous and responsible for his/her actions. If someone was acting under the belief that he or she was guided by a spiritual entity that had control of the person, this would bring into question the autonomy and hence the level of responsibility of the perpetrator and would thus necessitate an investigation of his/her mental capabilities. In the case of Copeland, analysts were clear that religious visions, through which Copeland felt he was acting on behalf of a higher power, were central to his deeds. Dr P. Gilluley, who assessed Copeland for his defence lawyers, noted that Copeland told him he was a "prophet" on a "mission" that would lead to Apocalypse and the arrival of Jesus on earth and that Copeland repeatedly backed up his claims with quotations from biblical scriptures (McLagan and Lowes 2003, 221–32). Dr John Basson, the medical director at Broadmoor, one of the United Kingdom's leading hospitals for the criminally insane, examined Copeland at length before his trial and stated that Copeland's belief in his mission from God drove him to commit his crimes, while his religious orientations gave him a delusional grandeur that made him certain he was right. In this certitude of righteousness, according to Basson, Copeland differed from right-wing political extremists who would recognize there was another point of view (McLagan and Lowes 2003, 253–4). According to McLagan and Lowes, it was Copeland's incorporation of Christian identity and biblical reading into his thinking that was crucial; "he became one of God's chosen people. Suddenly it gave him a purpose to live and, if need be, die for" (2003, 271).

Copeland was an isolated and disturbed loner, and those in the extreme right wing of the larger community who had contact with him were quick to dissociate themselves from his violent deeds (just as they appeared to have shied away from him beforehand because of his religious fanaticism). Yet he also illustrates how religious ideas and visions can influence individuals on their own in the enactment of violence. One cannot tell whether he might have eventually turned to violence even if he had not become fired up by his biblical obsessions. He was on the far right, a milieu that has produced a fair number of violent movements. Yet in Copeland's case it is evident that the impulses that moved him from political extremism to the commission of violent acts emanated from his immersion in the Bible and visits to extreme Christian websites that provided him with a sense of justification and legitimation for his acts and also, crucially, a sense of divine mission. They gave him the sense of delusional grandeur that Basson commented upon and that enabled him to feel he was communicating with God and acting as God's chosen agent to bring about the world God desired. Such a sense of grandeur elevated him to a level beyond normative morality – a position that one can also see in Asahara, who was, as I have noted elsewhere, also enveloped in a highly delusional sense of grandeur in which he saw himself as a chosen prophet, as a Christ-like figure and messiah (Reader 2000, 55, 169). That sense of grandeur at being chosen and having a divine mission elevated them to levels at which, in their minds, they could go beyond the realms of ordinary humans and act with impunity. It was such delusional views that made Copeland's fellow right-wingers shy away from him and that made him move from political extremism to a religiously oriented path of violence.

Punishment and the Denial of Innocence

In these various criminal deeds ranging across religious traditions, countries, and individuals, there are a number of recurrent themes, notably of the perpetrators seeing themselves engaged in a sacred mission – often as a sacred warrior and guided by God or some other spiritual entity – with the very commitment of deeds of violence in such terms serving as a way of either enhancing or proving their spiritual status. Those who commit such acts may also think, as a result, that those who are the targets of their violence deserve and merit their treatment, and this further serves to valorize and legitimate in the minds of perpetrators the deeds committed. When violence is internally directed (e.g., by Zen masters or Hindu gurus seeking to enlighten their disciples) the disciples are deemed to merit such violence (and even punishment) as a necessary means of transforming them. When externally directed, such violence may be portrayed as a form of punishment on unbelievers; it is a divine or spiritually ordained judgment, one that may take the form (as with Aum's doctrine of *poa*) of saving someone through stopping them from committing more sins or that may be framed as a punishment for sins committed, as with the Mormon "blood atonement" killings. While we may view the victims of Lundgren and the Laffertys as innocent, the killers saw them as sinners who could only be saved by losing their lives. Copeland viewed those he targeted as meriting violence because they fell outside of his vision of the sacred realms of a chosen white nation and because they represented the forces (such as homosexuality and non-white races) that threatened the world with "damnation." In Aum's view, Sakamoto, by opposing Aum, had hindered the truth and was therefore an agent of the forces of evil who deserved to be punished by forfeiting his life. Cohn's medieval millennialists who killed those they believed stood in the way of the advent on earth of the Kingdom of God likewise saw their victims as meriting punishment for their heinous stance, a view expressed also by the Ananda Marga disciple who thought that his guru had the right to kill anyone who threatened the cosmic order.

These are distinctive elements in what I am portraying here as "religious violence." For although it is a customary to describe acts of terror and violence as indiscriminate when they are carried out in public places, and for their victims to be portrayed as innocent, for those fired by religious zeal who perform such deeds, concepts of innocence and indiscriminate violence do not carry much sway. When violence is embedded in a framework of spiritualization and sacred mission, and especially when it is grounded in a polarized view of the world in which a sacred war against evil is deemed necessary, victimhood is neither random nor embedded in a framework of innocence. This is especially so when, as was the case with Aum, the "other" – the enemy against whom it is necessary to fight in this cosmic war – is seen as being part of a vast conspiracy against the "truth." Again, this is a common strand in the development of extreme religious perceptions of the world; Aum, in seeing the world in black-and-white terms, thought anyone not with them was against them, an enemy in a cosmic conspiracy (Reader 2000, 188–91) who deserved to be punished.

Such perceptions are common among apocalyptics, as is clear also in David Cook's recent study of contemporary Muslim apocalyptic literature, which is commonly framed around the notion of a vast Jewish conspiracy against Islam that is led by the Antichrist, against whom Muslims will have to fight. This conspiracy, however, is not just Jewish in nature; *everyone* is involved in it, and anyone not on the side of the Muslims is against them – and hence deserves to be punished (Cook 2008, 26).

Punishment – legitimated by the sacred status and righteousness (in their minds) of the perpetrators, frequently sanctioned by a spiritual entity or deity, and often involving the punishment not just of losing one's life in this world but also of further suffering in the hereafter (as with Aum's visions of some of its victims falling into Buddhist hells) – thus is an important and often underestimated element in the framing of violence carried out by those with religious agendas. It is evident in Aum's activities. It emerges, as well, in the attacks carried out by Mohammed Atta and his fellow hijackers on 11 September 2001. Atta's letter, entitled "The Last Night," was found after the attacks and showed clearly that Atta located his deeds within a framework of religious duty. David Cook argues that a key aim of the text was to "assist the 'martyr' through the difficult task of taking his own life (not to mention those of many others) in such a way that this act would be one of spiritual worship and not merely mass murder" (2002, 21). Drawing heavily on traditional Muslim literature, the letter emphasizes the pious nature of the deed to be carried out and speaks of the perpetrators being required by God to "slaughter the 'enemy,'" who are the "followers of Satan ... who have drunk of hell" (Cook 2002, 31–3, 43). As Bruce Lincoln has commented, a close textual analysis of Atta's letter "permits one to see how religious discourse construed mass murder and terrible destruction as religious practices" (Lincoln 2003, 8). Given that the perpetrators viewed themselves as martyrs who would receive the reward of entrance into paradise as a result, it is clear that the deed was seen as spiritually rewarding and enhancing, while those they attacked, like Aum's subway victims, were not innocent victims of an indiscriminate attack but were being punished for their "complicity" and failure to adhere to the truth.

Conclusions

In this chapter I have barely talked about Islam or the 9/11 attacks, which have in many ways formed the context within which so much of recent discussions of religion and violence, and indeed questions related to the concept of "radicalization," have been framed in recent times. Hector Avalos (2011, 137) has suggested that the "focus on religious violence after September 11 reflects an ethnocentric perspective" in which Western scholars became more interested in the topic because "we" were under threat. Avalos overstates matters in some ways, for prior to 9/11 there had been a fairly intensive focus on issues of religion and violence, among both academics and security forces around the world – but it was primarily focused on new and small-scale millennial movements in the run-up to the year 2000 and (in the aftermath of Aum) in connection with the possible use of non-conventional weapons (Reader 2012; Benjamin and Simon 2002, 229). David Benjamin and Stephen Simon, former advisers and high-level officials in counterterrorism in Bill Clinton's National Security Council, speak from the perspective of people deeply involved in high-level policy issues when they state that it was the Aum affair that opened the eyes of security agencies to an issue they had failed to acknowledge previously: "the killing power of religion" (2002, 439). As others have pointed out, after the Aum attack, there was a general consensus among security scholars and agencies that the futures of terrorism and radical extremism would be religious, apocalyptic, and indiscriminate, with terror groups henceforth moving away from traditional focuses on political goals towards

themes associated with worlds to come, mystical world transforma-
tions, and associations with divine rather than temporal authorities
(e.g., Hoffman 1998, 123; Stern 1996, 224; and Tucker 1996, 169).

After 9/11, however, after the bombings in Bali, Madrid, and London, and after the anger aroused by the "war on terror" conducted
predominantly in Muslim countries, this earlier orientation towards
analysing a relationship between various religions, extremism, terrorism, and violence in the context of small-scale groups and weapons
of mass destruction has largely been replaced by a singular focus on
Islam. That focus has led to a number of dangerous and problematic
assertions. The first is the immediate knee-jerk assumption that when
acts of horrific public violence occur, they must somehow be connected
with Islam. This was evident in the short period after news emerged
of the 22 July 2011 atrocities in Norway and before it became clear that
a Norwegian right-winger with possible extremist Christian mystical
leanings was behind the attacks. Before that realization, however, several "experts" had already announced that the acts were clearly carried out by Muslim fanatics or were somehow connected with Islamic
groups.[16]

The dangers of this kind of "response-mode" thinking, in which the
focus is always on the last great atrocity, seen as a marker or signifier
of the future(s) of terrorism and violence, are evident in the knee-jerk
responses to the Norwegian tragedy – and indeed, in the heavy focus
on Islam in discussions of religion, violence, and security affairs in
recent years. After the Aum affair, the inclination of policymakers and
security agencies to concentrate on millennial groups and chemical and
biological weapons played a role in the failure of US authorities to pay
attention to other potential areas of danger, contributing to the lack of
preparedness for an attack such as 9/11 (Benjamin and Simon 2002,
229). The dangers of post-9/11 "response-mode" thinking, similarly,
can lead not just to Islamophobia but to an overly simplistic narrowing
of the topic of study to one tradition as well. Yet, as the cases I have cited
here indicate, there is no one tradition that has a monopoly on violence
and extremism. Rather, there are identifiable patterns that stretch across
traditions and that resonate in seemingly different contexts. Copeland
was a racist and one of his target groups was the Muslims who lived in
Brick Lane in London, yet in the framing of his sacred mission and his
belief that he was carrying out the word of God he closely resembled
the extremists of the tradition he reviled. Aum's adherents and Ananda
Marga devotees saw the violence meted out to them by their guru as

rightful and sacred and saw any killings done in this context as appropriate acts.

When people believe that they are engaged in a cosmic struggle for truth and convince themselves of the righteous nature of their cause, when they see those who do not support them as enemies, and when they consider or recognize (based so often on religious traditions that affirm this point and provide plentiful examples to substantiate it) that violent acts can be spiritually enhancing and legitimate means of producing spiritual status, then violence becomes not just a readily accepted possibility but also a potentially sacred – and indeed even obligatory – act that punishes its victims as well as sanctifies its perpetrators. In such ways, violence and the sacred are intertwined not just metaphorically or symbolically but in very real, practical terms. To kill becomes, within this framework of interpretation, a deeply spiritual and compassionate deed that enhances the spiritual standing of the perpetrators and tells them that they are, like Nakagawa, not murderers but saviours and spiritual warriors battling against the evils of this world.

In these situations, contrary to Cavanaugh's suggestion, we are not dealing with policymakers intent on pushing forward their politically motivated agendas by inventing a category of "religious violence." Removing the "myth of religious violence," Cavanaugh argues, frees us to tackle the question that he thinks is most vital: "under what circumstances do ideologies and practices of all kinds promote violence?" (2009, 226). Yet valuable though this question might be, and laudable as it might be to expose the hypocritical ways nation states validate their own violence while demonizing that of others, removing the notion of "religious violence" from consideration undermines our potential for understanding and responding to it. As has been seen in this chapter, the category itself is a product of the deeds and thoughts of the actors who carry out the violence, and it needs to be discussed and recognized as such. Those who seek either to separate religion from violence on the grounds that religion is peaceful and "good" or to deny that there can be a category of religious violence are evading the reality of religion as a part of the human world and as a potential factor in and qualifying agent of violence. Certainly "religion" is not some fixed identifiable entity with a timeless nature; rather it is a conceptual category created by humans as a means of explaining or analysing the world. To that degree those who critique the concept of "religion" as an invented category are correct. But at the same time, I would argue that it remains a very useful category for helping us analyse what happens in the world. As this chapter indicates, it provides those who are concerned about public acts of violence with a means of identifying, assessing, and analysing certain specific and real patterns of activity and forming a better understanding of why they have occurred. If we ignore the religious nature of Aum, and the other people and groups I have discussed, it becomes impossible to understand their motives or to realize why the devotees of Aum risked life and limb making and using chemical and biological weapons. They had no identifiable political goals or worldly aims; what drove them were desires for spiritual awakening and the pursuit of a sacred mission and cosmic vision. The same goes for the others I have cited in this chapter.

It behoves us to take this seriously and recognize that, no matter what we think of their deeds, people such as Aum devotees, self-proclaimed Mormon prophets, Zen monks wielding sticks, medieval Christian millennialists, Bible-reading British racists, and the many other groups and individuals discussed in this book act as they do because they are motivated by religious impulses. Accepting this allows us greater scope to understand why such events occur and to gain a clearer insight into the ways in which such activists think. Portraying religion as innately good, talking of any examples of violence as evidence of the corruption of religion, or dismissing the idea of religious violence as a politically motivated invention are ways of avoiding the awkward question of why people brimming with religious enthusiasm and convinced that they are saving the world or carrying out the will of a supreme deity find it morally uplifting and spiritually rewarding to bomb and kill, or why they find it easy to espouse such radically extreme and violent paths of action. This does not mean that one turns a blind eye to any other form of violence or that one regards religious violence as worse than (say) secular, political, or nationalist-inspired violence; it simply means recognizing that religious violence is a significant reality whose study is essential for understanding why people can be deeply pious as they engage in acts of murder and violence against their fellow beings.

NOTES

1 Throughout this chapter, Japanese names are given in Japanese form (family name followed by given name).
2 Asahara was referred to by the terms *guru* and *sonshi* ("sacred master") by disciples.

3 The White House issued a press release on 17 September 2001 from George W. Bush saying that "Islam is peace," and this position was reiterated in later statements that claimed the attackers misrepresented Islam. Tony Blair also spoke similarly on several occasions, and the refrain was taken up by many others in public positions – such as Franco Frattini, then European Union Commissioner for Justice, Freedom and Security, who stated one should not use the term "Islamic terrorism" to describe suicide attacks and the like, arguing that those who perpetrate such attacks are in effect abusing the name of religion (*The Observer*, 14 May 2006, 11).

4 Keith Ward (2007) is another who, while accepting that religions can do bad deeds, considers that religion is primarily a "good" entity that at times manifests dark sides. But on the whole, according to Ward, its good outweighs its bad. Of course there are vociferous critics such as Richard Dawkins, Sam Harris, and Christopher Hitchens who present one-dimensional pictures of "religion" as dangerous and solely located within the realms of irrationality and violence. Like those of Ward, Kimball, and the politicians cited here, these depictions are so one-dimensional as to be of little use in analytical terms (see Reader 2008 for a broader discussion of the problems with such arguments).

5 In chapter 3 in this book Lorne Dawson presents yet another reading of the reluctance of academics to conceive of religion as a motivation for terrorist acts, and he also argues, for other reasons, that this is a mistake.

6 In making his claims Cavanaugh relies on Fitzgerald (2000), but Fitzgerald's argument has been widely criticized (e.g., Reader 2004a, b) Even Josephson (2012, 6), who otherwise supports this line of argument, notes that his new study on this topic was in part spurred by the inadequacy of earlier work such as Fitzgerald's. Josephson's (2012) account provides us with a more textually nuanced and scholastic analysis of how the terminology of religion was developed (or "invented," as he puts it) in nineteenth-century Japan. However, as the references I have cited in the text, notably Kramer (2013) and Shimazono (2004), indicate, the argument that Josephson makes about "religion" as a conceptual entity that did not exist in Japan until Western incursions in the mid-nineteenth century is open to much debate.

7 In this failing one should note that Cavanaugh is simply following Fitzgerald, whose attempt to substitute "ritual" for "religion" I have elsewhere shown to be deeply problematic and flawed (see Reader 2004a, b).

8 On this point Cavanaugh makes the claim that while religious violence is universally disapproved of, violence that is deemed secular may be praiseworthy, "especially when used for the purposes of bringing the blessings and peacefulness of liberalism to places like Vietnam" (2009, 208). This is

palpably absurd. One wonders where Cavanaugh has been over the past decades; while there was a sizeable body of opinion supporting the Vietnam War, there has actually been overwhelming criticism of it as well.

9 It should be noted that legal registration as a religious corporation (*shūkyōhōjin*) in Japan confers various privileges but not automatically. Groups have to actively apply for this status, and they must show they have a coordinated set of doctrinal teachings, practices, images of worship, and so on – all the trappings that would be seen as falling under the category of religion in a Western context. Aum, like many hundreds of other Japanese organizations, found no problem in claiming the name "religious" for itself.

10 Cavanaugh's only mention of Aum is on page 34 of his book, where, in a clear allusion to his later comments that imply one should use the term "ritual" rather than "religion" in the context of Japan, he says Aum was a melange of practices, failing to note that it had some clearly defined doctrines and teachings including concepts and interpretations of karma, concepts of multiple spiritual realms connected with the human realm, concepts of punishment, transcendence, and salvation, and so on. In framing Aum in such ways, along with portraying the Japanese context as one centred wholly on ritual and in which beliefs and doctrines appear to play no part, Cavanaugh is not too far away from the neocolonialist position that Japanese critics such as Shimada Katsumi (as well as myself) have suggested underpins Fitzgerald's argument about Japan, in which he uses blanket categories depicting a monolithic image of Japan and seemingly dismisses the notion that the Japanese have formulated complex religious ideas, concepts, philosophies, and the like (see Reader 2004b).

11 The term *harumageddon* (the Japanese version of Armageddon) appeared frequently in Aum rhetoric from around late 1988 after disciples alerted Asahara to the contents of the book of Revelation, as the images of a final cosmic war of good and evil he found therein appeared to fit with his own growing sense of apocalyptic disaster (Reader 2000, 141–2).

12 Aum drew inspiration from Hinduism, especially after Asahara visited India in 1986, while the name "Aum" itself – encapsulating images of destruction, preservation, and creation – came from Hinduism (Reader 2000, 61, 78–9).

13 This was especially so with the Tibetan Buddhist text the Kalacakra Tantra, which foretold a Buddhist saviour who would lead the forces of good against evil in a final war (Reader 2000, 91).

14 God, one might note, clearly does not worry about grammar or spelling ability when choosing people for his missions.

15 The court ruled that he was, and he was found guilty of murder, although he was then transferred to a hospital for the criminally insane.

16 See https://metranet.londonmet.ac.uk/fms/MRSite/Research/iset/ Suspect%20Communities%20Findings%20July2011.pdf for a report on a recent project that examines such issues in some depth. One Canadian university even issued on its website – very soon after the bomb went off and when only two deaths had been confirmed – a press release citing its "international security expert," Andre Gerolymatos (a professor of Hellenistic studies who has lectured widely about the Middle East, terrorism, and international politics), as saying he believed al-Qaeda is involved: "Until someone claims responsibility, those responsible are part of the numerous groups affiliated with al-Qaeda" (http://www.sfu.ca/pamr/issues-experts/2011/oslo-bombing.html, accessed 25 July 2011). Amazingly the comments were still accessible some weeks later, on 12 August 2011, after it became clear that the perpetrator was a virulently anti-Muslim Norwegian.

REFERENCES

Asahara Shōkō. 1991. *Tatagata abidanma: Shinri shōsha zettai saishō no hōsoku.* Vol. 1, *Daiūchū ni jissō.* Tokyo: Oumu Shuppan.

– n.d. *Vajrayana kōsu: Kyōgaku shisutemu kyōhon.* Internal unpublished 368-page training manual for senior Aum disciples, c. 1994.

Avalos, Hector. 2011. "Explaining Religious Violence: Retrospects and Prospects." In *Blackwell Companion to Violence,* ed. Andrew R. Murphy, 137–46. Malden, MA, and Oxford: Wiley-Blackwell.

Benjamin, Daniel, and Stephen Simon. 2002. *The Age of Sacred Terror.* New York: Random House.

Cavanaugh, William T. 2009. *The Myth of Religious Violence.* New York: Oxford University Press.

Chandler, Stuart. 2004. *Establishing a Pure Land on Earth: The Foguang Buddhist Perspective on Modernization and Globalization.* Honolulu: University of Hawai'i Press.

Cohn, Norman. 1970. *The Pursuit of the Millennium: Revolutionary Millenarians and Mystical Anarchists of the Middle Ages.* London and New York: Oxford University Press.

Cook, David. 2002. "Suicide Attacks or 'Martyrdom Operations' in Contemporary Jihad Literature." *Nova Religio* 6 (1): 7–44.

– 2008. *Contemporary Muslim Apocalyptic Literature.* Syracuse, NY: Syracuse University Press.

Crovetto, Helen. 2008. "Ananda Marga and the Use of Force." *Nova Religio* 12 (1): 26–56.

Earley, Pete. 1998. *Prophet of Death: The Mormon Blood Atonement Killings*. New York: William Morrow and Co.

Fitzgerald, Timothy. 2000. *The Ideology of Religious Studies*. New York and Oxford: Oxford University Press.

Gethin, Rupert. 2007. "Buddhist Monks, Buddhist Kings, Buddhist Violence." In *Religion and Violence in South Asia: Theory and Practice*, ed. John R. Hinnells and Richard King, 62–82. London: Routledge.

Gourevitch, Philip. 1998. *We Wish to Inform You That Tomorrow We Will Be Killed with Our Families: Stories from Rwanda*. New York: Farrar, Straus and Giroux.

Hayakawa Kiyohide and Kawamura Kunimitsu. 2005. *Watashi ni totte Oumu to wa nandatta no ka*. Tokyo: Popurasha.

Hinton, Alexander. 2005. *Why Did They Kill? Cambodia in the Shadow of Genocide*. Berkeley and Los Angeles: University of California Press.

Hoffman, Bruce. 1998. *Inside Terrorism*. London: Indigo.

Josephson, Jason Ānanda. 2012. *The Invention of Religion in Japan*. Chicago: University of Chicago Press.

Juergensmeyer, Mark. 2000. *Terror in the Mind of God: The Global Rise of Religious Violence*. Berkeley: University of California Press.

Kimball, Charles. 2002. *When Religion Becomes Evil*. San Francisco: Harper.

King, Richard. 2007. "The Association of 'Religion' with Violence: Reflections on a Modern Trope." In *Religion and Violence in South Asia: Theory and Practice*, ed. John R. Hinnells and Richard King, 226–57. London and New York: Routledge.

Krakauer, Jon. 2004. *Under the Banner of Heaven: A Story of Violent Faith*. New York: Anchor Books.

Kramer, Hans Martin. 2013. "How 'Religion' Came to Be Translated as *Shūkyō*: Shimaji Mokurai and the Appropriation of Religion in Early Meiji Japan." *Japan Review* 25: 67–89.

Lifton, Robert Jay. 1999. *Destroying the World to Save It*. New York: Holt.

Lincoln, Bruce. 2003. *Holy Terrors: Thinking about Religion after September 11*. Chicago: University of Chicago Press.

McLagan, Graeme, and Nick Lowes. 2003. *Killer on the Streets: The Terrifying True Story of a Killer and His Evil and Bloody Campaign*. London: Blake.

Mullins, Mark R. 2001. "The Legal and Political Fall-Out of the 'Aum Affair.'" In *Religion and Social Crisis in Japan: Understanding Japanese Society through the Aum Affair*, ed. Robert J. Kisala and Mark R. Mullins, 71–86. Basingstoke, UK, and New York: Palgrave Macmillan.

Pye, Michael. 1994. "What is 'Religion' in East Asia?" In *The Notion of "Religion" in Comparative Research: Selected Proceedings of the XVIth Congress of the*

International Association of the History of Religions, ed. Ugo Bianchi, 115–22. Rome: L'Erma di Bretschneider.
- 2002. "Modern Japan and the Science of Religion." In *Modern Societies and the Science of Religions*, ed. Gerard A. Wiegers and Jan G. Platvoet, 350–76. Leiden: Brill.
Reader, Ian. 1996. *A Poisonous Cocktail? Aum Shinrikyō's Path to Violence.* Copenhagen: NIAS Books.
- 2000. *Religious Violence in Contemporary Japan: The Case of Aum Shinrikyō.* Richmond, UK: Curzon Press; Honolulu: University of Hawai'i Press.
- 2001. "Consensus Shattered: Japanese Paradigm Shifts and Moral Panic in the Post-Aum Era." *Nova Religio* 4 (3): 225–34.
- 2004a. "Dichotomies, Contested Terms and Contemporary Issues in the Study of Religion." *Electronic Journal of Contemporary Japanese Studies* 2004. http://www.japanesestudies.org.uk/discussionpapers/Reader2.html.
- 2004b. "Ideology, Academic Inventions and Mystical Anthropology." *Electronic Journal of Contemporary Japanese Studies* 2004. http://www.japanesestudies.org.uk/discussionpapers/Reader.html.
- 2008. "Public Terror versus Public Good." In *The Edge of Reason? Science and Religion in Modern Society*, ed. Alex Bentley, 137–44. London: Continuum International.
- 2009. "Bodily Punishments and the Spiritually Transcendent Dimensions of Violence: Zen Buddhist Example." In *Dying for Faith: Religious Motivated Violence in the Contemporary World*, ed. Madawi Al-Rasheed and Marat Shterin, 139–51. London: I.B. Tauris.
- 2012. "Globally Aum: The Aum Affair, Counterterrorism and Religion." *Japanese Journal of Religious Studies* 39 (1): 179–98.
Shimada Hiromi. 2000. *Oumu: Naze shūkyō ga terorisumu o unda noka.* Tokyo: Transview.
Shimazono Susumu. 1997. *Gendai shūkyō no kanōsei: Oumu Shinrikyō to bōryoku.* Tokyo: Iwanami Shoten.
- 2004. "Kindai Nihon ni okeru 'shūkyō' gainen no juyō." In *Shūkyō saikō*, ed. Shimazono Susumu and Tsuruoka Yoshio, 189–206. Tokyo: Perikansha.
Stern, Jessica. 1996. "Weapons of Mass Impact: A Growing and Worrisome Danger." *Politics and the Life Sciences* 15 (2): 222–5.
Stevens, John. 1993. *Three Zen Masters: Ikkyū, Hakuin, Ryōkan.* Tokyo: Kodansha.
Suzuki, D.T. 1975. *Essays in Zen Buddhism, Vol. 1.* London: Rider.
Tucker, Jonathan B. 1996. *Chemical/Biological Terrorism: Coping with a New Threat Politics and the Life Sciences* 15 (2): 167–83.
Voix, Raphaël. 2008. "Denied Violence, Glorified Fighting: Spiritual Discipline and Controversy in Ananda Marga." *Nova Religio* 12 (1): 3–25.
Ward, Keith. 2007. *Is Religion Dangerous?* Oxford: Lion.

3 Trying to Make Sense of Home-Grown Terrorist Radicalization: The Case of the Toronto 18

LORNE DAWSON

Canadians really became participants, reluctantly, in the international war on Salafi-jihadist terrorism in the summer of 2006. Officially, the government had been engaged in this war in earnest for some time, and several Canadians or residents of Canada already had been arrested on terrorism charges.[1] But the fear of "home-grown terrorism," with real consequences for Canadians, was first driven home by the arrests of the group dubbed "the Toronto 18." On 2 June 2006, police teams raided several homes and a storage facility in Toronto and Mississauga, arresting 11 men and 4 youths. Two others, already serving prison terms for gun smuggling, were arrested as well; another man was arrested two months later. The group of young Muslim men were accused of participating in several plots to attack Parliament Hill and detonate truck bombs in front of the Toronto Stock Exchange, the Toronto office of the Canadian Security Intelligence Service, and an unspecified military base. They hoped, apparently, that their actions would avenge the deaths and injuries suffered by Muslims abroad at the hands of the United States and its allies and end Canada's involvement in the war in Afghanistan. Members of the group had been under investigation for some time and had been infiltrated by two CSIS informants (who were later transferred to the RCMP when the actual criminal investigation began). Several were ultimately trapped by an elaborate sting operation involving the delivery of a large shipment of fake fertilizer for building the bombs.

Long after the sensational news broke, many Canadians remained sceptical that there was a serious threat from home-grown terrorists. Most of the suspects were quite young, and charges were eventually stayed against four of the adults and three of the youths. In the absence of more information, because of a court-imposed publication ban, many

Canadians were inclined to dismiss the group as "a bunch of bravado-filled but bumbling incompetents who were not capable of carrying out their plans" (Teotonio 2010). Plus they questioned the role "played by two RCMP-paid infiltrators, suspicious they had been *agent provocateurs* who goaded the accused and fuelled the plots" (Teotonio 2010). Slowly but surely, however, as the remaining 11 either plead guilty or were convicted, and as the findings of the court cases, in particular the "Agreed Statements of Fact," became public, the reasons for doubt dwindled. It became clear that a catastrophe was narrowly averted, the police had not entrapped the offenders, and the terrorists, while amateurish, had acted with serious and sustained intent.[2] The threat to Canada from some of its own citizens was as real as that faced by Britain, the United States, and other countries in Europe, even though the offenders had failed to complete their plans. Since 2006 a number of other young Canadian Muslim men have been arrested on similar terrorism charges, and on 11 May 2010, Richard Fadden, director of CSIS, told the Canadian Parliament that the service "is investigating over 200 individuals in this country whose activities meet the definition of terrorism as set out in section 2(c) of the CSIS Act" (CSIS 2010).

What, in fact, do we know about these angry young men? Can we understand how and why the members of the Toronto 18 became radicalized? The copious news reports provide us with some insights into the lives, behaviour, and attitudes of these men. But only one quite limited attempt has been made to systematically place this group in the context of research on similar terrorist groups (see Silber and Bhatt 2007). In this chapter I begin the process of doing so more fully by presenting an overview of some of the unavoidable challenges faced by anyone who turns their hand to the task. To this end I do three things. First, I set the stage for the analysis by delineating three key methodological problems handicapping the study of radicalization in general. Second, I set the social profile of the members of the Toronto 18 in the context of what we know about terrorists from the global *mujahideen* and home-grown terrorists in Europe. This reveals the complexity of the nature of the phenomenon. Third, I broach the controversial issue of the role of religion in the process of radicalization and the case of the Toronto 18 in particular. This highlights one of the key interpretive conundrums. These three analyses have serious implications for making any generalizations about why and how individuals become radicalized. In the limited space available, however, I can do little more than frame what is at stake and the interpretive options available.

Methodological Problems Hindering Our Understanding

Anyone newly coming to the field of terrorism studies will soon confront two features of the field: first, the number of relevant studies since 9/11 has grown exponentially, and it is extremely difficult to sort the wheat from the chaff; second, surprisingly little real progress has been made in developing a systematic and scientifically credible understanding of the processes of radicalization leading to violence.[3] The reasons for the first development are obvious and warrant little attention here. The slow progress in understanding radicalization is more difficult to explain. It reflects, in part, the sheer complexity of the issues at hand and the need for a multidisciplinary approach to a multifaceted phenomenon. But it also stems from the impact of some persistent methodological problems in the study of all forms of terrorist radicalization: (1) the explanatory gap problem, (2) the primary data problem, and (3) the heterogeneity problem.

The Explanatory Gap Problem

The explanatory gap problem is not unique to terrorism studies, but it is noteworthy in this context because it is one of the key barriers facing policymakers pressured to know why and how people become terrorists and to provide solutions. Although scholars have called on an array of findings about relevant macro social, political, and economic conditions and various more micro psychological and social-psychological factors to make sense of terrorism, they have yet to explain why only a few individuals, from among the many subject to the same conditions, become terrorists (e.g., Della Porta 1988, 157; Horgan 2005, 83–4, 101; Noricks 2009, 13–36). This leaves us with a crucial gap in our analyses, and this holds true whether we are talking about permissive or predisposing conditions and attributes or more specific catalysts and precipitating factors (Crenshaw 1981; Horgan 2005; Noricks 2009). Researchers have been engaged in a massive process of finding, categorizing, and elaborating factors that, it was hoped, would allow us to predict people's involvement. In the process some of the seemingly necessary factors have been identified, but we have yet to discern what is sufficient.

The explanatory gap problem stems in part from a tendency to leap too readily from macro findings to micro implications, as well as a failure to use control groups. It is advantageous, for example, to have quantitative comparative studies demonstrating that there is no correlation, at the national level, between standard indicators of economic well-being and the people who have embraced terrorism. Contrary to popular opinion, for example, poverty is not a cause of terrorism (e.g., *9/11 Commission Report* 2004, 378; Krueger and Maleckova 2003; Berrebi 2009; Noricks 2009, 27–31). But as Noricks notes, these studies rely on macrolevel data and are not "able to really measure the significant motivator that redressing economic (as well as social) inequality seems to have been for all manner of leftist terrorist groups" (2009, 31). Surprisingly, when studies focus their attention on the more direct analysis of the nature and activities of specific groups and individuals, the approach is largely descriptive and historical. Speculations abound on the reasoning of terrorists and many important insights are available in the research literature, but the research is fairly idiosyncratic in character. There is limited recognition that similar behaviour has been studied systematically, experimentally, and in naturalistic settings by social psychologists and sociologists. Comparative analyses with these findings can act as a substitute for properly constituted control groups. But ideally, as Marc Sageman states (2004, 69), "The inability of specific factors, singly or in combination, to distinguish future mujahedin from nonmujahedin limits our ability to make statements that are specific to terrorists. Identification of variables specific to the creation, maintenance, and demise of terrorists requires comparison with a relevant control group of nonterrorists." Something like a control group is provided by Peter Beyer's study of 35 young Canadian Muslim men in this book. Beyer's findings provide some of the elements of an appropriate comparative context for making sense of the Toronto 18, helping us to further differentiate the kinds of variables that may have some real explanatory value in this case.

The Primary Data Problem

The explanatory gap problem is compounded, as some scholars of terrorism lament, by the deficient micro-level data available on processes of radicalization, especially for home-grown terrorists (e.g., Brannan, Esler, and Strindberg 2001; Horgan 2005, 2008; Smelser 2007, 90–1; Helmus 2009, 73; Dalgaard-Nielsen 2010). With well over a thousand books on terrorism published every year since 9/11, the best research available on jihadi radicalization is still based on anecdotes and the secondary analysis of limited data gathered from open sources, such as the books and articles of other researchers and the media (e.g., see Sageman 2004;

Pape 2005; Bakker 2006). As Andrew Silke documents (2008b, 101), "in only 1 percent of research reports have systematic interviews [with terrorists] been used to provide data." Since Silke came to this conclusion I am aware of only one academic study based on interviews with jihadi terrorists in Europe or North America, and that is Lorenzo Vidino's (2011) study of two jihadi terrorists from Morocco captured in Italy. In this instance, moreover, the interviews were conducted by security officials and Vidino's analysis is based on the copious transcripts. We also have acquired some important primary data on suicide bombers in the Palestinian-Israeli conflict (e.g., Post, Sprinzak, and Denny 2003; Merari, Diamant, et al. 2010; Merari, Fighel, et al. 2010) and in the Russian-Chechen war (e.g., Speckhard and Ahkmedova 2006). But the study of home-grown terrorist radicalization in the West continues to suffer from serious data problems. Given the legal and security barriers involved in accessing arrested and convicted terrorists and the issues of trust, for both terrorists and researchers, this is not surprising. Even if interviews can be conducted, there are serious questions about their credibility (see, e.g., Horgan 2005, 88–9; 2008; Speckard 2009; Dalgaard-Nielsen 2010, 811–12).

The Heterogeneity Problem

There are a number of analytically significant yet overlapping distinctions to keep in mind in seeking to understand any one instance of terrorism. In the first place it is crucial to distinguish between ethno-nationalist (e.g., Provisional Irish Republican Army, Front de libération du Québec, and perhaps the Liberation Tigers of Tamil Eelam), social-revolutionary (e.g., Red Brigades, Red Army Faction, Revolutionary Armed Forces of Columbia), and religious types of terrorism (e.g., Salafi-jihadist groups), and within these basic types between sub-variants such as left- and right-wing forms of terrorism, fundamentalist (e.g., anti-abortion actions in the United States), new religious forms (e.g., Aum Shinrikyō), and so on.

In addition, as John Horgan (2005, 30) points out,

Terrorist groups vary greatly not just in terms of their motivations, but also in size, capacity, resources, as well as their national composition and cultural background. While many of the late twentieth century's terrorist groups ranged in their ideologies from the religious to the overtly political, from the extreme right to the extreme left, terrorist groups also vary in terms of organizational structure, and hence may differ across issues to do with decision-making and targeting ..., weapons use, other tactics, and so on.

There are other less obvious but equally important distinctions as well: between foreign (or imported) and home-grown forms of terrorism, those occurring in and out of zones of conflict, and those rooted in larger social and political movements and semi-autonomous cliques. These differences matter. Much of the terrorist activity in zones of conflict, for example, especially suicide bombings, may be linked to personal experiences of trauma (Post, Sprinzak, and Denny 2003; Merari, Diamant, et al. 2010) and perhaps even to the effects of post-traumatic stress disorder (Speckhard and Ahkmedova 2006). This is patently not the case for the vast majority of home-grown terrorists. Similarly, the conditions surrounding the emergence of home-grown jihadi terrorism differ markedly from those of left-wing radicals in the 1970s and 1980s, when terrorist groups emerged gradually from escalating confrontations between protest movements and authorities (Wasmund 1986; Sprinzak 1990; Braungart and Braungart 1992; Della Porta 1995). The "bunch of guys," as Sageman (2008) calls most home-grown jihadist terrorists, is not radicalized through a gradual socialization to ever more violent tactics born of the frustrations experienced by members of a larger movement of social protest. The jihadists seem to revert to violence without any consideration of, or exposure to, more conventional forms of social action and protest. In addition, they are not part of a centralized organization, either in the straightforward sense that members of the Irish Republican Army or the Palestinian Liberation Organization are, or more amorphously, as members of the Red Brigades were in the 1970s or members of al-Qaeda are today. Rather they are semi-autonomous grass-roots groups responding to either a broader social movement or a set of ideas (e.g., Sageman 2008; Neumann 2009).

Failure to heed these distinctions can result in serious attribution errors when motivational inferences from one situation or type of terrorism are used to explain another. How much insight, for example, do we really gain into the motivation and radicalization of Zakaria Amara, one of the ringleaders of the Toronto 18, from studies of Hamas suicide bombers in Gaza or the West Bank (e.g., Brym and Araji 2006)? Both are Muslim, and both embrace violence, but the obvious contrast in their circumstances is as instructive as any similarities between them. Likewise, how much insight can be gained from studying the recruitment of young Somali American and Canadian immigrants to fight for al-Shabaab in Somalia? There is a superficial correspondence and media reports often conflated the two situations. But the contrast is probably even more instructive. The members of the Toronto 18, for example, did not experience anything like the conventional forms of marginalization and hardship so characteristic of the lives of many young Somalians, both in Somalia and since then in North America (e.g., Berns-McGown 1999; Weine et al. 2009).

Instances of home-grown terrorism, Silke (2008b, 119) argues, largely defy explanation in terms of the standard factors accounting for criminal behaviour in youth. Citing Farrington (2003, 224–5), he summarizes these factors as follows:

> The main risk factors for the early onset of offending before age 20 are well known … individual factors (low intelligence, low school achievement, hyperactivity-impulsiveness and risk-taking, antisocial child behaviour, including aggression and bullying), family factors (poor parental supervision, harsh discipline and child psychological abuse, inconsistent discipline, a cold parental attitude and child neglect, low involvement of parents with children, parental conflict, broken families, criminal parents, delinquent siblings), socioeconomic factors (low family income, large family size), peer factors (delinquent peers, peer rejection, low popularity), school factors (a high delinquency rate at school) and neighbourhood factors (a high crime neighbourhood).

"[M]ost of these factors," Silke observes, "are absent in the lives of *jihadis*, and indeed many terrorists appear to come from backgrounds that would normally protect against the onset of offending." This is not the case, however, for many of the Somali youth in North America. Many of the crimogenic factors are present in the more or less ghettoized Somali populations of Canada and the United States (e.g., Weine et al. 2009). Plus quite a few of these families have been traumatized by their experiences in the long and violent civil war in Somalia. They also maintain strong social and economic ties with their homeland, ties of loyalty that al-Shabaab recruiters exploit.[4]

Overall, then, every attempt to explain why home-grown terrorism occurs needs to be cognizant of these methodological problems and aim to ameliorate them.

The Toronto 18 in Comparative Perspective

In his path-breaking and highly influential book *Understanding Terror Networks* (2004) Marc Sageman tests the stereotype of jihadi terrorists. It is commonly assumed that such individuals are young, male, poor, not well educated, single, and from a strong religious background. Many, it is thought, must be suffering from psychological problems. Suicide bombers are thought to be fuelled by pent-up anger and frustration and struggling under the weight of psychological problems. It is these features, many contend, which make these individuals ideal targets for the extreme religious indoctrination that conditions them to sacrifice their lives for the cause. After examining the information available on 172 individuals known to be involved in the global *mujahideen* movement, Sageman comes to a significantly different conclusion. Recognizing some internal diversity in his sample, he divides the terrorists into four clusters (2004, 70): the Central Staff of al-Qaeda, those coming from core Arab states (Saudi Arabia, Egypt, Yemen, and Kuwait), members from the Maghreb (Morocco, Algeria, and Tunisia) and Maghreb families in France, and Southeast Asians (Indonesia and Malaysia). Most of his findings, however, are reported in more global terms.

The terrorists Sageman studied were not that young when they joined the jihad, the average being 25.69 years (2004, 92). They were, though, overwhelmingly male. These young men came from a variety of socio-economic backgrounds, but "about three-fourths ... were solidly upper or middle class" (2004, 74). The majority had gone to college. They were much better educated than their parents and the average population. Many were familiar with several countries and spoke several languages. Some did graduate from religious *madrassas*, but most "came from technical faculties such as science, engineering, or computer science." They were not the young, naive, and ethnocentric victims of systematic religious "brainwashing" (2004, 74–7). Occupationally, they were largely an upwardly mobile group, experiencing rising rather than falling expectations (2004, 78). The majority were married and had children. Psychologically, as numerous studies have shown (e.g., Victoroff 2005; Horgan 2005; Silke 2008b; Post et al. 2009), they were not psychopaths, sociopaths, or suffering from antisocial personality disorders, and there is little evidence to support more subtle diagnoses linking their behaviour to pathological narcissism, paranoia, or authoritarian personalities (Sageman 2004, 80–91). Rather, on the whole, they are pretty "normal" people (2004, 80–91). About a quarter of the sample had engaged in some petty crime (e.g., forging documents, credit card fraud, selling marijuana). But some of this was undertaken to raise funds for the jihad, and in other instances the individuals converted to fundamentalist views to expiate their sins and rehabilitate themselves (2004, 84). In the end, Sageman says (2004, 96), "members of the global Salafi jihad were generally middle-class, educated young men from caring and religious families, who grew up with strong positive values of religion, spirituality, and concern for their communities."

Most were recruited while they were living away from home, in Europe and elsewhere, and Sageman thinks this is significant, leading him to propose the following straightforward explanation for their conversion to extremism:

> They were isolated when they moved away from their families and friends and became particularly lonely and emotionally alienated in this new individualistic environment. The lack of spiritualism in a utilitarian culture was keenly felt. Underemployed and discriminated against by the local society, they felt a personal sense of grievance and humiliation. They sought a cause that would give them emotional relief, social community, spiritual comfort, and cause for self-sacrifice. Although they did not start out particularly religious, there was a shift in their devotion before they joined the global jihad, which gave them both a cause and comrades. (2004, 97)

The explanation is plausible and persuasive for many, but it runs afoul of two of the methodological problems. Hundreds of young men fit the profile offered, and yet only a few actually become terrorists. Thus the explanatory gap looms large. This gap stems, in part, from the lack of primary data. Sageman's analysis is uniquely comprehensive, but his data are derived exclusively from open sources (i.e., media reports, government reports, and court documents), which often are unreliable, incomplete, and subject to bias (Bakker 2006, 16–17). So while his study remains one of the best available, it is problematic.

The study is well known for another reason as well. Sageman's research reveals that pre-existing social networks of friends and kin are more relevant in accounting for recruitment to terrorism than any organized programs of outreach and brainwashing (2004, 99–135). As studies of new religious movements and social movements in general show, interpersonal relationships play a crucial role in influencing people to join (e.g., Lofland and Stark 1965; Stark and Bainbridge 1980; Wiktoro-wicz 2005; Munson 2008). In Sageman's words,

> Social bonds are the critical element in this process and precede ideologi-cal commitment. These bonds facilitate the process of joining the jihad though mutual emotional and social support, development of a common identity, and encouragement to adopt a new faith. All these factors are internal to the group. They are more important and relevant to the trans-formation of potential candidates into global mujahedin than postulated external factors, such as common hatred for an outside group. (2004, 135)

Edwin Bakker (2006), a Dutch counterterrorism professor, under-took a helpful replication and test of both aspects of Sageman's study with a sample of 242 jihadi terrorists and 28 known terrorist networks from Europe. His analysis of these largely home-grown terrorists con-firms many of Sageman's findings, but with a few significant twists. With regard to the networks, Bakker found they varied in size, range of operations, and degree of "success," but they were internally homo-geneous. The networks "tend to form around people who share age group, country of family origins, and the country in which they live" (2006, 34). A relationship of friendship or kinship between members when they joined, however, could only be documented in about 35 per cent of the sample (2006, 42), but, he insists, the findings tend to sup-port to Sageman's social network theory of how people join terrorist groups. Like Sageman's study, however, Bakker's analysis is hampered by the incomplete nature of the open sources of information on which he must rely.

Bakker's data on individual terrorists presents a less definite profile than Sageman's, and it draws out some key differences. The average age of 224 of 242 people studied (measured at the time of their arrest) was 27.3 years, but the statistical distribution, Bakker notes, is very spread out (2006, 41). Of the 72 people for whom he could "gather socioeco-nomic data, only three can be regarded as upper class, 30 middle class and 39 lower class." This distribution, however, reflects "the general socioeconomic character of Muslim immigrant communities in Europe" (2006, 37–8). Similarly, educational information was only available for 48 people, of which 42 completed secondary school and 15 of those fin-ished college or university. Many, however, were still students when they were arrested (2006, 38). Occupational information on 103 people revealed that 34 were unskilled workers, 19 were semi-skilled, and 12 had skilled jobs. Twelve others were entrepreneurs of some type, 17 were students, and 2 were (semi)professional athletes. Fifteen per cent were unemployed or had a long history of unemployment. That figure "is higher than the overall unemployment rate of the European Union, which is 8.2 percent, but it is lower than the unemployment rate for this age group. The EU [unemployment] figure for those under 25 is 17.7 percent" (2006, 39). There was reliable family information on only 66 people, with 39 married or engaged when they were arrested and 8 divorced. Twenty-five had children (2006, 40). But many of those arrested were too young to draw inferences (e.g., as young as 16 years old). Some information was secured as well on the religious backgrounds of 50 people. Fourteen were converts to Islam (mainly from Christianity), 11 were raised in religious families, and 25 "did not have a particularly religious childhood" (2006, 39). Almost a quarter of the sample had been arrested previously, but some of these criminal convictions were related to terrorist activities (e.g., illegal possession of firearms) (2006, 40). Finally, 11 people in the sample had a record of some mental illness, which is almost 5 per cent of the sample and rather high. But securing accurate information on this matter is problematic. Overall, though, most of the sample appears, once again, pretty "normal." A clear majority of European home-grown terrorists are young men in their 20s, with some education and economic means, and their family status and occupational histories are fairly diverse, as is typical for this age group.

Bakker calls attention to a number of variables that appear to be significantly different in his findings and Sageman's: the seemingly higher levels of criminality and mental illness for the European sample and the lower socio-economic status, levels of education, and occupations of the European terrorists. But much of the difference in the latter regard (clustering class, education, and occupation together since they tend to co-vary) stems from the predominance of Maghreb Arabs in the Muslim population of Europe. In his own work, Sageman repeatedly notes that this group tends to deviate from his findings for the three other clusters he differentiates in his study (i.e., the Central Staff of al-Qaeda, the core Arabs, and the Southeast Asians). In simple terms, the Muslim immigrants to European countries tend to come from the poorer states of North Africa and they came, legally and illegally, to fill low-level jobs in the economy. Many of them still live on the margins of these societies in relatively deprived conditions. This fact may well, of course, account for the relatively high levels of petty criminality and mental illness too.

Everything is qualified, however, by Bakker's admission that it was not possible to find adequate information on the education of European terrorists (2006, 46), and the "absolute number" of terrorists suffering from psychological disorders is actually "very low for both samples" (2006, 48). Closer reading reveals that the levels of criminality for the two samples are actually identical (i.e., 25 per cent), so much of this activity may be the result of radicalization rather than a precursor to it. A more consequential key difference is the finding, contrary to Sageman's theory, that "most of our 242 *jihadi* terrorists were not far from their families and friends, and in many ways were at home in the countries of recruitment ... Hence the two samples differ significantly on this issue" (Bakker 2006, 48).[5]

Another key difference, noted but not adequately explored in either study, is the variable "faith as youth." Sageman reports, for the significant portion of his sample for which information could be obtained, that 49 per cent "were described as religious children." He notes, however, that the large Maghreb cluster from his sample skews the results, creating the impression that a slight majority of jihadists were secular as youth. He seeks to deflect the implications of this finding by arguing that most of the Maghreb cluster is from France, a strongly secular country (2004, 77–8). He concludes, "The other three clusters robustly support the theory [that early exposure to strong religious views plays a role in creating jihadist terrorists], as 50 of 71 (70 percent) were described as religious as young men" (2004, 78). Bakker (2006, 46) comments on the weakness of Sageman's inference that living in France has secularized the Muslim immigrants and notes that in his sample, "the number of persons (not including converts) that were secular during their youth is twice as large as the number that were faithful during this phase of life (24 compared to 11)." He does not, however, systematically return to this point in his conclusions.

Finally, before turning to the Toronto 18, I will call attention to two additional points. First, most of the individuals Sageman examines are members of terrorist organizations with international networks of support. This also means they have received some formal training as terrorists and been subjected to programs of indoctrination. This is not true for most of the men Bakker studied. Their path to violence involved some kind of self-radicalization in small and local groups that had little or no contact with international terrorist organizations. They were heavily influenced by Salafi-jihadist propaganda, acquired online or through lectures, live and taped, by radical imams. But they had not travelled abroad to terrorist training camps. Second, as both Sageman (2004, 98) and Bakker (2006, 43, 53) conclude, the evidence suggests there is no typical terrorist or path to terrorism. Rather, many different kinds of people radicalize and in somewhat different ways. But this conclusion, introduced as a corrective to the preoccupation with finding a simple profile to meet the demands of counterterrorism, can be pushed too far. The insights into the complexity of the situation do not mean that there are no significant similarities and recognizable patterns, as a close reading of Sageman and Bakker reveals and as they affirm. We must keep the specific contexts of the groups in mind (e.g., home-grown versus foreign terrorists or religious versus ethno-nationalist terrorists), but the analytic demands faced by students of terrorism are not intrinsically any more complex than those faced by other scholars of social deviance (e.g., prostitution, white-collar crime, murder). Adequate data is always a problem, and in the study of social phenomena there will be exceptions to every finding, but this does not mean that we cannot delineate the generalizations essential to social science.

So what about the Toronto 18? How might the previous reflections inform our understanding of this group? My analysis will be limited to the ten men convicted in this case since there is no information readily available on the three youths for which charges were dropped, the one youth who was convicted, and the four adults whose charges were stayed. It is also derived from a variety of news reports and court documents, which poses some obvious limitations. A quick overview of the most pertinent comparative information is provided in Table 3.1.

The ages of those ten, at the time of their arrests, ranged from 18 to 30 years old. But the average age was 21.8, and nine of the ten were younger than 25 years old. Seven of the ten were born elsewhere: one each from Egypt, Afghanistan, Jordan, Somalia, and Saudi Arabia, and two from Pakistan, though the parents of the child born in Saudi Arabia are Pakistani. The remaining three were born in Canada with parents from Fiji, Pakistan, and the West Indies. Interestingly, six of the ten arrived in Canada when they were between the ages of nine and twelve, and one is reported as coming when he was a "youth." In terms of education, eight of the ten convicted had completed high school, and six had some exposure to university or college. When they were arrested, one had completed three years of a four-year degree before dropping out, two were full-time university students, and one was a part-time college student. I have no information on the education of two others, and I do not know their occupations either. For the eight remaining: one was a successful entrepreneur running his own software design

Table 3.1. Most Pertinent Comparative Data

	International Mujahideen	Home-grown European	Toronto 18 (ten adults convicted)
Age	25.7	27.3	21.8
Socio-economic status	Upper or middle class	Few upper, some middle, most lower class	Mainly middle to lower-middle class
Education and occupation	Most college/university, esp. sciences and engineering; upwardly mobile	Some college/ university; most low-skill to unskilled	6 of 10 college/ university (business and sciences)
Family status	Most married with children	Approx. 50% married, 25% children	2 married with children, 7 single (1 unknown)
Psychological state	Normal	Normal	Normal
Criminal record	25% petty crime	25% petty crime	1 with record
Religious background	Most religious families; 50% religious as children	Most nominally religious families; secular as children	3 somewhat religious families; rather secular childhoods
Where radicalized	Foreign country	At home (adopted country)	At home (adopted country)
Prior social ties	Strong role	Lesser but strong role	Lesser but strong role

business, one had a semi-skilled job and was a part-time student, two were university students, and four were unemployed. Otherwise, we have little sense of how to accurately classify any of the individuals in terms of their socio-economic status. The limited information available on the families suggests they largely came from the kinds of lower-middle-class to middle-class households typical of the two suburban areas where they lived (i.e., Scarborough and Mississauga). The majority, it is fair to say, had not experienced any real material hardship in their childhoods. Seven were single and two were married with kids, and there is no information for one person. Interestingly, the ringleaders, Fahim Ahmad and Zakaria Amara, were married and had children, even though they were just 21 and 20 years old respectively. Ahmad was unemployed, and Amara was underemployed. He worked as a gas bar attendant while attending classes at Humber College.

The courts determined that none of the ten convicted suffered from diagnosable mental illness or personality disorders, and there is no anecdotal evidence to the contrary. One of the lesser participants, Asad Ansari, is said to have been very depressed because financial limitations prevented him from taking up an offer to study computer science at the University of Waterloo. He chose instead to do a business degree closer to home but was dissatisfied and dropped out during his first year. Only one, Mohammed Ali Dirie, had a significant criminal record as a youth offender, as well as a prior conviction for smuggling firearms across the border from the United States (at the request of Fahim Ahmad). Likewise, only one, Shareef Abdelhaleem, the 30-year-old software designer, came from a devout family. His father had a PhD and was an Islamic scholar. Two others are said to have come from moderately religious families: Ahmad and Saad Gaya. But Ahmad's own comments make his family seem nominally religious at best. There is little information available on the religiosity of the other families, though they appear to have been fairly secular. There is some evidence, as well, that at least five of the ten came from less than stable family backgrounds, involving parental divorces, single-parent families, and in some cases many moves during childhood.

How then do the members of the Toronto 18 fit with the existing information on jihadist terrorists? On the whole they seem to fit the profile for home-grown European terrorists more than that for the international network of jihadists. They are younger, less well educated, and less worldly-wise than Sageman's sample. More of them are also single and from less religious backgrounds. Their relative youthfulness stands out. They are in fact much younger than the European terrorists in Bakker's study, but their socio-economic status and opportunities are probably better. The age factor, however, skews everything, since they were still too young at the time of their arrests to reasonably gauge what the future might have held. Like many Canadians in their late teens and early 20s, it seems fair to say that they were still just testing the waters and figuring out the possibilities while actually not doing much of anything in particular. In terms of conventional career aspirations, they seem to be a fairly aimless lot, with a few obvious exceptions, such as Saad Gaya and Shareef Abdelhaleem. When they were arrested Gaya was a good student pursuing a science degree at McMaster University, and Abdelhaleem was a successful entrepreneur. Abdelhaleem, however, is more or less an outlier, since he is between 6 and 12 years older than the others convicted. Yet, unlike Mohammad Sidique Khan of the London bombers, who is similarly older, Abdelhaleem was not one of the leaders of the Toronto 18. The Toronto 18 network of conspirators is also more ethnically diverse than most of the networks Bakker studied in Europe. All in all, a survey of the social data on the members of the Toronto 18 highlights the difficulty Sageman and Bakker had in developing a simple and effective social and psychological profile of jihadi terrorists. Yet we do still know that some common factors were involved in distinguishing this group of young men from others with similar experiences.

In line with the findings of Sageman and Bakker, the members of the Toronto 18 did come together as a result of pre-existing social networks. Many were friends and knew others in the group, and though everyone may not have known everyone else, the friendships played a strong role in encouraging individuals to become involved and to stay involved when doubts arose.

Contrary to Sageman's theory, however, it is questionable that most of the participants can be said to have been suffering from more loneliness or alienation than would be common among others in their age cohort. They were not isolated from or far away from their families, friends, and homeland, and the two ringleaders, Ahmad and Amara, had young wives and children. But nonetheless, were they "alienated" in some way? The amorphousness of this term, at least as commonly used in the radicalization literature, makes it difficult to determine if this was the case in any meaningful way. What would constitute evidence of alienation per se? The newspaper reports made a point of building up how ordinary and seemingly well integrated these young men were, identifying them as honours high school students who loved to play soccer and noting that their parents were hard-working homeowners. Neighbours and classmates would likely say of most members of the Toronto 18, "They were always such nice boys," a phrase Bramadat observes as being quite common in the post facto accounts of terrorists. Such accounts, which are common in the media coverage of radicalized young men, heighten the dramatic effect of the narrative. Such a frame of reference also highlights the absence of the standard crimogenic factors that even the public associates with youthful deviance. Simultaneously, and inconsistently, the same stories dwell on the early signs that these students were different because they were turning to religion with an unusual fervency, at least for Canadian teenagers and relative to their families. The implication is that this would have separated them from their other schoolmates. Ahmad and Amara, close friends at Meadowvale Secondary School in Mississauga, were active members of the Muslim Student Association, and they "helped form the 'Brothers of Meadowvale,' a group that created a blog to share their views on Islamic preaching and posted rambling rap lyrics with religious themes" (Teotonio 2010). Amara led Friday prayers and earned the admiration of many younger Muslims. Their mutual friend Saad Khalid formed the "Religious Awareness Club" and gave "impassioned sermons during lunch hour about jihad and martyrdom." After school they all hung out at the local Islamic centre, "where they railed about the suffering of the Ummah (the global community of Muslims) at the hands of the West" (Teotonio 2010). But does this kind of activity speak to their "alienation"? It is easy to read too much into these activities with hindsight, especially given the unusual behaviour that many teenagers indulge in to differentiate themselves. In seeking to discern the significance of these actions we must keep in mind the many different kinds of deviant identity play that some adolescents and young adults engage in to distinguish themselves from the rest of society.

In a six-page letter submitted to the court, Ahmad makes statements that support Sageman's account of how young men come to be radicalized. He stresses that as an only child he felt alone at home, with both his parents working multiple jobs, so he turned to the elders at a local mosque for support and advice, especially after some discriminatory treatment he felt he experienced as a Muslim in the wake of 9/11. Here and in chat rooms online, he found kindred spirits; he was encouraged to vent and turn to a more radical expression of his Muslim heritage. He professes that he was naive and sought to compensate for the inadequacies of his real life by indulging in a fantasy.

> [The mosque] was where I could get the attention that I wasn't getting from those closest to me. It was where I could be larger than life and not hear a word of criticism. I would say things, often terrible things, that I felt would get me attention in that fantasy world. It was easier to blame the authorities for hindering my job prospects than to face the reality that I had nothing to show on my resume. Looking for an escape is always easier than working for a solution, so I would often talk about participating in Jihad, especially in Afghanistan, as a way of avoiding having to deal with problems at home or going to school. By June 2nd of '06, I was a father of two, not so happily married, living in my in-laws' basement, and completely lost as to what to do in life. (Ahmad 2010, 3)

The image presented is compelling and undoubtedly provides us with some real insights into his condition. But these are the words of a convicted man seeking a lenient sentence from the court, so they must be treated with caution. Plus it remains to be seen whether they are equally pertinent to the motivations of other members of the Toronto 18 and other home-grown terrorists.

In this regard it may be important to note that seven of the ten adults convicted had arrived in Canada as youths who had already been socialized to other cultural and social realities. In one sense they were "home-grown," relative to many other jihadi terrorists. But in another sense they were not born and raised Canadians per se. They are actually 1.5 and not 2.0 immigrants, and this small difference may be a common and crucial factor in their radicalization. But precisely why and how is unclear at this time for lack of appropriate information. There are some signs that they did perhaps experience the classic dilemma faced by many children of immigrants, especially from cultures starkly different from the founding cultures of Canada. They may have felt torn between two worlds, two competing identity frameworks: the traditional cultures of their ethnic heritage and family, and the youth culture of the dominant society in which they lived every day (e.g., Anisef and Kilbride 2003; Awan 2007; Spalek 2007; Kamans et al. 2009; Githens-Mazer 2010). They rejected the former and came to see it as flawed (i.e., insufficiently Islamic), but they never quite fit in with the latter. But the explanatory gap is ever-present, since many other youths are subject to similar social conditions, and they are even involved in the same kinds of religious activities, but they are not radicalized to violence. Once again we need more and better primary data if we hope to resolve what happened in this regard.

At this juncture one final point warrants consideration, though there is no opportunity to develop it. As all students of social and religious movements know, care must be taken to differentiate between the experience, reasoning, and motivations of leaders of groups and the rank and file. In fact there is usually an apparent range of individuals that must be considered radiating out from the inner circle surrounding the inspirational leader to more marginal affiliates. This kind of analysis has yet to be undertaken in any systematic way with terrorist networks, especially home-grown groups. But Marieke Slootman and Jean Tillie (2006) and Petter Nesser (2010) have discussed ways of differentiating the types of people and motives involved. Using data from European jihadist terrorists, Nesser delineates an initial and useful typology distinguishing between the "entrepreneurs," the "protégés," the "misfits," and the "drifters." Whatever the merits of the typology, especially in the Canadian context, it is clear that something comparable should be introduced to the analysis of the Toronto 18. Awareness of the internal variations in motives and modes of commitment adds welcome nuance to our comprehension of the process of radicalization.

The Role of Religion in Home-Grown Terrorist Radicalization

As Ian Reader's chapter in this book makes clear, the role of religion in the radicalization of jihadist terrorists is one of the most disputed subjects in terrorism studies. Much of the debate, however, has been focused on suicide bombers in the Middle East, Chechnya, and other zones of conflict (e.g., Juergensmeyer 2000; Lincoln 2003; Pape 2005; Moghadam 2006; Jones 2008; Brym 2008). Coverage of this fascinating and unresolved debate exceeds our needs here, and it is unclear how relevant the findings would be for an understanding of home-grown jihadist terrorism in the West, particularly in Canada. The problem of the heterogeneity of terrorism comes into play. Still, important points can be made within the confines of the analysis presented so far. Sageman's study, for example, implies that religion plays an important role in the radicalization of jihadist terrorists while also noting, without adequately explaining, the anomalous data for European jihadists (2004, 93–4). Bakker's analysis implies religion is not a significant factor, since most European jihadist terrorists come from fairly secular backgrounds. Like Sageman, however, he stresses that in almost every case there is evidence of a marked increase in the devotion of individuals just prior to joining the jihad (2006, 49). Since his sample provides a natural point of comparison for understanding the Toronto 18, we need a better grasp of why these largely unreligious European youth become so religious and why this development is so strongly associated with the turn to radical violence.

Bakker is curiously mute on this point, whereas Sageman offers an explanation that is interesting but insufficiently substantiated (2004, 93):

> Lonely people look for companionship. In an expatriate community, especially in an unwelcoming non-Muslim Western country, the most available source for companionship with people of similar background is the mosque. Disillusioned with the society that excluded them and the empty promises of the Left [in Europe], second-generation or expatriate Maghreb Arabs went to the mosque and met new friends. Islam was a way to restore their dignity, gain a sense of spiritual calling, and promote their values.

But how do we know this was the case? No evidence is presented, and while this does seem plausible for foreign students and new immigrants far from their homes, is it equally plausible for the jihadi terrorists born and raised in Europe? As Bakker comments, they are not far from their friends, their family, and all that is familiar. Neither were the members of the Toronto 18. So in what sense can we say that both groups were driven by loneliness and alienation? Are these even the right concepts for discussing their situation? Loneliness may help explain why some individuals initially convert to Islam and maybe even a more cohesive form of Islamic fundamentalism, but is it relevant in explaining the further radicalization of some? Of the many people who turn to radical religion for solace, why do so few become radicalized to violence?

Sageman's argument reflects the general tendency of Western social scientists to discount the direct relevance of religious ideologies and desires as motive forces in the process of radicalization (e.g., Silke 2008b, 110–11; McCauley and Moshalenko 2011, 219–21). Implicitly, he seems to be assuming, without proof, that religious beliefs and practices, especially intense or fanatical ones, are only the secondary manifestation of some more primary cause or causes. When we encounter intense religious rhetoric and radical actions, the assumption seems to be that as social scientists we must discern the latent functions they serve. As Reader's and Bramadat's chapters suggest, the religious fanaticism is usually framed as either merely a symptom of something else or a convenient cover or justification for reprehensible actions, which are driven by other reasons or desires. The bulk of analysts who hold this very common view rarely apply the same reductive analysis to the nationalist or political rhetoric, sentiments, and aspirations of terrorists. They do not dwell on the comforting side effects of belonging to a political group or movement as the real reason for holding extremist views and undertaking violent actions. The disparity in treatment suggests an unquestioned Enlightenment assumption that nationalist or political causes are somehow prima facia more legitimate than religious ones. It also reflects the discomfort modern secular citizens of democracies feel in the presence of intensely held, supernaturally based beliefs.

Exercising caution, Sageman goes on to say, rather inconsistently,

> We should be careful not to ascribe a causal relationship to this increased devotion on the part of future mujahedin. This shift in faith may very well be a reflection of a more general process of engagement in the jihad. In this case, it would be more indicative of an effect rather than a cause of

the process. At this point, the evidence is still descriptive and does not yet justify conclusions about the contribution of this increased faith to the process of joining the global jihad. (2004, 93)

This is good advice and it highlights one of the most pressing interpretive conundrums faced by anyone seeking to explain home-grown terrorist radicalization. The methodological difficulty, however, should not be used to give short shrift to the examination of religious convictions and commitments as genuine sources of terrorism.

On the one hand, unlike Bakker, Sageman wishes to ascribe some significance to the youthful faithfulness of his sample. Presumably their childhood experience conditions them, as John Lofland and Rodney Stark (1965) argue in their famous step-model of religious conversion, to seek religious solutions to their own and the world's problems. But on the other hand, like Bakker, he wishes to discount the significance of the surge in religiosity prior to them becoming terrorists since it is difficult, in principle, to sort cause from effect. But the very way in which he frames the problem of causation is indicative of an assumption that political or other motivations are more primary than religious ones. Note his exact wording. The bias can be brought to the fore by posing an alternative example. If there is evidence that personal identity issues are more significant and consequential than political ones, for example, does this mean we should be sceptical about the sincerity and significance of the political rhetoric, motives, and goals of the terrorists in question? Operating out of a natural attitude of secularity (Schutz 1967), induced by their social experience as Westerners and their disciplinary training, the psychologists, political scientists, and international relations scholars who have dominated terrorism studies have repeatedly questioned the religious motives of jihadist terrorists, instead favouring their political ones; yet both are supposedly undergirded by what might generally be called identity needs and quests. Is this balance of perspectives sensible and helpful?

In the discourse on home-grown religious terrorism in particular, it is common for doubts to be raised about the causal role of religion for a number of reasons: many terrorists do not come from particularly religious backgrounds; their religious literacy is limited; many are recent converts to Islam (as was the case with Steve Chand and James Jahmaal in the Toronto 18); their turn to extremism happened rapidly; and they clearly have political and other motivations as well. In principle, and empirically, however, these considerations do not speak to the sincerity or significance of the religious beliefs and commitments of the terrorists. For decades the same reasons have been used to cast doubt on the veracity of conversion experiences of members of new religious movements, to justify violating their constitutional right to freedom of religious expression. But is a religious commitment of ten years' standing intrinsically (without other evidence) more sincere and influential than one newly undertaken? If so, how so, and how would we go about collecting the pertinent evidence? Given the great fervour typically displayed by new converts, one might well argue the reverse is often true. Similarly, what does knowledge of a religious tradition have to do with the authenticity and effectiveness of a commitment? The religious traditions of the world are riddled with struggles between pietists and theologians on this point, and sociologists have consistently found a low correlation between levels of religious knowledge and levels of religiosity. Is the rapidity of a conversion indicative of its insignificance? If so, then there is reason to call into question many of the paradigmatic conversion experiences (e.g., Saint Paul, Guru Nanak, Mohammad). There is no established correlation, and the speed with which one converts is a specious concern. Finally, the functional separation of religion from other spheres of life and society is a modern Western contrivance, one that serves the political interests of our societies. It is neither assumed nor normative in much of the rest of the world, and certainly not in most Islamic societies. The history of our own societies is replete with sectarian and millenarian movements that have sought to use political means to pursue religious ends. From their perspective everything is subsumed by religion. Thus the mixture of religious, political, and other motives tells us little about the sincerity of the religious pronouncements of terrorists, and consistent use of religious rhetoric may well be indicative of the dominance of religious over political objectives.

Concluding Remarks

Just how consequential is religion as a causal factor in cases of home-grown terrorism in North America? That is a question that must be answered on a case-by-case basis and not a priori. Certainly questions about the role of religion go to the heart of interpreting what happened to the Toronto 18. Most of the young men appear to have come from secular, nominal, or at best moderately religious backgrounds, yet they were bound together by an intense, coherent religious rhetoric and sense of purpose. They strove to live out the *mujahideen* ideal, in their own fashion, mixing the catchphrases of Islamic fundamentalism with the lingo of the gangster rap culture of urban youth. It is unclear, however, if they were willing to go further and embrace the ideal of martyrdom as well. They gloried in this notion, but Fahim Ahmad, one of the two leaders, never managed to put any of his grand plans into action, beyond running two rather amateurish outings in the woods to train, test, and select possible terrorists. Zakaria Amara, the other leader, raised funds, constructed a remote detonator, and arranged for the purchase of chemicals needed to build the bombs. But it is clear that he did not intend to drive any of the trucks containing the bombs, and on several occasions he started to make plans to flee the country either just before or after the bombings. The two young men caught unloading the bomb materials, Saad Khalid and Saad Gaya, seem to have been unaware of their role as the most likely drivers of the trucks, and they have not made any statements indicating their willingness to undertake suicide missions. Does this mean, as some commentators might suggest, that their religious commitment was, in a manner of speaking, half-baked? It is difficult to say, but I think it is safer to infer that the lack of clarity on these issues is indicative more of the youthfulness of the group and its relatively disorganized nature than the sincerity of the participants' religious motivations.

Given the age-old functional linkages between religion and identity (e.g., Mol 1976) and the role of the transcendent in sacralizing causes, it should come as no surprise that religious ideologies – no matter how unsavoury – can continue to play a role in the contention over ultimate ends in our cultures and lives. In their efforts to account for the radicalization of European Muslims in a globalizing and postmodern world, Olivier Roy (2004), Basia Spalek (2007), and Jocelyne Cesari (2008) point to the significance of the links between the need for identity and community, for a greater sense of purpose, for a youthful spirit of adventure, and for an anti-imperialist narrative. These linkages are probably equally pertinent in explaining the Toronto 18, as well as many other forms of contemporary youthful radicalism. To make sense of these themes, however, in terms of the actual lives and thoughts of these specific young men, we need more data, better data, and more exacting analyses.

NOTES

1 The most conspicuous cases were Ahmed Ressam, an Algerian immigrant caught smuggling explosives across the Canada-U.S. border in 1999, in a plot to blow up the Los Angeles International Airport, and Mohammad

Momin Khawaja, arrested in 2004 for his role in assisting a terrorist bombing conspiracy in England.

2 Most of the members of the Toronto 18 were convicted on some combination of the charges of participating in a terrorist group, training for terrorist purposes, and intending to cause an explosion; two were also convicted on the additional charges of smuggling firearms and one for counselling fraud.

3 Radicalism and radicalization are not consonant with terrorist violence per se. Rather, as stipulated by the Canadian Association of Chiefs of Police, for example, "Radicalization refers to the process by which individuals – usually young people – are introduced to an overtly ideological message and belief system that encourages movement from moderate mainstream beliefs towards extreme views" (Canadian Association of Chiefs of Police Prevention of Radicalization Study Group, "Building Community Resilience to Violent Ideologies," 2009, p. 5; https://www.cacp.ca/media/committees/efiles/16/422/RadicalizationEng.pdf). In line with most others in the field of terrorism studies, however, when I refer to radicalization I primarily have in mind the kind of processes that encourage violent behaviour and acts.

4 My observations stem from the comments of two well-known experts on Somalia and the Somalian diaspora in the United States: Dr Stevan Weine's presentations at the headquarters of the Canadian Security Intelligence Services in 2010 and at the 13th National Metropolis Conference in Vancouver in 2011, and Dr Kenneth Menkhaus's presentation at the Global Futures Forum held in Monterey, California, in 2011 (see Menkhaus 2009 as well).

5 Bakker's analysis is confusingly inconsistent on these points, stating in his conclusion to this section of his report that the difference in place of recruitment is "less explicit" and implying that the other differences noted are actually of greater significance.

REFERENCES

Ahmad, Fahim. 2010. R. V. Ahmad, Fahim. Exhibit #3: Written Submissions of Fahim Ahmad (Re: Sentencing). Ontario Superior Court.

Anisef, Paul, and Kenise Murphy Kilbride, eds. 2003. *Managing Two Worlds: The Experiences and Concerns of Immigrant Youth in Ontario*. Toronto: Canadian Scholars' Press.

Awan, Akil N. 2007. "Transitional Religiosity Experiences: Contextual Disjuncture and Islamic Political Radicalism." In *Islamic Political Radicalism: A European Perspective*, ed. Tahir Abbas, 207–30. Edinburgh: University of Edinburgh Press.

Bakker, Edwin. 2006. *Jihadi Terrorists in Europe: Their Characteristics and the Circumstances in which They Joined the Jihad.* The Hague: Netherlands Institute of International Relations, Clingendael.

Berns-McGown, Rina. 1999. *Muslims in Diaspora: The Somali Communities of London and Toronto.* Toronto: University of Toronto Press.

Berrebi, Claude. 2009. "The Economics of Terrorism and Counterterrorism: What Matters and Is Rational-Choice Theory Helpful?" In *Social Science for Counterterrorism: Putting the Pieces Together*, ed. Paul K. Davis and Kim Cragin, 151–208. Arlington, VA: National Defense Research Institute, Rand Corporation.

Brannan, David W., Philip F. Esler, and N.T. Anders Strindberg. 2001. "Talking to 'Terrorists': Towards an Independent Analytical Framework for the Study of Violent Substate Activism." *Studies in Conflict and Terrorism* 24: 3–24.

Braungart, Richard G., and Margaret M. Braungart. 1992. "From Protest to Terrorism: The Case of SDS and the Weathermen." In *Social Movements and Violence: Participation in Underground Organizations*, vol. 4 of *International Social Movement Research*, ed. Bert Klandermans and Donatella Della Porta, 45–78. Greenwich, CT: JAI Press.

Brym, Robert. 2008. "Religion, Politics and Suicide Bombing: An Interpretive Essay." *Canadian Journal of Sociology* 33 (1): 89–108.

Brym, Robert J., and Bader Araji. 2006. "Suicide Bombing as Strategy and Interaction: The Case of the Second *Intifada*." *Social Forces* 84: 1965–84.

Cesari, Jocelyne. 2008. "Muslims in Europe and the Risk of Radicalism." In *Jihadi Terrorism and the Radicalisation Challenge in Europe*, ed. Rik Coollsaet, 97–107. Aldershot, Hampshire: Ashgate.

Crenshaw, Martha. 1981. "The Causes of Terrorism." *Comparative Politics* 13 (4): 379–99.

CSIS. 2010. Remarks by Director Richard B. Fadden to the House of Commons Standing Committee on Public Safety and National Security. https://www.csis-scrs.gc.ca/cmmn/rmrks_hc_stndng_cmmtt_11052010-eng.asp.

Dalgaard-Nielsen, Anja. 2010. "Violent Radicalization in Europe: What We Know and What We Do Not Know." *Studies in Conflict and Terrorism* 33: 797–814.

Della Porta, Donatella. 1988. "Recruitment Process in Clandestine Political Organizations: Italian Left-Wing Terrorism." In *International Social Movement Research*, vol. 1, ed. Bert Klandermans, Hanspeter Kriesi, and Sidney Tarrow, 155–69. Greenwich, CT: JAI Press.

– 1995. *Social Movements, Political Violence, and the State: A Comparative Analysis of Italy and Germany.* Cambridge: Cambridge University Press.

Farrington, D.P. 2003. "Developmental and Life-Course Criminology: Key Theoretical and Empirical Issues – The 2002 Sutherland Award Address." *Criminology* 41: 221–55.

Githens-Mazer, Jonathan. 2010. "Mobilization, Recruitment, Violence and the Street: Radical Violent *Takfiri* Islamism in Early Twenty-first-century Britain." In *The New Extremism in 21st Century Britain*, ed. Roger Eatwell and Matthew J. Goodwin, 47–66. London: Routledge.

Helmus, Todd C. 2009. "Why and How Some People Become Terrorists." In *Social Science for Counterterrorism: Putting the Pieces Together*, ed. Paul K. Davis and Kim Cragin, 71–111. Arlington, VA: National Defense Research Institute, Rand Corporation.

Horgan, John. 2005. *The Psychology of Terrorism*. London: Routledge.

– 2008. "Interviewing Terrorists: A Case for Primary Research." In *Terrorist Informatics: Knowledge Management and Data Mining for Homeland Security*, ed. Hsinchun Chen, Edna Reid, Joshua Sinai, and Andrew Silke, 73–99. New York: Springer.

Jones, James W. 2008. *Blood That Cries Out from the Earth: The Psychology of Religious Terrorism*. New York: Oxford University Press.

Juergensmeyer, Mark. 2000. *Terror in the Mind of God: The Global Rise of Religious Violence*. Berkeley: University of California Press.

Kamans, Elanor, Ernestine H. Gordijn, Hilbrand Oldenhuis, and Sabine Otten. 2009. "What I Think You See Is What You Get: Influence of Prejudice on Assimilation to Negative Meta-Stereotypes among Dutch Moroccan Teenagers." *European Journal of Social Psychology* 39 (5): 842–51.

Krueger, Alan B., and Jitka Maleckova. 2003. "Education, Poverty and Terrorism: Is There a Causal Connection?" *Journal of Economic Perspectives* 17 (4): 119–44.

Lincoln, Bruce. 2003. *Holy Terrors: Thinking about Religion after September 11*. Chicago: University of Chicago Press.

Lofland, John, and Rodney Stark. 1965. "Becoming a World-Saver: A Theory of Conversion to a Deviant Perspective." *American Sociological Review* 30 (6): 862–75.

McCauley, Clark R., and Sophia Moshalenko. 2011. *Friction: How Radicalization Happens to Them and Us*. New York: Oxford University Press.

Menkhaus, Kenneth. 2009. "Current Somali Crisis and the Role of the Diaspora." Senate Hearings 11 March 2009. http://www.youtube.com/watch?v=WQ07pBEo_bg.

Merari, Ariel, Ilan Diamant, Arie Bibi, Yoav Broshi, and Giora Zakin. 2010. "Personality Characteristics of 'Self Martyrs'/'Suicide Bombers' and Organizers of Suicide Attacks." *Terrorism and Political Violence* 22: 87–101.

Merari, Ariel, Jonathan Fighel, Boaz Ganor, Ephraim Lavie, Yohanan Tzoreff, and Arie Livne. 2010. "Making Palestinian 'Martyrdom

Operations'/'Suicide Attacks': Interviews with Would-Be Perpetrators and Organizers." *Terrorism and Political Violence* 22: 102–19.

Moghadam, Assaf. 2006. "Suicide Terrorism, Occupation, and the Globalization of Martyrdom: A Critique of 'Dying to Win.'" *Studies in Conflict and Terrorism* 29 (8): 707–29.

Mol, Hans J. 1976. *Identity and the Sacred: A Sketch for a New Social Scientific Theory of Religion*. New York: The Free Press.

Munson, Ziad W. 2008. *The Making of Pro-life Activists: How Social Mobilization Works*. Chicago: University of Chicago Press.

Nesser, Petter. 2010. "Joining Jihadi Terrorist Cells in Europe: Explaining Motivational Aspects of Recruitment and Radicalization." In *Understanding Violent Radicalization*, ed. Magnus Ranstorp, 87–114. New York: Routledge.

Neumann, Peter R. 2009. *Old and New Terrorism*. Cambridge: Polity.

The 9/11 Commission Report. 2004. New York: W.W. Norton and Co.

Noricks, Darcy M.E. 2009. "The Root Causes of Terrorism." In *Social Science for Counterterrorism: Putting the Pieces Together*, ed. Paul K. Davis and Kim Cragin, 11–70. Arlington, VA: National Defense Research Institute, Rand Corporation.

Pape, Robert. 2005. *Dying to Win: The Strategic Logic of Suicide Terrorism*. New York: Random House.

Post, Jerrold M., Ehud Sprinzak, and Laurita M. Denny. 2003. "The Terrorists in Their Own Words: Interviews with 35 Incarcerated Middle Eastern Terrorists." *Terrorism and Political Violence* 15 (1): 171–84.

Post, Jerrold M., Farahana Ali, Schuyler W. Henderson, Stephen Shanfield, Jeff Victoroff, and Steven Weine. 2009. "The Psychology of Suicide Terrorism." *Psychiatry* 72 (1): 13–31.

Roy, Olivier. 2004. *Globalized Islam: The Search for a New Ummah*. New York: Columbia University Press.

Sageman, Marc. 2004. *Understanding Terror Networks*. Philadelphia: University of Pennsylvania Press.

– 2008. *Leaderless Jihad: Terror Networks in the Twenty-first Century*. Philadelphia: University of Pennsylvania Press.

Schutz, Alfred. 1967. *The Phenomenology of the Social World*. Boston: Northeastern University Press.

Silber, Mitchell D., and Arvin Bhatt. 2007. "Radicalization in the West: The Homegrown Threat." New York: New York City Police Department.

Silke, Andrew. 2008a. "Research on Terrorism: A Review of the Impact of 9/11 and the Global War on Terrorism." In *Terrorism Informatics: Knowledge Management and Data Mining for Homeland Security*, ed. Hsinchun Chen, Edna Reid, Joshua Sinai, and Andrew Silke, 27–50. New York: Springer.

– 2008b. "Holy Warriors: Exploring the Psychological Processes of Jihadi Radicalization." *European Journal of Criminology* 5 (1): 99–123.

Slootman, Marieke, and Jean Tillie. 2006. *Processes of Radicalisation: Why Some Amsterdam Muslims Become Radicals*. Amsterdam: Institute for Migration and Ethnic Studies, University of Amsterdam.

Smelser, Neil J. 2007. *The Faces of Terrorism: Social and Psychological Dimensions*. Princeton, NJ: Princeton University Press.

Spalek, Basia. 2007. "Disconnection and Exclusion: Pathways to Radicalisation?" In *Islamic Political Radicalism: A European Perspective*, ed. Tahir Abbas, 192–206. Edinburgh: University of Edinburgh Press.

Speckhard, Anne. 2009. "Research Challenges Involved in Field Research and Interviews Regarding the Militant Jihad, Extremism, and Suicide Terrorism." *Democracy and Security* 5: 199–222.

Speckhard, Anne, and Khapta Ahkmedova. 2006. "The Making of a Martyr: Chechen Suicide Terrorism." *Studies in Conflict and Terrorism* 29 (5): 429–92.

Sprinzak, Ehud. 1990. "The Psychosocial Formation of Extreme Left Terrorism in a Democracy: The Case of the Weathermen." In *Origins of Terrorism: Psychologies, Ideologies, Theologies, States of Mind*, ed. Walter Reich, 65–85. New York: Cambridge University Press.

Stark, Rodney, and William Sims Bainbridge. 1980. "Networks of Faith: Interpersonal Bonds and Recruitment to Cults and Sects." *American Journal of Sociology* 85: 1376–95.

Teotonio, Isabel. 2010. "Toronto 18." *The Toronto Star*. http://www3.thestar.com/static/toronto18/index.html.

Victoroff, Jeff. 2005. "The Mind of the Terrorist: A Review and Critique of Psychological Approaches." *Journal of Conflict Resolution* 49 (1): 3–42.

Vidino, Lorenzo. 2011. "The Buccinasco Pentiti: A Unique Case Study of Radicalization." *Terrorism and Political Violence* 23 (3): 398–418.

Wasmund, Klaus. 1986. "The Political Socialization of West German Terrorists." In *Political Violence and Terror: Motifs and Motivations*, ed. Peter H. Merkl, 191–228. Berkeley: University of California Press.

Weine, Stevan, John Horgan, Cheryl Robertson, Sana Loue, Amin Mohamed, and Sahra Noor. 2009. "Community and Family Approaches to Combating Radicalization and Recruitment of Somali-American Youth and Young Adults: A Psychosocial Perspective." *Dynamics of Asymmetric Conflict* 2 (3): 181–200.

Wiktorowicz, Quintan. 2005. *Radical Islam Rising: Muslim Extremism in the West*. Lanham, MD: Rowman and Littlefield.

4 Pluralism and Radicalization: Mind the Gap![1]

VALÉRIE AMIRAUX AND
JAVIERA ARAYA-MORENO

> [A]nd the more aware they become, however vaguely, of ambitions and of threats which transcend their immediate locales, the more trapped they seem to feel.
>
> C. Wright Mills (1959, 3)

> Although I had studied Pakistanis in the diaspora in Britain and Sufis in the North-West Frontier Province of Pakistan, what could I say about September 11 from the vantage point of the small places I knew well? This was the beginning and origin of my anthropological blues.
>
> Pnina Werbner (2010, 193–4)

Introduction

The issues of radicalization and religious extremism in Western contexts have been studied extensively over the last two decades by policy analysts, security agencies, think tanks, and social scientists. Most of the research approaches the issues from the angle of securitization.[2] In the multiple perspectives developed, however, the analyses have ignored a key aspect of these phenomena by failing to consider the critical linkages between, on the one hand, pluralism as a framework for contemporary life and the more mundane features of radicalization on the other. Although scholars have developed an extremely sophisticated understanding of radicalization – defined as a pathological outcome of socialization trajectories whereby an individual or group adopts extreme religious views and justifies acts of violence and terrorism based on these views (see chapter 1 by Bramadat in this volume; and Thachuk, Bowman, and Richardson 2008; European Commission 2005; Abbas 2007) – they have failed to investigate it adequately as a micro-phenomenon that is the product of ordinary interactions between people who do not know each other.

Radicalization here therefore effectively designates a process of reciprocal misunderstanding that will eventually evolve into more explicit resentment. If we wish to develop a better understanding of how pluralism is actually experienced by citizens living in religiously plural contexts, we suggest suspending, at least momentarily, a reflection centred on large abstract principles and disembodied discourses and instead returning to the examination of local practices, taking these local interactions seriously as sites in which one can observe the production of meaning. In a way, we are proposing a radical shift by postulating the link between processes of radicalization and the experience of pluralism, defined here as day-to-day constraint of being with others and not only as a taken-for-granted diversity or normative aspirations. Our emphasis on radicalization as a process refers to the "mundane" social interactions that tend to harden opinions and lead to negative views of the minority by the majority or negative views of the majority by the minority. These interactions can play significant roles in the formation of a radicalized consciousness. We are arguing, then, for a more pragmatic rather than theoretical approach, although the results will undoubtedly have significant theoretical implications.

Our hypothesis is that we can offer up new insights on pluralism and radicalization for the purposes of both scholarship and policy by shifting the focus of radicalization studies from an almost exclusive preoccupation with the extreme enactments, which produce violence and terrorism, to a much larger set of processes encompassing the daily interactions of individuals living in pluralistic societies. Radicalization from this perspective stems from the way people feel about sharing common space in a pluralist neighbourhood (whether a courtyard, a sidewalk, a mall, a playground, or a line at the bank or post office) and the way they react to the constant exposure to otherness and differences. This broader framing brings us to the unspoken and silent social routine in which hate, love, rejection, or isolation emerge, influence social life, and eventually degenerate into strong hostility towards those who gradually come to embody difference. Pluralism and democracy, to which it is linked, are often primarily addressed as philosophical issues or legal objects of study (Morag 2002). This chapter proposes to connect the present global "time of anxiety and suspicion" (Nussbaum 2012) with aspects of social interaction in daily life, as well as with the meanings and emotions that stem from these interactions. This repositioning prevents us from entering into abstract discussions about whether multiculturalism or interculturalism are right or wrong, or better or worse than secular republicanism; such arguments only further entrench the artificial juxtaposition between, on the one hand, the threat of radicalization and extremism and, on the other, the ideals of justice and equality.[3]

Clearly the surveillance and study of a small number of people who preach hatred and encourage violence in the name of any religious message must remain a priority for both security personnel and scholars. However, we are arguing for the need to move beyond case studies or event-related analyses to fully seize the epistemological and theoretical dimensions of the radicalization process by, somewhat paradoxically, leaving aside a principles-based mode of thinking and returning to the examination of daily experiences and practices to assess the practical features of the roots of radicalization. This analysis begins with the sense that there seems to be a cleavage, or at least a tension, between the normative or official representation of religious pluralism and individuals' daily experiences of it. Many people in the West posit religious pluralism as an intrinsic feature of late-modern Western societies, and yet little if any scholarship has examined how ordinary people live and perceive it. Both pluralism and radicalization should therefore be considered not only as dialectically related (as Bramadat argues in chapter 1 of this book) but as primarily rooted in ordinary and daily routines that deserve at least some serious attention and examination.

This chapter will undoubtedly leave readers with more questions than answers, given that it is largely a call to action and not a report on results. Nonetheless, we would argue the urgency of reorienting some of the social scientific research on the process of radicalization. In the first part of the chapter, after a systematization of different conceptions of religious pluralism, we propose the concept of *situated religious pluralism*, both as a theoretical construction and as an empirical object. In the second part, we assess recent works on radicalization, showing how they tend to conceive of the process in a manner that is too disconnected from the many sociological complexities of individuals, contexts, and situations, largely because they neglect an ethnographic approach to the issue. We then discuss the possibilities for the study of radicalization offered by adopting ethnographic methodologies and conceiving of situated religious pluralism.

What Does It Take to Make an "Ordinary Trap" Operational?

Our thinking about this issue started with a simple question that we initially asked ourselves as citizens rather than as social scientists: when it comes to analysing radicalization in religiously plural contexts, why is it so difficult to link ordinary practices with big political questions? C. Wright Mills (1959) called the former daily routines "troubles," a term he juxtaposed against broader political "issues."[4] Mills's framework is helpful here in many respects, mostly because it invites us to think in sociological terms about how critical social questions rely on the improvement of individuals' basic capacities of observation and imagination. With this distinction between the particular "troubles" and the general "issues," the question is how to document the link between religious pluralism as a feature of liberal democracies and radicalization, generally conceived of as a risk to liberal democracies. Discussions about radicalization almost always conjure up horrifying images, often supported and further consolidated by news coverage, fictional literature, and other aspects of popular culture (see Beer and Burrows 2010). There is obviously a matter of scale that shapes this response. As Werbner (2010) notes, talking about her own doubts as an anthropologist working on Islamic militancy in the West, events such as 9/11 (2001) and the London (2005) and Madrid (2004) bombings – and effectively all global terrorist acts – defy easy understanding. Thinking of anthropologists like her, working on "small places," Werbner writes, "we mostly encounter the normal and the quotidian, not the extraordinary and world shattering" (Werbner 2010, 193). Large-scale terrorist acts seem to embody the opposite of the everyday and the local; they are hardly intelligible and always occur as unexpected catastrophes. Indeed, for anthropologists, and, we could add, all ethnographers, they evince the dilemma of how to move from the quotidian to the cataclysmic (Werbner 2010, 194). The difference in the scale of events notwithstanding, the Western public has been educated to integrate such events into the fabric of their daily lives. For instance, through a powerful and convincing security discourse implemented in the media coverage, 9/11 has been framed as a defining moment for Western societies. This integration does not, however, imply that the meaning of 9/11 has been brought into the fabric of people's daily lives or that they are aware of the disjuncture between their lives and the complex issues associated with 9/11. In this chapter, following Mills, we call this habit of conflating "big issues" with immediate "troubles" the "ordinary trap," into which Western secular citizenries are locked. The ordinary trap refers

Figure 4.1. "Le vote anti-minarets"
© Chappatte dans "Le Temps" (Genève), www.globecartoon.com

to situations in which an individual might think about life-threatening terrorist plots or cells while remaining, in daily life, enmeshed in a mostly anonymous and normal life, totally disconnected from violent radicalization. In so doing, however, these individuals are nevertheless living the realities of religious and cultural pluralism that play a role in the process of radicalization on a daily basis.

The case of the Swiss minaret ban offers a good illustration of this ordinary trap of confusing the local and the global, reality and fear, in which most Europeans and North Americans find themselves locked.[5] In November 2009, the bill calling for banning the building of minarets was passed, with the support of 57.5 per cent of the voters. The irony of the new law did not escape some citizens. On 1 December, Chappatte, a regular cartoonist at the Swiss daily newspaper *Le Temps*, published a caricature showing a Swiss couple in front of a typical Alpine house located on a beautiful mountainside obviously far removed from the construed threat of Islam as well as interactions with Muslims (Figure 4.1). A journalist is asking them, "Is Islam disturbing you?"

Figure 4.2. Poster
© Ry Tweedie-Cullen

The image is indeed a witty response to the widely reproduced and quite influential poster issued by the Swiss People Party, who initiated the anti-minaret campaign. The image on the poster (Figure 4.2) exhibits a Swiss flag covered in tall black minarets, which resemble missiles, in front of which stands a woman draped in black, a large *Stopp* written beneath her.[6]

In short, the minaret has become emblematic of the threat of Islam and an Islamic takeover of Europe. In addition, the female figure veiled head-to-toe in black in the foreground of the image also constitutes an exotic fiction in a country where 90 per cent of the 400,000 Muslims originate from Kosovo and Turkey, where such garments are not customary. The Chappatte cartoon articulates the discrepancy between the alleged threat depicted in the "Stopp" political poster (the issue) and the reality regarding Islamic places of worship in Switzerland (the trouble). At the time of the vote, although there were an estimated 150 mosques or prayer rooms in Switzerland, only four of them featured minarets and only two others had plans to construct minarets (Cumming-Bruce and Erlanger, 2009). The point is evidently that while the stereotypically characteristic Swiss couple in the comic have never actually been "troubled" by mosques or minarets, and probably never directly by Muslims, the "issue" constructed and communicated through the campaign (i.e., the Islamicization of Switzerland) not only is intelligible to them but echoes a pattern that we also find proliferating in other European countries, for instance by extreme-right parties such as in France. Here is the anatomy of the ordinary trap: when we are asked to answer "yes" or "no" to a question that has no meaning in our daily universe and with which we have never had a direct experience (as for instance when MPs in Iceland anticipated in February 2011 the possible prohibition of the burka on the island before the garment had even made an appearance there, as reported by the *Reykjavik Grapevine*), we still answer. This response confirms Mills's claim: "and the more aware they become, however vaguely, of ambitions and of threats [issues] which transcend their immediate locales, the more trapped they seem to feel" (Mills 1959, 3).

The liberal focus on rights and representation has probably contributed to the neglect of the lived dimensions of the debates on multiculturalism and pluralism, elucidating the chasm between rhetoric and reality. This liberal emphasis has certainly made it difficult for many of us see that expectations regarding recognition also imply struggles over principles and values, as well as struggles over ways of living, customs, and even senses. Mills's distinction between troubles and issues is crucial here. Troubles occur within the character of the individual, within the range of his immediate relations with others – for example during the process of a conversation or interaction regarding some mundane immediate concern – whereas issues, to state it in simple terms, involve a public matter, as when some people believe that values or principles cherished in specific societies are being threatened. Issues are, however, not so easy to identify in the immediate and everyday environments of ordinary people. Other social scientists have articulated similar distinctions using different terms. For example, Geertz (1963) addressed the tension in many societies between primordial attachments and emerging civil sentiments. The latter denote a generalized commitment to an overarching and somewhat alien civil order revolving around practical demands for political efficacy, social justice, and economic progress. The former refer to specific and familiar identity markers such as kinship, race, religion, geographic proximity, and language. These primordial concepts are in a way irrational. They are constructed by history and often appear as the product of centuries of gradual sedimentation. They consist, as Geertz (1963) notes, of "congruities of blood, speech, customs" (9), and "they consist of an unreflective sense of collective selfhood that in turn is rooted in the non-rational foundations of personality" (128). Primordial sentiments and the attachments they produce rest on perceptions and beliefs. Both Mills and Geertz juxtapose the realm of individual personal experience to the realm that transcends the local environments of individuals and the range of their personal lives and understandings, such as in the example of the Islamic threat to Swiss culture discussed previously. The ensuing question of interest in this chapter is what are the major "issues" – in the sense of the term offered by Mills – experienced in religiously plural societies that connect the process of radicalization with the key "troubles" of private individuals? Ordinary "troubled" scenes of daily life and urban legends – echoing "issues" – offer a relevant focus for trying to answer this question. In Montreal, and more particularly in the Outremont neighbourhood, a story circulates, told either by people who live in the neighbourhood or by those who are just passing through it. One never knows if it is true or just a fiction designed to ridicule a minority, but it narrates an allegedly typical and frequent scenario involving a visible religious minority, ultra-Orthodox Jews, and the non-Jewish population in Outremont. The story can involve a man or a woman or both and usually takes place on a Friday evening in a street where Hassidim live: a Jewish man or a Jewish woman, sometimes together or even with children, approaches the passerby-cum-storyteller to ask him or her in English (a part of the narrative that has political connotations in a society in which some perceive the dominant French language as being under siege) to help turn on some lights, the heating, or electrical appliances, or even make a phone call, because the onset of Shabbat means that practising Jews can no longer undertake these daily gestures.[7] The passerby enters the house, fulfils the request, and continues to walk home. Although not everyone can recount such a story, we contend that such interactions are far from rare (indeed one of the authors has had such an experience). In her remarkable master's thesis, Alton (2011) dedicates a full chapter to these "Sabbath Hands," gentiles helping observant Jews, a phenomenon she situates in a larger historical tradition known by Jews as the "shabbos goy" (84).

This account sets the stage for the way we would like to invite scholars to deal with radicalization in its complexity, to situate it as one possible outcome of a reciprocal process of interactions that can potentially increase the distance between groups and harden their representations of their differences. Individuals living in plural contexts are exposed to such daily interactions that have been neglected by analysts. Unfortunately, these are precisely the experiences that develop into full-blown conflicts in the public arenas of Parliament or the media and constitute "the missing link" between, on one side, religious pluralism defined as a constraining condition of life and, on the other, radicalization conceived as a process generated by micro-interactions potentially leading to increased discrimination and xenophobia. As Bramadat noted,[8] the meaning attributed to this interaction is potentially open, depending upon the convictions and behaviour of both the Jewish family and the passersby and their knowledge of each other's traditions; consequently, this particular interaction in Outremont could "mean" many things. It could be an opportunity to build communication (exchanges of knowledge, jokes, etc.), or on the contrary it could enlarge the gap by underlining cultural differences on both sides. This openness to interpretation is, indeed, precisely what we seek to establish, since it is one of the goals of the larger project from which our present reflection arises, to provide the Québécois public discussion on interculturalism and reasonable accommodation with empirical evidence of its day-to-day accomplishment.

The first episode of the first season (2007) of the popular Canadian television show *Little Mosque on the Prairie* offers another good example of such an intersection between troubles and issues involving the Muslim community, both as an empirical subject of experience and as a represented community in the political imaginary.[9] The scenario is simple: a young Muslim man, Amar, trained as a lawyer, has been hired to serve as the local imam in a recently opened prayer room in the basement of an Anglican church in Mercy, a small town in Alberta. Waiting in line for the check-in counter at the Toronto airport, he is talking on his cell phone with his mother, who apparently does not understand the rationale for his decision to give up his law career. Playing on ambiguity in the dialogue, the script makes a woman in the same queue believe that the future imam is certainly a terrorist, as all the details of his life (change of career, stay in Afghanistan, Islamic education in a Muslim country, etc.) provided in the short conversation clearly situate him on the map of Islamic radicalism. As a vigilant, suspicious, and responsible citizen, the woman thus calls the airport security and Amar is detained for interrogation, providing other opportunities for Zarqa Nawaz, the series's creator, to highlight how stereotypes and representations shape the construction of meanings.

Interactions such as the ones briefly described here do take place all the time in cosmopolitan cities such as Montreal. However, although such scenes are usually associated with Muslims, similar experiences occur to each of us every day without our necessarily being aware that we are experiencing pluralism in its most direct form. People belonging to different religious communities continuously cross each other in daily life. Despite public controversies and political discussions about differences between Québécois interculturalism and Canadian multiculturalism, micro-adjustments are constantly being made or denied in situations where non-believers and believers of various religious traditions share public spaces and cope with features of another person's religious identity or practice, cognizant or not of what we might call the interpersonal economy associated with the interactions between people. Let us think of a few examples drawn from fieldwork conducted in Montreal by students working with us on the PLURADICAL project. Most doctors will for instance let women perform prayers for their dying babies next to their beds in the main rooms of a public hospital's neonatology services, but some will not.[10] Most schools or subsidized daycare centres will respect pupils' specific ethnic or religious dietary requirements, whereas others will not.[11] These few situations in which individuals decided to deny believers the right to certain practices were mostly "minor troubles" that were turned into "big issues" by the public attention drawn to them, as for instance in 2007–8 during the work of the Bouchard-Taylor Commission.[12] Whether these incidents are the result of daily indifference, ideological opposition, or ignorance, the examination of routine social life suggests – notwithstanding the panic that seems to run through Québécois and Canadian public opinion every time such sensitive topics make the headlines – that there is, in fact, very little resistance to the accommodation of religious convictions in the dominant population.

Considering multicultural democracy as a way of being – rather than just as a set of principles and norms – means that it entails primarily and simply the experience of living with others. Citizens engaging with democracy must be willing to engage with disagreement and differences, not just in the political realm but also with regard to socioeconomic and cultural differences. So for a democracy to qualify as multicultural, the emphasis should be on the responsibility of every citizen to adequately navigate pluralism. Recently, however, the road to democracy has been getting narrower with the further entrenchment of restrictive notions of "us" and "them" and the concomitant shift backward towards assimilationist positions on the part of larger segments of the public. We see this in the political situation in Europe, for instance, as illustrated by the rise of the extreme right in national polls and the normalization of a certain hostility to cultural/religious difference, notably through the denunciation of multicultural policies (Lentin and Titley 2011). In the last decades a majority of Western governments have pleaded for the extension of multiple sets of rights as the most effective way to implement a just and stable multicultural society; however, this is disconnected from social expectations that regard recognition as more than rights, that it also encompasses struggles over values and ways of living. In 2009, several cities in Northern Italy – where the daily experiences of religious pluralism are, as in Switzerland, not very common – started a systematic campaign, sometimes supported by legal decisions, to "de-ethnicize" (our terminology) Italy's historical town centres, legally banning kebab shops, phone kiosks that enable migrants to call abroad, and pubs and bars of "an ethnic nature." As with the examples explored earlier, this movement in Italy demonstrates the ways that claims about "multiculturalism gone wild" circulate in one context and very quickly get adopted into another (Lentin and Titley 2011). The full list of instances of such paranoia would be quite long, of course. One would need to add to this list discriminatory comments made by politicians in the 2012 Quebec provincial election. As well, one would want to include Quebec's Herouxville controversy in which (as in similar Italian and Swiss cases) the level and type of religious diversity were imagined to be far greater, more problematic, and more immediate than they actually are in reality, thereby provoking formal political statements meant to constrain this (negligible or absent) diversity.[13] All of these comments and policy statements are part of the ongoing discussion – the "issue" – of reasonable accommodation in the province, and yet all of them are also linked to what we might call the "contagion phenomenon" that is also evident in EU member states where similar stories make the headlines and show the convergence of divergent European national traditions: the centrality of the headscarf controversies in various contexts (France, Germany, Italy, Great Britain), later the bans on the burka (France, the Netherlands, Belgium), the "burkinis" being socially rejected and locally banned from Italian swimming pools and French beaches in the summer of 2009, the sharia tribunal debates and decisions in Ontario and England, and the anxieties that erupted in France and Quebec in the spring of 2012 when concerns were expressed about the presence of halal food in public schools meals program (Amiraux and Koussens 2012). Moreover, the press coverage of the "global problems with Muslims in Western contexts" certainly contributes to the problematization of Islam as a tradition that is incommensurable with democracy and liberalism. Interestingly, most often, when radicalization appears in the research literature, it is common for commentators to associate these tensions between Muslim immigrants and their host societies with the onset of the "pre-radicalization" phase in which individuals become receptive to the radicalization message and process.[14] "Radicalized" individuals will thus appear as having "failed to integrate into a pluralistic, tolerant democracy, or they have turned away and integrated into a radicalized subculture that has taken root through a perversion of the freedoms afforded by multiculturalism" (Parent and Ellis 2011, 79).

The process of radicalization has been associated almost exclusively with its final result – terrorist attacks – and with its concomitant social formation: religious fundamentalisms.[15] Ordinarily, radicalization refers to some exceptional, abnormal, unusual, and unexpected situation. The figure of the home-grown terrorist is presented as the culmination of this process and positioned as being beyond reason. How could we reasonably understand why the "Toronto 18," the young Muslim Canadians discussed by Lorne Dawson in chapter 3 of this volume, would plan to detonate truck bombs in the centre of the city in which they had spent their lives, gone to school, and socialized with non-Muslim friends? How can we understand their behaviour, and that of other "terrorists" in Western contexts, other than through the effect of some "pathological drift" of their lives (Collovald and Gaïti 2006)?

However, beyond studies of socialization trajectories, as Dawson suggests in this volume, very little is known about how radicalization takes root in ordinary people. Indeed, if we establish that both religious pluralism and radicalization processes are related – and this relationship is somehow assumed when the latter is mainly analysed as the pathological reaction of inadequately integrated religious believers[16] – we should also recognize that radicalization processes often begin to take root in the complex soil of micro-societal interactions about which we know very little. In other words, radicalization must be assessed as a reciprocal and relational dynamic and not exclusively as the outcome of deviant unilateral trajectories of socialization. The emphasis thus needs to be put on the responsibility of reciprocal (mis)perceptions and (mis)representations that *need* to be talked about because they nurture feelings of hostility among social actors. The necessity to take seriously what ordinary people are experiencing is crucial in understanding the roots of radicalization in a pluralist context. The following section reflects further on these challenges, starting with a return to definitional issues.

Situating Religious Pluralism and Radicalization

Although modern political thinking conceives of religious pluralism as a positive value that accompanies the privatization of religion,[17] for most living in cosmopolitan contexts it is a daily challenge, "a critical civil issue for citizens" (Eck 2007, 760), an often unconscious constraint or negotiation we cannot escape. Defining religious pluralism to make it a useful analytical tool, rather than an abstract descriptive category of a desired condition of modern liberal democratic societies, demands thinking about it in ways that cover the three dimensions of religious pluralism highlighted by Beckford (2003, 74): "First, societies differ in the extent of their religious *diversity*. Second, the degree to which various religious groups enjoy *acceptance* or recognition in the public sphere varies country to country. Third, support for the moral or political *value* of widening the public acceptance of religions is also variable."

The trend to take pluralism for granted is particularly visible in the statistics and quantitative data that help scholars, politicians, and citizens to know who lives where. Ethnic neighbourhoods typify the global metropolis: "Chinatown" is expected to appear in every tourist guide of major cities in the United States; and Outremont has been relabelled the "Orthodox Jewish neighbourhood" of Montreal in such guides. Both claims speak to geographical "facts" but also to contestable political claims. Scholars working on religious minorities, in response, have questioned the reliance on categories that fail to accurately reflect the internal plural identities of believers.

Our approach to religious pluralism is that it should be conceived as an experience in which a situation is constantly and dynamically being redefined. Here we are reminded of Berger and Luckmann (1967, 117), who define pluralism as a situation in which social actors face a competition between global meanings of daily life and their institutional form. Also related is Thomas's insistence on the dichotomy between a "definition which a society has provided" for an individual and "the spontaneous definitions of the situation" made by the individuals (Thomas 1923, 42).[18] In these perspectives, religious pluralism operates practically both as a frame for action and as a situation in itself.

We suggest that religious pluralism is a "reality test" – a moment in which people have to justify their position and reach an agreement (Boltanski and Thévenot [1991] 2006, 40). Again, as related in the empirical illustrations we mobilized in the first section, our proposal aims at charting and making legible what most other visions of religious pluralism exclude. The various examples we mentioned earlier, from the Shabbat hands to doctors preventing parents from mourning their dead children in hospitals or the other controversies over accommodation, refer to the practical accomplishment of the encounter between individuals adjusting their respective convictions about the other in the course of the interaction. At this scale, religious pluralism is no longer a simple normative set of principles or a taken-for-granted reality but rather a practice experienced by subjects in a specific interactive setting, visible to the outside "in language differences or in modes of dress, eating, and socializing" (Wuthnow 2005, 5). In this way we might begin to think of religious pluralism even more as an ordinary condition of life in modern Western democratic societies, a fact for inhabitants who have no option but to experience it.

As well, modern pluralistic societies are distinguished by the formal regulatory structures, the sets of rules and norms that organize the public life of religious plural societies and that directly affect religious groups (Côté 2003; Saris 2010). Interactions occurring in public spaces are of course connected with it. Social interpersonal practices do not take place in a void but are framed by normative and institutional discourses. Ammerman (2010, 155) contends that there is nothing new in this situation:

> [P]luralism ... is the natural state of religion, everywhere and always. I want to suggest that our questions are best asked in terms that take at least some religious diversity for granted. Our task is not to delineate stages along a path from unity to diversity, nor to outline possible institutional responses to the loss of a place of singular privilege in a society. Our task is to examine how multiple religious ideas, groups, and practices constitute the dynamic social reality in any given place and time.

With such a definition, we could accept that *pluralism* is rather *pluralisms* (Beckford 2003; Marty 2007), that it is not only a social challenge and a normative ideal but also a political, civil issue, encountered in diverse ways every day by citizens of liberal democracies.

We propose to apply this theoretical framework to the phenomenon of radicalization. For twenty years, and more significantly since 9/11, radicalization has been a major theme in discussions about the current state of religious minorities (see chapters 5, 6, and 7 by Beyer, Jamil, and Jakobsh, respectively, in this volume). The emphasis in the literature on religious pluralism on home-grown, second-generation terrorist threats stands as a perfect example. According to the dominant narrative, important factors intervene in the socialization (the school, the religious group, the neighbourhood, the socio-economic status), as well as the identity formation processes (through interactions, meetings, events, discourses), of these young men. The vast list of publications that have adopted this perspective demonstrates the popularity of a vision that frames radicalization as the result of the combination of multiple structural variables (historical, political) and personal characteristics (psychosocial conditions) (Stroink 2007; Krueger 2008). Unfortunately, these two forces rarely meet in scholarship. At some point, the ability of an individual to manage multiple cultural identities, his or her "pluralistic skills" so to speak, determines his or her chances of becoming a "radical." Addressing Islamic radicalization in Europe, Roy (2007, 52) summarizes the current view by saying that home-grown radicals "all share common patterns. They speak European languages, are Western educated, and many have citizenship of a European country. They have had a 'normal' Western teenager's upbringing, with no conspicuous religious practices, often going to night-clubs, 'womanising' and drinking alcohol. None have previous religious training." Yet for some reason these young men become alienated from, and eventually hostile to, this very culture and lifestyle.

Recognizing that pathways to radicalization are multiple, public reports often recognize the absence of a single factor that could be considered "causal" in the radicalization process (Precht 2007, 32). Terrorists and radicals are mostly "unremarkable" (Silber and Bhatt 2007). This literature – mostly published as public reports produced by government agencies[19] – sees radicalization as the result of successive steps with no identifiable timeline or set format. Generally, it addresses radicalization as a phenomenon that must be eliminated rather than understood.[20] The "Causal Factors of Radicalisation" report, published by the Transnational Terrorism, Security, and the Rule of Law (2008) research project and financed by the European Commission, distinguishes for instance between *causes* (context, psychological characteristics, network dynamics, etc.) and *catalysts* (recruitment and trigger events) in understanding the trajectories of radicals. There is, however, a strong emphasis by the authors on the phenomenon of the "identity crisis" as a cause of a radicalized trajectory. Here, religious radicalization results from the individuals' search for identity: they are "faced with the processes causing a crisis either of the model of the secular state and the privatization of religion, or else of the globalization of religious processes with the ensuing crises of identity" (Filoramo 2003, 42). Radicalization is conceived as the ultimate violent outcome of failed processes of social integration. But this concentration on the deviant perspective ends up being very restrictive. Studies of radicalization tend to draw their conclusions from ideal typical figures: well-educated middle-class men suffering from identity crises are put forth as more susceptible to radicalization processes than others, but the authors often fail to adequately consider the complex and exact nature of the social relations and experiences that might underwrite such deviant choices. In terms of the approaches adopted for the study of radicalization, academics interested in criminology and terrorism have collaborated significantly (LaFree and Freilich 2012, 4) to develop scales and sophisticated questionnaires able to predict radical behaviour. Other approaches include analyses of personal documents of terrorists – letters, manifestos – and especially the reconstruction of terrorists' lives to identify common features, with an intense interest in discerning the typical pattern of behaviour. The focus is squarely on the post hoc analysis of individuals who have become violent.

However, studies of those many radicalization trajectories that do not lead to terrorism or violence are rare.[21] Even scanter are studies that examine radical tendencies in majority populations. In February 2007, the Quebec prime minister established the Consultation Commission on Accommodation Practices Related to Cultural Differences, led by Gérard Bouchard and Charles Taylor (see Bouchard and Taylor 2008), which worked for 15 months to map the accommodation practices in place in the region, identify the main challenges, look at other contexts confronted with similar situations, launch a consultation with the population, and finally formulate recommendations to the government. The committee's public hearings were broadcast on television in Quebec for months. The debates related to *accommodements raisonnables* clearly illustrated how the majority was adopting more and more extreme positions towards Quebec's minority communities (Potvin 2008). Our wider definition of radicalization allows us to factor such discourses of stigmatization from the dominant population into analyses of violent and non-violent radicals.

Radicalization studies, we argue, are looking twice over in the wrong place. First, they have adopted an overly restrictive theoretical definition of the phenomenon: radicalization as an individual trajectory. Second, they largely make a methodological choice that excludes ex ante an ethnographic approach. Moreover, affective experiences such as distrust, humiliation, betrayal, and other feelings or emotions that should be taken into account when looking at what one might call the radicalization of all members of society are rarely significant factors in the analysis of such processes.[22] It seems, however, that radicalization as a reciprocal process is also a matter of feelings, as the Bouchard-Taylor Commission demonstrated. The next section suggests ways in which scholars might approach radicalization in a more productive manner.

Pleading for an Ethnographic Approach to the Study of Situated Religious Pluralism and Radicalization Processes

Ethnography is a way to produce data, essentially concerned with concrete social interactions that take place in given contexts. This approach might diminish the pathologizing tendency evident in most studies of radicalization. As Hemmingsen (2011, 1211) has pointed out, ethnography "enables the researcher to move beyond the extraordinary and spectacular and to begin to shed light on the everyday and the real life" of all members of a society, not just those who seem to qualify as *radicals*. An ethnographic approach can make sense of actors' actions, situating them in a given context wherein social interactions are considered as constituents of social phenomena and not only as outcomes (Thomas 1923). It implies reconsidering the development of in situ observation and simple conversations with people who experience religious pluralism and those whose experience could have led them to develop a rejection of others.

The potentialities of an ethnographic approach for the study of radicalization can be illustrated by some recent empirical ethnographic studies. For instance, Buckser (2005, 142), in his ethnographic work on social interactions between two Jewish communities with strong doctrinal differences, concludes that these opposite doctrinal views are not translated into antagonistic relations in practice. Similarly, the fieldwork carried out by Hemmingsen (2011, 1208), with individuals suspected of planning terrorist acts in Denmark, provided her with "a heterogeneous collection of qualitative data consisting of observations, conversations, and semi-structured research interviews." This collection of data forced her to change the object of her study, the focus shifting from the examination of "terrorists" to that of a "shared identity" or a "milieu." A last example of ethnographies developed in the context of radicalization studies is the work by Kenney (2011), who undertook research in a Muslim neighbourhood of Ceuta, often described as home to Spanish people with terrorist inclinations. In his research he "tried to illustrate how ethnographic research can better inform our understanding of this marginalized community and, by extension, other places and problems of interest to counter-terrorism scholars."[23]

With these studies in mind, three questions emerge from this plea for the adoption of an ethnographic approach to the study of situated religious pluralism and radicalization: What should one look at? Where should one look? And how should one look at it? Consistent with our definition of situated religious pluralism, we should focus on those ordinary experiences in which common individuals experience "othernesses." As mentioned earlier, public parks, sidewalks, and public transportation constitute major places to experiment with situated religious pluralism. Such places are the *where to look*. In these sites, ordinary social interactions that lead to the experience of what Mills calls troubles could be identified, studied, and understood; and one might ask, do encounters between people visibly belonging to different religious communities inevitably develop into "failed interactions" (Goffman 1959)? When or how do they escape this path?

The ethnographic approach to radicalization does not mean, however, that the institutional dimension of religious pluralism may now be excluded. Although this dimension has been central to researchers' analyses of religious pluralism, the links with radicalization *processes* remain largely understudied, whereas the state's decisive role in shaping national regulatory regimes has been well documented (D'Antonio and Hoge 2006). In this context, and to consider the institutional dimension of religious pluralism when positioning interactions, we should also take into account policies of regulation, as long as their practical – expected or unexpected – effects are considered, in education or hospitals for instance (Fortin 2006). Public discourses contribute to framing social interactions in which religious pluralism may complicate interactions. Analysing the *accommodements raisonnables* controversies, Potvin (2008) demonstrates the difference between specific practical conflicts and the ones described in the media, and how this transposition from private to public discourses constitutes a radicalization of the positions, encouraging racist postures. Specifically, Potvin identifies the emergence of positions that are definitive and closed, lacking nuances, and which involve a tendency to make generalizations, to depict the other as inferior, and to express the wish for the expulsion of some offending party.[24] This also makes public discourse an answer to the question about *where to look* when studying radicalization from an ethnographic perspective. This calls for paying special attention to affect. Throughout the *accommodements raisonnables* crisis, the emotional involvement of ordinary citizens was clear and explicit. Radicalization processes take root in these primordial sentiments and primary instincts that modern governance is trying to pacify. Geertz's study of Javanese patterns of feeling (Geertz 1960, 1973) is helpful here as it underscores the power and the place of emotion in society: "What the cockfight says is a vocabulary of sentiment – the thrill of risk, the despair of loss, the pleasure of triumph. Yet what it says is not merely that risk is exciting, loss depressing, or triumph gratifying, banal tautologies of affect, but that it is of these emotions, thus exampled, that society is built and individuals are put together" (Geertz 1973, 449). Ethnography makes it possible to understand those social routines and processes in which contradictory *feelings* emerge (hate, love, contempt), which eventually lead to interactions between individuals and groups that produce complex feelings of rejection, isolation, or sympathy. Emotions are social and matter, says Elster (1999), because they are triggered by belief and can short-circuit the rationality of choice. However brief they are, they induce certain ways of acting and constantly relate to social norms. In most of the attacks where home-grown terrorists have been implicated, the common readings of their motivations evidence the problems associated with drawing definitive conclusions about their trajectory and ought to lead us to ask broader questions not just about the kinds of social interactions in which these individuals are situated but also about the effects of hostile public discourse on their sense of belonging to the neighbourhood.[25]

Regarding the question of *how to look* at radicalization processes from the perspective of situated religious pluralism, we suspect, along with Hemmingsen (2011, 1209), that "[t]he more time spent in the field, the less useful concepts such as *terrorism*, *terrorist*, and *radical* [will] bec[o]me." Blom (2011) makes a very sophisticated statement in her work on Pakistani jihadists when she challenges the academic literature on suicide bombing; she explains how these studies usually rely on questionable sources and material and produce a representation of a martyr who is always extremely motivated to die and accepting of death. She then suggests an *emic* approach that would, by taking the conceptions and representations people have of these phenomenon as the starting point of the analysis, go beyond such generalizing discourses and, more significantly, overcome the *individual* trajectories of suicide bombers (Blom 2011). As Werbner (2010) and Elster (2005) state, about the London 7/7 and the 9/11 terrorists respectively, underlining the uncertain efforts of public agencies to discern the main motives of suicide bombers from the videos they left behind is the recognition that we may never really know what mattered most to them and the constraints within which they were living.

Conclusion

This chapter has both a theoretical and a methodological objective. The former involved thinking about how the definitions of pluralism and radicalization often overlook the crucial role of what we have described as the constraining context (pluralism in this case) and the complex reciprocal processes of social interaction, where potential reciprocal alienation might begin in the fomenting of radicalization. The methodological shift we propose focuses on situations, rather than individual or structural factors, and may offer stimulating avenues for researching both pluralism as a condition of life and radicalization as a particular response to this condition of life. By looking at ordinary unease, at the day-to-day emotions emerging in the course of interactions in a pluralistic society, between people ignorant of or unfamiliar with another's moral universe, we seek to avoid the classical and exclusive emphasis on pathological trajectories of radicalization and the functionalist modes of explanation that are often attached to studies with this focus.

We argue for the adoption of an ethnographic approach in the study of radicalization, which would generate a new definition of the object studied, its nature and the identification of innovative fields to be observed. Radicalization processes are certainly more complex and more encompassing than those postulated in the theorization of the homegrown second-generation threat, and we should develop an approach consistent with this complexity. Such a shift will require "a fundamental alteration of the sociological consciousness" (Ball 1972, 66).

As some of the authors cited have expressed, radicalization remains an enigma (Blom, Bucaille, and Martinez 2007; Boltanski 2012). It is factually impossible to know the reason people decide to die as suicide bombers (Bozarslan 2004). "It is an enigma wrapped in a puzzle"

(Elster 2005), and the home-grown terrorist phenomenon continues to surprise us by the difficulty we have in reading the rationale behind these trajectories. Early in 2012, Mohammed Merah moved from petty crime to violent terrorism, killing and wounding French soldiers from the same North African background as himself as well as Jewish schoolchildren and a rabbi. As most of the media said, he had various faces, and making sense of his trajectory is problematic. Changing the scale, method, and theoretical design of research on pluralism and radicalization will not give us the power to anticipate future crises. If we begin with the assumption that personal consistency and clear predictability are non-existent (in "us" as well as "them"), then we will avoid the pitfalls of the profiles and predictive models that are currently the emphases of the dominant paradigm in the research on terrorism and radicalization. As the Merah case makes clear, even someone on the radar of the French intelligence services, known by local and national law enforcement agencies, may nonetheless commit terrible acts of brutality that we cannot anticipate. As most scholars of Salafism and radical Islam would say, he was disconnected from any terrorist cell and more of a maverick than a member or follower of any group. The social and political conditions that made his violent gesture possible remain mysterious (Burgat 2012). As we suggest, this intellectual knot, and the broader social fabric of which Merah is just a thread, would certainly be better addressed with a shift of perspective, by paying attention to how he and many others like him interact with others in the pluralist context that is the defining feature of the modern West. By being able to make connections between what is exceptional and what happens routinely, the outcome of terrorism and the situation in which it arises, the "issues" and the "troubles," we can find some important clues to understand what has so far been an enigma.

NOTES

1 This essay stems from three years of reflection on the study of religious pluralism by V. Amiraux that led to the implementation of the PLURADI-CAL team, funded by the Fonds de Recherche Société et Culture du Québec (2011–13). J. Araya-Moreno has been associated with the project since its inception. All information related to the PLURADICAL team can be found at valerieamiraux.com. The authors wish to thank Dr Valérie Behiery for letting us benefit from her precious editing talents, making

this text available for an English-language public. They also warmly thank
Paul Bramadat and Lorne Dawson for helping them to make the argument
clearer and stronger, thanks to their rich comments.

2 See for example the studies released by the Change Institute (2008) or
Transnational Terrorism, Security, and the Rule of Law (2008), among
many others. The literature on terrorism and radicalization is vast and
cannot be exhaustively referenced here. We invite interested readers to
consult the endnote bibliographies that the PLURADICAL team has made
available on the website mentioned in note 1.

3 We are alluding to the "multiculturalism gone wild" discourse that has
become a key issue in the European Union since 2001, especially in Great
Britain and the Netherlands. This trend to equate multiculturalism with
a series of problems, assumingly related to religious diversity, reflects the
impact of 9/11 (see Lentin and Titley 2011 and Silj 2010).

4 "Perhaps the most fruitful distinction with which the sociological imagination works is between 'the personal troubles of milieu' and 'the public issues of social structure.' This distinction is an essential tool of the
sociological imagination and a feature of all classic work in social science"
(Mills 1959, 8).

5 We could have taken the burkini discussion during summer 2009 in Italy
or the burka plus national identity discussion in France that started with
the Council of State decision to deny French nationality to a Moroccan
woman because of her radical practice of her religion (i.e., the wearing of a
niqab), which ended up with a law forbidding people to hide their faces in
public in October 2010.

6 The image from the poster was reproduced in the international press.

7 A few Québécois novels have addressed this issue of learning how to
know your immediate neighbors better. The best-known are the novels
of Zipora (2006) and Faroud (2012). Of course, several scholars have been
working on these neighbourly interactions, often in relationship with legal
questions; see Shaffir (2002) and Van Praagh (2008).

8 Paul Bramadat, personal communication with the authors, 10 June 2012.

9 Different studies have analysed Zarqa Nawaz's television program (see,
e.g., Khan 2009 and Bibler 2008).

10 We are here referring to the way the prayer is performed (using for
instance specific accessories such as incense or candles or involving loud
and long hours of wailing, large numbers of people, uninterrupted loud
reading of a sacred text), not the prayer per se. In this specific example,
the woman was requesting the use of a prayer carpet in the middle of
a highly sanitized room. This case was reported by a doctoral student

working on Muslim women and their access to health services in Montreal hospitals.

11 As in the case of the Centre à la petite enfance (public child care center) Gros Bec, where a preschool teacher had made an informal agreement with a Muslim father not to give pork to his son (Rioux and Bourgeoys 2008). This agreement was later discussed during the *accommodements raisonnables* debate because it generated a legal decision. This case points to the common existence of such informal and interpersonal agreements between parents and teachers. *CDPDJ* c. *Centre à la petite enfance Gros Bec*, 2008 QCTDP 14.

12 The commission was created by the prime minister of Quebec in February 2007 and asked to assess the practice of reasonable accommodation related to cultural differences.

13 See http://www.cbc.ca/news/canada/montreal/quebec-town-may-scrap-immigrant-code-1.925377.

14 "Pre-radicalization describes the many general background factors that make individuals receptive to extremism just before the actual radicalization process begins" (Precht 2007, 34).

15 See, for example, the reports released by the Change Institute (2008) or Transnational Terrorism, Security, and the Rule of Law (2008).

16 See the list of recommendations given in most of the reports on terrorism and counterterrorism initiatives in Western contexts produced by the Change Institute (2008) or Transnational Terrorism, Security, and the Rule of Law project (2008).

17 This positive valence of choice when it comes to religion (freedom of conscience as a freedom to believe or not to believe) is particularly explicit in the literature on the Islamic headscarf in Western contexts. The umbrella of choice makes religious convictions more intelligible to secular publics (Amiraux 2009; Fernando 2010).

18 "Definition of the situation" is probably Thomas's stronger contribution to the sociology of interaction. It is a clear invitation to look at on the one hand the meaning of situations and on the other the situated meanings within them as the actors are experiencing them. As a consequence, actions as well as interactions stem directly from this definition of the situation. The notion of the latter here does not refer simply to the conditions in which something is happening: a situation is not a scene or a stage. It is a process by which the point of view of the actor is central, which echoes Nussbaum's idea mentioned earlier in this chapter. Functional consequences are not at the core of Thomas's interests: the definition of situation expresses his interest in looking at "existential causality," which offers a very different locus of explanation than the one usually offered to understand social conducts (Ball 1972). The process of situational definition is "a causal agent itself in

the social conduct of self-determining, volitionally active persons, located in situations they construct and invest with meaning" (Ball 1972, 65). This is what we would like to map by working on situated religious pluralism: the way actors located in their day-to-day business define the situation in which they are located. Nothing can be taken for granted and there is so to say no "personal consistency" to be looked at in such a perspective.

19 Sageman (2008) is a good illustration of this trend, working for the US State Department on profiling from a psychological perspective.

20 Out of the 20,000 pieces of literature about terrorism analysed by Lum, Kennedy, and Sherley (2006), only seven were based on a rigorous scientific strategy and were able to provide effective policy recommendations.

21 Non-violent radicalization processes are also defined with reference to violence. For example, Bartlett, Birdwell, and King (2010, 8) define non-violent radicalization as "the process by which individuals come to hold radical views in relation to the status quo but do not undertake, or directly aid or abet terrorist activity."

22 Consider Jacob Levy's warning: "the danger of bloody ethnic violence, the reality that states treat members of minority cultures in humiliated ways, the intentional cruelty of language restrictions and police beatings and subtler measures which remind members of a minority that they are not full citizens or whole persons, there are the focus of attention" (Levy 2000).

23 Just as the notion of *situation* helps elucidate and provide new definitions of pluralism, Goffman's notion of *footing* can be helpful when it comes to ethnography of radicalization. *Footing* is a concept he developed which suggests that the "[p]articipant's alignment, or set, or stance, or posture, or projected self is somehow at issue." The notion entails that inside a unique *frame* "[a] change in footing implies a change in the alignment we take up to ourselves and the others present as expressed in the way we manage the production or reception of an utterance. A change in our footing is another way of talking about a change in our frame for events." According to this theoretical perspective, social interactions in the context of religious pluralism – and that could include processes of radicalization – are *footed* in specific settings on multiple stages (Goffman 1981, 128).

24 She in particular looks at the Multani case.

25 The emphasis on the multiplicity of the potential interpretations of daily routines and specific gestures in the US context of the war on terror is illustrated well in the successful TV series *Homeland*. The show narrates the complex story of a US Marine returning to the States after he was a prisoner of al-Qaeda. *Homeland*'s plot is inspired by a successful Israeli TV series (*Hafutim*) in which three Israeli soldiers return home after 17 years as prisoners in Lebanon.

REFERENCES

Abbas, Tahir. 2007. *Islamic Political Radicalism*. Edinburgh: Edinburgh University Press.

Alton, Caitlin J. 2011. "Cultural Diversity in Mile End: Everyday Interactions between Hasidim and Non-Hasidim." Master's thesis, Concordia University.

Amiraux, Valérie. 2009. "L' 'affaire du foulard' en France: Retour sur une affaire qui n'en est pas encore une." *Sociologie et sociétés* 41 (2): 273–98.

Amiraux, Valérie, and David Koussens. 2012. "Délires franco-québécois sur la viande halal." *Le Devoir*, 26 March.

Ammerman, Nancy T. 2010. "The Challenges of Pluralism: Locating Religion in a World of Diversity." *Social Compass* 57 (2): 154–67.

Arnsperger, Christian, and Hervé Pourtois. 2000. "Reason, the Public Sphere and the Challenges of Religious and Cultural Pluralism." *Revue Philosophique de Louvain* 98 (1): 1–5.

Ball, Donald W. 1972. "The 'Definition of Situation': Some Theoretical and Methodological Consequences of Taking W.I. Thomas Seriously." *Journal for Theory of Social Behavior* 2: 61–82.

Bartlett, Jamie, Jonathan Birdwell, and Michael King. 2010. *The Edge of Violence: A Radical Approach to Extremism*. London: Demos.

Becker, Howard. 1998. *Tricks of the Trade: How to Think about Your Research While You're Doing It*. Chicago: University of Chicago Press.

Beckford, James A. 2003. "The Vagaries of Religious Pluralism." In *Social Theory and Religion*, ed. J.A. Beckford, 73–102. Cambridge: Cambridge University Press.

Beer, David, and Roger Burrows. 2010. "The Sociological Imagination as Popular Culture." In *New Social Connections: Sociology's Subjects and Objects*, ed. Judith Burnett, Syd Jeffers, and Graham Thomas, 233–52. New York: Palgrave Macmillan.

Berger, Peter, and Thomas Luckmann. 1967. *The Social Construction of Reality: A Treatise in the Sociology of Knowledge*. New York: Doubleday.

Bibler, Susan. 2008. "Subverting Discourses of Risk in the War on Terror." In *Risk and the War of Terror*, ed. Louise Amoore and Marieke de Goede, 218–32. New York: Routledge.

Blom, Amélie. 2011. "Les 'martyrs' jihadistes veulent-ils forcément mourir? Une approche émique de la radicalisation autosacrificielle au Pakistan." *Revue Française de Science Politique* 61 (5): 867–91.

Blom, Amélie, Laetitia Bucaille, and Luis Martinez, eds. 2007. *The Enigma of Islamist Violence*. New York: Columbia University Press.

Boltanski, Luc. 2012. *Énigmes et complots*. Paris: Gallimard.

Boltanski, Luc, and Laurent Thévenot. (1991) 2006. *On Justification: Economies of Worth*. Princeton, NJ: Princeton University Press.

Bouchard, Gérard, and Charles Taylor. 2008. "Building the Future: A Time for Reconciliation." Final report of the Commission de consultation sur les pratiques d'accommodement reliées aux différences culturelles. Quebec: Gouvernement du Québec.

Bozarslan, Hamit. 2004. *Violence in the Middle East: From Political Struggle to Self-sacrifice*. Princeton, NJ: Markus Wiener Publishers.

Brown, Mose. 2011. *Raising Brooklyn: Nannies, Childcare, and Caribbeans Creating Community*. New York: New York University Press.

Buckser, Andrew. 2005. "Chabad in Copenhagen: Fundamentalism and Modernity in Jewish Denmark." *Ethnology* 44 (2): 125–45.

Burgat, François. 2012. "Jihadisme des uns et jihadisme des autres." *Politis* 1197 (5 April).

Cefaï, Daniel. 2002. "Qu'est-ce qu'une arène publique? Quelques pistes pour une approche pragmatiste." In *L'héritage du pragmatisme*, ed. Daniel Cefaï and Isaac Joseph, 51–81. Paris: Éditions de l'aube.

Change Institute. 2008. "The Beliefs Ideologies and Narratives." *Studies into Violent Radicalisation*. http://ec.europa.eu/home-affairs/doc_centre/terrorism/docs/ec_radicalisation_study_on_ideology_and_narrative_en.pdf.

Collovald, Annie, and Brigitte Gaïti. 2006. *La démocratie aux extrêmes: Sur la radicalisation politique*. Paris: La Dispute.

Côté, Pauline. 2003. "Autorité publique, pluralisation et sectorisation religieuse en modernité tardive." *Archives de Sciences Sociales des Religions* 121: 19–39.

Croft, Stuart. 2012. *Securitizing Islam: Identity and the Search for Security*. Cambridge and New York: Cambridge University Press.

Cumming-Bruce, Nick, and Steve Erlanger. 2009. "Swiss Ban Building of Minarets on Mosques." *The New York Times*, 29 November.

D'Antonio, William V., and Dean R. Hoge. 2006. "The American Experience of Religious Disestablishment and Pluralism." *Social Compass* 53 (3): 345–56.

Dewey, John. 1927. *The Public and Its Problems*. Chicago: Swallow.

Eck, Diana L. 2007. "Prospects for Pluralism: Voice and Vision in the Study of Religion [Editorial Material]." *Journal of the American Academy of Religion* 75 (4): 743–76.

Elster, John. 1999. *Strong Feelings: Emotion, Addiction and Human Behaviour*. Cambridge: MIT Press.

– 2005. "Motivations and Beliefs in Suicide Missions." In *Making Sense of Suicide Missions*, ed. Diego Gambetta, 233–58. Oxford: Oxford University Press.

European Commission. 2005. "Terrorist Recruitment: Addressing the Factors Contributing to Violent Radicalisation." Brussels. http://eur-lex.europa.eu/LexUriServ/LexUriServ.do?uri=COM:2005:0313:FIN:EN:PDF.

Faroud, Abla. 2012. *Le sourire de la petite juive*. Montreal: VLB Éditeur.

Fernando, Mayanthi. 2010. "Reconfiguring Freedom: Muslim Piety and the Limits of Secular Law and Public Discourse in France." *American Ethnologist* 37 (1): 19–35.

Filoramo, Giovanni. 2003. "Religious Pluralism and Crises of Identity." *Diogenes* 50 (3): 31–44.

Fortin, Sylvie. 2006. "Urban Diversity and the Space of the Clinic: Or When Medicine Looks at Culture ..." *Medische Antropologie* 18 (2): 365–85.

Geertz, Clifford. 1960. *The Religion of Java*. Glencoe: The Free Press.

– 1963. "The Integrative Revolution: Primordial Sentiments and Politics in the New States." In *Old Societies and New States: The Quest for Modernity in Asia and Africa*, ed. C. Geertz, 105–57. New York: The Free Press of Glencoe.

– 1973. *The Interpretation of Cultures*. New York: Basic Books.

Goffman, Erving. 1959. *The Presentation of Self in Everyday Life*. New York: Doubleday Anchor Books.

– 1974. *Frame Analysis*. New York: Harper and Row.

– 1981. *Forms of Talk*. Philadelphia: University of Pennsylvania Press.

Hemmingsen, Ann-Sophie. 2011. "Salafi Jihadism: Relying on Fieldwork to Study Unorganized and Clandestine Phenomena." *Ethnic and Racial Studies* 34 (7): 1201–15.

Honneth, Axel. 1995. *The Struggle for Recognition: The Moral Grammar of Social Conflicts*. Cambridge: Polity Press.

Kaplan, Stephen. 2002. *Different Paths, Different Summits: A Model for Religious Pluralism*. Lanham, MD: Rowman and Littlefield.

Kenney, Michael. 2011. "Hotbed of Radicalization or Something Else? An Ethnographic Exploration of a Muslim Neighborhood in Ceuta." *Terrorism and Political Violence* 23: 537–59.

Khan, Sarah. 2009. "The Many Faces of Muslim Women in Canada: A Re-constructed Image in CBC's *Little Mosque on the Prairie*." PhD diss., University of Ottawa.

Krueger, Alan B. 2008. "What Makes a Homegrown Terrorist? Human Capital and Participation in Domestic Islamic Terrorist Groups in the U.S.A." *Economics Letters* 101: 293–6.

Kymlicka, Will. 1998. *Finding Our Way: Rethinking Ethnocultural Relations in Canada*. Oxford: Oxford University Press.

LaFree, Gary, and Joshua D. Freilich. 2012. "Editor's Introduction: Quantitative Approaches to the Study of Terrorism." *Journal of Quantitative Criminology* 28: 1–5.

Lentin, Alana, and Gavan Titley. 2011. *The Crises of Multiculturalism: Racism in a Neoliberal Age*. London and New York: Zed Books.

Levy, Jacob. 2000. *The Multiculturalism of Fear*. Oxford: Oxford University Press.

Lum, Cynthia, Leslie Kennedy, and Alison Sherley. 2006. "The Effectiveness of Counter-terrorism Strategies." *Campbell Systematic Reviews* 2: 1–51.

Marty, Martin E. 2007. "Pluralisms." *Annals of the American Academy of Political and Social Science* 612: 13–25.

McClure, Kristie. 1992. "On the Subject of Rights: Pluralism, Plurality and Political Identity." In *Dimensions of Radical Democracy: Pluralism, Citizenship, Community*, ed. Chantal Mouffe, 108–25. London: Verso.

Mills, C. Wright. 1959. *The Sociological Imagination*. New York: Oxford University Press.

Morag, Patrick. 2002. "Rights and Recognition: Perspectives on Multicultural Democracy." *Ethnicities* 2 (1): 31–51.

Mose Brown, Tamara. 2011. *Raising Brooklyn: Nannies, Childcare, and Caribbeans Creating Community*. New York: New York University Press.

Nussbaum, Martha C. 2012. *The New Religious Intolerance: Overcoming the Politics of Fear in an Anxious Age*. Cambridge, MA: Belknap Press of Harvard University Press.

Parent, Richard B., and James O. Ellis. 2011. "Countering Radicalization of Diaspora Communities in Canada." Working Paper nos. 11–12, Metropolis British Columbia.

Phillips, Anne. 2007. *Multiculturalism without Culture*. Princeton, NJ: Princeton University Press.

Potvin, Maryse. 2008. "Crise des accommodements raisonnables: Une fiction médiatique?" Montreal: Athéna Editions.

Precht, Tomas. 2007. "Home Grown Terrorism and Islamist Radicalisation in Europe, From Conversion to Terrorism: An Assessment of the Factors Influencing Violent Islamist Extremism and Suggestions for Counter Radicalisation Measures." Research report funded by the Danish Ministry of Justice. http://www.justitsministeriet.dk/sites/default/files/media/Arbejdsomraader/Forskning/Forskningspuljen/2011/2007/Home_grown_terrorism_and_Islamist_radicalisation_in_Europe_-_an_assessment_of_in fluencing_factors__2_.pdf.

Rioux, Marc, and Rodolphe Bourgeoys. 2008. "Enquête sur un échantillon de cas d'accommodement (1998–2007)." Rapport remis à la Commission de consultation sur les pratiques d'accommodement reliées aux différences culturelles. Quebec: Gouvernement du Québec.

Roy, Olivier. 2007. "Islamic Terrorist Radicalisation in Europe." In *European Islam: Challenges for Society and Public Policy*, ed. Samir Amghhar, Amel Boubekeur, and Michael Emerson, 52–60. Brussels: Center for European Policy Studies.

Sageman, Marc. 2008. *Leaderless Jihad: Terror Networks in the Twenty-first Century*. Philadelphia: University of Pennsylvania Press.

Saris, Anne. 2010. "La gestion de l'hétérogénéité normative par le droit étatique." In *Appartenance religieuse, appartenance citoyenne: Un équilibre en tension*, ed. Paul Eid, Pierre Bosset, Micheline Milot, and Sébastien Lebel-Grenier, 141–77. Quebec: Presses de l'Université Laval.

Scott, Alan, Edwin Amenta, and Kate Nash, eds. 2012. *The Wiley-Blackwell Companion of Political Sociology*. Malden, MA: Blackwell Publishing.

Shachar, Ayelet. 2001. *Multicultural Jurisdictions: Cultural Differences and Women's Rights*. Cambridge: Cambridge University Press.

Shaffir, 2002. "Outremont's Hassidim and Their Neighbors: An Eruv and Its Repercussions." *Jewish Journal of Sociology* 5 (1): 33–50.

Silber, Mitchell D., and Arvin Bhatt. 2007. "Radicalization in the West: The Homegrown Threat." New York: New York City Police Department.

Silj, Alessandro. 2010. *European Multiculturalism Revisited*. London and New York: Zed Books.

Stroink, M. 2007. "Processes and Preconditions Underlying Terrorism in Second-generation Immigrants." *Peace and Conflict: Journal of Peace Psychology* 13 (3): 293–312.

Taylor, Charles. 1994. *Multiculturalism: Examining the Politics of Recognition*. Princeton, NJ: Princeton University Press.

Thachuk, Kimberley L., Marion E. Bowman, and Courtney Richardson. 2008. *Homegrown Terrorism: The Threat Within*. Center for Technology and National Security Policy, National Defense University. http://www.isn.ethz.ch/ Digital-Library/Publications/Detail/?lng=en&id=134894.

Thomas, William Isaac. 1923. *The Unadjusted Girl*. Boston: Little, Brown and Co.

Transnational Terrorism, Security, and the Rule of Law. 2008. "Causal Factors of Radicalisation." Contextual paper, Work package 4. http://www. transnationalterrorism.eu/tekst/publications/Causal%20Factors.pdf.

Van Praagh, Shauna. 2008. "View from the Succah: Religion and Neighbourly Relations." In *Law and Religious Pluralism in Canada*, ed. Richard Moon, 20–40. Vancouver: UBC Press.

Weinstock, Daniel. 1992. "Le défi du Pluralisme." *Lekton* 3 (2): 7–28.

– 1993. "Libéralisme, nationalisme et pluralité." *Philosophiques* 19 (2): 117–45.

– 2009. "Frayed Federation: Challenges to Canadian Unity in the Wake of Trudeau's Failed Nation-Building Project." In *The Ties that Bind: Accommodating Diversity in Canada and the European Union*, ed. John E. Fossum, Johanne Poirier, and Paul Magnette, 279–99. Brussels: Peter Lang.

Werbner, Pnina. 2010. "Notes from a Small Place: Anthropological Blues in the Face of Global Terror." *Current Anthropology* 51 (2): 193–221.

Wuthnow, Robert. 2005. *America and the Challenges of Religious Diversity*. Princeton, NJ: Princeton University Press.

Zipora, Malka. 2006. *Lekhaim! Chroniques de la vie hassidique à Montréal*. Montreal: Les éditions du passage.

5 Securitization and Young Muslim Males: Is None Too Many?

PETER BEYER

Introduction

The context of this chapter is the idea and fear of what sometimes is called "home-grown radicalism," "home-grown terror," or more specifically and simply, the radicalization of young Muslim males in Western countries. Since 9/11, many of the more spectacular violent and terrorist events in Europe and North America have been perpetrated by young Muslim males who grew up in the West, including the Madrid train bombings in 2004, the assassination of Theo van Gogh in Amsterdam in 2004, the London subway and bus bombings of 2005, the attempt to set off a car bomb in Times Square in New York in 2010, and the murder of three soldiers, three Jewish children, and a rabbi in France in 2012. In Canada, the "point-to" event has been the arrest of the "Toronto 18" in June 2006, 11 of whom were eventually convicted on "terrorism"-related charges. All of those convicted were young Muslim men[1] who had either been born in Canada or arrived as children aged 12 or younger (i.e., they are part of the "1.5 generation") (Teotonio and Javed 2010; chapter 3 by Dawson in this volume).

Two sorts of questions commonly arise from this context: How widespread is such radicalization among young Muslims, specifically in Canada? And, to the degree that it happens, what factors can be associated with such radicalization, that is, what "causes" it? Much more pointedly in this regard, if such radicalization occurs predominantly – but by no means exclusively – among young *men* (generally adolescents and young adults in their 20s), and if the radicals under scrutiny are at least nominal Muslims, what does Islam have to do with it? The fear, in other words, is that there is something about Islam that specifically

facilitates this particular sort of radicalization in contemporary circumstances and, even more sharply focused, that this radicalization may
be a lethal mix of the "excess testosterone" of young maleness with
"excess religion."

In an effort to address such questions, this chapter seeks to determine
both how susceptible young Canadian Muslim men may be to such
radicalization and what Islam has to do with it. It does so by examining the results of a research project conducted by the author and his
collaborators between 2004 and 2006, a project that included in-depth
interviews with a sample of 35 young, (at least nominally) Muslim men
who grew up in Canada. The sample is not representative since the
participants self-selected for the project and were recruited only on six
central Canadian university campuses, but it is arguably indicative of
the sorts of profiles of young Muslim men that are significantly present
in this Canadian subpopulation. Although the sample will have inevitably missed certain types of profiles, the degree of saturation reached
in the interviews (see later) suggests that these profiles have a very
minor presence among Canadian men in their late teens and 20s who
self-identify as Muslim or are at least of Muslim families.

Model Factors in Radicalization

As the other chapters of this book demonstrate, the literature on the sort
of radicalization at issue here is already significant and is growing fast.
In order to provide a framework for the current analysis, however, I use
Mina al-Lami's summary of explanations for radicalization offered in
a report written for a project funded by the New Security Challenges
program of the British Economic and Social Research Council (ESRC)
(Al-Lami 2009; see also Bartlett, Birdwell, and King 2010). Al-Lami lists
"the [five] key explanations given for the 'radicalization' of Muslims
in the West": socio-economic deprivation, the search for identity, social affiliations, political marginalization and grievances, and radical
rhetoric. Very briefly, the first assumes a positive association between
radicalization and being poor, unemployed, or underemployed and
having low educational attainment. The second refers to the phenomenon of young Muslim men of immigrant background being "caught
between two worlds," the Muslim world of their parents or families,
which they reject, and the Western world around them, which rejects
them. They feel like they belong to neither. Radicalization is posited as
offering a positive way out of this dilemma. The third means essentially

that young Muslim men "hang with the wrong crowd" or get absorbed in radicalized networks, sometimes featuring charismatic individuals as leaders. The fourth refers to the exclusion of these young men from political influence, whether in their own communities where their elders dominate or at the level of the national political process. This includes the inability to affect Western foreign policy that is perceived to be directed against "their people" and "their religion." Finally, the fifth factor points to the existence of discourses of radicalization available broadly in the environment, whether local, national, or transnational, whether physical or virtual.

A central difficulty must be associated with these factors. Although they are each entirely plausible, the evidence for their existence is mostly taken from individuals that have become radicalized. Establishing the most important factor at work, therefore, requires, as it were, "reverse engineering." The research focuses on radicalized individuals who reflect on their own personal histories. The stories they tell are in many ways like "conversion stories" from the New Religious Movements literature, which means that they often follow a script that is itself a symptom of someone who has converted to what others call a radicalized perspective and identity and may not be a reliable account of the causes of radicalization. That is, with hindsight, a radical sees himself as having been "lost" according to certain criteria, setting the stage for being "found" according to other corresponding criteria that he now accepts. Nonetheless, such accounts do tell us something reliable about what has happened in these individual cases, and therefore the commonalities across narratives can be taken as at least somewhat trustworthy. There is in any case little evidence to discount them entirely. Several further difficulties associated with these accounts include whether such evidence can or cannot distinguish between sufficient and necessary conditions of radicalization, namely whether all of the five factors mentioned earlier have to be present or only some; one might also wonder whether other critical factors are missing from such radicalization stories because the people involved have difficulty admitting or recognizing them; and finally, we need to question whether or not the presence of all factors necessarily results in a significantly higher degree of radicalization among the population under scrutiny.

With these challenges in mind, the following analysis looks for these five factors in the Canadian sample of 35 young Muslim men and also looks for other factors or commonalities that may or may not be associated with radicalization *or* that may be taken as possibly counter-indicative for radicalization. In this regard, particular attention will be paid to the role and nature of Islam in the lives of these 35 individuals, none of whom has become radicalized in any admitted or detectable way. They thus contrast quite clearly with those very few young Canadian Muslim males who have experienced radicalization, including almost all of the Toronto 18 discussed in Lorne Dawson's chapter in this volume.

The Research Project: Religion and Immigrant Youth in Canada

The Religion and Immigrant Youth in Canada project conducted 197 semi-structured in-depth interviews with persons between 18 and 27 years old who came from immigrant families, had grown up in or were born in Canada, and identified as having a Muslim, Hindu, or Buddhist background. They were recruited between spring 2004 and spring 2006 on six university campuses in Toronto, Ottawa, and Montreal. Previous research with Canadian census data had shown that the population with this background and within this age range had postsecondary education exposure of 80 to 95 per cent depending on religious identity and gender (Beyer 2005; Beyer and Martin 2010). Recruiting on university campuses therefore made sense since the aim was to collect as broad a sample as possible, with the realization that no such sample could be random and therefore representative. Inevitably, therefore, the project will have missed including persons without university or postsecondary exposure, and it did not include adolescents. The latter fact is important because the interviews confirmed that people in the target age groups had often changed a great deal as they were growing up and many had changed recently, especially as it concerned religion. The resulting sample included 93 Muslims, 35 of whom were men and 58 women. Hindus and Buddhists made up the rest of the sample. In the case of both the Muslim men and women, the researchers judged that they had "reached saturation": that is, later interviews failed to reveal significantly new patterns with respect to the central questions asked, and therefore one can assume that whatever response patterns were not picked up by the project will have only a very minor presence in the target population or they will be of such a nature that participants were unlikely to reveal them. Unfortunately, radicalized individuals may well have qualified on both counts. They may constitute the proverbial "needle in the haystack," but that may be a good argument for paying greater attention to the "haystack." In other words, the results of the research project did not allow us to say anything about the presence of radicalized individuals, but it might say a great deal about the vast majority of young Muslim males in Canada. In this regard, it is worth noting that a good number of those convicted among the Toronto 18 also had postsecondary education and therefore could, in principle, have been recruited into our project (see Dawson's chapter 3 in this volume). Indeed recruitment for the project took place exactly during the two years before their arrest in June 2006, in the age range in which almost all of them were at that time, in the city that they inhabited, and on the postsecondary campuses that some of them actually had attended.

The main purpose of the project was to see how the participants related to the religions of their family heritage. The core question to all participants was how were they contributing to the reconstruction of their religion, here Islam, in the Canadian context? In less technical language, it asked what their relation was to religion and to the religion of their family heritage in particular. In this context, interviews also included discussion of how they conducted their lives in Canada; how comfortable or uncomfortable they felt; how accepted or integrated they felt; how they identified culturally as well as religiously; what they thought about Canada as a country; what negative experiences they had had growing up or at the time of the interviews; what they thought were the main problems facing them, their religion, Canada, the world; and what role religion and their religion did or should have in all of these matters. They were asked about their expectations and aspirations, the socioeconomic situation of their families, their political orientations, their social networks including religious networks, their attitudes to other religions and people without religion, to whom or what they looked for guidance in matters religious, and their attitudes to multiculturalism and religious diversity. In various ways, therefore, the questioning probed all five of the aforementioned factors but added the significant focus expressly on religion, on Islam, what that meant for them, what that implied, and its place in the world. In some limited respects, then, this research can serve as a near equivalent to the control groups, at least in the Canadian context, that are missing from most research into homegrown terrorist radicalization (see chapter 3 in this volume).

A Demographic Profile of 35 Muslim Men[2]

In Canada at the time of the 2001 census – notably two months before 9/11 – almost 84 per cent of Muslim males born in Canada and between the ages of 21 and 30 had some form of postsecondary schooling (Beyer 2005; Corak 2008). It is from this large segment of the Muslim population that our sample of 35 Muslim males was drawn. All of them were at the time of their interviews either enrolled in university or had already graduated, an unsurprising characteristic given they were recruited through university campuses.

In age, they ranged from 18 to 27, with an average age of 21.4 years. Only 5 of them were 25 years or older, whereas 11 of them were under 20. As such, they were on average a very young group. This feature of the sample is also reflective of the overall population in the sense that the vast majority of the second generation of Muslim immigrants in 2001 was still quite young: 86 per cent of them were still under the age of 20; and 96.5 per cent were under the age of 30. Even among the overall Muslim population, which includes the 1.5 and second generations of our sample, 45.3 per cent were under the age of 25 (Statistics Canada 2003, 2004). As a reflection of their young age, the Muslim male participants, for the most part, will not have settled into a definitive adult identity, including quite possibly as it concerns religion. None of them was married (two of the Muslim women were), and relatively few had full-time jobs and were already actively engaged in pursuing careers.

Like the Muslim women,[3] the men or their families had their origins in a wide variety of countries around the world. The vast majority came from Muslim-majority countries, especially the countries of North Africa and the Middle East (12) or Pakistan and Bangladesh (13). One gave India as his country of origin, five Iran, one Guyana, two East Africa, one Somalia, and one Sri Lanka. The only country-of-origin subgroup that was different from the others was the five whose families came from Iran. As with the six Muslim women with the same origin (Beyer and Ramji 2013, chapter 6), these five were uniformly very little involved with religion, and four out of five were expressly non-religious, even anti-religious. In spite of the fact that a few participants averred that South Asian Muslims were on average more "extreme" in their Islam than, for instance, those from North Africa and the Middle East, this sample of 35 men did not show any consistent pattern in this regard.

Again, as with the Muslim women, while the clear majority of the men were Sunni or from Sunni families, a significant portion was also one variety or another of Shi'a. Twenty-one were Sunni, ten were Twelver Shi'a (including the five Iranians and one Sunni who had converted to Twelver Shi'ism), two were Ismaili, one Ahmadi, and one came from a mixed Shi'a/Sunni family. None indicated that they or anyone in their immediate families was an adept of Sufi forms of Islam. Again, with the exception of the Iranians, subdivision of Islam was not a reliable predictor of religious involvement, understanding of Islam, or importance of religion in the lives of individuals.

Classifying the Muslim Males

Analysis of the interviews divided the respondents into overall classification schemes for each religion, mainly as heuristic devices to give points of reference for comparing the different individuals within each religious identity group to one another. The various classifications within these schemes are not ideal types in a Weberian sense but rather descriptive labels of convenience whose sole purpose is to assist in the comparison. In the case of the Muslims, a ten-point classification scheme running from non-believers/express atheists to the most sectarian and highly practising should be seen, on the one hand, as a kind of continuum of involvement from low to high and, on the other, as a rough grouping into the non-involved, the somewhat to moderately involved, and the highly involved, with gradients according to certain criteria within each of these broader categories. The ten-point gradient also allows different ways of dividing the group into low, medium, and high. In addition, the classification scheme is not theoretically derived; rather it emerged from the analysis of the data of the interviews. Others doing the analysis may well have come up with a different and potentially just as valid scheme. Its justification is in how and what it helps us see, not because there would have been no other way of seeing.

Figure 5.1 shows a graph of how the 35 Muslim men fell along the ten-point scale, comparing them with the Muslim women. A comparison of the distribution in this figure with the corresponding classification of the Muslim women shows both differences and similarities. Concerning differences, proportionately more men than women were in one of the three non-religious categories: 31 per cent of men compared to 17 per cent of women. Correspondingly, more women than men were in the middle three, somewhat to moderately involved classifications: 26 per cent of men as compared to 33 per cent of the women. On the high end of the scale, categories 7–10 included 43 per cent of the men and 50 per cent of the women. If we group the categories somewhat differently, into lower (1–5) and higher (6–10), the distinction being the presence or absence of self-described regular practice, then the outcome is again similar, slightly in favour of the women. With this grouping, 60 per cent of the men but 65 per cent of the women engaged in regular Islamic religious practice.[4] On the whole, then, the data appear to

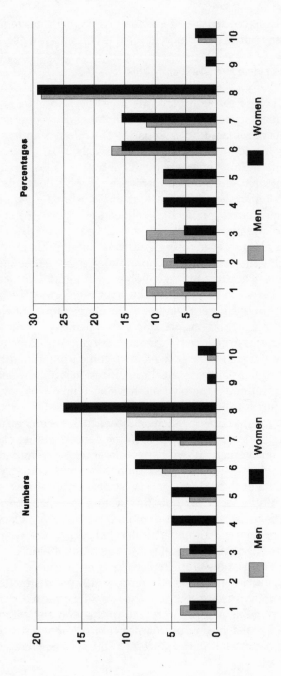

Figure 5.1. Ten-point Classification Distribution of Muslim Participants, Men and Women

be consistent with the common conclusion that women are somewhat more religiously involved than men (see, for example, Collett and Lizardo 2009). In this case, however, what is particularly significant is the greater polarity among the men between the non-religious and the highly involved and the very high percentages of both sexes that are significantly or highly involved, from half to two-thirds of the sample depending on how one groups them. On the higher end of the scale, the difference between men and women is not that large. In this regard, it should be noted that the nature of the participant recruitment process would favour people who care about religion and therefore are more likely to be involved in religion; but given that this process was not different for the Buddhists and the Hindus in the overall sample, the high proportion among the Muslims of the highly involved in all likelihood means that, on average, young Muslim adults in Canada are more religious by their own standards (and those of most others in society) than those of the other two religious identities. For most, Islam is important; for a great many, it is at the centre of their identities.

Non-Muslims and Non-religious Muslims

Those in the sample who did not identify as Muslims or declared themselves to be non-religious Muslims (i.e., Muslim identity but little belief or practice) are important in the present context because they help pose the question with regard to radicalization: does religion, here Islam, bear any *necessary* relation to this process? In this regard, one might begin by noting that among these 35 men, being raised in a non-religious household correlated almost perfectly with being non-religious as an adult (or young adult); but the reverse was not as consistently the case. All the highly religious Muslim men received strong religious socialization, but over half of the non-religious grew up in a similar atmosphere. More significant, however, is that with respect to at least one of the five factors summarized by al-Lami (2009), namely political marginalization and grievances, a small group of the non-religious displayed evidence of these factors being present more clearly than did any of the more religious participants. Yet even in these cases, the evidence was muted.

An example is Ali. He was in most senses a very secular person by his own admission, but he was also fairly critical of aspects of Canadian society. With regard to multiculturalism as policy and reality, he was one of those who felt that multicultural policy was either an exercise in Canadian self-deception or simply subtle racism. In tune with John

Porter's thesis from the 1960s, that Canada managed its cultural diversity through the establishment of a vertical mosaic (Porter 1965), he felt that "Canada likes to play the multiculturalism card a lot, but, I mean, look at the classes in Canada: whites on top." To an extent, this opinion was a reflection of the discrimination that he felt he and his father had experienced, his father because of "his accent and his name," he himself because he was not white. Moreover, even though he did not consider himself to be very religious (he said he was more spiritual), he felt Islam had something to offer that Canadian society had a tendency to negate: the Canadian environment militated against the maintenance of a strict and traditionalist Islam, and he found this depressing. In spite of rejecting Islam for himself, he nevertheless felt that it had value and that compromising it for the sake of fitting into Canadian and Western society would be a tragic outcome. To illustrate his perspective he referred to the commonly observed phenomenon in Canadian cities of young Muslim women who combine hijab on the head with more "fashionable" clothing on the body. What he said when asked if he thought the Muslim second generation of which he was formally a part would fall away from their religious heritage is worth quoting at some length:

> I think they're already starting. I think ... most second generation Islamic people I have seen in Canada are very hypocritical. They'll wear the veil, but then they'll wear the tightest clothing you've ever seen. I mean, if ... you're ... going to wear revealing clothing and then a veil, that's just hypocritical. I think that's the kind of internal conflict many people run into. Essentially [it's] "I want to fit into society" and [in this society] sexuality is what is considered a plus, you know, being beautiful and blah, blah, blah. Whereas, my original culture is one where women should be judged based on her mind and her personality rather than her appearance ... I've seen the conflict many times. My cousins who came from Iran when they were eight or ten ... went to public schools ... and they were ostracized for wearing the veil ... They still believe in Islam and everything but they don't wear the veil, and they've loosened up a lot and very much become westernized in order to fit in and to be able to make friends ... [Islam and Western ways are] two completely different ideologies and when you try to merge them, it just doesn't work. And if you try, you're going to have to really make some severe compromises ... [H]istorically, Islam was the religion of the people because it was such an easy religion, it was fair to everyone. Relatively. And if you look at the West, it's selling another dream, you know, the American dream they sell us. Forget who you are, join who

we are, essentially sell your soul in order to be successful ... And I find a
lot of people are coming here and trading that off.

From our data, it is difficult to determine to what extent Ali is correct
about his Muslim generation in Canada. Suffice it to say that the larger
number of our participants disagreed with his assessment.

Although Ali's comments might seem to reflect a kind of political
and cultural alienation, he does not seem to have felt particularly out
of place or marginalized in Canada and certainly had no desire to live
somewhere else such as his native Iran, where he said that the younger
generation was becoming a lost generation without a future. He was
confident about the future and ambitious in his goals and prospects.
Most of his friends were white or Iranian (largely his relatives), and he
experienced no prejudice from them. He considered himself to be "both
Canadian and Iranian," but Iranian first from a cultural perspective.
His pride in Iranian culture and history was as strong as his inability to
relate to Islam or religion. He was not so much "caught between two
worlds" as someone who was secure in his cultural identity as an Iranian living in Canada. Lack of a clear identity, as for most of his fellow
participants, was not a perceived problem.

Another example was Rashad, also non-religious, who had had
negative experiences with Canadian authorities as a result of mistaken
identity. He felt such an experience was common:

So polite racism is just – you listen to the radio or we watch CBC, the beautiful CBC, and you feel wow everything's so beautiful, but really when
you're in the system ... places for you to develop, to get bigger, or to be
treated the same ... ah ... it's different. And, mind you, I could pass as
Argentinean. I could pass as Mexican, but they still, they see my name and ...
they bother me.

Rashad was by no means the only participant who reported discriminatory experiences while growing up in Canada; but he was one of the
few who drew from it the conclusion that this was indicative of an alienating and fundamental flaw in Canadian society. To some degree, one
could conclude that he did feel politically alienated, that this was not
something over which he and others like him could have an influence.
Like Ali, however, as well as the other nine participants who fell into
this broad category of non-religious, Rashad gave no indication that he
was somewhere on the road to any kind of radicalization. Nonetheless,

it is possibly significant that where political alienation might be seen to be manifesting itself in the sample, it was among the non-religious, not the religious, and even then only ambiguously.

Highly Involved Muslim Men

Turning now to the majority of the Muslim men who fell on the higher end of our classification scale, what is striking is the virtual absence of the five "radicalization" factors summarized by al-Lami and quite a number of indicators that would point in the opposite direction. As an introduction to what this means, we can take a statement from the most ardent of the group: Ahmed, 25 years old at the time of the interview, put Islam at the very centre of his life and identity, was punctilious about every aspect of Islamic practice, and had gone so far as to change career paths so that he would not have to work with women outside his family. Here is an exchange that occurred after he was asked about the place of religion in Canadian society:

> AHMED: [R]ight now I think the status quo respects the Canadian heritage and I guess the foundation of religion which was brought by the Catholics and Protestants and whatnot. So they do get a little more preference in terms of, you know, schooling, their school system and whatnot. It's a little bit more accepted. But I find that the status quo really helps foster diversity and it doesn't infringe upon the rights of minority religions such as my own. Anything, anything which would I guess make religion more political or make it more, more official in ... Canadian society may infringe upon minority groups, I think.
> INTERVIEWER: Do you believe that you can practise your religion fully in Canada ... without any obstacles?
> AHMED: Yeah, there's nothing here that really prevents me from practising religion in its entirety.
> INTERVIEWER: Do you also feel accepted as a full and equal member of Canadian society?
> AHMED: Yeah.

Like the other classification groups, the men of the four highly involved categories display both an internal continuum and individual and qualitative differences among themselves. What centrally distinguishes them is that they consider Islam to be not only important but central, as the axis around which their lives are organized and in terms of which they make their meaning. All the participants in this group believed and practised regularly; this included above all praying regularly every day, usually trying to do so at the five (sometimes three) prescribed times or more often, and attending Friday communal prayers at a mosque. A further consistency was fasting during Ramadan along with the core dietary restrictions of avoiding pork and alcohol. Zakat and hajj (i.e., charitable and religious payment and pilgrimage to Mecca, respectively) were intentions limited by their stage in life and the fact that few of them had significant incomes, since they were mostly full-time university students. Their profession of faith comprised principally the shahadah (i.e., the profession of faith) and other variously described core belief items, including above all the centrality and truth of the Qur'an and the Sunna or traditions of the Prophet Muhammad. Their moral code included refraining from sexual activity outside marriage and dating before marriage, disapproval of homosexuality, insistence on marrying either a Muslim woman or one from a religion of the book (which men could do, but not women), and determination to raise their children as Muslims. Azim, who stated that Islam was "the most important thing in my life" and who defined religion as "a set of laws in order to live your life," described the principal teachings of Islam in the following manner:

> [T]he main thing is believing in one God and not ... having any other God ... mixed in with it. Believing in all the messengers that he sent in order to pass down the message. Just keeping good moral character ... [F]asting and prayer are all mentioned [in the Qur'an and] are important [and] will make you more righteous and better, but it's things to help you to stick to the one pillar of Islam which is to believe in one God.

Zohair put it much more simply: "if someone was to ask me ... about Islam then I would tell them about ... the five pillars and ... the six articles of faith." In terms of the main sources of authority, of what to believe and what to do in Islam, those who expressed an opinion were unanimous that the Qur'an was central, followed closely by the traditions of the Prophet and, for Twelver Shi'as, prominent scholars of this tradition.

Besides these formal sources, which a great many of them accessed directly without interpretive intermediaries, the most commonly mentioned sources were books and websites along with members of their personal networks, principally family members, and among these, mostly parents and elders. Use of the Internet for both accessing primary sources and seeking advice was particularly prominent. One could say that it ranked second after the influence of family and friends. Relatively few participants gave priority to local imams or other community leaders whom they knew directly. Muhammad, as one example, gave a rather typical reply to the question of where he would go if he had a religious question: "First I'd ask my parents. My parents would probably direct me to family friends who really know a lot about the religion. Or if not, just ask questions to relatives." Or, as Abdul put it, "most of my religious knowledge comes from my dad ... when I got older, I did a lot of it on my own, like I read on the internet, I read books and stuff like that, but my basis comes from my dad."

This last quote points to a strong commonality among the highly involved: Without exception, they grew up in households where Islam was important; they received a religious upbringing or their parents presented devout models for them. Although in some cases the participants said that they were somewhat more observant than their parents, at least one of the parents in each case was still highly observant. None grew up in the sort of non-religious environment that some of the non-religious participants experienced in their childhood, and none had what two or three of the moderately involved described as "liberal" parents. If this sample of 35 men were to be seen as representative, they support the idea that, with minor and inevitable exceptions, religious socialization may be a necessary but not sufficient condition for religious offspring, at least among immigrant Muslims in Canada.

In terms of "radicalization" factors, what these characteristics among the highly involved indicate is that they were, without obvious exceptions, not disconnected and alienated from their parents and the first generation. Nor, as we shall illustrate shortly, were they particularly alienated from the surrounding society, not even, it seems, to the minor extent that Ali and Rashad (mentioned earlier) were. Moreover, their social networks were usually mixed, with combinations of Muslims and non-Muslims, of visible minority and non-visible minority friends, and, for the majority of them, of men and women.

As Figure 5.1 shows graphically, those Muslim men classified as 6 or higher constitute the majority of the sample, with the classification 8 men being by far the single largest category. One might say that the classification 8, and generally also the 7, men represent a kind of standard. That said, because the classification system was generated inductively, from the data, it may be that the high number of participants in classifications 7 and 8 is merely an artefact of that analytic process, that it shows a lack of refinement at that point in the scale more than it does a commonality in the role and character of Islam in these participants' lives. Although other researchers analysing these data may indeed have come up with a different sort of heuristic classification, the cogency of the one we offer here lies in a set of observable characteristics that together demonstrate significant aspects of what it may mean to be a young devout Muslim in today's Canadian society. Adapting an expression that is becoming popular in French and Quebec debates about the "accommodation" of religious diversity, namely the idea of *laïcité ouverte*, we suggest that what the number 7 and 8 participants – and even the 9 and 10 classification, as Ahmed demonstrates – embody what could be called a *religiosité ouverte*.

The religiosity in this phrase refers to the common features of their Islam, as already outlined. Among the 15 participants in classifications 7–10, none deviated significantly from this model, although they did put emphasis on different aspects. Najib, a Canada-born 18-year-old of Pakistani origin, was very rule-oriented; practising Islam meant not doing forbidden things. He put it like this:

> This world is just a test; if I do well in it, if I do everything that I'm given ... then I'll go to heaven. And I try my best now, and I know everything I did wrong before, the *haram* that I've done, Allah will forgive me, I hope He does ... so that's how I view everything, I try not to do anything wrong.

Karim, 20 years old and also Canada-born from a Pakistani family, put the emphasis on broader moral principles. He stated as follows:

> Most important teachings? As a philosopher, the one thing I can't give up is belief in God. Everything else is debatable ... If I give that up, then I fear my whole philosophical system would be nonsensical ... Most important practices: the way in which you treat other people, kindness and things like that ... Those are the primary objectives, and then secondary objectives would be praying, fasting, the rituals.

A critical aspect of this Islam-centredness, however, and what makes it an "open religiosity," is how these Muslims see themselves and Islam in relation to and in the context of the surrounding society. Relevant aspects of this situatedness are the attitudes to other religions, which is to say religious diversity, to the secular nature of Canadian society, to their own place as devout Muslims in that society, and to the role of religion/Islam in political life, including in relation to militancy and the political expression of Islam in the state. Summarizing these aspects, those in higher classifications almost all accepted religious diversity and, in that context, were generally positive about the idea of Canada as a multicultural society; they accepted or had few problems with living in a secular or nominally Christian country; they participated and expected to participate fully; they wanted to be thoroughly woven into the life of that society through their studies, their careers, and their social relations; and they almost uniformly rejected any direct political role for religion and Islam in Canada, although they had mixed opinions on this question in Muslim-majority countries. On each of these items there were, of course, exceptions and significant variation.

A closer look at how some of the interviewees expressed this combination of strong religiousness with openness to full participation in the wider, largely secular society can put some flesh on these basic ideas. Shabib, another 20-year-old from a Pakistani family, put the combination succinctly with relation to the second generation, which he represented:

> I'm noticing here in the university, a lot of young Muslims, especially ... second-generation immigrants, second-generation Canadians, they're responding to the initial, I guess, ghettoization of the community by asserting their place in this society ... [W]e have this tradition [Islam], ... this total package ... [and] what we're seeing is that this package can be applied right here, right? And part of this package is this feeling of belonging, this feeling that this is my home too.

Implied in this statement is the idea that Islam or the Muslim identity not be restricted to a compartment of life, that, for instance, the way to be religious was to be Muslim in private while keeping that aspect hidden or bracketed in public. Abdul, a 22-year-old Shi'a man from an Indian family, put his opposition to this orientation and his acceptance of a religiously pluralistic society like this:

> The problem with Canada I find [is] that the religious aspect or the spiritual aspect ... is totally gone in our society ... You can't have a Christian government or a Muslim government because we have a multicultural society, but you shouldn't have an anti-God society either, where even mentioning God is kind of like taboo. I don't agree with that; I think we have to become more spiritual in our society.

Hussain, a 19-year-old Shi'a participant, put it another way:

[R]ight now, personally I don't think that a lot of Canadians are religious; a lot of them don't care about religion, which I find is really sad, whether it's Christianity, Judaism, or Islam, or whatever religion, I think that more people should be ... more caring for religion.

The explicit attitude to other religions in this society was generally accepting without thereby weakening the central status that Islam had for individuals. As an example, the same Shi'a participant replied to the question of whether some religions were better than others, saying, "No. I don't think so. They're all doing the same thing, basically." He elaborates later:

I don't judge a person by their religion or their background, because ... if people aren't going to do that to me, I'm not going to do that to them. I have a lot of friends that are Christian, friends that are Jewish, I don't mind it ... It doesn't conflict with me. I'm talking to the person, not to the religion itself. I have nothing against the religion. I'm Muslim, I chose that religion on my own.

Others put the same idea in somewhat different ways. Bahir and Hakim said,

I don't know what God's plan is for [people of other religions]. Like, everyone has their own life and ... everyone's judged accordingly, right? So whether you're spiritual or not ... there are a lot of good people. You know, there are good people, being Hindu or Muslim or even within Muslims there are bad people, it's just the way they are, ... like their character alone is good ... And I can't just tell them, okay, you're going to hell. (Bahir)
[Y]ou got to understand that since the last thirty or forty years, Islam has absolutely exploded, right? Absolutely exploded. So I wouldn't say that there's one [religion] better than the other, but if it continues this way, then it's going to be the dominant religion ... so let's leave it at that. (Hakim)

The issue of living this Islam in what is largely a secular – at most nominally Christian – society was also understood in a variety of ways, but it included the idea that people ought to be free to practise their religion as fully as they wished. These Muslim men felt that freedom of religious practice was a reality in Canada for themselves and others; the secular or non-Muslim context could nonetheless be seen as a challenge. Bahir, whose life was so centred on Islam that he might possibly have been classified as a 9 rather than just an 8, put it this way:

> [In Canada] you're free to practise and do what you want to do ... It's a very good country for that, you're able to practice your own religion ... you're able to be a Muslim ... [T]he only thing is you're also surrounded with all the other influences too, which makes it harder for a Muslim to be a Muslim.

Hussain, the 19-year-old Shi'a, felt that, in terms of religious tolerance, Canada was "perfectly fine" and averred that "[r]ight now Canada, it's basically taking care of all religions at the same time, which I think it's doing a very good job at it." Abbud, however, a Somali Muslim, was somewhat less sanguine, stating that he could practise Islam to its fullest in Canada but

> that it's tough. It takes a lot of determination, it takes a lot of energy ... You can practice your religion, but you're going to have to face a lot of hurdles and downright discrimination against you; especially if you're a woman.

The general understanding of the relation between religion and politics was that the two should be separated. There was unanimous rejection among the highly involved participants of religiously inspired violence and what many described as religious extremism. Several participants, however, held a nuanced view of the religio-political relationship. One exception even negated the general attitude, wishing that religion and politics could be united in Canada as elsewhere. He was the other participant who could have been classified as a 9, if his sectarian orientation had not been accompanied by the fact of a religiously and culturally quite mixed circle of friends. Najib, a recent convert to Shi'a Islam from a Sunni family, declared outright that religion and politics should be fused and even declared that

> if Ayatollah [Sistani][5] was running the country, like, well, not running it, but if he was the leader of the country, he would make laws and tell everybody that this is in the Qur'an and this is how you should act upon it. So, I think that would be ideal.

Not surprisingly, this participant approved of the government of the Islamic Republic of Iran. He was not the only one, but the others who did so (none of whom were Iranian) qualified their approval by stating that Iran had gone too far or was not living up to the ideal. Abdul, the 22-year-old Shi'a who thought that Canada should be more spiritual, also had this opinion about Iran:

> [T]he thing I like about Iran, but the thing that's not done properly, is that there's two bodies, of the people and there's the religious[6] ... In Iran right now, the religious overrules the people which is not right ... In my ideal Islamic society, there should be a democratically elected representative, but there should also be a council of learned scholars, Islamic scholars who can decide ... whether or not the laws proposed by the house are in accordance with Islamic law, but they shouldn't be able to overrule them. It would be like an equal [relation], like the House and the Senate in the States. It has to pass in both houses before it can be law ... [I]n our [Canadian] society the religious is overpowered by the secular and in Iran ... it's the religious [that] overpowers the secular, but it has to be a balance because you have to respect people who are following [other religions or other versions of Islam].

In that context, he also said that "Islam in government, if it's done correctly, I think is good; but I haven't seen it done correctly, ever." A stronger negative opinion was expressed by Hussain, the 19-year-old Shi'i quoted earlier. He felt that religion should have more of an influence in Canadian society, but not a specific religion; and he thought that in countries like Saudi Arabia and Iran, where religion has a strong role in the political sphere, it is "people who are misinterpreting religion governing." Besides these qualified opinions, there were also those among the highly involved who, unlike the convert to Shi'ism, were convinced that religion and politics should not mix. Abbud, the Somali Muslim already quoted, was quite unequivocal. He stated that "when religion's applied to politics, or when religion is applied with nationalism or racism, a lot of evil things happen." Elaborating, he said,

> [U]nfortunately, ... even in countries where they have Muslim Islamic movements that are political, it's never good to have the dominant religion in power or influencing over minorities. It's just not. I hate to say this, it's just not. That doesn't mean you should restrict religious people from

politics ... But to have a religious party ... aligned so much with religion is not a good thing for society, especially when you have minorities, especially when you have racial minorities that don't belong to that dominant religion.

Of note in most of these opinions, and consistent with the attitudes of the great majority of the highly involved Muslims, is that their situation – as highly religious people in a religiously diverse society – influences how they see this question of religious influence in any society: they cannot and are not against such influence but mostly want it to be non-specific, not tied to a particular religion such as their own or that of the nominally Christian majority. Their generally positive evaluation of religious diversity, or at least their acceptance of that diversity, correlates with this way of seeing religious influence. It is an important aspect of their "open religiosity."

Conclusions

The evidence from this research project is, of course, only a beginning. Much of what it revealed is at best suggestive, subject to further study and verification. Relatively little research has been done on this section of the Canadian population, and what has been done is equally a first step. That said, this other research so far has not found contradictory evidence with respect to the central questions posed here (Eid 2007; Karim 2009; Moghissi, Rahnema, and Goodman 2009). There is little evidence that the factors of radicalization discussed here are significantly present among young adult Muslim men in Canada, especially of the 1.5 and second generations from immigrant families. To be sure, basing an argument on the absence of evidence is not ideal, given that no research project has been designed and carried out to date in Canada which had this objective specifically in mind. A partial exception is Jamie Bartlett and Carl Miller's (2011) comparative analysis of the views and experiences of violent radicals and non-violent radicals in the United Kingdom, Canada, Denmark, France, and the Netherlands, along with a control group of 70 ordinary young Muslim men in Canada. In addition, the young adults about whom we have reported here are just that: young. By their own accounts, who they were at the time of the interviews often differed from who they were during their usually barely surpassed adolescence, and therefore it is entirely possible that new developments will occur in the future or perhaps in many cases have already occurred, given that the data are now already six or more years old.

Expressing such caveats, however necessary, does not mean that the sample of young Muslim men who participated in this research is unrepresentative in some consequential way. With reasonable certainty, they tell us what sorts of profiles exist in significant numbers in Canada, even if we cannot draw too many conclusions about the relative distribution of those profiles, which ones are dominant, and which are not. In short, the data we have collected tell us that the factors shown by other research to be associated with radicalization thus far do not appear to be significantly present in the young Canadian Muslim male population and therefore that there is little evidence of a strong possibility for radicalization beyond the very isolated few, such as the 11 convicted in the wake of the Toronto 18 arrests in 2006 and Ottawa resident Mohammad Khawaja, convicted in 2009 of plotting a terrorist attack in the United Kingdom. Recently a few others have joined this group, for example the three high school friends from London, Ontario, who became involved in terrorism in Africa. Ali Medlej and Xristos Kasiroubas died in the 16 January 2013 terrorist attack on the Tiguentourine gas plant in Algeria by an offshoot of al-Qaeda in the Islamic Maghreb from northern Mali. Their friend Aaron Yoon was imprisoned in Mauritania on the charge of associating with known terrorists. It is the very rarity of these instances in the Canadian context, however, and the fact that two of those radicalized were converts to Islam, that made the story so newsworthy.

To summarize, then, the relation between the research results reported here and al-Lami's five factors of radicalization: the 35 participants did not seem to be leading lives of socio-economic deprivation; they were not and did not perceive themselves to be particularly marginalized in Canadian society, whether as the children of immigrant families or as Muslims. They recognized that they were members of minorities but not especially marginalized minorities. Like most people in their age group, they were indeed on the search for adult identity, but they did not seem to be particularly pessimistic about finding that identity or of being on the way to it. Their social affiliations tended not to be with the "wrong crowds," groups, or individuals with only certain characteristics that might encourage their own radicalization or feeling of belonging only outside the dominant society. Their political marginalization, to the extent that they expressed any at all, was muted; and to the degree that there was evidence for it, it was among the non-religious or less religious, not among the devout Muslims. Finally, while they undoubtedly had access to radical rhetoric, given that they were for the most part active users of the worldwide communications technologies where almost anything of this nature can easily be found, such involvement did not seem to have had any noticeable impact on them – at least as far as they were willing to admit.

Absence of radicalization, of course, does not mean that any of them could not in the future be subject to it; their identities in their late teens and early 20s were, after all, still in most cases rather fluid. And, as Lorne Dawson demonstrates (see chapter 3 in this volume), the profiles of the Toronto 18 in many senses match those of our 35 participants, meaning that the absence of identifiable radicalization factors does not preclude radicalization in individual cases. On the whole, however, it is far more likely that, in absence of factors favouring radicalization, nothing of the sort is going to happen to any of them. Above all, as other research has shown (see Bartlett, Birdwell, and King 2010; and Bartlett and Miller 2011 as examples), degree of implication in religion, here Islam, appears to bear no consistent relation to radicalization one way or another and, if this sample can be taken to be in any sense indicative, likely acts more as an immunizing factor than one that correlates with susceptibility to radicalization.

NOTES

1 The oldest was 30 at the time of arrest, the youngest was 17; most were in their early 20s. Four had converted from Christianity or Hinduism; the rest grew up as Muslims.
2 The following section includes revised portions of chapter 5 in Beyer and Ramji (2013).
3 For analyses of the Muslim women in our sample, see Beyer and Ramji (2013, chapter 6); Ramji (2008a, 2008b).
4 Grouping the participants into low, medium, and high, but counting those in category 6 as among the high yields a similar result: the men would be 31 per cent in low, 9 per cent medium, and 60 per cent high; the women, by contrast, 17 per cent low, 17 per cent medium, and 65 per cent high.
5 As a follower of Ithna Ashari (Twelver) Shi'ism, he chose as his religious authority or *marja* ("source of imitation") the Grand Ayatollah Sistani (see www.sistani.org), who lives in Najaf, Iraq, and is considered by many the preeminent Shi'a cleric of that country and even among all contemporary Grand Ayatollahs.

6 The reference is to the parallel sets of governmental structures of the Islamic Republic of Iran, one republican and including a directly elected president and legislature, the other consisting of appointed Shi'a clerics and including the Council of Guardians, the Council of Experts, and the Supreme Leader (*Faqih*). The latter have veto power over the former and control the armed forces as well as the judiciary.

REFERENCES

Bartlett, Jamie, Jonathan Birdwell, and Michael King. 2010. *The Edge of Violence: A Radical Approach to Extremism*. London: Demos.

Bartlett, Jamie, and Carl Miller. 2011. "The Edge of Violence: Towards Telling the Difference between Violent and Non-violent Radicalization." *Terrorism and Political Violence* 24: 1–21.

Beyer, Peter. 2005. "Religious Identity and Educational Attainment among Recent Immigrants to Canada: Gender, Age, and 2nd Generation." *Journal of International Migration and Integration* 6 (2): 171–99.

Beyer, Peter, and Wendy K. Martin. 2010. *The Future of Religious Diversity in Canada*. Ottawa: Citizenship and Immigration Canada.

Beyer, Peter, and Rubina Ramji, eds. 2013. *Growing Up Canadian: Muslims, Hindus, Buddhists*. Kingston and Montreal: McGill-Queen's University Press.

Collett, Jessica L., and Omar Lizardo. 2009. "A Power-control Theory of Gender and Religiosity." *Journal for the Scientific Study of Religion* 48 (2): 213–31.

Corak, Miles. 2008. "Immigration in the Long Run: The Education and Earnings Mobility of Second-generation Canadians." *IRPP Choices* 14 (13): 1–30.

Eid, Paul. 2007. *Being Arab: Ethnic and Religious Identity Building among Second Generation Youth in Montreal*. Montreal and Kingston: McGill-Queen's University Press.

Karim, Karim. 2009. "Changing Perceptions of Islamic Authority among Muslims in Canada, the United States and the United Kingdom." *IRPP Choices* 15 (2): 1–30.

Al-Lami, Mira. 2009. *Studies of Radicalisation: State of the Field Report*. Politics and International Relations Working Papers 11, January. www.rhul.ac.uk/politics-and-IR.

Moghissi, Haideh, Saeed Rahnema, and Mark J. Goodman. 2009. *Diaspora by Design: Muslim Immigrants in Canada and Beyond*. Toronto: University of Toronto Press.

Porter, John A. 1965. *The Vertical Mosaic: An Analysis of Social Class and Power in Canada*. Toronto: University of Toronto Press.

Ramji, Rubina. 2008a. "Being Muslim and Being Canadian: How Second Generation Muslim Women Create Religious Identities in Two Worlds." In *Women and Religion in the West: Challenging Secularization*, ed. K. Aune, S. Sharma, and G. Vincett, 195–205. Aldershot, Hampshire: Ashgate Publishing.

– 2008b. "Creating a Genuine Islam: Second Generation Muslims Growing up in Canada." *Canadian Diversity / Diversité canadienne* 6 (2): 104–9.

Statistics Canada. 2003. *Religion (95) and Immigrant Status and Period of Immigration (11) for Population for Canada, Provinces, Territories, Census Metropolitan Areas and Census Agglomerations 2001 – 20% Sample Data. Catalogue No. 97F00022XCB01004.* Ottawa: Statistics Canada.

– 2004. *Religion (18), Immigrant Status and Period of Immigration (9), Age (7), Ethnic Origin (15), Ethnic Origin Single/Multiple Response (3), Total Income Groups (9) and Sex (3) for Population, for Canada and Selected Census Metropolitan Areas, 2001 Census.* Ottawa: Department of Canadian Heritage.

Teotonio, Isabel. 2010. "Toronto 18." *The Toronto Star*. http://www3.thestar.com/static/toronto18/index.html.

6 The Impact of Securitization on South Asian Muslims in Montreal

UZMA JAMIL

Introduction

> When I realized that they [September 11 attackers] were Muslim, I felt that I was no longer able to feel like everyone else ... I was all of a sudden part of the "other" category. Since the first time I came to Canada, I did not feel welcome. I felt fear.
>
> (cited in Hussain 2002, 11)

Although this Muslim woman's sentiments were expressed almost a decade ago, these concerns about fear and belonging continue to resonate today for many Canadian Muslims living in the post-9/11, war-on-terror (WOT) context. Public anxiety about home-grown terrorism and radicalization after the Toronto 18 case has added to these concerns. Unlike Dawson's chapter 3 which specifically addresses the Toronto 18, this chapter focuses more broadly on Muslims in Canada. Of course, the vast majority of them are not involved with terrorism or radicalization, but they are, nevertheless, often perceived to be socially and politically implicated by the society around them.

Muslim communities have been present in Canada since the early 1900s, with a large wave of arrivals in the past 20 or 30 years. However, their visibility as minorities has changed over time. In this respect, 9/11 marks a turning point. Negative perceptions of Muslims as "foreign" or "different" existed before 2001 as well, but their association with violence and terrorism became much more strongly defined within polarizing discourses of "us" and "them" in WOT rhetoric (Razack 2008). Although I focus on the "post-9/11" period in this chapter, this social and political context is not divorced from broader processes within which both majority and minority groups define themselves as part of Canadian society.

In the first chapter of this book, Bramadat defines securitization as "the way the state and society frame the individuals and groups drawn to radical religious subcultures." I suggest that securitization affects more than the individuals and groups drawn to radicalization. Securitization is part of the contemporary sociopolitical context which shapes the way Muslim communities are perceived in society, particularly the ways in which they are collectively identified as "guilty by association" and viewed as potential threats, terrorists, fifth columnists, or a danger to national security (Bakht 2008).

In addition, Muslims are often assumed by the majority groups in society to be homogeneous and defined almost entirely by their religious identity. Even the potential for violent radicalization of young Muslim men is thought to hinge upon their religiosity, despite evidence to the contrary (Beyer, chapter 5, this volume). Other elements such as their racial, national, or ethnic backgrounds, class, age, country of origin (in some cases), geographic location, and profession, among other characteristics, all seem to fade against the perceived importance of their religious identity. The research results presented in this chapter challenge these generalizations by focusing on the complexity of what it means to be a Muslim, South Asian, parent, man, woman, child, neighbour, and so forth living in Montreal. These distinct identity markers each play significant roles in the lives of these individuals, though it is the religious marker that typically attracts the attention of the broader society.

Drawing on two community-based research studies conducted by researchers from the McGill University Transcultural Research and Intervention team, this chapter focuses on the impact of securitization associated with the WOT on the lives of South Asian Muslims in Montreal. In particular, I examine how Pakistani and Bangladeshi Muslim families of working-class backgrounds understand, communicate about, and cope with the WOT and the Iraq and Afghanistan wars (Rousseau and Jamil 2010). I compare their responses to the experiences of middle-class respondents in Montreal and also discuss the significance of doing research with Muslim communities strongly affected by securitization (Jamil and Rousseau 2012). As an academic and a community-based researcher, I also situate myself in this context, on this topic. We are all living in the same sociopolitical context, and as a racialized Muslim woman I am also part of the researched.

The Impact of the WOT: Fear, Social Perceptions, and Profiling

Most community studies about Muslims in the post-9/11 context focus on American Muslims, which is not surprising. The United States was the target of the 9/11 terrorist attacks and the leader in the subsequent military interventions in Iraq and Afghanistan. The combination of domestic and foreign policies focused on national security and anti-terrorism, including the Patriot Act and the creation of the National Security Entry-Exit Registration System, which targeted South Asian, Middle Eastern, and Arab communities as "suspect communities" (Maira 2009; Ngyuen 2005).

Among the social and psychological effects, American Muslims have experienced increased negative stereotyping, bias, suspicion, and discrimination as their loyalty and belonging as citizens and members of society has been interrogated by others (Bayoumi 2008; Ewing 2008; Ibish et al. 2003). In different Muslim communities around the country, people report feelings of fear, worry, anxiety, and insecurity (Cainkar 2009; Hallak and Quina 2004).

Although Canada's role in the WOT is different than that of the United States, Canadian Muslims reported some of the same perceptions and experiences of heightened scrutiny, negative stereotyping, and discrimination (Antonius 2002; CAIR-CAN 2002a; Helly 2004). In the aftermath of the 2001 terrorist attacks, a community-based study of 181 Canadian Muslim women from all ethnic groups reported fear and anger on multiple levels, including fear about "potential terrorist attacks in Canada, personal safety, backlash, [and the] future of their children in Canada" (Hussain 2002, 10). Participants questioned their sense of belonging in Canada and their religion. Interestingly, some of this self-examination may have led to positive affirmation of their religious identity as a response, as reflected in a survey conducted by the Canadian Council on American-Islamic Relations. Twenty-two per cent of respondents in the 2002 survey said they had become more committed Muslims and more involved in community affairs and had more opportunities to dispel stereotypes about Islam and Muslims (CAIR-CAN 2002b).

With the passage of time, many Muslims continue to be concerned about discrimination and intolerance from other Canadians, although it is important to observe that the available data makes it difficult to distinguish between different ethnic or racial groups within the broader Muslim community. In an Environics survey of Muslims in 2006–7, about 66 per cent of respondents said they were worried about discrimination, while 31 per cent said they had had bad experiences as a result of their race, ethnicity, or religion in the past two years (Environics 2006, 82). In a study in Atlantic Canada, Muslims of different ethnic and racial backgrounds felt Canadian-born whites looked at Arabs and Muslims more closely and with more suspicion than they used to before 9/11 (Crocker et al. 2007, 49). The results of these two studies suggest undefined, but intertwined, feelings among Muslims about the way they are perceived within Canadian society. In general, and almost regardless of where the studies are based and who conducts the investigation, one sees a common theme: especially in the wake of 9/11, many Muslims feel that they are perceived negatively or are under greater scrutiny by majority groups in Canadian society.

Recent polls conducted within the majority group population confirm the presence of these negative perceptions of Muslims. A recent poll by Ipsos Reid found that 60 per cent of people surveyed felt there was increased discrimination against Muslims, in comparison to ten years ago (Chung 2011). In a March 2012 survey conducted by the Association of Canadian Studies, 52 per cent of 1,522 Canadians polled expressed high levels of distrust towards Muslims, saying that they can be trusted "not at all" or "a little" (Boswell 2012). Among French Canadians, the percentage was higher, with 70 per cent of respondents expressing little or no trust in Muslims.

The Quebec context is distinctive. Many within the majority groups in Quebec are concerned first and foremost about their minority status in English Canada. The French language in Quebec is not just a linguistic identity but the central component of its cultural identity as well. This shapes how majority groups in Quebec relate to minorities. Their concerns about their own status are often manifested in public anxiety about the allegedly unassimilable nature of Muslims as racial and religious "others." The Hérouxville code of conduct and some of the inflammatory and often aggressive rhetoric associated with the public hearings in the Bouchard-Taylor Commission on Reasonable Accommodation in 2007 captured this public anxiety and the majority perception that Muslims present a challenge to the secularism and gender equality so closely associated with Quebec's national identity (Jamil 2013). The Final Report of the commission concluded, however, that this fear of the dilution of Quebec identity was reflective of the anxiety of francophone Québécois in relation to English Canada (Bouchard and Taylor 2008, 185). It also held the media responsible for fuelling this public anxiety even though there were actually only a small number of cases in which residents sought reasonable accommo-dation (Bouchard and Taylor 2008, 74).

In addition to these commonly articulated public concerns, many Muslims feel they are victims of community profiling by the govern-ment. Community organizations, such as the People's Commission on Immigration and Security Measures in Montreal, report increased incidents of racial/religious profiling of Muslims by the government (People's Commission on Immigration and Security Measures 2007), although it is difficult to prove that they are the direct result of the Anti-Terrorism Act. After all, profiling is often done without formal justification and at the discretion of law enforcement officials (Bahdi 2003; Crocker et al. 2007, 20). While the Anti-Terrorism Act does not specify racial, ethnic, or religious groups in its text, some legal schol-ars nevertheless argue that the potential for discrimination exists in its implementation precisely because of the discretion given to police and other bodies to determine what constitutes "terrorists" and "terrorist activity" (Bhabha 2003; Roach 2002). Furthermore, the lack of police sta-tistics on racial, ethnic, or religious profiles of people they stop, search, or make contact with also makes it difficult to prove racial profiling (Wortley and Tanner 2004).

These results suggest that there is a gap between actual experiences of individuals and the much more widespread belief held by many in these communities that they are targets of profiling by security agen-cies. A 2004 survey by the Canadian Council on American-Islamic Relations (CAIR-CAN) on visits by national security officials to Cana-dian Muslims highlights this gap. Only a small number of respon-dents (37 out of 467) reported that they were contacted by national security government officials. However, a much larger number (83 out of 195) said that they were personally acquainted with someone who had been contacted by security officials (CAIR-CAN 2004, 3), and the organization states that these numbers are probably under-reported. As Paul Bramadat notes in the first chapter, the survey has been criticized for some serious methodological flaws (e.g., there were no controls over who could take the survey or how many times; the 83 people who said they knew someone who was contacted could have been referring to a small number of the same individuals; the 467-person sample was neither random nor representative), but the popularity of this survey within the community does call attention to the perceptions of threat within Canadian Muslim communities, per-ceptions which are supported by individual experiences of targeting or profiling at the airport shared in other small, qualitative studies (Nagra 2010; People's Commission on Immigration and Security Measures 2007).

In conclusion, data on the impact of the WOT on Canadian Muslims is uneven, but it highlights several key themes. First, although there are differences between the American and Canadian contexts, Muslims in Canada have also been affected by 9/11 and they continue to deal with the negative social effects of the WOT context in the form of increased scrutiny, negative bias, or discrimination. Second, these negative perceptions of Muslim communities are linked to their concerns about discrimination as racialized minorities in Canadian society. Third, there is a strong perception among many Muslims of being profiled and targeted as a community in the securitization context associated with the WOT.

It is important to bear in mind the relationship between individual experiences and community perceptions in trying to understand Canadian Muslim experiences in the WOT context. While many individual Canadian Muslims feel they are scrutinized, stereotyped, discriminated against, and profiled, whether by the government or by society after 9/11, many also believe that their communities as a whole are experiencing such ill treatment because they are Muslims. This second belief is confirmed and sustained by aspects of the public response to every new high-profile incident, such as the Toronto 18 case, as well as more mundane events such as passersby insulting a Muslim woman wearing the hijab. Both may be understood as consequences of the WOT. Indeed, they are intertwined, making it difficult to say which is a reflection of securitization and which is the result of "regular" social discrimination. Nevertheless, they are both part of the experiences of Canadian Muslims as individuals and as a part of their communities.

Muslim and South Asian Communities in Montreal

According to the 2011 National Household Survey (which replaced the census), the population of the island of Montreal is approximately 1.6 million (Statistics Canada 2011). The Montreal metropolitan area has the third-largest visible minority population in Canada, after Toronto and Vancouver (Statistics Canada 2008, 27). About 30 per cent of the population in the Montreal metropolitan area is made up of immigrants, with the largest concentration in the city of Montreal (Ville de Montréal 2009). Although South Asians are the largest visible minority group in Canada, blacks and Arabs are the two largest visible minority groups in Quebec (Statistics Canada 2008, 18). The Muslim population in Canada has increased exponentially in the last 20 years, driven primarily by immigration. According to the 2011 National Household Survey (NHS), there were 1.05 million Muslims in Canada in 2011, 221,000 of whom lived in Montreal and were mostly foreign-born. There are approximately 155,000 Pakistanis in Canada according to the NHS. Montreal has a small Pakistani population of about 12,000, in contrast to the largest one in Canada (90,000) in the Toronto area. The Bangladeshi community in Canada is much smaller in comparison, at about 34,000, according to the 2011 NHS. Of this number, approximately 7,100 live in Montreal (Statistics Canada 2011).

Two groups of South Asian Muslim respondents from two community studies are discussed in this chapter. The first study is based in the neighbourhood of Parc Extension in Montreal and includes working-class Pakistani and Bangladeshi families. I use both "working class" and "Parc Extension" as descriptions of the context within which these families live because the neighbourhood is a distinct environment which I describe later. The second study focuses on middle-class Pakistanis who live in more affluent parts of Montreal and in the suburbs. Overall, I have used the distinction of working class/Parc Extension and middle class in this chapter as a way to represent the social and economic position of these South Asian Muslim respondents within Montreal and Quebec society. While socio-economic status (SES) is commonly employed to refer only to income, education, and profession, here it is used to refer to a combination of factors such as their histories of migration and settlement as refugees or as immigrants, the length of their residence in Canada, their educational background, and professions.

For the Parc Extension study, researchers interviewed 15 Bangladeshi and 5 Pakistani working-class families. One parent and one child were interviewed in each family. The adults ranged in age from mid-20s to mid-50s. Most of them were in their 30s, were married, and had children. Approximately three-quarters of the respondents had completed college or university in their country of origin. About half of the respondents were unemployed. Most respondents came to Canada as refugees in the 1990s, with only a few arriving in the twenty-first century (Rousseau and Jamil 2010, 602).

Parc Extension is a low-income, multi-ethnic neighbourhood inhabited primarily by South Asian and Greek communities. In recent years, it has also become home to large numbers of other visible minorities.

There are about 11,000 South Asians who live in the neighbourhood, including about 2,000 Pakistanis and 1,700 Bengalis, based on 2006 census data (Paquin 2008, 33, 24–5). Many of them work in low-paying factory jobs or in local ethnic grocery stores or receive social assistance from the government. The Parc Extension neighbourhood was chosen as a field site for the first study because it has a concentrated South Asian Muslim population with similar experiences of settling and living in Montreal. Education and income levels are relatively low in comparison to the rest of the city. Only 15.4 per cent of the adult population in Parc Extension holds a university degree, in contrast to 31.8 per cent of the adult population in Montreal (Paquin 2008, 35). About 41.4 per cent of the total population lives below the poverty line (Paquin 2008, 50). The unemployment rate is 18.1 per cent in Parc Extension, while it is 8.8 per cent for Montreal (Paquin 2008, 44).

There were 20 middle-class Pakistani adults in the second study, all of whom lived in other parts of Montreal or in the suburbs. The respondents ranged in age from early 20s to late 60s, although most were over 40. The majority were middle-class, were married, and had children. Most of the respondents had university degrees and were employed as professionals or small-business owners. Almost all were Canadian citizens and had arrived in Canada either as graduate students or as immigrants. The earliest group of arrivals (four people) had come to Canada in the mid- to late-1960s. About three-quarters of respondents had been living in Canada for at least 20 years (Jamil and Rousseau 2012, 376).

Community Experiences

The study with working-class families in Parc Extension focused uniquely on parent-child understanding, reactions to the Iraq and Afghanistan wars, and the WOT. Interviewed in 2006 and 2007, most parents were reticent to discuss these political events, as were some of the children and youth, both in the course of their interviews and in their families. Some parents avoided discussing the topic in their interviews and stated that they avoided political discussions in their families as well. They found it difficult to explain the complexity of the political situation, particularly to younger children, and they did not want them to be affected negatively. In almost all cases, parents felt that their children were too young to be exposed to news or discussion about the wars or terrorism, regardless of the age of the child. These parents also believed that the school should not discuss these political events with their children, fearing that it might either trigger tensions among students at school or create loyalty conflicts for their children. However, a few parents were more comfortable discussing the topic in their families, and their children in turn reflected this orientation. They also supported classroom discussions on the topic (Rousseau and Jamil 2010, 605).

One Pakistani couple acknowledged their inability to express the moral complexity of the situation in talking with their children about the wars. They had four children, ranging in age from 6 to 18 years old.

> We don't discuss anything with the children because we ourselves can see that this is not fair. But the children are young, they will be disturbed by it ... We don't want any negativity to take root in our children's minds.

These parents felt that the war in Iraq was unjust and that the people of Iraq were suffering as a result. But their desire to protect their children and their own inability to explain the situation meant that they decided it was best to avoid talking about the issue in their family. Their oldest daughter, a college student, echoed this avoidance as well. Referring to discussions at school, she said, "As soon as someone says September 11th, I just want to tune out. I just don't like to hear about it. Because the thing is, I feel really bad." She felt that although her teachers talked about Americans who were killed in the World Trade Center, they did not talk about the suffering of the people in Iraq. "But I just don't like talking about it because I know they feel sorry for their people and I feel sorry for my people, so that's why I don't like getting into a discussion," she stated (Rousseau and Jamil 2010, 604).

Her comment suggests a strong emotional identification with Iraqis as fellow Muslims and as "my people." It may reflect not only her sympathy for their suffering but also a parallel identification with their position of powerlessness in an unjust war which has ripple effects for all Muslims, echoing her parents' feelings about the injustices of the war on Iraq. Though she "feels really bad" about the suffering of Iraqis, she may also have similar feelings about her own position of being silenced at school and not being able to talk about the pain and sadness she feels about the wars and the suffering of Muslims globally. On one level, her comment suggests a self-protective response. On another level though, it reflects the fluid and nuanced ways in which boundaries between "us" and "them" are created against the backdrop of the global WOT.

Family and Community Coping Strategies

In describing their everyday life, working-class respondents spoke of the challenges of living in Parc Extension, trying to find a job, making a living, accessing health care and social services, and taking care of their families. Dealing with the impact of terrorist events and the wars in Iraq and Afghanistan on top of these challenges was difficult for many. Not surprisingly, there was a strong association between their feelings of helplessness in daily life and expressed helplessness in dealing with the WOT conflicts. A few parents, although acknowledging the challenges of their living situation in Parc Extension, also talked about their strategies to survive and to protect their children, avoiding discussion of political events such as terrorism or war in their families (Rousseau and Jamil 2010, 606).

However, these feelings of helplessness among these Parc Extension residents were complex. For example, some felt that they could not do anything as individuals because politicians held all the power. As one Bengali mother stated, "We are like common people. What can we do? If we want to save, how can we? Because the political people, they are destroying the world, intentionally, they are destroying" (Rousseau and Jamil 2010, 606).

Some favoured the role of the community as a form of agency to counter feelings of individual helplessness. For example, a Pakistani mother felt the Muslim community should speak up and challenge the current sociopolitical climate and its negative effects on Muslims like them.

> Why are we in the community suffering? ... This should not be happening to us. And there needs to be a solution to this. And that is, from within the Muslim community, there should be an organization that can make people aware in Quebec, make them understand that [the suffering of Muslims] is not right. (Rousseau and Jamil 2010, 606)

Among the families interviewed in Parc Extension, many children and youth had mixed reactions which incorporated agency and helplessness. When asked what they felt they could do, some youth said that they needed to understand what was going on and to be informed about it. Others stated that that was not enough and that they needed to have a voice, either by communicating with God through prayer or by speaking up personally or collectively. "You can do something if all the kids in America like get together and tell President Bush to stop that, as long as if we like talk to him ... he is going to understand, I think so," said a ten-year-old Bengali girl from a working-class family. Other children proposed more specific strategies such as talking with their friends or speaking up if one of them made a joke about Muslims being terrorists (Rousseau and Jamil 2010, 606).

In many Parc Extension families, the parents' feelings of helplessness were linked with their children's anxieties and fears. In a Bangladeshi family where the mother expressed anxiety about coping with the WOT conflicts, her 13-year-old daughter also described her worries. "I worry that it's going to happen to my family, every day, like anyone, my grandmother, my grandfather ... I'm afraid that there is going to be an earthquake or they are going to get bombed or something like that" (Rousseau and Jamil 2010, 607). Her comment indicates a diffuse anxiety which may be an echo of the majority's anxiety about being the victims of a terrorist attack in North America. Yet the reference to being bombed may also suggest a parallel with the bombing in Iraq and Afghanistan and the death of civilians in those countries. However, since her extended family and grandparents live in Bangladesh, a country not involved in the WOT conflicts, her pervasive anxiety may also reflect a broader concern for the safety of the global Muslim community.

The close relationship between the ways adults and children discussed these issues in this neighbourhood may not be surprising. The findings also offer alternative methods of interpreting how parents experience and discuss tensions evoked by the fraught global and local sociopolitical contexts. The results of this study confirm an earlier pilot study with immigrant schoolchildren in Parc Extension in which researchers described how students negotiated between divergent home and school understandings of the Iraq war, demonstrating their individual feelings of sadness along with a belief in their ability to promote empathy for others (Rousseau and Machouf 2005; cf. Rousseau and Jamil 2010, 608).

In contrast to these working-class Parc Extension respondents, the middle-class respondents who lived in other parts of Montreal emphasized the importance of countering negative perceptions of their communities by presenting a positive image through their own individual behaviour. Some took part in activities such as being involved in different volunteer or community groups, interacting with people from other communities, or giving alternative perspectives to media representations of Islam, Muslims, or Pakistanis to their colleagues or friends in everyday conversations. "So that makes me very hopeful that if on our part of our community we do our work and present a positive image and be a bit more engaged in the society, they [other people] will reciprocate," said one middle-class Pakistani woman in her 50s.

Some of the differences in the responses and coping strategies of the working-class families from Parc Extension and the middle-class respondents from more affluent areas of Montreal and the suburbs may have to do with the differences in their position within society. The middle-class group had been living in Canada for many years and felt they were more established and comfortable, financially, professionally, and in their social circles. In contrast, the Parc Extension respondents faced more challenges. They struggled to make ends meet financially, as many were unemployed or underemployed, as well as trying to take care of their families in response to the negative social perceptions of their neighbourhood and of their communities.

Doing Research in the WOT Context

Conducting research with Muslims in North America is extremely complicated because of the heightened sense of vulnerability many report in the aftermath of 9/11. For many, views on political issues such as war and terrorism are inevitably associated with their loyalty and belonging, with disastrous consequences for some who speak out against the wars (Maira 2009). This climate makes people wary of trusting others and of speaking openly for fear that they will be labelled as disloyal citizens or as "the enemy within" (Smith 2010, 32). Although the situation for Canadian Muslims may be different than that for American Muslims, the presence of a paid community informant in the Toronto 18 case may have reinforced the same fears in Canada. In recruiting participants and conducting interviews, researchers found some hesitation to speak about the WOT, 9/11, terrorism, or the wars in Iraq and Afghanistan.

Many respondents in Parc Extension declined to participate in the study once they heard about the topic. Many asked if their information would be given to the government. Despite assurances from the researchers that it was an academic study, many still declined to participate. Among those who did agree to be interviewed, they were concerned about their interviews being (audio) recorded. Many people tended to answer questions in indirect ways, avoiding any overt political statements or opinions on the wars. In contrast to the Parc Extension communities, middle-class Pakistani respondents seemed less reluctant to speak about the topic of the WOT or terrorism. Whereas some had initial concerns, almost all of the people approached ultimately agreed to be interviewed. In their interviews, many people also offered complex political analyses of American foreign policy in the Middle East and South Asia, although they avoided discussing Canada's military role in Afghanistan, a topic which might have been perceived as being too sensitive.

We can understand these variations in comfort level in talking about potentially sensitive political topics in several different ways. One explanation might be rooted in the difference between the working-class Parc Extension respondents and the middle-class respondents from elsewhere in the city regarding their feeling of relative security or vulnerability in their position within the host society. Here it is important to bear in mind that some of the Parc Extension respondents were refugee claimants at the time of the interviews and were concerned about weakening their applications. The fear of being perceived as "suspect" in the eyes of the Canadian government was, understandably, a concern for them. Coming as refugees from countries with some history of state control over public, political discourses, they may also have been less likely to feel comfortable expressing their personal political views in Canada. Others had originally come as refugees even if their status had become more stable now as permanent residents or Canadian citizens. In contrast, the middle-class respondents had been Canadian citizens for many years, in addition to having originally come to Canada as immigrants or as graduate students in some cases. Yet, although they spoke openly about some political events, they avoided discussing the role of Canada in the Afghanistan war, indicating that some issues were still too sensitive (Jamil and Rousseau 2012, 376–8).

These results reflect findings from an earlier community study in which Pakistanis in Parc Extension expressed feelings of vulnerability and a pervasive sense of insecurity (Rousseau and Jamil 2008). This feeling of vulnerability may have contributed to their reluctance to speak openly about politically sensitive topics to researchers who were perceived as outsiders. However, it is also important to note that the arrests of the Toronto 18 were made during the same time period as the recruitment of research participants through local community networks. In particular, shortly after the arrests in June 2006, it was revealed that a local man from the Toronto Muslim community, Mubin Sheikh, was working as a paid informant in the case (Teotonio 2010).

This revelation may have reinforced a collective feeling of fear among the Parc Extension respondents, some of whom might not distinguish between researchers and government informants.

The social and political scrutiny experienced by Canadian Muslim communities is both a core concern of the research and something that creates a common ground between myself and the community I am researching. While I am "protected" as an academic in a position of power in some ways, in other ways I share the vulnerability of the communities that I do research with because I am also a racialized, Muslim woman living in a city in which it is not at all uncommon to hear negative comments in public discourse about people in my racial, ethnic, and religious communities. In addition, researchers have a responsibility to be careful about how the data is used, given that any knowledge gathered regarding Muslims is sensitive and might be misconstrued by people unfamiliar with the nuances and histories of the communities involved.

The Significance of Living in a Securitized Context

Like many other Muslims in North America, these South Asian Muslims in Montreal have also experienced and continue to experience increased scrutiny, suspicion, and negative perceptions after 9/11, despite the number of years that have passed since the terrorist attacks. Many respondents both identified this negative visibility – their sense that after 9/11 they were much more visible to others around them, as Muslims, as Pakistanis, or as minorities, than ever before – and argued that this visibility created problems for them. "The Pakistani community became, in a certain way, it became more important ... more visible after 9/11," said one middle-class respondent, age 65. He had lived and worked as a teacher in Montreal for about 40 years. He felt there was a significant change in public and government perceptions of Pakistanis over the years. He remembered the friendly and welcoming attitude of the Canadian immigration official who had interviewed him when he applied for permanent residency in the 1960s. Now, he felt there were only negative views which linked the entire community to terrorism in the minds of most people in Quebec society. However, while he was extremely conscious of the ways he believed his community was perceived, he had not experienced anything negative personally.

In contrast, a Pakistani woman in her early 40s from Parc Extension and her daughter (age 18), both of whom wore the hijab, described some incidents of harassment. In one incident on the street, Québécois college girls tried to pull off the mother's hijab. Her daughter, who was 13 years old at the time, was teased at school by her classmates who said to her, "Are you the daughter of Osama bin Laden?" or "Saddam Hussein is your father!" Although both the mother and daughter have continued to wear the hijab since 2001, the mother was very conscious of the negative perceptions of Muslims around her. "We are not viewed positively. Everywhere we go, we noticed that the situation of the past does not exist anymore," she said (Jamil and Rousseau 2012, 381–2), alluding to the relatively positive environment they experienced between their arrival as refugees in 1999 and the cultural mood that has developed during the decade after 9/11.

These two examples suggest that, even as the participants in both studies are all very much aware of the negative visibility of their communities as a whole, middle-class and working-class respondents in Montreal may differ significantly in the extent to which they feel affected as individuals by the broader process associated with securitization. In particular, the relative security of the lives of the middle-class respondents may play a protective role in the way they both experience and respond to securitization. However, the marginalization and everyday vulnerabilities experienced by the working-class respondents in Parc Extension would not provide this kind of insulation. These differences are significant and merit further examination by others.

Overall, as these research results demonstrate, many Muslims have experienced a significant sense of vulnerability after 9/11. This has led to a strong sense of self-consciousness of their actions and words reflected in their hesitation to participate in research studies, as well as in what research participants are willing to discuss in interviews. Another indication of respondents' concerns is evident in the way some Muslim parents try to protect their children from the negative social and psychological effects of religious, ethnic, and racial stereotyping. Whereas some do it by avoiding discussion of the WOT and the moral complexity of the Iraq and Afghanistan wars in their families, others are more engaged with challenging negative stereotypes and encouraging discussions in classrooms and with their peers.

Alongside these issues, however, are a number of outstanding questions about the purpose and significance of research about Muslim communities in the context of securitization. What does it contribute to the broader public discourse which has such fixed and limited ways of categorizing Muslims? Can such research challenge these limitations without falling into essentializations? How will such studies be read by different audiences, academic and non-academic, insider and outsider? What does it mean to be a Muslim scholar investigating the securitization of Muslim communities? I believe these questions are worth considering collectively, as scholars and policymakers.

Conclusion

In conclusion, these community studies describe the impact of the securitization context for South Asian Muslim families in Montreal. They also highlight the importance of examining how local contexts play a role in shaping Muslim experiences in Canada, despite the negative visibility of Muslim communities in the West after 9/11. These internal nuances help to challenge the homogenization of Muslim communities as objects of study and as objects of securitization. However, we also run the danger of focusing solely on Muslim communities and overlooking the fact that it is the interactions between these Muslim minority and non-Muslim majority groups in Canadian society which create securitization in the first place. For this reason, future research that interrogates the social and political dynamics which shape the relationship between majority and minority communities may be a fruitful way to understand how to go about creating a stronger and more resilient society.

REFERENCES

Antonius, Rachad. 2002. "Un racisme 'respectable.'" In *Les relations ethniques en question: Ce qui a changé depuis le 11 septembre 2001*, ed. J. Renaud, L. Pietrantonio, and G. Bourgeault, 253–71. Montreal: Les Presses de l'Université de Montréal.

Bahdi, Reem. 2003. "No Exit: Racial Profiling and Canada's War against Terrorism." *Osgoode Hall Law Journal* 41 (2–3): 94–318.

Bakht, Natasha. 2008. *Belonging and Banishment: Being Muslim in Canada*. Toronto: TSAR.

Bayoumi, Moustafa. 2008. *How Does It Feel to Be a Problem? Being Young and Arab in America*. New York: Penguin Press.

Bhabha, Faisal. 2003. "Tracking 'Terrorists' or Solidifying Stereotypes? Canada's Anti-Terrorism Act in Light of the Charter's Equality Guarantee." *Windsor Review of Legal and Social Issues* 16: 95–136.

Boswell, Randy. 2012. "More than Half of Canadians Mistrust Muslims, Poll Says." *Postmedia News*, 20 March.

Bouchard, Gérard, and Charles Taylor. 2008. "Building the Future: A Time for Reconciliation." Final report of the Commission de consultation sur les pratiques d'accommodement reliées aux différences culturelles. Quebec: Gouvernement du Québec.

Cainkar, Louise. 2009. *Homeland Insecurity: The Arab American and Muslim American Experience after 9/11*. New York: Russell Sage Foundation.

CAIR-CAN. 2002a. *Life for Canadian Muslims the Morning After: A 9/11 Wake-up Call*. Ottawa: Canadian Council on American-Islamic Relations.

– 2002b. "Survey: More than Half of Canadian Muslims Suffered Post-9/11 Bias." 5 September. Ottawa: Canadian Council on American-Islamic Relations.

– 2004. *Presumption of Guilt: A National Survey on Security Visitations of Canadian Muslims*. Ottawa: Canadian Council on American-Islamic Relations.

Chung, Amy. 2011. "Canadians Less Tolerant after 9/11: Poll." *Vancouver Sun*, 7 September.

Crocker, Diane, A. Dobrowolsky, E. Keeble, C.C. Moncayo, and E. Tastsoglou. 2007. *Security and Immigration, Changes and Challenges: Immigrant and Ethnic Communities in Atlantic Canada, Presumed Guilty?* Ottawa: Status of Women Canada.

Environics. 2006. *Focus Canada: The Pulse of Popular Opinion*. http://www.environicsinstitute.org/uploads/institute-projects/focus%20canada%20 2006-4%20report.pdf (accessed 26 February 2014).

Ewing, Kathryn P., ed. 2008. *Being and Belonging: Muslims in the United States since 9/11*. New York: Russell Sage Foundation.

Hallak, Maram, and Kathryn Quina. 2004. "In the Shadows of the Twin Towers: Muslim Immigrant Women's Voices Emerge." *Sex Roles* 51 (5–6): 329–38.

Helly, Denise. 2004. "Are Muslims Discriminated against in Canada since September 2001?" *Journal of Canadian Studies* 36 (1): 24–47.

Hussain, Samira. 2002. *Voices of Muslim Women: A Community Research Project*. Mississauga, ON: Canadian Council of Muslim Women.

Ibish, H., K. Carol, S. Kareem, W. Marvin, and A. Stewart. 2003. *Report on Hate Crimes and Discrimination against Arab Americans: The Post-September 11 Backlash*. Washington, DC: American-Arab Anti-Discrimination Committee.

Jamil, Uzma. 2007. "The Stranger Within: Rethinking Distance and Proximity of Researcher as Community Member." In *Researching with Communities: Grounded Perspectives on Engaging Communities in Research*, ed. A. Williamson and R. DeSouza, 209–18. London and Auckland: Muddy Creek Press.

– 2013. "National Minority and Racialized Minorities: The Case of Pakistanis in Quebec." *Journal of Ethnic and Racial Studies* (26 July). http://www.tandf online.com/doi/pdf/10.1080/01419870.2013.814801.

Jamil, Uzma, and Cecile Rousseau. 2012. "Subject Positioning, Fear and Insecurity in South Asian Muslim Communities in the War on Terror Context." *Canadian Review of Sociology* 49 (4): 370–88.

Maira, Sunaina. 2009. *Missing: Youth, Citizenship and Empire after 9/11*. Durham, NC: Duke University Press.

Nagra, Baljit. 2010. "Flying without Citizenship: Canadian Muslim Youths' Experiences of Security and Surveillance at Airports and Borders." Paper presented at the American Sociological Association Annual Meeting, San Francisco, California, 13–19 August.

Ngyuen, Tram. 2005. *We Are All Suspects Now: Untold Stories from Immigrant Communities after 9/11*. Boston: Beacon Press.

Paquin, Christian. 2008. *Profile de la population du territoire de Parc-Extension*. Montreal: CSSS de la Montagne.

People's Commission on Immigration and Security Measures. 2007. *People's Commission on Immigration Security Measures: Final Report*. Montreal. http://www.peoplescommission.org/en/commission/report.php (accessed 31 May 2011).

Pew Forum on Religion and Public Life. 2011. *The Future of the Global Muslim Population: Projections for 2010 to 2030*. 27 January. http://www.pewforum.org/2011/01/27/the-future-of-the-global-muslim-population/ (accessed 11 December 2011).

Razack, Sherene. 2008. *Casting Out: The Eviction of Muslims from Western Law and Politics*. Toronto: University of Toronto Press.

Roach, Kent. 2002. "Canada's New Anti-terrorism Law." *Singapore Journal of Legal Studies*: 122–48.

Rousseau, Cécile, and Uzma Jamil. 2008. "Meaning and Perceived Consequences of 9/11 for Two Pakistani Communities: From External Intruders to the Internalization of a Negative Self-Image." *Anthropology & Medicine* 15 (3): 163–74.

– 2010. "Muslim Families' Understanding and Reaction to 'the War on Terror.'" *American Journal of Orthopsychiatry* 80 (4): 601–9.

Rousseau, Cécile, and Anousheh Machouf. 2005. "A Preventive Pilot Project Addressing Multiethnic Tensions in the Wake of the Iraq War." *American Journal of Orthopsychiatry* 75: 466–74.

Smith, Jane I. 2010. "Islam in America." In *Muslims in the West after 9/11: Religion, Politics and Law*, ed. Jocelyne Cesari, 28–42. London and New York: Routledge.

Statistics Canada. 2006. *"Pakistani" and "Canada." Ethnic Origin (101), Age Groups (8), Sex (3) and Selected Demographic, Cultural, Labour Force, Educational and Income Characteristics (309), for the Total Population of Canada, Provinces,*

Territories, Census Metropolitan Areas and Census Agglomerations, 2006 Census – 20% Sample Data. Ottawa.

– 2007a. *Population and Dwelling Counts, for Canada, Provinces and Territories, and Census Subdivisions (Municipalities), 2006 and 2001 Censuses – 100% Data (Table). Population and Dwelling Count Highlight Tables. 2006 Census. Statistics Canada Catalogue no. 97–550–XWE2006002.* Ottawa. Released 13 March 2007.

– 2007b. *Ethnic Origins, 2006 Counts, for Canada, Provinces and Territories – 20% Sample Data (Table). 2006 Census. Ethnocultural Portrait of Canada Highlight Tables.* Ottawa.

– 2008. *Canada's Ethnocultural Mosaic, 2006 Census.* Ottawa: Ministry of Industry.

– 2011. *National Household Survey Data Tables. Statistics Canada Catalogue no. 99–010–X2011032.* Ottawa. Released 8 May 2013.

Teotonio, Isabel. 2010. "Toronto 18, Parts 1 and 2." *Toronto Star*, 3–4 July.

Ville de Montréal. 2009. *Profil sociodémographique: Agglomération de Montréal.* Montreal: Division des affaires économiques et institutionnelles.

Wortley, Scot, and Julian Tanner. 2004. "Discrimination or 'Good' Policing? The Racial Profiling Debate in Canada." *Our Diverse Cities* 1 (Spring): 197–201.

7 The Sikhs in Canada: Culture, Religion, and Radicalization

DORIS R. JAKOBSH

Introduction

On 23 June 1985 an explosive device tore through the cargo hold of Air India Flight 182 over the Atlantic Ocean as the jet approached the coast of Ireland. The passengers had boarded the plane in Montreal en route for Delhi, India, via London, England. All 329 people on board were killed. A second bomb killed two Japanese baggage handlers moving luggage to another Air India plane at New Tokyo International Airport in Narita, Japan, 54 minutes before Flight 182 exploded (Jiwa and Hauka 2006). Canadian law enforcement determined that the main suspects in the bombing were members of a Sikh militant group known as the Babbar Khalsa, based in Canada. Although a number of members were arrested and tried, including Ripudaman Singh Malik and Ajaib Singh Bagri, both residents of British Columbia, Inderjit Singh Reyat was the only person convicted in 2003. He was found guilty of manslaughter for his involvement in the building of the bombs and was sentenced to 15 years in prison (Major 2010; Commission of Inquiry 2007). Malik and Bagri were acquitted for lack of solid evidence and because of various investigative and legal errors made by the Canadian security services, law enforcement, and Crown attorneys (R. v. Malik and Bagri 2005). The extended media coverage of the investigations, the trials, and the inquiries into what went wrong put the Sikh community in Canada in the spotlight. Whether they were affiliated with the militant Babbar Khalsa group or not, Canadian Sikhs bore the brunt of suspicion and the negative press surrounding the bombing of Air India Flight 182. Though the incident occurred over two decades ago, suspicions of radicalization and the need for securitization continued to be associated with the Sikhs in Canada (Parent and Ellis 2011, 51–4). The continued valorization of Babbar Khalsa founder Talwinder Singh Parmar, who masterminded the Air India catastrophe, as a "martyr of the faith" among some segments of the Sikh community has also fanned the flames of fear with regard to radicalized religio-cultural expressions within the Canadian Sikh community (Bolan 2011; Milewski 2007).

In this chapter, I will examine some of the potential factors contributing to violence and radicalization among Sikhs in Canada. I begin, however, with words of caution with regard to terminology and seemingly simple tendencies to qualify and categorize "Sikhism." While arguing that religion and culture are not easily delineated from one another, within both contemporary and historical milieus, I will delineate what have often been portrayed as "cultural" and "religious" characteristics associated with Sikhs. Notions of honour and hyper-masculinity will be examined within the contexts of the family and community, gurdwara politics and administration, caste as well as sectarian and ideological divisions. In terms of "religious" characteristics, I will turn to the formation of the Khalsa and understandings of martyrdom within Sikh history. Finally, I examine recent "dramatic denouements" (Bromley 2002, 12), specific time frames in which Sikh collective identity has perceived itself as threatened: the political and religious upheavals of 1984, the Air India bombing of 1985, 9/11, France's debates around laïcité, Quebec's Bill 94, and most recently the tragic events that took place in Oak Creek, Wisconsin. These varied religio-cultural factors, heightened moments of insecurity, convictions, and ideologies, have had the potential to play significant roles in the fomenting of violent action or radicalization in parts of this diaspora community.

Before we can even begin to address the specific factors noted earlier, we need to consider the implications of the language used to discuss this issue, especially for the minority community of Sikhs in Canada who are already facing some forms of overt discrimination. This discrimination stems in part from what might be called the "marked body" (Puar and Rai 2004, 81) of at least a portion of the male Sikh community: those who choose to wear some or all of the external symbols of Sikhism, most particularly the turban and kirpan.

The terminology often used to address the issue of violence in the Sikh community can be highly problematic. As Andrew Silke notes, identifiers such as "terrorist" (and one could add "radical," "fundamentalist," and "security risk") are far from neutral descriptors, nor are their meanings universally accepted. Some communities, after all, see members of groups like the Babbar Khalsa "not as 'terrorists' but rather as 'freedom fighters,' 'rebels' or 'the resistance.' One cannot avoid the fact that applying the label 'terrorist' is often a value judgment (and a negative one) and is often a label imposed from outside of the communities and culture that the terrorists belong to" (Silke 2008, 116; see also Reader's chapter 2 in this volume). Mark Juergensmeyer's well-known study of the rise of contemporary movements of religious violence came to similar conclusions: many "terrorists" emphatically insisted they were instead "freedom fighters" fighting in the name of justice and righteousness (2000, 9; see also chapter 1 by Bramadat in this volume).

Even seemingly innocuous terms with regard to Sikh identity, widely used by both Sikh and non-Sikh observers, such as "conservative," "orthodox," and "moderate," are open to wide-ranging interpretation. The term "orthodox" is potentially misleading, since it implies a value judgment and comes from a Christian context in which "right belief" (the literal meaning of orthodox) has historically been understood as fundamental for salvation (Jakobsh and Nesbitt 2010, 34). However, the term is widely used and often refers to those who have undergone initiation into the Khalsa order, correctly identified as *amritdhari* Sikhs. These Sikhs have committed to observing the specific external signifiers of Sikh identity known as the five Ks – uncut hair (*kes*), steel bracelet (*kara*), dagger or sword (*kirpan*), breeches worn as underwear (*kachhera*), and the small round comb worn in the hair (*kangha*) – alongside all other injunctions specified in the Sikh Code of Conduct (*Sikh Rahit Maryada*). At times, however, the term "orthodox" may also refer to those who are *outwardly* recognizable as Sikhs but who in fact have not followed through in the "key ritual moment in the life of a committed Sikh," namely, that of initiation into the Khalsa order (Mahmood 2005, 56), while still upholding some or even all of the five Ks. In India, this group constitutes the bulk of the Sikh populace and is known as *kesdhari* Sikhs.

However, caution must be exercised in attempting to delineate, define, and categorize particular aspects of Sikh practice and identity. Words are not value-free and are themselves central to creating a "powerful web of discourse" that must remain central to the study of any culture. Categorizations, terms, and delineations often taken for granted as "easy and obvious markers of our social lives are, in fact, merely the storefronts for great webs of highly complex social systems of historical, political, economic, and cultural force … [W]ords have histories and are political realities" (Smith 2008, 191–2). For example, the term "moderate" in reference to Sikh identity has been variously used. "Moderate Sikhs" often identified those who rejected violent means to establish a Sikh state in the 1980s and 1990s (Minahan and Wendel 2002). The term has been used for Sikhs "for whom adaptation and change are a necessity," in direct opposition to "traditionalists" or "radicals" (Singh and Tatla 2006, 185). In Canada, "moderate" may be used to identify those Sikhs who are not "conservative" or not "fundamentalist" (Gurpreet Singh 2008), including Sikhs who reject some or all of the external manifestations of Khalsa identity (especially uncut hair). They are often defined as *sahajdharis* within Punjabi Sikh identity parlance; the term *sahajdhari* itself has undergone numerous shifts in meaning, being defined variously as "slow adopter" or, in generalized terms, a "non-Khalsa Sikh." Moderate has also referred to Sikh congregations (*sangats*) that have broken with tradition in allowing for the usage of tables and chairs in the sharing of the Sikh communal meal known as *langar*, conventionally eaten in rows on the floor as a sign of egalitarianism (Gurpreet Singh 2008). In yet another context, an Indian matrimonial site profiles potential Sikh brides as "moderate," without referencing any particular aspects of Sikh identity (Bandhan n.d.).

More broadly speaking with regard to religious categorization in general, each classification of religion, whether "Muslim" or "Hindu," "Christian" or "Sikh," among others, is subject to interpretation and varies widely in practice across the dimensions of time and place. The open-endedness and ambiguity inherent in categorizing specific behaviour makes it difficult to assign analytical meaning to specific "traits" of any particular religion or culture (Zubaida 1995; see also Jamil, chapter 6, this volume). The categorization problem becomes even more marked when attempting to ascertain the specific meanings of traits within an increasingly globalized world. Religious, ethnic, or cultural characteristics within diasporic locales are often brought into a more defined comparative focus through a process of intensified differentiation in relation to dominant cultures. In other words, the modern world may be characterized as being propelled "by a new set of disjunctures" (Appadurai 1996, 41). This is particularly the case with regard to issues of "meaning" or "identity" (Robertson 1992, 29), whether religious, ethnic, or cultural. Traditional distinctions made between "the local" and "the global" are being challenged widely, with terms such as the "glocal" or the process of "glocalization" referring, "in the subjective and personal sphere, to the construction and invention of diverse localities through global flows of ideas and information" (Eade 2000, 47;

Robertson 1995). Within this theoretical context, glocalized dimensions of identity politics become difficult to ascertain; the simple compartmentalization of specific behaviour, attitudes, even beliefs in referring to specific religions or cultures, however appealing because of its tendency towards intellectual neatness, is more than likely incongruous with many of the lived realities of members within these groups. Hall insists on the need for a complex "multisited" analysis of how identities are "created, circulated, debated, and contested across social contexts and levels of scale" (Hall 2004, 109). Simply put, religious, cultural, and ethnic identities are not, and never have been, neat and tidy categories.

Thus when distinctions such as "culture" and "religion" are made in this chapter I must stress that these distinctions are not universally accepted. In some cases, religion is simply presented as a proxy for culture (Stulz and Williamson 2001, 3). Or, as a recent study of Punjabi Sikh Canadian youth has shown, "culture and religion are so intertwined, it has become increasingly difficult for members of the Punjabi-Sikh community to identify what is in accordance with their faith, and what is *merely* cultural" (Gill 2007, 12 [italics mine]; see also Nayar 2004, 250). It would seem that religion is valued as something "more" than culture, but what this valuation actually refers to is difficult to determine. For example, Gill observes that there "is no specific reference in the *Guru Granth Sahib* that prohibits dating, yet this [dating] is justified as not being in alignment with 'Sikh values,' thus making it inappropriate" (Gill 2007, 12). Another example of the blurring of religious and cultural identities can be seen in the phenomenon known as bhangra, traditionally a rural dance form and today a symbol of essential *Punjabiat* (Punjabiness). Although having no direct ties to Sikhism, bhangra is often showcased at Sikh religious functions. In some cases it is simultaneously endowed with the central purpose of articulating and projecting Sikh, Jat Sikh (the dominant Sikh caste), and Punjabi culture and identity. In other words, bhangra has "emerged as a key marker of tradition" for Sikhs (Ballantyne 2006, 131; Jakobsh 2012; Katrak 2002). There is a rather nebulous and inextricable linkage between that which is "Sikh" religion and that which is "Punjabi" culture (I.P. Singh 1977, 70).

A fluid understanding of Sikh identity – as religious, cultural, regional, and national identity – is not a contemporary phenomenon. Harjot Oberoi describes Sikh identity in the eighteenth and nineteenth centuries as having as much to do with caste affiliation, kinship ties, and regional loyalties as with religion. Then as now, many Sikhs cut their hair, rejected the external signifiers of the Khalsa order, and adhered to heterogeneous beliefs, practices, and rituals drawn from the varied traditions surrounding them. He adds that "far from a single Sikh identity, most Sikhs moved in and out of multiple identities grounded in local, regional, religious and secular loyalties ... [and] several competing definitions of who constituted a Sikh were possible" (Oberoi 1994, 24–5). North Indian religious identities developed in conjunction with one another, without the need for rigid compartmentalization of one from the other (Smith 1981, 15). British colonizers simply interpreted what they considered to be a most puzzling amorphous state of affairs as Indians being confused over their religious identity (Geaves 1998, 22)!

This is not only the case with regard to Sikh identity within historical Punjab. W.H. McLeod has postulated that in referencing the earliest waves of Sikhs entering their new diasporic homelands, including Canada, caution should be applied in portraying these new immigrants as "Sikh," not only because this cohort included Hindus and Muslims but also because of the absence of "clear cut normative identities" in Punjabi villages of the early twentieth century (McLeod 1989, 42). Moreover, Canadian officials and the media often generically labelled all Indian immigrants as "Hindu" or "Hindoo" upon arrival in Canada. Some, though not all, Sikh pioneers did understand Sikhism as a distinct category that existed under the wider umbrella of Hinduism, accepting that their identities ought to be understood as complex and multiple (Johnston 2005–6, 15).

Within the early Sikh Canadian milieu, Sikhs within different caste groups also had varied loyalties in terms of their Sikh identity. Members of an agricultural sub-caste known as Mahton Sikhs left a village in Punjab named Paldi, migrated to Canada, and established *another* Paldi in British Columbia. Historically, Mahton Sikhs identified themselves primarily as followers of Guru Nanak (Nanak *Panthis*) as opposed to identifying with the Khalsa order of the tenth Sikh guru, Guru Gobind Singh (Verma 2002, 53). Understandings of distinct religious difference, particularly vis-à-vis the Khalsa Sikh ideal (complete with the external signifiers – the five Ks) have long been an essential element of Sikh self-definition, and the *privileging* of the Khalsa identity over and above other "narratives of Sikh identity" appears, according to Anjali Roy, to be a post-1984 phenomenon (Roy 2008, 4). Roy is referring to that highly charged period of intense self-reflection and concentrated preoccupation with Sikh identity of the 1980s and early 1990s, before and after the rise of Sikh militancy under the leadership of Jarnail Singh Bhindranwale. Importantly, the "strategic invocation of the pure Khalsa narrative of Sikhism after 1984 also illustrates the dynamic nature of Sikh identity and how it has been constantly changing over the centuries" (Roy 2008, 4).

Beyond raising and acknowledging the complexity of the impact of some of the major issues of Sikh identity, customs, characteristics, and history of the Sikh diaspora in Canada, the scope of this chapter will not allow a deeper analysis of the ways in which these often ill-defined, constantly shifting, and rather consequential terms are employed, especially in the context of a discussion of the Sikh community, radicalization, or violent action. My hope is that this necessarily rudimentary overview would remind us of the need to guard against oversimplification, essentialism, and either subtle or blatant bias against the Sikh "other."

The Sikhs – Religio-cultural Perspectives

Regardless of the country where Sikhs are found, in India or within the vast Sikh diaspora, they have always been a minority. In India, Sikhs constitute about 2 per cent of the entire population, roughly 22 million people. In Canada, the most recent census figures indicate that Sikhs form just less than 1 per cent of the populace (Statistics Canada 2001, 18). Projections for 2031, however, predict that Sikhs may constitute from 2 to 2.3 per cent of the Canadian populace (Statistics Canada 2010, 25). The consistent and acute minority status of Sikhs worldwide has led to a "minority within a minority" mentality among them, or what Khyati Joshi calls a "double-minority" mentality (2006a, 4). This perception, based on "scripts or macronarratives" (Crenshaw 1988, 20), has been used to connect historical events to those of the present, underscoring a self-understanding among Sikhs of being a community under siege or potentially under siege from the varied, though always dominant, forces surrounding them (Baixas and Simon 2008). This perceived need to protect Sikh identity has led in many cases to increased attention on what it means to be Sikh.

Within Canada, a recent poll on attitudes towards religious groups among Canadians has underscored this Sikh macro-narrative. Sikhs have consistently been perceived and presented as inherently violent, despite years of active attempts by the Sikh community to improve their relations with other Canadians. Responding to the poll, Palbinder Shergill, a Vancouver lawyer, observed that the "patient work trying to overcome the widespread view of Sikhs as dangerous seemed to be paying off" – until recently. Shergill (Geddes 2009) notes that with recent Air India verdicts Sikhs have faced a "huge resurgence" of resistance to their distinctive practices, a problem that they thought had been laid to rest years earlier (ibid.).

Culture

As noted earlier, distinguishing between Sikh culture and Sikh religion is fraught with difficulties. However, wide-ranging scholarship has tended towards clearly defining both entities as separate. I will do so here as well, to clarify potential factors involved in the radicalization of segments of the Sikh diaspora community in Canada.

Scholars have highlighted two Punjabi Sikh traits, among others, that are inextricably intertwined with characteristics associated with the most dominant Sikh caste in Canada and India, namely, Jat Sikhs. Jats have traditionally been identified as the landowning caste in Punjab, and the traits in question are a preoccupation with honour (*izzat*) and a propensity towards hyper-masculinity (Judge 1993; Mooney 2010; Singh and Tatla 2006, 182). Both are highly complex and require considerable contextualization, but I would also suggest that they offer at least partial explanations for the violent reprisals or radicalization of a small number of Sikhs.

Honour

In an early study, Joyce Pettigrew defines honour or izzat as that "complex of values regarding what was honorable" (1975, 58–9). Izzat has a number of important components associated with it, namely, the honoured name of the family (especially the behaviour, practices, and reputation of women), the community, and even the homeland. In many ways, North Indian society remains highly feudalistic. When honour is at stake, singularly or collectively, individuals or groups may take matters into their own hands and mete out whatever punishment is considered appropriate for a perceived loss of honour. This may or may not include violent action. Vestiges of these attitudes and practices can be seen within the Canadian context among Sikhs, including some of the violent altercations in gurdwaras, instances of domestic violence, and gang warfare (Sangra 2008).

Another value generally associated with notions of honour, especially for women, is that of modesty or propriety (*sharam*). For Punjabi males, izzat has traditionally been reflected on an individual level through wealth, status, and actions but also through the behaviour of kin, most especially that of their wives, daughters, and sisters. Together, izzat and sharam play an important role in maintaining the traditional patriarchal framework of Punjabi society (Mooney 2010). A popular Punjabi maxim notes that "a man's *izzat* is his women's *sharam*." Loss of honour and a lack of modesty are traditionally associated with female behaviour. Importantly, beyond the individual, loss of izzat represents a loss of family honour, which in turn leads to a decline in the family's social standing in the community (Kang 2006, 154–5). For this reason, regulations surrounding females are generally more stringently applied than are those related to males. It must, however, be noted that honour as a social construct is deeply imbricated in differentiations based on class, socio-economic status, geographic locales, and education (Toor 2009, 245) as well as caste. These factors must also be taken into account in the structuring and negotiation of izzat (Dwyer 2000, 483). While not discounting the centrality of the trope itself within this exploration of gendered social codes and behaviours, I must also caution that the complex, layered, and nuanced nature of izzat can far too easily be essentialized and racialized and lead to the denigration of whole communities.

Hyper-masculinity

Closely related to the notion of honour is hyper-masculinity. A commonly heard phrase used to describe powerful Punjabi Sikh males is "Sher-Punjabi," or "lions of the Punjab." Factors associated with hyper-masculinity involve the maintenance of highly patriarchal value systems, but they may also include deeply held notions of male dominance, homophobia, and the attitude that "boys will be boys" alongside a sense of pride in heavy drinking (Singh and Tatla 2006, 177). This is the case even though at least within Sikh scripture, many egalitarian principles are stressed and the Sikh Code of Conduct officially condemns intoxicants of all kinds (Dharam Parchar Committee 1994).

Studies have shown an increase in hyper-masculinity during the times of political upheaval and radicalization that occurred among Sikhs during the 1980s under the leadership of Jarnail Singh Bhindranwale in Punjab. According to anthropologist Veena Das, Bhindranwale exhorted his followers to distance themselves from the "feminine" character of Mahatma Gandhi's principle of non-violence, symbolized by the *charkha* (spinning wheel), and instead to become bearers of weapons (Das 1992, 250–2). "The danger," according to Das, "is not of a heroic confrontation with a masculine other, but that the feminine other will completely dissolve the masculine self of the Sikhs" (1992, 251). In other words, at least within this context, radicalized identities are created by and in turn bolster hyper-masculine notions of the ideal Sikh. As I shall point out, honour and hyper-masculinity as social constructs may be closely aligned to violence and securitization.

Violence, Honour, and Sikh Institutions

Family

Notions of honour, as mentioned previously, largely centre on maintaining the family name, most particularly with regard to restraints placed on Sikh women. Hall notes that the restrictions and overt disciplinary actions surrounding the ideology of family honour generally focus on the control of female sexuality in "protecting the 'gift' of female purity and virginity until it can be given away at marriage. The bodies of unmarried women are the sites on which the dynamic struggles of sociocultural reproduction within Sikh communities are fought" (Hall 2002, 168). In one of the first major studies focusing on British Sikh women, Rai (2011) refers to the double standards that operate in the social control mechanisms of male and female Sikh behaviour. Females, as noted earlier, are intricately tied to notions of chastity, honour, and family prestige; these are "considered to be a woman's *shingar* (ornaments) and she should not lose them at any cost" (Rait 2005, 53).

Violence can occur when it is perceived that a female member is bringing dishonour to the family by dating or marrying outside of her caste group. Although rare, honour-based violence against women to the point of death can occur, as a recent and highly publicized case in Canada has shown (Sarin 2006). Similarly, unions formed with non-Sikhs are contrary to regulations within the *Sikh Rahit Maryada* (Dharam Parchar Committee 1994). This is especially the case with female Sikh and male Muslim unions. While there are numerous and highly complex reasons for the tensions between Sikhs and Muslims (Sian 2011, 120; Gurharpal Singh 2010), two historical connections are often made: two of the Sikh gurus died at the hands of Muslim authorities, and Sikh partition narratives have "the Muslim enemy" as "oppressing, abusing and forcefully converting the Sikh collective" (Sian n.d., 11–15). Another contemporary narrative of "forced conversion," based on Sikh perceptions of "predatory Muslim males" seeking to coerce and groom "vulnerable Sikh girls" (Sian n.d., 4), is also relevant. However, caution must be exercised in making these comments since family relations and community ties are not only restrictive but also provide invaluable support and enhance the lives of Sikh women (Hall 2002, 169).

Community

In December 2004, a young female Sikh playwright, Gurpreet Kaur Bhatti, caused an uproar in the British Sikh community in Birmingham, where her play *Behzti* (Dishonour) was to have its debut. The play was cancelled, Bhatti's life was threatened, and she was forced into hiding for months. The play depicted scenes of rape that took place within a gurdwara (Wason 2005). Although some compromises were reached with representatives of the local Sikh community and the theatre before the opening night of *Bhezti*, largely peaceful protests also included incidents of violence.

While many Sikhs condemned the violence and supported Bhatti's play (Gurharpal Singh 2004), the incident raised important insights into the perceived need to protect Sikh identity and the potential for violence when community sensibilities are offended (Grillo 2007). It also raised questions regarding the extent to which Sikhs or non-Sikhs (the playwright was herself a Sikh) may take licence in portraying the Sikh community.

The role that Sikh groups played in fomenting the violence that occurred has not been adequately examined. *The Times* reported that the Sikh Federation, a group formed after the banning of the International Sikh Youth Organization (under the United Kingdom's Terrorism Act of 2000) took part in the demonstration and were potentially responsible for acts of violence (Grillo 2007, 12). The *Behzti* incident was writ large on numerous websites, thus moving the discourse into the milieu of the glocal, reaching far beyond Birmingham.

Gurdwara Politics

Given the very real discrimination the early Sikhs faced upon arrival in Canada, many attempted to blend into Canadian society by replacing traditional Punjabi clothes with Western attire, cutting their hair, and rejecting other aspects of the Khalsa Sikh identity (Johnston 1999). Early Sikh migrants worshipped in gurdwaras without covering their heads, disgraceful behaviour within the Indian context and also within the Canadian contemporary Sikh milieu (Bains and Johnston 1995).

With the arrival of new waves of immigrants after World War II, many of the practices adopted by these early Sikhs came to be challenged. The 1950s witnessed the first split within the Canadian Sikh community. While most gurdwaras consisted of clean-shaven Sikhs, some members began to argue that gurdwara management committees should be restricted to Sikhs following the Khalsa form. Other gurdwaras allowed clean-shaven Sikhs to serve as elected officials. These divisions intensified with increased immigration in the 1960s and 1970s. Many of these new immigrants were Khalsa Sikhs who viewed the practices of earlier Sikh immigrants as far too lax. During and after the Punjab disturbances in the 1980s and with increased immigration, many of these new immigrants brought their political perspectives and dreams of a separate state of Khalistan with them to Canada. Intracommunal conflicts became increasingly tense, especially in Vancouver. Clashes between pro- and anti-Khalistan Sikhs often took place within gurdwaras, which continue to be the major sites of political wrangling between the two groups (Jakobsh 2012).

Largely as a result of these political battles, new questions with regard to Sikh identities came to be posed. These same issues continue to divide Sikhs today. As I have shown, Sikh identity is not uniform; it consists of many layers, each of which (caste, time of arrival, orthodox or modern, etc.) assumes different prominence depending on the extent of glocalization. For the most part, Sikhs have been content to live with diverse understandings of what it means to be a Sikh. However, since the 1980s, discussions among Sikhs about identity issues have become polarized between those who are "observant Sikhs" (generally understood to be Khalsa Sikhs) and those who are "unobservant" Sikhs (sahajdhari Sikhs), the latter also considering themselves to be devoted Sikhs.

Administration

Local gurdwaras play important roles for Sikhs in terms of the everyday workings of the community. For the most part, each *sangat* acts as an entirely autonomous institution, with elected officials on a management committee maintaining the affairs of each gurdwara. There is no one umbrella administrative organization worldwide regulating gurdwaras, or even just in Canada (P. Singh 1990; Mann 2001). Gurdwaras are often run by a small number of families who exert a tremendous control over the offerings that are brought into the gurdwara by devotees (Kalsi 1995). In larger gurdwaras, those offerings can amount to millions of dollars every year. As such, it is not difficult to imagine how the control over gurdwara administration and finances often comes to be combined with struggles over authentic Sikh practices and the contemporary articulation of Punjabi values such as honour.

Caste

While the "Sikh public narrative of caste" (Behl 2009, 16) maintains that their gurus eliminated all caste inequalities and even the caste system itself among Sikhs, in fact, as with many other socio-religious groups in India, caste continues to have a strong hold on Sikhs. The Sikh caste hierarchy is roughly composed, beginning with the top of the hierarchy, of Jats, then Khatris, followed by various artisan castes, including Tarkhans or Ramgharias, and finally by Dalits or outcastes. Marginal Sikhs have consistently experienced the "constant 'drip-drip' of subtle, yet equally damaging acts of caste prejudice" by the wider Sikh community (Lum 2012, 190). Casteism within diasporic contexts may in fact be on the increase, as a result of dominant castes needing to maintain the status quo and accompanying privileges, especially in light of the economic and educational progress by Dalits (Lum 2012, 190–4) and an expanding religio-social assertion from the margins.

Caste often overrides all other facets of identity, including religion (Jaspal 2011, 34). In the Punjab, despite egalitarian tenets enshrined within the Sikh Code of Conduct, lower-caste Sikhs are often forced to worship in distinct gurdwaras and have separate cremation grounds (Lal 2009, 226; World Sikh Organization of Canada 2008). Some of these practices, particularly with regard to distinct places of worship, have continued within diasporic contexts (Singh and Tatla 2006, 77–81).

Many lower-caste Sikhs follow what mainstream Sikhs (largely Jat) consider to be heterodox practices while still claiming full membership *as Sikhs* or understand themselves as having marginal ties with the wider Sikh community though others stress that they are simply "Ravidassias" (Takhar 2005; Lum 2010, 2012). Ravidassias follow a number of Sikh teachings, including the veneration of Sikh scripture, which contains 41 poems, but view their founder as Guru Ravidass, not Bhagat Ravidass as do mainstream Sikhs, who reserve the term "Guru" for their ten masters. An example of caste identities and heterodox versus mainstream practices clashing occurred in Vienna, Austria, on 25 May 2009 when a violent reprisal between two Sikh groups took place.

Six men from the mainstream Sikh community armed with a gun and knives attacked a group of lower-caste Ravidassia Sikhs who were followers of Sant Niranjan Das, whose centre is known as the Dera Sach Khand in Punjab. Das was visiting the new gurdwara built by his followers in Vienna. The clash led to two deaths and many injuries, including the killing of Das's deputy, Sant Rama Nand, also visiting Vienna. Sant Niranjan Das was one of the seriously wounded. The response in Punjab was swift; various regions in Punjab erupted in waves of violence between supporters of the Dera Sach Khand and "mainstream" or upper-caste Sikhs (M. Singh 2009).

Some mainstream Sikhs, however, deny that this clash can be attributed to caste, continuing to uphold a non-caste, egalitarian narrative as central to the very essence of Sikhism. Instead of caste, the heterodox or "blasphemous" teachings of the Ravidassias have been identified as the root cause of any problems between these groups. Thus, the violence in Austria and that ensuing in Punjab have in some cases been presented as morally justifiable (Mehta 2009). However, some Sikhs from the mainstream community condemned these "acts of fanaticism" as being "against the basic tenets of the Sikh faith" (Williams 2009).

Canada has one of the largest populations of Ravidassia Sikhs outside of India (Gurmukh Singh 2009), and the Vienna incident may be a wake-up call for the possibility of increased radicalization among Canadian Sikh caste groups. According to Dalit lobbies, the bloodshed in Vienna "has blown holes in the argument that caste [is] an Indian phenomenon, firmly showing that it had spilled out on a global platform along with the diaspora ... Caste has moved beyond India with the Indian diaspora" (Ghildiyal 2009). One Indian media outlet maintained that the "hardline" stance, or pro-Khalistani character, of the perpetrators of these violent acts stemmed from the mobilizing efforts of upper-caste Sikh groups in Europe and Canada (Dogra 2009). According to Lum, the Vienna attacks "acted as a trigger that released pent-up Chamar anger at their lack of equal status and treatment within Sikhism" (2012, 198). Clearly, these developments point to potential arenas for radicalization among Sikh castes within the global context.

Sectarian/Ideological Divisions

In January 2010, the Akal Takht, the highest Sikh temporal seat, issued a startling edict. The former *Jathedar* (head) of the Akal Takht, Ragi Darshan Singh, was to be excommunicated for his "blasphemous" teachings that questioned the historical veracity of specific incidents

associated with the life of the tenth guru of the Sikhs, Guru Gobind
Singh. Given the stature of the former leader, this was a novel event
in the history of Sikhism. The edict included specific instructions to
Sikhs worldwide that they were to break all relations with Ragi Darshan Singh (Jagmohan Singh 2010). However, many Sikhs, both in India and North America, continued to support Singh, a well-loved and
respected theologian and skilled musician (T.S. Singh 2007). Supporters
and detractors turned to the Internet to voice their concerns, including a
pro–Ragi Darshan Singh Facebook page. Dissent, however, moved well
beyond the virtual realm and led to violent altercations in gurdwaras,
most recently when Singh was invited to the Sikh Lehar Centre, a major
gurdwara in Brampton, Ontario. Prominent lawyer Manjit Mangat was
injured by an anti–Ragi Darshan Singh protester as Mangat attempted
to mediate the situation (Aulakh 2010b). This is not the first violent incident of its kind. Gurbaksh Singh Kala Afghana, another controversial Sikh whose writings question specific Khalsa Sikh observances and
were banned by the highest Sikh authorities in Punjab, has also sparked
violent altercations between his supporters and his denouncers in various Canadian gurdwaras (Vision TV 2007).

Cynthia Keppley Mahmood has noted that infighting, whether
through verbal assaults or physical violence, is as characteristic among
Sikhs as is external solidarity (1996, 152; Razavy 2006, 88–90). This is
particularly the case when those considered to be "wayward" or guilty
of blasphemy *as* Sikhs may be perceived as bringing dishonour to the
community or to time-honoured Sikh beliefs and practices. These incidents underline the complexity and consequences of radicalized perspectives on religion and society, upheld by a small number of Sikhs
who may resort to violent actions. These highly publicized events have
tended to reinforce the wider Canadian public's branding of the entire
Sikh community as radical, essentially hostile and violent (even to one
another). This in turn feeds into what I described earlier as a powerful
and deeply held minority mentality among many Sikhs that suggests
that the community is perpetually under siege by the dominant forces
surrounding them.

Religion

The Khalsa

The early developing Sikh tradition stressed the extreme *interiority* of
religious devotion that was open to all, regardless of caste, religious

affiliation, gender, or status. According to the early Sikh gurus, pilgrimages, the adornment of sacred threads or any other religious identifiers, asceticism, and any form of organized and hierarchical forms of religion, particularly religious insignia, were useless in the quest for liberation – indeed they were barriers. *Only* through pure, unmediated, religious devotion and love of the Divine could the spiritual quest be attained.

Nevertheless, one of the unique features of Sikhism came to be the ideal of the saint-soldier of the Khalsa order. Developments in the sixteenth century led to wider understandings of the gurus as being representatives of *both* religious and political authority (McLeod 1997, 32–3). This culminated in the inauguration of the Khalsa order in 1699. Men were, then as now, initiated into this order through a rite known as *khande di pahul*, and their membership displayed through the clearly defined external and militarized signifiers known today as the five Ks. This is not to say that the interior aspects of religious devotion stressed by the early gurus were rejected. They were not. They were clearly a part of the newly defined religio-political ideal; those initiated into the Khalsa were to be warrior-saints. *Nam simran*, repetition of the divine Name, was to be incorporated into every aspect of life, including that of the newly established Khalsa warrior.

The centrality of a martial identity for Sikhs is one factor that may lead to violent action. However, most Sikhs will insist that any form of violence is only to be carried out in the name of defending the defenceless. This includes, for some Sikhs, defending the honour of Sikhism, its institutions, and its tenets. The defence of Sikhism may justify violent action, as shown by both the clash in Vienna and the Air India bombing by militants. In this regard, a strong and shared cultural sense of honour may interact with sectarian religious sentiments (Dorn and Gucciardi 2011, 62) and lead to radicalization.

It must also be stressed that while upholding the importance of the Khalsa ideal, the Sikh Code of Conduct defines a Sikh far more inclusively. It states that anyone who has faith in one God, the ten gurus and their teachings, and the primacy of the Guru Granth Sahib (the scripture of the Sikhs) and does not adhere to any other religion is a Sikh. It does, however, continue to say that a Sikh is one who believes in the necessity and importance of initiation into the Khalsa (Dharam Parchar Committee 1994, chapter 10). With regard to Sikh identities in Canada, though the ideal of the Khalsa Sikh is held high through Baisakhi processions celebrated in many major cities, non-Khalsa Sikhs, identifiable in that they cut their hair and (in the case of males) do not wear the turban, constitute the bulk of the Sikh populace. These two religious identities, Khalsa and non-Khalsa Sikhs, have tended to coexist with relative ease within most Sikh communities and families.

Martyrdom

Closely tied to Sikhism's religious ideals is the notion of martyrdom. As in Islam, Sikhism has its roots in the notion of death "bearing witness" to a righteous cause. As the gurus of the Sikhs gained increasing political power within their spiritual domains, they began to draw the ire of the dominant systems surrounding them. According to Sikh tradition, two Sikh gurus were martyred for the cause of righteousness. Indeed, Sikh historical accounts maintain that the ninth master, Guru Tegh Bahadur, was beheaded as a result of his intercession with the authorities for the religious rights of a group of Hindus who were being coerced to convert to Islam. His death is understood as a significant factor in the creation of the Khalsa order by his son, Guru Gobind Singh, who believed Sikhs should not only fight for the sake of righteousness but also be *recognizable* as Sikhs in the defence of righteousness.

Martyrdom as an institution continues to fascinate and inspire the veneration of many Sikhs who believe that instances of martyrdom foster piety and bravery, particularly among young Sikhs. Some gurdwaras contain particularly violent and graphic pictures depicting instances of Sikh martyrdom, both historical and contemporary martyrs (Fenech 2000). As "heirs to a faith which exalts heroism and lauds the death of martyrs, young Sikhs receive a nurture which strongly encourages a martial spirit" (McLeod 1997, 238). The Sikhs, according to Bhindranwale, are a race whose "history is written in the blood of martyrs" (Das 1992, 251). As I explore later, both the warrior-saint ideal and martyrdom have in recent history combined under varied circumstances and led to the radicalization of at least segments of the Sikh populace in various parts of the Sikh diaspora, including in Canada.

"Dramatic Denouements" and Identity Politics among the Sikhs

According to David Bromley, "dramatic denouements" may occur when a segment of society, or a particular group with a collective core identity, feels threatened enough to take a stand against that which is considered to be threatening. This may include mobilizing so that power positions are reversed or "restor[ing] what they avow to be the appropriate moral order" (Bromley 2002, 11). There have been a significant number of dramatic denouements for Sikhs within the past 25 years, and the most significant of these will be explored in terms of Sikh identity politics and the potential for radicalization and violent reprisals.

1984

Lehar in Punjabi, or "the Sikh struggle," a term used to capture the wider events and aftermath surrounding 1984 for Sikhs the world over, cannot be overemphasized in any discussion of contemporary Sikhism (Rai 2011, 1). A short summary of the events may be helpful. In late 1983 a group led by the charismatic Sikh preacher Jarnail Singh Bhindranwale took sanctuary in and fortified the complex of the Golden Temple. When the Indian Army mounted an assault on the complex, code-named "Operation Blue Star," on 5 June 1984 to flush out Bhindranwale and his followers, one of the most painful episodes of modern Sikh history occurred. Many innocent Sikh lives were lost and the complex was severely damaged. The political situation intensified when two Sikh bodyguards assassinated Prime Minister Indira Gandhi on 31 October 1984 as an act of revenge against her decision to send troops into the Golden Temple complex. In Delhi in particular, but also in many other regions, mobs began roaming the streets, especially in areas with large numbers of Sikhs. Many Sikh homes and businesses were burned to the ground, and outwardly recognizable Sikhs, particularly outwardly recognizable Sikh males, were killed, maimed, and burned in the streets. Around 3,000 Sikhs in Delhi alone died at the hands of rioting mobs (Tully 1986).

The Sikh community was shocked that these acts of violence could have taken place despite the significant police and army presence and despite government awareness of the carnage. Sikhs were also faced with the realization of their precarious situation as a small minority within the larger Hindu majority. The subsequent years were a time of political and religious uncertainty for Sikhs both in India and within the Sikh diaspora; they were also a time of intense re-evaluation about Sikh identity and the future of Sikhism (Mahmood 1996). Whereas much of the anguish surrounding this tumultuous time has subsided in Punjab, within some Sikh communities outside of India – particularly in Canada and the United Kingdom – the dream of a separate state called Khalistan has continued to be nurtured. The events of 1984 continue to be defining moments for Sikhs worldwide, both within the context of a Sikh collective memory and in the personal memories of many Sikh families. Indeed, it has been argued that a specific Sikh identity in the diaspora has only emerged in response to the violence of 1984 (Shani 2008; Dusenbery 1995).

Within India, as Indian prime minister Manmohan Singh recently attested (Armstrong 2010), the movement to create Khalistan is virtually non-existent. However, as noted, the events of 1984 continue to play a critical role for many Sikhs in diasporic locales. Though largely rejecting the violent means associated with the creation of a Sikh homeland, the Sikh diaspora has instead turned its focus to human rights abuses in India and a perceived need to keep the "memory" of 1984 alive for subsequent generations. Two recent student conferences commemorating the 25th anniversary of the events of 1984 were organized at UC Berkeley, "After 1984," and at Fresno State University, "Remember 1984: Reflect. Respond. React." They illustrate "patterns of Khalistan revivalist sentiment and discourses of victimhood" and reflect the need of young North American Sikhs to engage with their histories and identities (Verma 2011, 44).

Giorgio Shani notes that after 1984 a localized Sikh identity was replaced by a globalized identity in the Sikh diaspora.

Sikhs in the diaspora, many not even born in 1984, were, however, more willing to speak about an event which they had only experienced or "witnessed" through the media. Prominent Sikh political activists I interviewed admitted that they had been radicalized by Operation Blue Star and in some cases had only become *kes-dhari* Sikhs after the "critical event." Operation Blue Star thus enabled them to rediscover their "Sikh" roots. The violence of 1984 was, for them, perfectly in keeping with an Indian state strategy of oppression of ethno-national minorities. (2008, 95)

Sikh Baisakhi processions, especially in British Columbia and Ontario, attest to the continued fascination of some Sikhs with upholding the dream of Khalistan (Milewski 2007). In Vancouver and Toronto, these annual celebrations include the honouring of Babbar Khalsa members, a group officially listed as a terrorist organization by the Canadian government. While the grievances of older generations who had personal connections to the events of 1984 are perhaps understandable, what is significant is that some second- and third-generation Canadian Sikhs now perceive themselves as the carriers of the collective memory of 1984 (Aulakh 2010a). These grievances are quietly, or at times not so quietly, nurtured by various factions and elements within the community. This includes extensive references to 1984 on Sikh Internet sites, pictures of the two "martyrs" who were responsible for the killing of Indira Gandhi carried on procession floats (Sin 2008), and the prevalence of Khalistan T-shirts at Baisakhi processions (Verma 2011). It also includes consistent rhetoric against the Indian government and its Hindu majority, as well as a recent petition in the House of Commons by Sukh Dhaliwal, a Sikh MP, asking Ottawa to recognize the sectarian violence that occurred in India as a "genocide" of the Sikhs (MacNair 2010).

It would appear that the radical nature of the Khalistan movement has become increasingly marginalized. But as one Sikh journalist has noted, one must be cautious, for the perceived need to protect "community honour" in this regard continues to exist (Gurmukh Singh 2010). Recent threats made to Ujjal Dosanj, the former Sikh premier of British Columbia, and continued vitriolic denunciation of Kim Bolan, the *Vancouver Sun* journalist who has followed the movement for 20 years, would support Gurmukh Singh's call for vigilance. Dosanj, Bolan, and others insist that the ongoing glorification of violence and vestiges of radicalization from the Khalistan movement exists at least within the margins of the Sikh community (Aulakh 2010a).These observations do cast doubt on whether the separatist movement and Sikh radicalization is "dead" (Milewski 2007; Cernetig 2010).

I would suggest that beyond the question of Khalistan, what remains, at least within small segments of the Sikhs in Canada, the United States of America, and the United Kingdom, is an increasing focus on a more conservative, traditionalist, or perhaps even "radicalized" Sikh identity (Shani 2008). On university campuses across Canada, for the majority of Sikh youth, their religious identity as Sikhs is not the sole and probably in most cases not even the central feature of their own self-understanding. But there exists at the same time a more traditional, even marginal interpretation of what a small portion of youth (and adults) believe to be the "purest tenets" of Sikhism. This may entail the embrace of teachings stemming from centres such as Damdami Taksal, closely associated with Jarnail Singh Bhindranwale, the Sikh religious leader who was at the helm when militancy reigned in Punjab in the 1980s. These groups disseminate and uphold a highly conservative, marginal Khalsa identity that is largely rejected by the majority of Sikhs in the diaspora, including within Canada.

An increased concern with constructing the Khalsa Sikh identity is also observable on the World Wide Web (Jakobsh 2012). When Sikhism and Sikh identity are defined or described, for the most part, images and content focus almost exclusively on Khalsa Sikh identity, namely, Sikhs wearing the five Ks. In many ways, the creators of these sites are becoming "new authorities" actively involved in constructing a highly particular version of Sikh identity online. In some ways their efforts are reminiscent of traditional apologetics stemming from traditional Sikh institutions of authority in India, yet in their modern media-savvy methodology and mode of presentation, they are ultimately incompatible with Sikhism in the traditional Punjabi context. The language used here is highly compatible with liberal, multicultural values, stressing instead the new lingua franca of "human" or "religious" rights to uphold a Khalsa Sikh identity (Jakobsh 2012).

Air India

As pointed out earlier, the events surrounding the bombing of Air India Flight 182 are fraught with difficulties for the majority of Canadian Sikhs, who have distanced themselves from the radicalized actions of the few. Still, many Sikhs in Canada are concerned that the terrorist actions of a few continue to be unfairly associated with the Sikh community at large (CBC 2007). This has led to renewed perceptions among the Sikhs that they are the victims of discrimination from members of the broader society. These perceptions, along with memories of 1984 and its aftermath, remind the community of its minority status both in India and abroad.

One important aspect of the 1985 Air India bombing requiring further study is the extent to which "the silent majority" of Sikhs is prevented from voicing its objections to the perpetrators of this act (Gurpreet Singh 2011a) or from coming forward with additional information on this tragic event, possibly out of fear of violent reprisals.

9/11

The literature on discriminatory attacks on religious and ethnic minorities in the post-9/11 era has focused, understandably, on the anti-Muslim backlash in the United States. However, Sikhs wearing the outward symbolism and garb of the Khalsa were also affected by the events of that September morning in significant ways (Gohil and Sidhu 2008;

Shani 2008; Stromer 2006). Many were misidentified as turban-wearing Muslims, and consequently one of the first victims of the anti-Muslim backlash in the United States was a Sikh, Balbir Singh Sodhi, who was shot to death in Mesa, Arizona. Racist violence has spread beyond the borders of America into Canada, with turban-wearing Sikhs living in fear of harassment, discrimination, and hate crimes, including the vandalism of their sacred spaces, such as gurdwaras (Sikh Coalition 2014). The "otherness" of outwardly visible Sikhs wearing the five Ks (especially the turban and kirpan) has often led to Sikhs being identified as terrorists (Jaideep Singh 2003; Ahluwalia and Pellettiere 2010). Increased incidents (both reported and unreported) of Sikhs facing overt discrimination at airports and other public places since 9/11 have made the Sikh community critically aware of public perception of Sikhs having a connection with Muslim extremists (Pluralism Project n.d.; Puar and Rai 2004).

Like the events of 1984, 9/11 has been a wake-up call for Sikhs, particularly Khalsa Sikhs, deepening self-perceptions as a perpetual minority group under siege. The events of 1984 heightened the conviction that India was not and could never be a "Sikh" homeland, and the response to 9/11 has served as a painful reminder for many Sikhs that they can never truly be "home" within North America either.

In Canada, Sikhs have once again entered into a new era of intense re-evaluation of their place within Canadian society. This is particularly evident among young, Canadian-educated Sikhs seeking to be recognized as Sikhs and gain protection of their religious and ethnic particularities. Sikhs have made great strides within Western academic circles in that they are identified as a community which is clearly distinct from Islam and Hinduism; as Juergensmeyer (1979, 13–15) observed, early portrayals of Sikhism present an ideal lesson in syncretism, given Hinduism and Islam's influence on Sikhism's origins and development. The need to clearly distinguish Sikhs from other Indo-Canadian groups has become pivotal. In other words, Sikhs have made great efforts to delineate themselves from with the wider "South Asian" Canadian community.

France's Laïcité/Quebec's Bill 94

In post-9/11 France, the findings of the Stasi Commission in 2003 (investigating the extent to which the principle of *laïcité* was being applied in France) prompted the passage of a law in 2004 to strictly uphold *laïcité* by banning all religious symbols or religious garb in the public school system. While the law did not specifically target Sikhs, turbaned Sikh schoolchildren attending state schools were severely affected, and six schoolboys were expelled (Shani 2011, 63–4). The law also extended the prohibition of religious garb or symbols to identification photographs for important documents, which had adverse consequences for Sikhs wearing turbans. This situation, clearly perceived by Sikhs as discriminatory, has mobilized Sikhs worldwide; European Sikhs in particular see their loss of religious rights as a direct contravention of the European Convention on Human Rights, Article 9. A "Right to Turban Campaign," initiated by Sikh activists, has been situated within larger claims of rapidly eroding rights, increased hate and bias crimes, and other discriminatory laws in general (Right to Turban n.d.). In France, however, Sikh activists' tactics to protect their rights are unique. Namely, it is the Sikhs' right to "belong to a transnational, sovereign religio-political body: the *Khalsa* [and] what is at stake is not freedom *per se* but *sovereignty and identity*" (Shani 2011, 64). Thus, France's imposition of *laïcité* is perceived as a "forced conversion" of sorts to secularism and a rejection of the Khalsa identity which Sikhs, since the time of Guru Gobind Singh, have shed blood to maintain. In other words, the honour of the Khalsa is on the line.

In a similar vein, on 18 January 2011 four Sikhs representing the World Sikh Organization of Canada who were taking issue with Quebec's Bill 94 (or the Niqab Bill) were invited to appear at the National Assembly in Quebec before a legislative committee (Séguin 2011). While supportive of Muslim women's rights to the niqab, they also came to argue that the bill would have negative consequences in terms of wider religious rights in Quebec. As they approached the Assembly they were asked by the guards to remove their kirpans because they were classified as weapons and would set off the metal detectors. The four Sikhs refused, insisting that it was their right as Sikhs to carry their kirpans as religious symbols at all times. The guards at the National Assembly stood their ground, and representatives of the World Sikh Organization of Canada lost their opportunity to contribute to the wider discussion surrounding Bill 94. Sikhs argue that they have fought long and hard for their religious freedoms to be recognized within all sectors of Canadian governance. If the spate of newspaper and Web responses are any indication of the ways this incident has been interpreted in the Sikh community, their fears of being under siege have simply been confirmed (Dhillon 2011).

Oak Creek, Wisconsin

On 5 August 2012, white supremacist and army veteran Wade M. Page walked into the suburban gurdwara in Oak Creek, Wisconsin, a suburb of Milwaukee, and opened fire on Sikhs who were gathered for worship. Page killed one woman and five men before turning his gun on himself. More than any other time in recent Sikh American history, given the magnitude of Page's killing spree, Sikhs have rightly been fearful for their continued safety in the United States. Although the reasons for Page's targeting of the Sikhs is not yet clear, his supremacist leanings and affiliations with neo-Nazi music bands were known to authorities (Goode and Kovaleski 2012). In seeking to understand the tragic event, the mainstream media in the United States immediately turned its attention towards the Wisconsin Sikh community and understanding Sikhism's beliefs and practices, as well as the history of the Sikhs in America. The Sikh community's response was remarkable on many levels. While deeply shaken by the extent of the violent shooting, the Wisconsin Sikh community itself responded with astounding graciousness, stressing forgiveness of the man who had killed in their midst and inviting the larger public to grieve with them, thus highlighting the major tenets of the Sikh faith. Interfaith vigils honouring the victims were held across America, and T-shirts appeared with the slogan "We are all Sikhs. America Stands Together" (Rootsgear 2012). Beyond the immediate response of the Wisconsin community, analysts, both Sikh and non-Sikh, used mainstream media outlets to insist that the ensuing discourse move beyond mere rhetoric of "randomness" and "senseless acts of violence" to seeing the attack as another tragic example of the violence and hate crimes that Sikhs and other minority religious groups have come to experience since 11 September 2001 (Sen 2012). After 9/11 Sikhs took great pains to educate their fellow Americans that they were *not* Muslims. But following the Wisconsin shooting, Sikh spokespersons were careful not to focus on issues of "misrecognition" or "mistaken identity" (Amardeep Singh 2012), cognizant of the message's insidious subtext that Muslims are more appropriate targets of hate crimes (Kaur and Singh 2012). Moreover, scholar Mark Juergensmeyer insisted that the shooting be understood as ongoing hate crimes in the defence of "the purity of white Christian society against the evils of multiculturalism that allow non-white non-Christians an equal role in America society" (Juergensmeyer 2012). Sikhs effectively began using this incident to highlight what they consider to be systematic inequities against them in the United States, including exclusionary policies against turbans and beards within the New York Police Department (H. Singh 2012) and the US military (Kaur 2012), as well as unfair mainstream media coverage of the Wisconsin shootings (N. Singh 2012).

However, many Sikhs also view this incident as a turning point in Sikh American relations with wider American society. According to I.J. Singh, "after the Wisconsin killings, the national response was dramatically swift and different. The news coverage was superbly awesome. News anchors visibly struggled to learn the distinct Sikh traditions so as not confuse them with Muslims or others. Fundamentals of the Sikh faith and a bit of their colorful history were on air the [sic] almost 24/7 for several days" (I.J. Singh 2012). Moreover, the outpouring of support and interest in Sikhs across the United States was unsurpassed in terms of allowing Sikhs to represent themselves as loyal American citizens.

At the same time, in Punjab, demonstrators were burning American flags to protest this violent incident. Sikhs in the United States immediately condemned the burning of the flag and instead demanded an apology from the Punjab government for the desecration of the American flag, highlighting their allegiance to the United States. Commentators blamed the flag burning on "Hindu supremacists ... looking for racial divisions, hatred, and violence against American Sikhs" (Amrik Singh 2012). The incident is indicative of substantive differences in terms of values and world views between Sikh diasporic communities and those in India. Sikhs in the United States, having received positive attention through the Wisconsin shootings, hastened to distance themselves from the violent reprisals in Punjab. And yet, according to Kiranjot Kaur, a member of the highly authoritative Shiromani Gurdwara Parbandhak Committee (SGPC) in India, the parliamentary body for Sikhs responsible for religious sites in Punjab, incidents such as the Wisconsin shootings "have a big impact here [in India]. They give rise to a sense of insecurity within the community here like over there" (Burke 2012). Clearly, the political, religious, and social ramifications and consequences stemming from the Wisconsin shootings go far beyond the bounds of one particular gurdwara, city, and country.

Conclusions

As noted earlier, the trend towards religious particularization is not unique to Sikhs in Canada or the United States. Gurharpal Singh observes in a recent report on Sikhs and Muslims in Britain a distinct shift from a primarily ethnic to a religious identification for Muslims, influenced by the aftermath of the Iranian revolution in 1978, the Rushdie affair in 1988, the two Gulf Wars in 1991 and 2003, 9/11, and the 7/7 bombings in London. In the Sikh diaspora community, corresponding shifts took place largely beginning with the Khalistan movement in the 1980s, along with an increased awareness of Sikh identity since the rise of the Hindu Right in India, particularly after the demolition of the Babri Mosque on 6 December 1992. Another important factor included the Indian census of 2001 enumerating religious affiliation for the first time, allowing Sikhs to be decisively recognized as Sikhs (Gurharpal Singh 2010; Moliner 2007).

Within the Canadian context, a similar trend towards particularization of identity has been elaborated on by theorists of multiculturalism, under such theoretical constructions as the "politics of recognition" (Taylor 1994) and the "politics of difference" (Young 1990). This form of identity politics can best be understood as Sikhs constituting their own distinct ethno-religious national identity (free, at least for some, of the demand for the recognition of Sikh nation state) within a multicultural, multi-ethnic, multi-religious Canada. While the ramifications of a renewed focus on Sikh ethno-religious particularities demand additional research, other questions also arise – namely, to what extent are global Sikh diasporic manifestations of nationalisms influencing one another? One important site of comparison may be the United Kingdom given that a growing number of animosities and clashes have been documented between Sikh and Muslim youth (Sian n.d.; Gurharpal Singh 2010). Questions arise then as to the extent that these enmities – and their reliance on one another – may be influencing Sikh and Muslim identities in other diasporic contexts such as Canada. To what extent (if at all) are radicalized Muslim identity politics in the United Kingdom, for example, encouraging radicalization among Sikhs as well?

Many questions thus remain. Is radicalization occurring among Sikhs? There is no one answer. Sikhs have often been characterized as a "model minority" group (Puar and Rai 2004). They have contributed positively to Canadian society, through their political involvement and the often enviable economic success of the community as a whole. Sikhs, however, also have an "image problem," given many of the issues raised in this chapter. Sikhs, alongside Muslims, according to Puar and Rai, have tended to "test the ambivalence" inherent in multiculturalism given their highly visible and "marked bodies" (2004, 81). Moreover, in the post-9/11 world, religion has become increasingly

racialized, compounding perceived associations of Sikhs with terrorism (Joshi 2006b, 211). Thus, racism, ethno-religious discrimination,
and general biases against Sikhs cannot be underplayed in looking to
explain the kinds of radicalization one might witness within the community. Such explanations might also help those who seek to determine
whether or not the state's and society's securitization could be justified.
Moreover, homeland politics or backlashes against the community –
similar to those that have taken place since 9/11 as well as the recent
Wisconsin shooting spree – alongside political interference in Sikh
identity politics within wider diasporic contexts will almost certainly
be reflected within the Canadian Sikh community. Clearly, Sikh perceptions of being an oppressed minority (and very real instances thereof)
have a long and tenuous history (K. Singh 2009). Equally important are
deeply held and highly honoured ideals of defending the worldwide
Sikh community at all costs, including Sikh religious practices and the
identity markers that perpetually maintain the "otherness" of the Sikhs.

REFERENCES

Ahluwalia, Muninder K., and Laura Pellettiere. 2010. "Sikh Men Post-9/11:
   Misidentification, Discrimination, and Coping." *Asian American Journal of
   Psychology* 1 (4): 303–14.
Appadurai, Arjan. 1996. *Modernity at Large: Cultural Dimensions of Globalization.*
   Minneapolis: University of Minnesota Press.
Armstrong, Jane. 2010. "'Distorted' Multiculturalism to Blame of Rise in Sikh
   Extremism." *Globe and Mail*, 21 April.
Aulakh, Raveena. 2010a. "Sikh Preacher Determined to Keep Speaking." *To-
   ronto Star*, 5 April. http://www.thestar.com/news/gta/2010/04/05/sikh_
   preacher_determined_to_keep_speaking.html (accessed 11 October 2010).
– 2010b. "Sikh Separatism: Still Alive and Festering in Canada." *Toronto Star*,
   3 May. http://www.thestar.com/news/gta/2010/05/03/sikh_separatism_
   still_alive_and_festering_in_canada.html (accessed 11 October 2010).
Bains, T.S., and H. Johnston. 1995. *The Four Quarters of the Night: The Life-
   journey of an Emigrant Sikh*. Montreal and Kingston: McGill-Queen's
   University Press.
Baixas, Lionel, and Charlène Simon. 2008. "From Protesters to Martyrs: How
   to Become a 'True' Sikh." *South Asia Multidisciplinary Academic Journal*, special issue – Nb. 2, "'Outraged Communities': Comparative Perspectives on
   the Politicization of Emotions in South Asia." http://samaj.revues.org/1532
   (accessed 20 July 2011).

Ballantyne, Tony. 2006. *Between Colonialism and Diaspora*. London: Duke University Press.

Bandhan. n.d. "Matrimony Profiles for Moderate Sikh Brides." Bandhan matrimony search. http://www.bandhan.com/female/moderate/sikh/ (accessed 2 September 2011).

Behl, Natasha. 2009. "Sikh Politics, Caste, and Narrative Identity in Postcolonial India." Paper presented at the American Political Science Association 2009 Annual Meeting, Toronto, 3–6 September. http://papers.ssrn.com/sol3/papers.cfm?abstract_id=1449406 (accessed 9 May 2011).

Bolan, Kim. 2011. "Surrey Vaisakhi and Sikh 'Martyrs.'" *Vancouver Sun* Staff Blogs, *The Real Scoop*, 24 April. http://blogs.vancouversun.com/2011/04/24/surrey-vaisakhi-and-sikh-martyrs/ (accessed 23 May 2013).

Bromley, David G. 2002. "Dramatic Denouements." In *Cults, Religion and Violence*, ed. David G. Bromley and J. Gordon Melton, 11–41. Cambridge: Cambridge University Press.

Burke, Jason. 2012. "Sikh Golden Temple Memorial Reopens Old Wounds in India." *Guardian*, 2 October. http://www.theguardian.com/world/2012/oct/02/sikh-golden-temple-memorial-india (accessed 4 October 2012).

CBC. 2007. "Sikh Community Unfairly Labeled 'Terrorists' after Air India Bombing, Inquiry Told." CBC News, 8 December. http://www.cbc.ca/news/canada/sikh-community-unfairly-labelled-terrorists-after-air-india-bombing-inquiry-told-1.691393 (accessed 12 September 2011).

Cernetig, Miro. 2010. "Zero Tolerance Can Be the Only Stance for Politicians." *Vancouver Sun*, 20 April.

Commission of Inquiry. 2007. "Terrorism, Intelligence and Law Enforcement – Canada's Response to Sikh Terrorism." Commission of inquiry into the investigation of the bombing of Air India Flight 182 – DOSSIER 2. https://members.ialeia.org/files/docs/dossier2_ENG.pdf (accessed 8 November 2011).

Crenshaw, Martha. 1988. "The Subjective Reality of the Terrorist: Ideological and Psychological Factors in Terrorism." In *Current Perspectives on International Terrorism*, ed. Robert O. Slater and Michael Stohl, 12–46. London: Macmillan Press.

Das, Veena. 1992. "Time, Self and Community: Features of the Sikh Militant Discourse." *Contributions to Indian Sociology* 26 (2): 245–59.

Dharam Parchar Committee. 1994. *Sikh Rahit Maryada*, English version. http://www.sgpc.net/sikhism/sikh-dharma-manual.html (accessed 1 September 2011).

Dhillon, R. Paul. 2011. "Quebec Intolerance Raises Its Ugly Head with Kirpan Decision." *Link*, 13 February. http://thelinkpaper.ca/?p=4245 (accessed 10 January 2012).

Dogra, Chander Suta. 2009. "Deras: Something Burning." *Outlook Magazine*, 9 June. http://www.outlookindia.com/article.aspx?240620 (accessed 10 July 2011).

Dorn, A. Walter, and Stephen Gucciardi. 2011. "The Sword and the Turban: Armed Force in Sikh Thought." *Journal of Military Ethics* 10 (1): 52–70.

Dusenbery, V.A. 1995. "A Sikh Diaspora? Contested Identities and Constructed Realities." In *Nation and Migration*, ed. P. van der Veer, 17–42. Philadelphia: University of Pennsylvania Press.

Dwyer, C. 2000. "Negotiating Diasporic Identities: Young British South Asian Muslim Women." *Women's Studies International Forum* 23 (4): 475–86.

Eade, J. 2000. "Giddens and Robertson on Globalization." In *Globalization: The Reader*, ed. J. Beynon and D. Dunkerly, 46–8. New York: Routledge.

Facebook. n.d. "Fateh, Professor Darshan Singh! We Support You." https://www.facebook.com/pages/Fateh-Professor-Darshan-Singh-We-Support-You/476315710384 (accessed 30 August 2011).

Fenech, Louis E. 2000. *Martyrdom in the Sikh Tradition: Playing the "Game of Love."* Delhi: Oxford University Press.

Geaves, Ron. 1998. "The Borders between Religions: A Challenge to the World Religions Approach to Religious Education." *British Journal of Religious Education* 21 (1): 20–31.

Geddes, John. 2009. "What Canadians Think of Sikhs, Jews, Christian, Muslims …" *Maclean's Magazine*, 28 April. http://www.macleans.ca/news/canada/what-canadians-think-of-sikhs-jews-christians-muslims/ (accessed 4 March 2011).

Ghildiyal, Subodh. 2009. "Vienna Clash May Put Caste in Global Spotlight." *Times of India*, 26 May. http://timesofindia.indiatimes.com/india/Viennaclash-may-put-caste-in-global-spotlight/articleshow/4577105.cms?referral=PM (accessed 29 April 2011).

Gill, Jagjeet Kaur. 2007. "Exploring Issues of Identity among Punjabi-Sikh Youth in Toronto." Ceris working paper, no. 53. Toronto: Joint Centre of Excellence for Research on Immigration and Settlement – Toronto. http://canada.metropolis.net/policypriority/family_e.htm (accessed 18 November 2010).

Gohil, N.S., and D.S. Sidhu. 2008. "The Sikh Turban: Post-911 Challenges to This Article of Faith." *Rutgers Journal of Law and Religion* 9 (2): 1–60. http://lawandreligion.com/sites/lawandreligion.com/files/sidhu.pdf (accessed 22 March 2011).

Goode, E., and S.F. Kovaleski. 2012. "Wisconsin Killer Fed and Was Fueled by Hate-driven Music." *New York Times*, 6 August.

Grillo, Ralph D. 2007. "License to Offend? The Behzti Affair." *Ethnicities* 7 (1): 5–29.

Hall, Kathleen D. 2002. *Lives in Translation: Sikh Youth as British Citizens*. Philadelphia: University of Pennsylvania Press.
– 2004. "The Ethnography of Imagined Communities: The Cultural Production of Sikh Ethnicity in Britain." *Annals of the American Academy of Political and Social Science* 595 (January): 108–21.
Jakobsh, Doris R. 2003. *Relocating Gender in Sikh History: Transformation, Meaning and Identity*. Delhi: Oxford University Press.
– 2011. *Sikhism*. Dimensions of Asian Spirituality Series. Honolulu: University of Hawai'i Press.
– 2012. "'Sikhizing the Sikhs': The Role of 'New Media' in Historical and Contemporary Identity Construction within Global Sikhism." In *Sikhs Across Borders: Transnational Practices of European Sikhs*, ed. Knut Jacobsen and Kristina Myrvold, 141–64. London: Continuum.
Jakobsh, Doris R., and Eleanor Nesbitt. 2010. "Sikhism and Women: Contextualizing the Issues." In *Sikhism and Women: History, Texts and Experience*, ed. Doris R. Jakobsh, 1–34. Delhi: Oxford University Press.
Jaspal, Rusi. 2011. "Caste, Social Stigma and Identity Processes." *Psychology and Developing Societies* 23 (1): 27–62.
Jiwa, Salim, and Donald J. Hauka. 2006. *Margin of Terror: A Reporter's Twenty-year Odyssey Covering the Tragedies of the Air India Bombing*. Toronto: Key Porter Books.
Johnston, Hugh. 1999. *The Encyclopedia of Canada's Peoples*. http://multiculturalcanada.ca/Encyclopedia/A-Z/s4/1 (accessed 2 January 2010).
– 2005–6. "Group Identity in an Emigrant Worker Community: The Example of Sikhs in Early Twentieth-century British Columbia." *BC Studies: The British Columbian Quarterly* 148 (Winter): 3–23.
Joshi, Khyati Y. 2006a. *New Roots in America's Sacred Ground: Religion, Race, and Ethnicity in Indian America*. New Brunswick, NJ: Rutgers University Press.
– 2006b. "The Racialization of Hinduism, Islam, and Sikhism in the United States." *Equity & Excellence in Education* 39 (3): 211–22.
Judge, Paramjit. 1993. *Punjabis in Canada: A Study of Formation of an Ethnic Community*. Delhi: Chanakya.
Juergensmeyer, Mark. 1979. "The Forgotten Tradition: Sikhism in the Study of World Religions." In *Sikh Studies: Comparative Perspectives on a Changing Tradition*, ed. Mark Juergensmeyer and N. Gerald Barrier, 13–23. Berkeley, CA: Berkeley Religious Studies Series.
– 2000. *Terror in the Mind of God: The Global Rise of Religious Violence*. Berkeley: University of California Press.
– 2012. "Christian Terrorism Comes to Milwaukee." *Religion Dispatches*, 6 August. http://www.religiondispatches.org/dispatches/guest_blog

gers/6263/christian_terrorism_comes_to_milwaukee/ (accessed August 10, 2012).

Kalsi, Seva Singh. 1995. "Problems of Defining Authority in Sikhism." *DISKUS* 3 (2): 43–58. http://www.basr.ac.uk/diskus/diskus1-6/KALSI3_2.TXT (accessed 8 July 2011).

Kang, Neelu. 2006. "Women Activists in Indian Diaspora: Making Interventions and Challenging Impediments." *South Asia Research* 26 (2): 145–64.

Katrak, Ketutt. 2002. "Changing Traditions: South Asian Americans and Cultural/Communal Politics." *Massachusetts Review* 43 (1): 75–88.

Kaur, Valerie. 2012. "U.S. Military, Open Your Doors to Sikhs." *Washington Post*, Guest Voices, 8 August, http://www.faithstreet.com/onfaith/2012/08/08/us-military-open-your-doors-to-sikhs/11450 (accessed 10 August 2012).

Kaur, Valerie, and Simran Jeet Singh. 2012. "Two Sikh Americans: Let's Retire 'Mistaken Identity.'" *Washington Post*, Guest Voices, 8 August. http://www.faithstreet.com/onfaith/2012/08/10/two-sikh-american-activists-lets-retire-mistaken-identity/10590 (accessed 13 August 2012).

Lal, Madan. 2009. "Gurudom: The Political Dimension of Religious Sects in the Punjab." *South Asia Research* 29 (3): 223–34.

Lum, Kathryn. 2009. "A Minority within a Minority: The Ravidassia Sikhs, Sikhs in Europe Network." http://www.sikhs-in-europe.org/index.php?option=com_docman&task=cat_view&gid=38&Itemid=60 (accessed 29 November 2010).

– 2010. "The Ravidassia Community and Identity(ies) in Catalonia, Spain." *Sikh Formations* 6 (1): 31–50.

– 2011. "Caste, Religion and Community Assertion: A Case Study of the Ravidasias in Spain." In *Sikhs in Europe: Migration, Identities and Representation*, ed. Knut A. Jacobsen and Kristina Myrvold, 179–200. Farnham, Surrey: Ashgate.

MacNair, Adrian. 2010. "Sikh Genocide Petition Has No Place in Canada." *National Post*, 10 June. http://fullcomment.nationalpost.com/2010/06/10/sikh-genocide-petition-has-no-place-in-canada/ (accessed 17 April 2011).

Mahmood, Cynthia Keppley. 1996. *Fighting for Faith and Nation: Dialogues with Sikh Militants*. Series in Contemporary Ethnography. Philadelphia: University of Pennsylvania Press.

– 2005. "Sikhs in Canada: Identity and Commitment." In *Religion and Ethnicity in Canada*, ed. P. Bramadat and D. Seljak, 52–68. Toronto: Pearson Education Canada.

Major, Honourable John C. 2010. "Air India Flight 182: A Canadian Tragedy." Report of the Commission of Inquiry into the investigation of the bombing of Air India Flight 182. Ottawa: Ministry of Public Works and Government

Services. http://epe.lac-bac.gc.ca/100/206/301/pco-bcp/commissions/
air_india/2010-07-23/www.majorcomm.ca/en/reports/finalreport/
default.htm (accessed 9 January 2010).

Mann, G.S. 2001. "Sikhism in the United States of America." In *The South Asian Religious Diaspora in Britain, Canada and the U.S.A.*, ed. Harold Coward, John R. Hinnells, and Raymond Brady Williams, 259–76. Albany: SUNY Press.

McLeod, H. 1997. *Sikhism*. London: Penguin.

McLeod, W.H. 1989. "The First Forty Years of Sikh Migration: Problems and Possible Solutions." In *The Sikh Diaspora: Migration and Experience beyond Punjab*, ed. N.G. Barrier and V. Dusenbury, 29–48. Columbia, MO: South Asia Books.

Mehta, Pratap Bhanu. 2009. "Monopoly Religion." *Indianexpress.com*, 26 May. http://archive.indianexpress.com/news/monopoly-religion/466059/0 (accessed 10 June 2010).

Milewski, Terry. 2007. "Sikh Politics in Canada: World Sikh Organization." 28 June. http://archive.today/CjIpC (accessed 11 April 2010).

Minahan, James, and Peter Wendel. 2002. "Sikhs." In *Encyclopedia of the Stateless Nations: Ethnic and National Groups around the World*, vol. 4, S–Z, 1720–6. Westport, CT: Greenwood.

Moliner, Christine. 2007. "*Frères ennemis*? Relations between Panjabi Sikhs and Muslims in the Diaspora." *South Asia Multidisciplinary Academic Journal* 1: 1–16. http://samaj.revues.org/135 (accessed 19 August 2011).

Mooney, Nicola. 2010. "Lowly Shoes on Lowly Feet: Some Jat Sikh Women's Views on Gender and Equality." In *Sikhism and Women: History, Texts and Experience*, ed. Doris R. Jakobsh, 152–82. Delhi: Oxford University Press.

Nayar, Kamala E. 2004. *The Sikh Diaspora in Vancouver: Three Generations amid Tradition, Modernity and Multiculturalism*. Toronto: University of Toronto Press.

Oberoi, Harjot. 1994. *The Construction of Religious Boundaries: Culture, Identity and Diversity in the Sikh Tradition*. Delhi: Oxford University Press.

Parent, Richard B., and James O. Ellis. 2011. "Countering Radicalization of Diaspora Communities in Canada." Centre of Excellence for Research on Immigration and Diversity working paper series 11–12. Vancouver: Metropolis British Columbia. http://mbc.metropolis.net/assets/uploads/files/wp/2011/WP11-12.pdf (accessed 3 January 2012).

Pettigrew, Joyce. 1975. *Robber Noblemen: A Study of the Political System of Sikh Jats*. London: Routledge and Kegan Paul.

Pluralism Project. n.d. "Discrimination and National Security Initiative: Project Description." http://www.pluralism.org/affiliates/kaur_sidhu/index.php (accessed 15 November 2011).

Puar, Jasbir K., and Amit S. Rai. 2004. "The Remaking of a Model Minority: Perverse Projectiles under the Specter of (Counter) Terrorism." *Social Text* 22 (3): 75–104.

R. v. Malik and Bagri. 2005. "British Columbia Supreme Court 350, Docket CC010287." http://www.courts.gov.bc.ca/Jdb-txt/SC/05/03/2005BCSC0350.htm (accessed 9 January 2012).

Rai, Jasdev. 2011. "Khalistan Is Dead! Long Live Khalistan!" *Sikh Formations* 7 (1): 1–41.

Rait, Satwant Kaur. 2005. *Sikh Women in England: Their Religious and Cultural Beliefs and Social Practices*. Stoke on Trent, UK, and Sterling, NY: Trentham Books.

Razavy, Maryam. 2006. "Sikh Militant Movements in Canada." *Terrorism and Political Violence* 18 (1): 79–93.

Right to Turban. n.d. "United Sikhs: Recognize the Human Race as One." http://www.unitedsikhs.org/rtt/ (accessed 9 September 2011).

Robertson, R. 1992. *Globalization: Social Theory and Global Culture*. London: Sage.

– 1995. "Glocalization: Time-space and Homogeneity-heterogeneity." In *Global Modernities*, ed. M. Featherstone, S. Lash, and R. Robertson, 25–44. London: Sage.

Rootsgear. 2012. "We Are All Sikhs." http://www.rootsgear.com/product.php?p=407 (accessed 1 October 2012).

Roy, Angali Gera. 2008. "Rethinking Diaspora." *Transforming Cultures Ejournal* 3 (1): 1–25. http://epress.lib.uts.edu.au/journals/index.php/TfC/article/view/672/601 (accessed 21 August 2011).

Sangra, Baljit. 2008. *Warrior Boyz*. Documentary film. Toronto: National Film Board of Canada.

Sarin, Vic. 2006. *Murder Unveiled*. Documentary film. Force Four Entertainment Inc., first aired by Canadian Broadcasting Corporation's *The Fifth Estate*, 6 February 2006.

Séguin, Rhéal. 2011. "Invited to Quebec Legislature, Sikhs then Barred for Carrying Kirpans." *Globe and Mail*, 18 January. http://www.theglobeandmail.com/news/politics/invited-to-quebec-legislature-sikhs-then-barred-for-carrying-kirpans/article1874725/ (accessed 5 March 2012).

Sen, Rinku. 2012. "Not Senseless, Not Random: The Deadly Mix of Race, Guns & Madness." *Colorlines: News for Action*, 6 August. http://colorlines.com/archives/2012/08/how_long_before_islamophobias_toxic_spread_destroys_america.html (accessed 12 September 2012).

Shani, Giorgio. 2008. *Sikh Nationalism and Identity in a Global Age*. London: Routledge.

– 2011. "Securitizing 'Bare Life': Critical Perspectives on Human Security Discourse." In *Critical Perspectives on Human Security: Rethinking Emancipation and Power in International Relations*, ed. David Chandler and Nik Hynek, 56–68. New York: Routledge.

Sian, Katy. n.d. "Forced Conversions within the British Sikh Diaspora." Unpublished paper, Centre for Ethnicity and Racism Studies (CERS), School of Sociology and Social Policy, University of Leeds. http://www.sociology.leeds.ac.uk/assets/files/research/cers/final%20cers%20working%20paper%20katy.pdf (accessed 29 August 2011).

– 2011. "Understanding Inter-Brasian Conflict: Sikhs and Muslims in the Diaspora." *Sikh Formations: Religion, Culture, Theory* 7 (2): 111–30.

Sikh Coalition. 2014. "One Step Forward. Half a Step Back." http://sikhcoalition.org/images/documents/onestepforward_bullying_report.pdf.

Silke, Andrew. 2008. "Holy Warriors: Exploring the Psychological Processes of Jihadi Radicalization." *European Journal of Criminology* 5 (1): 99–123.

Sin, Lena. 2008. "Sikh Assassins of Gandhi Defended as 'Martyrs.'" *Vancouver Province*, 12 April. http://www2.canada.com/topics/news/national/story.html?id=1c98a96b-08ce-40c4-ac62-257df4e41399&k=45712 (accessed 2 July 2011).

Singh, Amardeep. 2012. "Beyond Recognition and Misrecognition: The Shooting at Oak Creek Gurdwara." 5 August. http://www.electrostani.com/2012/08/on-recognition-and-misrecognition.html (accessed 12 August 2012).

Singh, Amrik. 2012. "Sikh Americans Decry American Flag Burning in India and Demand Apology." *Examiner.com*, 11 August. http://www.examiner.com/article/sikh-americans-decry-american-flag-burning-india-and-demand-apology (accessed 2 October 2012).

Singh, Gurharpal. 2004. "Sikhs Are the Real Losers from Behzti." *Guardian*, 24 December. http://www.theguardian.com/stage/2004/dec/24/theatre.religion (accessed 19 February 2007).

– 2010. "The Adab – 'Respect' Research Programme: A Perspective on Muslim-Sikh Relations in the United Kingdom and Causes of Tensions and Mistrust between the Two Communities." *Faith Matters*. http://turbancampaign.com/resources/muslimsikh_relations.pdf (accessed 8 July 2011).

Singh, Gurharpal, and Darshan Singh Tatla. 2006. *Sikhs in Britain: The Making of a Community*. London: Zed Books.

Singh, Gurmukh. 2009. "Dalits in Canada Call Vienna Killing 'Act of Terrorism.'" *Thaindian News*, 25 May. http://www.thaindian.com/newsportal/world-news/dalits-in-canada-call-vienna-killing-act-of-terrorism_100196938.html (accessed 13 August 2011).

- 2010. "Sikh Violence Wanes in Punjab, Grows in Canada." *National Post*, 7 May. http://fullcomment.nationalpost.com/2010/05/06/gurmukh-singh-sikh-violence-wanes-in-punjab-grows-in-canada/ (accessed 9 June 2010).

Singh, Gurpreet. 2008. "Sikh Moderates Must Unite to Overcome Religious Fundamentalism." *Georgia Straight*, 18 December. http://www.straight.com/news/sikh-moderates-must-unite-overcome-religious-fundamentalism (accessed 5 February 2009).

- 2011a. "In Solidarity with the Air India Victims." *Georgia Straight*, 26 June. http://www.straight.com/news/gurpreet-singh-solidarity-air-india-victims (accessed 22 November 2011).

- 2011b. "Community Split on Resolution Banning Non-baptized Sikhs from Running Guru Nanak Temple." *Georgia Straight*, 12 July. http://www.straight.com/news/gurpreet-singh-community-split-resolution-banning-nonbaptized-sikhs-running-guru-nanak-temple (accessed 22 November 2011).

Singh, Hainder. 2012. "Allow Sikhs to Wear Turban, Beard in NY Police Department." *Sikh Siysat Network*, 12 August. http://www.sikhsiyasat.net/2012/08/12/allow-sikhs-to-wear-turban-beard-in-ny-police-department/ (accessed 21 August 2012).

Singh, I.J. 2012. "Wisconsin Killings: Threatening Clouds, Silver Linings." *Huffington Post*, 29 September. http://www.huffingtonpost.com/ij-singh/ (accessed 2 October 2012).

Singh, Indera Pal. 1977. "Caste in a Sikh Village." In *Caste among Non-Hindus in India*, ed. Harjinder Singh, 66–83. Delhi: National Publishing House.

Singh, Jagmohan. 2010. "Former Jathedar of Akal Takht Excommunicated from Sikh Community." *Punjab Newsline Network*, 29 January. http://www.sikhnet.com/discussion/viewtopic.php?f=2&t=3316 (accessed 1 September 2011).

Singh, Jaideep. 2003. "The Racialization of Minoritized Religious Identity: Constructing Sacred Sites at the Intersection of White and Christian Supremacy." In *Revealing the Sacred in Asian and Pacific America*, ed. Jane Naomi Iwamura and Paul Spickard, 87–106. New York: Routledge.

Singh, Khushwant. 2009. "Religious Bias against Sikhs Rising, Claims Group." *Times of India*, 17 September. http://timesofindia.indiatimes.com/news/world/indians-abroad/Religious-bias-against-Sikhs-rising-claims-group/articleshow/5019796.cms (accessed 17 January 2012).

Singh, Madhur. 2009. "Austrian Murder Sparks Protests in India." *TIME*, 26 May. http://content.time.com/time/world/article/0,8599,1900882,00.html (accessed 14 November 2010).

Singh, Naunihal. 2012. "An American Tragedy." *New Yorker*, 13 August. http://www.newyorker.com/online/blogs/newsdesk/2012/08/an-american-tragedy.html (accessed 15 August 2012).

Singh, Pashaura. 1990. "Sikh Traditions in Ontario." *Polyphony: Bulletin of the Multicultural History Society of Ontario* 12: 130–6. http://www.tgmag.ca/magic/mt36.html (accessed 1 September 2011).

Singh, T. Sher. 2007. "The Gift." *Sikhchic.com*, 3 June. http://www.sikhchic.com/article-detail.php?cat=4&id=217 (accessed 2 September 2011).

Smith, Leslie E. 2008. "What's in a Name? Scholarship and the Pathology of Conservative Protestantism." *Method and Theory in the Study of Religion* 20 (3): 191–211.

Smith, Wilfred Cantwell. 1981. *Towards a World Theology: Faith and the Comparative History of Religions*. London: Macmillan.

Statistics Canada. 2001. "Population by Religion, by Province and Territory, 2001 Census." http://www.statcan.gc.ca/tables-tableaux/sum-som/l01/cst01/demo30a-eng.htm (accessed 4 January 2012).

Statistics Canada. 2010. "Projections of the Diversity of the Canadian Population, 2006–2031." http://www.statcan.gc.ca/pub/91-551-x/91-551-x2010001-eng.pdf (accessed 4 January 2012).

Stromer, Mark. 2006. "Combating Hate Crimes against Sikhs: A Multi-tentacled Approach." *Journal of Gender, Race & Justice* 9 (3): 739–66.

Stulz, R.M., and R. Williamson. 2001. "Culture, Openness, and Finance." Dice Center working paper no. 2001–02. http://papers.ssrn.com/sol3/papers.cfm?abstract_id=263507 (accessed 9 April 2012).

Takhar, O.K. 2005. *Sikh Identity: An Exploration of Groups among Sikhs*. Aldershot, Hampshire: Ashgate.

Taylor, Charles. 1994. "The Politics of Recognition." In *Multiculturalism: Examining the Politics of Recognition*, ed. A. Gutman, 25–74. Princeton, NJ: Princeton University Press.

Toor, Sunita. 2009. "British Asian Girls, Crime and Youth Justice." *Youth Justice* 9 (3): 239–53.

Tully, Mark. 1986. *Amritsar: Mrs. Gandhi's Last Battle*. London: Jonathan Cape.

Verma, Archana B. 2002. *The Making of Little Punjab in Canada: Patterns of Immigration*. Delhi: Sage.

Verma, Rita. 2011. "Making Meaning of 1984 in Cyberspace: Youth Answering Back to Reclaim Sikh Identity and Nationhood." *Sikh Formations* 7 (1): 43–56.

Vision TV. 2007. "The Heretics: Cast Out of the Temple – Gurbaksh Singh Kala Afghana." *360 Vision*, 9 May.

Wason, Anjali. 2005. "A Matter of Words." *Samar: South Asian Magazine for Action and Reflection* 19. http://samarmagazine.org/archive/articles/184 (accessed 6 August 2010).

Williams, Matthias. 2009. "Is Caste Behind the Killing in Vienna and Riots in Punjab?" *India Insight*, 26 May. http://blogs.reuters.com/india/

2009/05/26/is-caste-behind-the-killing-in-vienna-and-riots-in-punjab/ (accessed 3 January 2012).

World Sikh Organization of Canada. 2008. "Caste Concerns in Cremation Grounds – Totally Contrary to Sikh Teachings." 13 June. http://www. worldsikh.ca/news-release/caste-concerns-cremation-grounds-totally-contrary-sikh-teachings (accessed 11 October 2011).

Young, Iris Marion. 1990. *Justice and the Politics of Difference*. Princeton, NJ: Princeton University Press.

Zubaida, Sami. 1995. "Is There a Muslim Society? Ernest Gellner's Sociology of Islam." *Economy and Society* 24 (2): 151–88.

8 Religion, Politics, and Tamil Militancy in Sri Lanka and the Diaspora

AMARNATH AMARASINGAM

As the civil war raged in Sri Lanka (1983–2009), the Canadian government became increasingly concerned about the presence of radical elements in the large Sri Lankan Tamil community in Canada. The concern was largely justified, given that the Liberation Tigers of Tamil Eelam (LTTE), declared a terrorist organization by Canada in 2006, was very active in the diaspora in Canada and elsewhere in the world. Under the cover of a series of organizations (e.g., the World Tamil Movement), the LTTE had been raising funds and other kinds of support for their war effort for some years. As Bell (2004, 27) noted during the war, "When it comes to fundraising, the Tamil Tigers are unrivalled. They have used every conceivable tactic – government grants, front companies, fraud of every type, migrant smuggling and drugs." According to successive CSIS reports, the LTTE received anywhere between $1 million per month to $2 million per year from the Canadian Tamil diaspora (Bell 2004, 27; see also Hoffman et al. 2007) which, according to recent census figures and community estimates, numbers between 150,000 and 200,000 people. Diaspora leaders also have been accused of engaging in sophisticated propaganda campaigns, the radicalization of youth in the community, and political lobbying for the Tigers. The international propaganda war conducted by the LTTE, Chalk (1999) observed, was far more sophisticated than any counter-campaign the government in Colombo, Sri Lanka, was able to organize (see Purdy 2003 as well).

Tamil immigrants have largely adapted well to their new and distant home in Canada, yet many in the diaspora community remain deeply invested in the fate of their relatives and friends in Sri Lanka. Since, as Purdy (2003) noted, "most terrorism-related activity in Canada are extensions of foreign conflicts," diaspora groups, the Tamils included, have increasingly come under the scrutiny of Canadian security agencies. According to Hoffman and colleagues (2007, 1–2), diaspora groups are worrisome for six reasons: (1) there is a real fear that members of diaspora communities will launch violent attacks against host countries; (2) a lack of host-country integration may make individuals vulnerable to terrorist recruitment; (3) diaspora groups have been effective fundraisers for terrorist organizations; (4) diasporas facilitate the procurement of weapons; (5) host states provide opportunities for propaganda campaigns that are impossible in native countries; and (6) diaspora groups can effectively lobby their governments to put pressure on the government of their native country. All of these concerns undoubtedly led the Canadian government to prioritize keeping a close eye on developments in the Canadian Sri Lankan Tamil diaspora, though it should be noted that Hoffman's fifth and sixth points deal with activities that fall within the accepted parameters of behaviour in most liberal democracies (see, for example, Keck and Sikkink 1998).

Worries about this diaspora community were heightened by a number of additional factors. First and foremost, at the broadest level there is the long association between ethno-religious conflicts and intractable violence, and often more specifically terrorist campaigns. Public perceptions are shaped by what happened in Northern Ireland, Bosnia, Malaysia, Nigeria, Pakistan, Iraq, the Israeli-Palestinian conflict, and elsewhere. The alignment of religion with other significant differences seems to magnify and aggravate the levels of hostility involved in conflicts and perhaps also the ferocity of the carnage. The fearful legacy of the long and bloody wars of religion that ravaged Europe in the wake of the Protestant Reformation continues to inform Western worries on this count. Second, these very worries seemed to be justified by the current threat posed by the worldwide campaign of terrorism unleashed by Salafi-jihadist groups inspired by al-Qaeda. Third, and more specifically, worries about the Sri Lankan Tamil diaspora in Canada were heightened by the emergence of home-grown Muslim radicalization, resulting in the bombings in Madrid and London, and the numerous arrests made for plots to perpetrate violent acts elsewhere, including the Toronto 18 plot in Canada in 2006 (see Dawson, chapter 3 this volume). Fourth, specific concerns about the Canadian Sri Lankan Tamil diaspora were increased by the escalating violence and desperation evident in the dying days of the conflict in Sri Lanka in 2009 and by the extended and surprisingly successful demonstrations launched in Canada and around the world by members of the Tamil diaspora. The fear was that the pattern of home-grown radicalization in "defence of Islam" would be replicated in the Tamil community, especially given the past proclivity of the LTTE to use terrorist tactics such as suicide bombings (Swamy 1994; Bloom 2007) and the mounting urgency of their plight as the Sri Lankan armed forces closed in on areas under their control. Various elements of the 2009 demonstrations, especially in Toronto, were worrisome in this regard: the presence of the LTTE flags, portraits of the charismatic LTTE leader Velupillai Prabhakaran, and the blockade of the Gardiner Expressway.

However, apart from a few arrests of individuals involved in funnelling funds and arms to the LTTE (e.g., Suresh Sriskandarajah and Ramanan Mylvaganam), no significant element of the Tamil community appears to have radicalized to violence as feared. Rather, with the defeat of the LTTE, the Tamil diaspora is no longer solely mobilized to provide financial support to the separatist conflict in Sri Lanka. In general, through continued demonstrations, newly formed organizations like the Transnational Government of Tamil Eelam (TGTE), and changes in individual identity, members of the Tamil diaspora are adopting new strategies aimed at disassociating Tamil nationalism from the LTTE, rebranding it in the language of human rights, and marketing it as a transnational sociopolitical movement.

In this chapter I provide an account for the discrepancy between the worries and the realities of the situation by clarifying two points. The first is simply that despite the fairly uniform religious differences of the conflicting parties in the Sri Lankan civil war, the Buddhist Sinhalese versus the largely Hindu Tamils, religion was not a prime motivator of violence, at least not on the part of the Tamils. This point is fairly well known to those who have studied the Sri Lankan conflict, but it is easily overlooked or misunderstood by others. The second is that there is some evidence that the militancy of Sri Lankan Tamil youth in Canada has been blunted by their fairly pervasive adoption of non-traditional forms of religiosity, namely the loose forms of new spirituality so characteristic of many other North American youth. Contrary then to popular conception, even among academics and government officials, the role of religion in this conflict is both less consequential than commonly thought and yet more consequential, in unanticipated ways, in determining the degree and type of radicalization present in the Sri Lankan Tamil diaspora in Canada.

The violent struggle in Sri Lanka is often misread as yet another instance of an ethno-religious conflict, similar to the strife in Northern

Ireland. Consequently, the potential for radicalization in the Canadian Tamil diaspora is often framed in terms of our existing and dominant conceptions of the role of religion in immigrant communities. Traditional religious beliefs, practices, and commitments often intensify in immigrant communities, at least for a generation or two, in response to the identity and resettlement needs of the community (see, e.g., Ebaugh and Chafetz 2000). Religion often operates as a social anchor and means of sustaining one's culture in a foreign and sometimes hostile host society (Min 2010; Williams 1988). This is especially the case for refugee communities (McLellan 1999), where people have been compelled to flee their native lands. Under these circumstances religious identity is often at the core of the ongoing sense of solidarity of refugees with compatriots in their country of origin, especially if religious differences factored significantly into the persecution of their people in the homelands (e.g., the solidarity many Muslims feel with the Palestinian cause or their co-religionists in Bosnia and Chechnya). But religion was not a key identity marker and source of radicalization and violence in this particular case, and as far as the children of the Sri Lankan Tamil immigrants are concerned, traditional religious commitments have not played a significant role in their adaptation to Canadian society or continued support for their cause in Sri Lanka. However, I argue that there may be a noteworthy correlation between the assimilation of young Tamils to the broader patterns of new spirituality and universalism in the West (and hence moving away from and not closer to traditional patterns of religiosity) and the preference for casting off militancy in favour of a new transnational social movement to promote and protect the interests of the Tamil population in Sri Lanka.

To this end, I will examine the role of religion in (1) the origins of the civil war in Sri Lanka; (2) the self-conception of the LTTE; and (3) the lives of Tamil youth and young adults in Canada. In so doing, I demonstrate that there is a strong historical link between politics and religion in Sri Lanka, but that linkage is exclusive to the Sinhalese, whose leaders promoted the convergence of Buddhist revivalism and Sinhalese nationalism. This merger of religion and ethnicity, however, was not replicated by most Tamil nationalist/militant movements in Sri Lanka, who were largely Hindu. The Tamils were united, often in opposition to the Sinhala nationalists, by their shared language and culture and not Hinduism per se. These discussions are of necessity brief, and my argument with respect to the Tamil diaspora in Canada is still rather conjectural. But the analysis is anchored in a larger study of post-war diaspora politics in the Sri Lankan Tamil community in Canada. The study is the first of its kind, entailing interviews with over 130 people, primarily youth but also organizational leaders, law enforcement officials, and NGO workers (Amarasingam 2013).

Religion, Ethnicity, and Politics in Sri Lanka

The close proximity of Sri Lanka to India has meant that Indian religious, cultural, and social influences have always been significant. But this Indian influence should not be exaggerated, as the Palk Strait also provided the country with "some isolation from the vagaries of Indian politics" (de Silva 1997, 9). Sri Lanka has a population of approximately 20.3 million people, according to the 2012 island-wide Sri Lankan census (the first since 1981), and this population is fairly diverse, ethnically and religiously. According to the 2012 census, the majority ethnic group in Sri Lanka are the Sinhala (75 per cent), the vast majority of whom (around 90 per cent) are Buddhist. The Tamil community in Sri Lanka, roughly 15 per cent of the total population, consists of Sri Lankan Tamils (11.2 per cent of the total population) and Indian Tamils (4.2 per cent). The vast majority of the Tamil population in Sri Lanka is Hindu (around 80 per cent), but there are a significant number of Christians. The Moors of Sri Lanka (Muslims) are also an important ethnic group and make up about 9 per cent of the population. They are called Moors not because they have any direct connection to the people of North Africa but because the "Portuguese gave this name to all the Islamic communities they encountered on the Indian Ocean littoral" (de Silva 1997, 3–5). The smaller ethnic groups (1 per cent in total) consist of the Burghers (descendants of European settlers), the Malays (descendants of settlers from the Malay Peninsula, arriving during the Dutch and British colonial period), and the Veddas (the indigenous peoples of Sri Lanka).

In addition to Indian influence, for over 400 years, all or parts of Sri Lanka fell under the control of successive European powers: the Portuguese (1505–1658), the Dutch (1658–1796), and the British (1796–1948). For our purposes, the British colonial period is most significant in providing a context for the Hindu and Buddhist revivals of the nineteenth century. Indeed, as de Silva (1997, 198) notes, "the Buddhist revival is perhaps better described as the Buddhist reaction to the missionary onslaught." However, while the Buddhist revivals of the nineteenth and twentieth centuries were characterized by a kind of fusion of religious and ethnic identity, the Hindu revival cannot be seen in the same light. As Tamil militancy arose after independence in 1948, it largely took on a secular quality. Although Buddhism played an important role in Sinhala nationalism in the twentieth century, it often *manifested itself* in secular policies as well. In other words, Sinhala nationalism, while intimately tied to Buddhism (see the later discussion), was often put into practice through land colonization, language legislation, and educational policies which were discriminatory. Although these policies could indeed have produced a religious response from the island's (largely Hindu) Tamil population, this did not occur, and the Tamil nationalist response, particularly in its turn to militancy, was largely secular.

It goes without saying that Tamil and Sinhala nationalisms are deeply wound up in the history of Sri Lanka. The Buddhist revivalists of the late nineteenth and early twentieth centuries were convinced that they were recovering a lost ideal from the Anuradhapura period.[1] However, many scholars note that this "lost ideal" likely never existed. Tamil nationalists, for their part, were equally adamant that "Dravidians"[2] had established settlements in Sri Lanka long before the Sinhala. While scholarly discussions continue about the exact nature of ancient Sri Lanka, there seems to be some consensus that both the Sinhala and Tamil versions of the past are modern inventions (Indrapala 2007). In other words, part of the nationalist thrust has been to paint historical figures as precursors to contemporary nationalist sentiments and movements.

The nineteenth and twentieth centuries in Sri Lanka brought on successive waves of Hindu and Buddhist revivals. The central figure of the Hindu revival was the Tamil literary scholar Arumuka Navalar (1822–79), who spent several decades seeking to recover the teachings of Saiva Siddhantam (the Tamil school of Saivism) (Ambalavanar 2006). Navalar wanted to reduce the "alien" cultural and religious domination of Christians on the island, and as Little (1994, 41) notes, his "remarkable achievements were all motivated by a passion to break the missionary monopoly over the schools in the Tamil area." An important aspect of Navalar's campaign was the absence of hostility towards the Sinhala people or the Buddhist faith. Navalar did not link Hinduism with Tamil ethnic identity. Later biographers interpreted his "advocacy of social reform, 'as aspirations to national or political awakening and leadership,' as rejection of British and colonial rule, and an incipient national leadership for Eelam." However, Hellmann-Rajanayagam argues, "nothing could be further from the truth" (1989, 249).

While Navalar's religious revival neither evinced enmity towards Sinhala populations nor strongly linked itself with an ethnic identity, the same cannot be said for the Buddhist revival of the nineteenth century. According to the Sinhala, the *Mahavamsa*, a historical poem about the great kings of Sir Lanka compiled in about the fifth century, testifies to the fact that they were the original inhabitants of the island, and much attention is paid to the account of one monarch in particular, Dutthagamini. His story encourages the view that the Sinhala and Tamil people are long-standing enemies (DeVotta 2004, 26), and it centres on his defeat of the Chola king, Elara,[3] who ruled Sri Lanka from the ancient capital of Anuradhapura. In the account, Dutthagamini is not at peace with himself following the brutal defeat of the Chola king, and eight arahants are sent to provide comfort and ease his mental anguish. They do so by convincing him that he went to war "not for personal glory but for the sake of the Buddhist religion" (Kent 2008, 19–20). In other words, the point of the story, as Grant (2009, 48) notes, is that the "overthrow of the Tamil king is required first and foremost because Sri Lanka cannot be united unless the monarch is Buddhist." For many contemporary Sinhala nationalists then, the Dutthagamini epic is not a thing of the past. Modern activist bhikkhus have uncritically called on the story of Dutthagamini to justify their actions, and so as Grant (2009, 49–50) makes clear, "the ghost of Dutthagamini has lived on, reclothed in modern dress – and now also equipped with modern weapons."

An important later figure in the Sinhala-Buddhist revival was Anagarika Dharmapala (1864–1933). He was a fierce opponent of colonialism and sought to articulate the deep-seated fears of the Sinhala population. Dharmapala looked to the *Mahavamsa* to confirm the intimate and historical relationship between the Sinhalese people and Buddhism. His writings are a mixture of ethnic supremacism, anti-colonialism, and Buddhist glorification. Given historical realities, his anti-colonial tirades may be justified. However, as DeVotta (2004, 31–2) points out, "his rhetoric, whether intended to do so or not, legitimated extremism and helped catalyze the chauvinism that followed. It was jingoist and exclusivist and showed no regard or tolerance for non-Buddhists."

Walpola Rahula (1907–97) also had a significant influence on Sinhala-Buddhist nationalism in the early twentieth century. Rahula was an internationally respected scholar of Buddhism, but his book *The Heritage of the Bhikku* (1946) was a "virtual manifesto for Sinhala Buddhist nationalism, linking the identity of the Sinhalas with the land and religion, and declaring a willingness to resort to violence to defend the Sinhala interest" (Grant 2009, 81). He argued that prior to colonization the Sangha was revered and socially engaged. Under the British, they had lost much of their social influence and had become reclusive, a plight that can only be corrected by gaining independence from colonial rule (Seneviratne 1999, 168–88). Rahula (1974, 95) was also highly critical of Sinhala, who, having internalized a Western notion of private religion, thought that bhikkhus should stay out of politics.

While the intellectual groundwork had been laid for Sinhala-Buddhist majoritarianism, its full consequences would not be felt until after independence in 1948. During the colonial period, American missionaries had instituted an excellent education system in the north of Sri Lanka through which many Tamils had become literate in English. Indeed, whereas many Sri Lankans learned English in order to compete for elite jobs, those not fluent in English found economic opportunities largely out of their reach (DeVotta 2004, 43–4). Such proficiency in English had placed the Tamils in a particularly advantageous position in relation to Sinhala populations. In 1946, for example, Sri Lankan Tamils made up only 11 per cent of the total population (de Silva 1997, 4). However, they made up 33 per cent of the civil service, 40 per cent of the judicial service, and 31 per cent of university students (DeVotta 2004, 46–7). Such developments help to make clear why Sinhala nationalism manifested itself in secular ways, even as it was closely tied to Buddhist revivalism.

Ethnic tensions were on the rise by the mid-twentieth century. With its profound defeat in the 1952 election, the Sri Lanka Freedom Party (SLFP), under S.W.R.D. Bandaranaike, became determined to take power in the 1956 election. He brought to the 1956 election an intimate understanding of the political usefulness of communal tensions. As Richardson (2005, 144) points out, Bandaranaike "discovered that appeals on behalf of Sinhalese language, religion, culture and interests caught the imagination of people who had been previously apathetic." Bandaranaike declared that the 1948 independence of Sri Lanka from Britain was not yet complete. The issue of language was one of the most important heading into the election. Following independence, it was assumed that Sinhala and Tamil would be given equal significance as the language of administration in a united Sri Lanka. However, Bandaranaike stated that, if the SLFP were elected, only Sinhala would be given official status. As Ross and Savada (1988) note, "Bandaranaike introduced a dangerous emotionalism into the election with his 'Sinhala only' platform, which labelled both Tamil and English as cultural imports."

The year 1956 was significant for two other reasons as well: first, it was the year of the Buddha Jayanti, the 2,500th anniversary of Buddha's entry into *parinibbana* (complete enlightenment, or final nirvana). As the Buddha is thought to have prophesied that his *dhamma* would endure for 5,000 years, it was believed that at this midpoint, Buddhism would undergo a remarkable period of renewal. The event, celebrated in May 1956, further solidified the bond between Sinhala nationalist and religious identities. Second, the Buddhist Committee of the Enquiry, established by the All Ceylon Buddhist Congress, published *The Betrayal of Buddhism*, arguing that Buddhism needed to be restored to its rightful place. The report asserted not only that Buddhism suffered greatly under British rule but also that little had changed with independence.

With Bandaranaike's election victory in 1956, it was clear to many observers that the conversation the country was having about itself was changing in tone and character. As Bond (1988, 90) points out, the election of Bandaranaike "established a link between the government and the Buddhist religion that has been essential to the political and religious history of Sri Lanka since that time." It was also evident that Bandaranaike's opportunism would backfire. In Bandaranaike's estimation, the fires of Sinhala and Tamil emotion could be stoked and snuffed out at will. He reasoned that Sinhala passions would be abated following the passage of Sinhala-only legislation. Once things had calmed, he could then seek to appease the Tamil population. It would prove to be a profound misreading of the political climate.

Shortly after the election victory, Bandaranaike proposed the Official Language Act, which declared Sinhala to be the only official language in Sri Lanka. It would become a long-running symbol of Sinhala nationalism and would solidify in the minds of many that the Sinhala leadership could not be trusted to uphold the rights of minority populations (DeVotta 2002, 2004, 2005). There was immediate backlash to the Language Act by Sri Lankan Tamils, represented by the Federal Party, who argued that the legislation placed their language, culture, and economic position in jeopardy. The Federal Party launched a *satyagraha* (non-violent protest)[4] beginning in June 1956, when around 200 Tamils assembled on Galle Face Green across from Parliament and were soon attacked by Sinhala protesters, who beat and pelted them with stones, wounding and hospitalizing many.

Bandaranaike, perhaps a little taken aback by the violence, spoke to the Sinhala crowd outside Parliament, telling them, "I will give you the Sinhalese language. Give me one thing. Co-operate with me and go home peacefully" (quoted in DeVotta 2004, 83). After the assassination of Bandaranaike in 1959 by a Buddhist monk,[5] his widow, Sirimavo Ratwatte Dias Bandaranaike, carried forward much of her husband's policies and aggressively enforced the Sinhala-only act. What made matters worse was a government policy to hire Sinhala into government service (see Table 8.1). While ethnic tensions continued to simmer, it is also important to remember that Tamil militancy was non-existent throughout the 1950s and 1960s. In May 1972, Bandaranaike and the United Front used their overwhelming majority to introduce a new constitution. The new constitution made the country a republic, officially changed the name of the island from Ceylon to Sri Lanka, declared Sri Lanka to be a "Unitary State," gave Buddhism a "foremost place" in the country, and made it the state's duty to "protect and foster Buddhism." In the very same month that the constitution was passed, the Federal Party, the Tamil Congress, and the Ceylon Workers' Congress formed the Tamil United Front (TUF).

Perhaps the single most important issue which aggravated ethnic tensions, leading many Tamil youth to throw their support behind militant movements, was the matter of university admissions (de Silva 1998, 130–2). In the 1960s, students were educated in one of three language streams: Sinhala, Tamil, or English. There existed, then, three different sets of entrance exams, which would be evaluated by three sets of examiners. In the late 1970s, critics alleged (but it was later shown to be baseless) that Tamil students benefited from the favouritism of the Tamil-language examiners. In order to balance this perceived bias, a language-based system of standardization was introduced, which inevitably favoured Sinhalese students. The numerical scores of applicants in each of the three languages were adjusted to fit a common scale,

Table 8.1. Percentage of Tamils in Government Service

Employment	1956	1965	1970
Administrative service	30	20	5
Clerical service	50	30	5
Engineers and doctors	60	30	10
Armed forces	40[6]	20	1
Labour force	40	20	5

The Tamil population in Sri Lanka was never more than 12 per cent throughout these years.
Courtesy of DeVotta (2004, 126).

which was based on the number of applicants in each language. As Sinhala youth were more numerous than Tamils in Sri Lanka, it meant that the scores of Sinhala students were raised in relation to Tamil and English applicants. While this was initial evidence that ethnicity would begin to trump merit in determining entrance into higher education, with the "district quotas," introduced in 1974, the message became clear. "Under this system, residents of 'backward' districts were given preferential admissions treatment. Under criteria devised by the Education Ministry, these were mostly districts with heavy Kandyan and Muslim populations" (Richardson 2005, 297). The district quotas had a significant impact on the number of Tamils admitted to university science programs. In a single year, the number of admissions dropped by a third (for a detailed analysis of the university admissions issue, see de Silva [1978]).

Sirimavo Bandaranaike, more concerned with promoting her Sinhala-Buddhist agenda, failed to foresee how militancy would come to reshape the nature of Tamil politics in Sri Lanka. Two of the early militant groups trace their origins to Velvettiturai (VVT), a conservative fishing community in the far north of Sri Lanka. The Tamil Eelam Liberation Organization (TELO), as early as 1971, held meetings, stockpiled weapons, and experimented with bomb making. The founder of the second militant group – initially called the Tamil New Tigers and later the Liberation Tigers of Tamil Eelam (LTTE) – a shy, hitherto unknown youth named Velupillai Prabhakaran, was also from Velvettiturai. The LTTE, whose membership leading up to the 1977 elections was likely no more than 40 individuals, would, in the 1980s and 1990s, grow to be one of the most innovative and feared rebel movements in the world.

Alongside the rise of Tamil militancy, the Tamil United Front was, to put it mildly, also undergoing changes in its political objectives. In May 1976, a convention was held in the Northern Province Constituency of Vaddukoddai, during which the TUF reconstituted itself as the Tamil United *Liberation* Front (TULF) (Kearney 1985; Siriweera 1980). The insertion of the word "liberation" reflected the growing sentiment that fairness, political rights, and economic opportunities would not be guaranteed to Tamils as a minority population within a united Sri Lanka. The TULF manifesto for the 1977 elections makes it clear how far Tamil-Sinhala relations had deteriorated in the previous seven years:

What is the alternative now left to the nation that has lost its rights to its language, rights to its citizenship, rights to its religions and continues day by day to lose its traditional homeland to Sinhalese Colonization? What is the alternative now left to a nation that lies helpless as it is being assaulted, looted and killed by hooligans instigated by the ruling race and by the security forces of the State? ... There is only one alternative and that is to proclaim with the stamp of finality and fortitude that we alone shall rule over our land our forefathers ruled. Sinhalese imperialism shall quit our homeland. (quoted in Richardson 2005, 294)

While a full examination of the course of the civil war cannot be undertaken here (see, e.g., Wilson 2000 and Swamy 1994), it should be sufficient to point out that following communal violence during the late 1970s and throughout the 1980s – including the riots of 1977 and 1981, the "pogroms" of Black July 1983, and subsequent Indian involvement in the training and funding of Tamil militant groups – the civil war reached levels of destruction that were hitherto unforeseen. Consequently, the LTTE became one of the most feared rebel groups of the twentieth century, equipped with an air force, a navy, an intelligence wing, and an international propaganda and funding structure, as well as close to 10,000 well-trained cadres ready to die for the cause of national liberation (Hellmann-Rajanayagam 1994; Swamy 1994; Weiss 2011). While it is officially a secular movement, some have argued that there was a decidedly religious aspect to the cultural symbolism evoked by the LTTE to rally support for its cause among fellow Tamils; we now turn to a brief discussion of that view.

Was the LTTE a Religious Movement?

The academic literature related to the role of religion in the LTTE remains scattered and unsystematic (see, e.g., Schalk 1997a, 1997b; Roberts 1996, 2005a, 2005b; Hellmann-Rajanayagam 2005). As the LTTE was officially a secular organization, academics and journalists who interviewed members of the Tiger leadership, or even regular cadres (with some exceptions), rarely asked questions about religious identity. In my own interviews with ex-LTTE cadres now living in Canada, they noted that there was a conscious effort to keep the LTTE as secular as possible. As one former member pointed out,

Anybody could practice whatever religion they wanted. Prabhakaran was very careful about that. Religious freedom for everybody. But, the Tigers themselves don't have a religious ideology. Tigers are *simply* about nationalism. People try to give a socialist perspective. This and that perspective.

But, it was Tamil nationalism. There did not have to be a religious motivation, because religion never played a part in Tamil politics. Compare it to Tamil Nadu or even the Sinhala politics in the south of Sri Lanka. Even before the LTTE, Chelvanayakam[7] was born Christian. He didn't have to change his religion to lead the Tamils.

The latter point is important: Tamil churches and Tamil Christians provided a significant basis of support for the Tigers and, as such, the LTTE could not reasonably profess to be an exclusively Hindu movement (see Hoole 2001, 449; Abayasekera 2001). Rather, the LTTE leadership argued that religious differences were needlessly dividing the Tamil community, which should remain unified around an ethnic and linguistic identity.

Some scholars note, however, that even as the LTTE remained a secular organization, comfortable with uniting different religious groups around a strong Tamil ethnic identity, they were still influenced by age-old cultural and religious symbolism and terminology in framing their nationalist movement. As Roberts (2005a, 494) argues, for example, approaching LTTE ideology from a "deep cultural" perspective has the potential to reveal much about the movement. A basic example of this, of course, is the influence of the Chola kingdom of South India in providing the figure of the tiger for the LTTE flag. Similarly, developments ranging from the adoption of the concept of *maveerar* (great heroes) to the decision to bury the LTTE dead – known as *nadukal* (hero stones or, literally, "planted stones") – have roots in the religious practices of South India (Roberts 2005b, 75).

According to Roberts, the LTTE's contention that it never buries its dead, but rather "plants them" as seeds to be reborn, is clearly influenced by South Indian Saivite culture. As he argues, "Tamil Saivism in effect underlines a basic proposition 'in Hindu thought,' namely that 'life is born out of darkness; Death himself is the Creator'" (2005b, 76). For Roberts, as well as other scholars such as Peter Schalk, it is not entirely accurate to label the LTTE as fully secular even if they make these claims. Schalk goes so far as to say that the LTTE rejects religion because its understanding of it is too narrow. He asserts, "[T]he self-understanding of the LTTE is that it is beyond religion, not for and not against religion, even though we, as outsiders, can see that LTTE concepts are de facto heavily influenced by Hindu and Christian terms. The LTTE leaders are not historians of religion and are therefore unaware of this influence ... [but] the self-understanding of the LTTE is no reason for us as outsiders to accept this self-understanding as a true depiction of its concepts" (1997b, 155–6).

Although contemporary scholars of religion shy away from telling research participants what their beliefs are really about, for Schalk, who has written more than anyone else on the LTTE's religio-political ideology, the LTTE is no doubt involved in a process by which politics is sacralized through notions of liberation, martyrdom, and sacrifice for the nation. While Schalk argues that the LTTE is secular movement, he also notes that it uses religious terminology to express the idea of Tamil Eelam as an ultimate value. As he notes, "In the culture where the LTTE was working, ultimacy/non-contingency is expressed in religious terms and the LTTE takes it over" (Schalk, personal communication, 23 July 2012). In this sense, conceptions such as *cutantiram* (independence), *tiyakam* (donation; the giving up of life), or *velvi* (sacrifice) are "holy aims" for the LTTE. As Schalk (1997b, 156–7) notes, "the most important step towards a religion was to stipulate an ultimate aim for which many young men and women have given their lives. All members of the LTTE swear to give their lives for this aim, that is cutantiram … [and] where there is an ultimate aim, there is religion." Based on this premise, Schalk (1997b, 152) goes so far as to suggest that the LTTE should be seen not as "a religious movement with political aspirations but a political movement with religious aspirations."

Schalk's broad working definition of religion is similar to Thomas Luckmann's (1967) notion of "invisible religion." For Luckmann, human beings, once they transcend their biology and begin establishing objective and morally binding systems of meaning, are already engaging in religious practice. Luckmann's theory, perhaps rightly, has been criticized for subsuming all of human activity as religious. Peter Berger (2011, 97), Luckmann's friend and colleague, recently wrote in his intellectual memoir, "I once asked Luckmann who would not be religious by his definition. He replied, 'A dog.'" Similarly, under Schalk's framework, there could never be a non-religious political movement for as soon as such a movement begins speaking of ultimate goals, dying for the cause, or sacrifice, it would have to be deemed religious.

For scholars such as Roberts and Hellmann-Rajanayagam, in contrast, it is not so much that the LTTE is sacralizing politics as it is deeply influenced by the religious and cultural (including secular) contexts in which it arose and formulated a conception of itself. As Roberts (2005b, 76) notes, "Without such evocative religious traditions to draw on, the LTTE's spin-doctors in cultural production would have possessed no foundations to work on. Without being existentially part of this world, they could not themselves believe in the webs they spin. Both the effective demagogue and the effective priest are already immersed in their respective congregations. It is their belief in the ingredients of their cause that secures affective effect." While the work of these and other scholars has expanded our understanding of LTTE ideology, more work is needed to better understand the interplay between religious, ethnic, and nationalist formulations. However, with the defeat of the LTTE, and the Sri Lankan government's destruction of LTTE sites (particularly cemeteries), future studies will prove difficult, if not impossible (Haviland 2011).

Tamil Youth and Changing Religious Identity: Service, Social Justice, and Spirituality

While I have thus far explored the interaction between religion and politics in the conflict in Sri Lanka, in this section I consider some of the ways in which Tamil diaspora activism as a social movement has religious and spiritual elements "at its edges" (Demerath and Schmitt 1998, 390). As James Beckford has noted, some social movements have quite openly adopted religious resources in their formulation (anti-slavery, temperance, pacifism, etc.). However, he points out, "the direct contribution of religion toward social movements is only one side of the coin. The other, less understood side concerns the processes whereby religious, or at least spiritual, issues emerge in social movements. This is a relatively neglected area of study" (Beckford 2003, 239; see also Hannigan 1990, 1991, 1993). In order to adequately address this neglected area, we must first examine theoretical advances in understanding the process of globalization and what such large-scale processes mean for the construction of individual and national identity.

There has been much debate in academic circles about the consequences of globalization, particularly around the question of whether globalization encourages the homogenization or heterogenization of identities. For our purposes, it is important to note that processes of globalization have not precluded the persistence of national identities. Rather, as Scholte (2005, 231) argues, "national identities have come increasingly to take substate, transstate and suprastate forms as well. Indeed, many individuals have acquired a plurinational sense of self." According to Scholte, globalization has, perhaps counter-intuitively, encouraged the growth of what he calls "micro-nations" (which, for example, include groups like the Tamils in Sri Lanka and the Québécois in Canada). He argues that micro-national commitments persist because (1) globalization has reduced the relative power of the state, (2) micro-national movements have often gone global or transnational to advance their cause, and (3) globalization has encouraged a reactive stance from the point of view of micro-nations (Scholte 2005, 234–6). Similarly, Roland Robertson and others have argued that globalization has brought increasing attention and reflection on perhaps the quintessential non-territorial identity – that of humankind itself (Robertson 1992; Scholte 2005, 241–4).

While these conceptions of humankind and micro-nationalism may seem to contradict each other, they are, Robertson believes, integral to globalization itself. According to Robertson (1992, 100), we are, in the contemporary world, "witnesses to – and participants in – a massive, twofold process involving the *interpenetration of the universalization of particularism and the particularization of universalism.*" In other words, as Beyer (1994, 27) succinctly points out, "Central to the very idea of globalization is that subunits of the global system can constitute themselves only with reference to this encompassing whole ... But conversely, the global whole becomes a social reality only as it crystallizes out of the attempts of subunits to deal with their relativizing context."

This dialectic is important for understanding how Tamil youth in Canada navigate their ethnic and religious identities in a globalized context. I argue that Tamil youth have reconstructed their ethnic and religious identities in a few identifiable ways: their global *ethnic* identification (a kind of transnational diasporic nationalism) has altered how they experience the religions of their upbringing, and their internalization of more universalistic *religious* sensibilities (a kind of moralistic, human-rights-oriented spirituality) has influenced how they frame *ethnic* nationalism. It should be noted that their adoption of these kinds of religious sensibilities has contributed to a decline in attachment to their inherited religious traditions as well. Because of space constraints, however, I limit my examination to the way the internalization of a kind of moralistic spirituality – or what can tentatively be called a "spiritual cosmopolitanism" – has influenced how Tamil nationalism is framed by some in the diaspora. It perhaps has the additional effect of blunting the drive towards radicalization, in the conventional sense associated with other ethno-religious groups embroiled in conflict. The new religious sensibilities adopted in the Canadian context tend to foster, as will be shown, a turn away from militancy in favour of developing a more cosmopolitan social movement focused on human rights abuses and the need for sociopolitical reform in Sri Lanka.

Many respondents I spoke with expressed a deep and ongoing interest in spirituality, which they defined in a variety of ways during interviews. As these respondents noted, it was their "spirituality," rather than their Hindu or Christian upbringing, which influenced how they viewed the Tamil struggle as well as other conflicts around the world. For them, spirituality was *not solely* about how it is stereotypically understood: spiritually desperate seekers creating a hodgepodge world view characterized by an evanescent commitment to meditation, yoga, New Age beliefs, Buddhist philosophy, and private contemplation. Rather, spirituality was also a social ethic consisting of a commitment to social justice, a oneness with nature, volunteerism, involvement in civic associations, and a safeguarding of human rights (see, for example, Lynch 2007; Chandler 2011). While many of these aspects of spirituality may exist in Hinduism and Christianity, respondents pointed out that the religious leadership in the Canadian Tamil diaspora was not doing a commendable job in highlighting them. Instead, the perception remains among Tamil youth that religious institutions are primarily concerned with ritual and, as such, are void of the resources needed for them to be socially involved and social-justice-oriented individuals in today's complex geopolitical landscape.

Changes taking place in contemporary religion are multifaceted and have proven hard to predict. As Roof (1999, 4) pointed out over a decade ago, "Trends and events stretch our imagination, even as we try to predict the direction of religious change. Some indicators point to institutional religious decline, others to a profound spiritual ferment, confusing the picture and making it difficult to describe what is really happening." Of course, much research today shows that contemporary religious change, including among Tamil youth in Canada, is characterized both by institutional decline and spiritual rejuvenation. Even as inherited traditions are important and somewhat colour the course and character of individual lives, even as they engage in Diwali celebrations and attend temple pujas from time to time, the lives of Tamil youth are also saturated with notions of inwardness, the experiential, service to others, and social justice. As Roof (1999, 41) argues, "Tradition as memory and authority, or as a means of organizing the past in relation to the present, is eroded in a secular world; religious scripts that once communicated deep meanings, symbolic frames of reference, and defined modes of action must now compete with other stories in a pluralistic and media-saturated society that encourages a mixing of religious themes." This has resulted in a shift "from a world in which beliefs held believers to one in which believers hold beliefs" (Susan Harding, quoted in Roof 1999, 42). Many of my respondents indicated that their "turn to the spiritual" was based on a corresponding view of religion as out-of-date and bereft of spirituality.

As many sociologists of religion have pointed out, the late-modern context in which Tamil youth live their lives is one in which we cannot assume that inherited religious and cultural identities will simply pass from one generation to the next. These traditions may be carried forward with minor changes but may just as easily be abandoned altogether. Indeed it is these kinds of trends that Roof seeks to understand with a process he terms "retraditionalizing":

> Here the emphasis is not on reinterpreting words or symbols embedded in a religious narrative but on the fact that new traditions arise and should be recognized as serious alternatives. It points to the rise of more universal and humanistic meaning systems that now compete with the historic religions. These new discourses are sensitive to concerns about human dignity and equality, to suffering of all kinds, to fears of disasters and destruction, to human potential ... as opposed to trends toward moral relativism, narcissism, and emotivism, retraditionalizing calls attention to newly emerging, culturally pervasive ethical formations. (Roof 1999, 171)

For our current purposes, particularly in examining whether diaspora politics is influenced by religious or spiritual sensibilities, retraditionalizing is significant.

For many I interviewed, the local, ritualized, and often limited nature of their own Tamil traditions are seen as insufficient to address the needs of individuals who wish to fashion a more global ethic. Given that their identities and political sensibilities are transnational, it should not surprise sociologists of religion that their religious beliefs go beyond the borders of their faith with equal ease. As Roof makes clear, retraditionalizing is characterized by a concern for equality, human rights, tolerance, and inclusivity. This does not mean, of course, that such an ethic of humanity or an increasingly cosmopolitan world view precludes any commitment to nationalism. Levitt (2008, 785) argues, "While, in theory, cosmopolitanism seeks an allegiance to humanity writ large, in reality everyone belongs to social groups, networks and culture ... every contemporary cosmopolitan is somehow rooted somewhere.

Each individual cobbles together his or her own combination of universal and particularistic ethnic, national and religious elements." Such cobbling together was highly prevalent throughout my field research. One 1.5-generation Tamil man, who volunteers a lot of his time with Tamil diaspora organizations, put it this way:

I'd like to say I'm spiritual, but not exactly very religious. I think religion divides people, right? I come from a Hindu background, but I don't really differentiate myself as a Tamil Hindu. I'm very tied to my Tamil identity, but I don't really associate myself with any specific religion. But I'm spiritual, I'm just not religious. I believe that there is a God. And I believe that, you know, there is obviously something that runs us. And I respect that and I respect people who commit a lot of time, you know, trying to make a change in the world. And I respect those who serve fellow human beings, so I see spirituality in that way. But I don't see being faithful to God by going and pouring milk on, you know, the altar and calling it being religious when there are kids in the world that really need that milk. Why throw it down the drain? So I see – like my spirituality comes from helping somebody that is in need. So whether it's people back home [in Sri Lanka], whether it's somebody in Darfur, or whether it's, you know, somebody that is at a Salvation Army shelter, if you're helping a person that is in need, you're basically serving God. That's the way I see it. To me that's what it means to be spiritual.

Another 1.5-generation Tamil man who has also been extensively involved with Tamil diaspora groups in Canada, described a similar view of spirituality from the standpoint of service to others. As he noted,

I think I've realized there are things about spirituality that I need to pursue, like service is a huge deal for me. Service – to others and to be of help to others and to offer that help to others. That's a huge deal for me, I think. I really don't subscribe myself to the Sathya Sai Baba school, but one of my favorite sayings of his is, "Hands that help are holier than the lips that pray." And I truly believe that. People can say they can do five different things. People will write that they'll do three of those things but will anyone do at least one of those things in action? So to commit yourself and to keep your word and to put it into action is very important to me. If there's one thing, that would be it. That's one of the major things I've discovered ... How are you going to give back? That [Ralph Waldo Emerson] line, "To know that one life has breathed easier because you've lived." You know, that makes all the difference.

This is in line with Smith's (2009) research on religion and American youth. Much like with many of my Tamil respondents, Smith points out that when individuals were asked if it was easy to know what is right and wrong in their daily life, most respondents noted that it was easy. Smith (2009, 46) states, "Many hardly had to even think about it. When then asked how hard it is to know right and wrong – regardless of how difficult it is to do what is morally right – again, nearly everyone said it is easy. Morality is like common sense; unless you are actively resisting it, it is not hard to know what to do or to do it." Smith says that youth today are, in essence, philosophical consequentialists: if individuals hurt other people, it is plainly wrong; if they help others, it is the right thing to do. However, Smith notes, many youth cannot explicate *why* they think hurting others is morally reprehensible. As he argues, "To them it is just obvious ... They did not appeal, for instance, to God's will, natural law, utilitarian principles, the Bible, or any other supposed source of universal moral truth to justify this belief. 'Don't hurt others' functions instead as a kind of free-floating, unjustified supposition that informs intuitive moral feelings and opinions" (2009, 47).

It is these kinds of spiritual and cosmopolitan beliefs – variously described by Roof, Levitt, Smith, and others (e.g., Ammerman 1997; Appiah 1998) – that also influenced many of my respondents' views on the conflict in Sri Lanka. In other words, virtually none of the Tamil youth I spoke with thought that Hinduism or Christianity, first, had anything to do with the civil war in Sri Lanka and, second, had an influence in forming their own opinions about the future of the conflict. Yet ironically one second-generation Tamil man in Toronto, who did not fully support the LTTE, felt an attachment to them arising out of his broader sense of what is morally correct for human beings. As he pointed out,

I understand why people consider Prabhakaran a prophet or whatnot, because he has moved a lot of Tamils with his words and his bravery, but I am very secular in terms of what I think in politics as well. Why I think I have an attachment to the LTTE is because I feel like no one stood up for us and the LTTE is the only one who actually did that. I don't know if that was very helpful for – we lost 80,000 people – but it's just the principle. We are being treated badly and, you know, you have to say something to that, you have to do something against that, I believe, and I think the LTTE did that, so I'm glad. Well, I'm not sure if it was a good idea or not, but based on that principle, I think it was a good idea, so I would side with them.

When asked about how he viewed the relationship between religion and politics, another respondent, a second-generation Tamil man who was heavily involved with the demonstration in Toronto from January to May 2009, responded after some reflection that his spirituality was very important.

> Like on a personal level, yes, I think it is really different from ... I want equality and I would love to believe, I would really love to believe that if we role reversed everything, if Tamils were the majority in Sri Lanka and I was still of Tamil descent and Sinhalese were the ones being discriminated against, I really really would love to believe that I would support the Sinhalese cause in that scenario. So in that case, yes. I don't believe I am in this cause because I am a Tamil. I believe I am in this cause because of my spiritual values and my value of human life and my morals in dictating what is right and wrong.

To conclude, then, while much of my field research with Tamil youth and organizational leaders sought to understand whether and how Tamil nationalism, as a social movement, was being carried forward in the diaspora, I was also intrigued by the question of whether religious identity in some way coloured how individuals conceived of Tamil nationalism. The civil war in Sri Lanka is at times, and somewhat simplistically, seen as a conflict between Hindu Tamils and Sinhalese Buddhists. Transferring such a framework onto diaspora activism makes little sense. Indeed, I argue here that it cannot be assumed that Tamil diaspora activism is influenced simply by inherited religious traditions (be it Hinduism or Christianity). Rather, Tamil youth are equally, if not more, influenced by broader religious changes in the North American landscape, which inevitably colours how they view the conflict in Sri Lanka, the plight of minority populations in the country, and the role of the diaspora going forward.

Most often, research in the sociology of religion, and especially into the relationship between religion and ethnicity, has emphasized the ways in which religion helps to preserve ethnic identity (Williams 1988; Sheth 1995; Min 2010; McLellan 1999; Park 2004), helps to link people across space and time through a chain of memory (Tweed 1997;

Hervieu-Leger 2000), and helps to socialize migrants into the politics and culture of the receiving country (Guest 2004; Kurien 1998; Ebaugh and Chafetz 2000, 2002; Bramadat and Seljak 2009). As Levitt (2008, 768), speaking of the American example, points out, "Commitments to religious identities and religious organizations facilitate the acquisition of an American cultural toolkit for immigrants and their children: a new language, a new political and civic culture, and new loyalties. Religious networks, celebrations, rituals and organizations serve as a forum in which many first- and second-generation Americans become schooled in American politics and lay claim to public recognition and government assistance for their communities."

During my interviews with Tamil youth (particularly the activist segments of the community), I was struck by the fact that they were undergoing many of the changes to their religious identity that sociologists of religion have shown to be commonplace in the broader North American context (see, for example, Roof 1999). Much of what Tamil youth seem to be experiencing with respect to the religion of their upbringing is supported by the exhaustive academic literature on intergenerational transmission of religious identity, but there is more to the story (see, for example, Ebaugh and Chafetz 2000). This is a key point, as scholarship on religious identities in North America remains bifurcated. Mainstream, white, and middle-class individuals are thought to undergo large-scale religious changes. They become more secular, adopt "spiritual-but-not-religious" sensibilities, and practise a syncretistic form of religion. However, studies of religious identity in ethnic or immigrant communities are often limited to understanding generational differences in religious practice or the relationship between religion and ethnicity. It is too often assumed that the religious changes experienced by immigrant populations and their children are somehow contained and are, in some way, free from the influence of the large-scale changes scholars see taking place in the broader religious landscape.

This approach is not only short-sighted, but it also hinders our ability to more fully understand diaspora activism, the role of religion in imported conflicts, and processes of radicalization and de-radicalization. As I have argued, while religion was indeed important for Sinhala-Buddhist nationalism in Sri Lanka, it played very little role in helping to articulate or sustain Tamil nationalism and Tamil militancy, even as the majority of Tamils in Sri Lanka and in the diaspora are Hindu. As such, it is problematic to understand the potential for violent radicalization in the Canadian Tamil diaspora through dominant conceptions of the role of religion in immigrant communities or even the scholarly literature on the role of religion in Salafi-jihadist radicalization. This is not to suggest, however, that "religion" plays no role whatsoever. Not only have traditional religious ideas and communities been involved in the history of tensions in Sri Lanka, but indeed, as I have begun to show in this chapter, broadening our understanding of religion to encompass spiritual, moralistic, and cosmopolitan sensibilities and employing this framework to understand Tamil nationalism and activism among diaspora youth does lead to unique insights. In unexpected ways, then, it may be that in the post-LTTE and post-war context, these new forms of spirituality and cosmopolitan identity influence the course and character of the new transnational and peaceful political activism of most members of the Tamil diaspora.

NOTES

1 Anuradhapura was the religious and political capital of Sri Lanka for 1,300 years starting in the fourth century BCE.
2 A term used to describe a diverse group of people belonging to a large family of languages spoken especially in southern India and northern Sri Lanka that includes Tamil, Telugu, Malayalam, and Kannada.
3 The Chola kingdom ruled South India from the 300s BCE to 1279 CE. As K.M. de Silva (2005, 13) has noted, by the third century BCE, Dravidian intrusion into Sri Lankan affairs increased. Around the second century BCE, the Chola king Elara usurped power at Anuradhapura and ruled for 44 years.
4 It would be wrong to suggest that such instances of resistance are *religious* because terms like *satyagraha* were used by Federal Party activists. The term, developed by Mahatma Gandhi during India's independence movement, was used by Federal Party activists to link the Tamil struggle against "Sinhala colonization" with India's struggle against the British. It is also important to note that many members of the Federal Party, including S.J.V. Chelvanayakam, were Christian.
5 The monk, Talduwe Somarama, reportedly killed the prime minister because of Bandaranaike's reluctance to pursue Sinhala nationalist reforms more aggressively. Bandaranaike's signing of the Bandaranaike-Chelvanayakam Pact in 1957 (which afforded some level of autonomy to the Tamil people) as well as the passing of the Tamil Language (Special Provisions) Act in 1958 (which allowed for the use of Tamil in education

and administration in the Northern and Eastern Provinces) are commonly cited as catalysts leading to the assassination.

6 While DeVotta places the percentage of Tamils in the armed forces at 40 per cent in 1956, other scholars argue that this is much too high. Horowitz (1980, 67), for example, suggests that Tamils probably did not make up more than 12 per cent of the armed forces prior to 1956.

7 S.J.V. Chelvanayakam is a deeply admired figure in post-independence Tamil politics. In 1949, he formed the Illankai Tamil Arasu Kachchi (Federal Party) and remained the central figure advocating for Tamil rights in Sri Lanka until his death in 1977 (see Wilson 1994).

REFERENCES

Abayasekera, Jeffrey. 2001. *The Role of the Churches: A Historical Perspective.* Marga Monograph Series on Ethnic Reconciliation no. 17. Ethul Kotte: Marga Institute.

Amarasingam, Amarnath. 2013. "Pain, Pride, and Politics: Social Movement Activism and the Sri Lankan Tamil Diaspora in Canada." Diss., Wilfrid Laurier University.

Ambalavanar, Darshan. 2006. "Arumuga Navalar and the Construction of a Caiva Public in Colonial Jaffna." PhD diss., Harvard University.

Ammerman, Nancy. 1997. "Golden Rule Christianity: Lived Religion in the American Mainstream." In *Lived Religion in America: Toward a History of Practice,* ed. David D. Hall, 196–216. Princeton, NJ: Princeton University Press.

Appiah, Kwame Anthony. 1998. "Cosmopolitan Patriots." In *Cosmopolitics: Thinking and Feeling beyond the Nation,* ed. Pheng Cheah and Bruce Robbins, 91–114. Minneapolis: University of Minnesota Press.

Beckford, James A. 2003. "Social Movements as Free-floating Religious Phenomena." In *The Blackwell Companion to Sociology of Religion,* ed. Richard Fenn, 229–48. Malden, MA: Blackwell Publishing.

Bell, Stewart. 2004. *Cold Terror: How Canada Nurtures and Exports Terrorism around the World.* Mississauga, ON: John Wiley and Sons.

Berger, Peter L. 2011. *Adventures of an Accidental Sociologist.* New York: Prometheus Books.

Beyer, Peter. 1994. *Religion and Globalization.* London: Sage.

Bloom, Mia. 2007. *Dying to Kill: The Allure of Suicide Terror.* New York: Columbia University Press.

Bond, George D. 1988. *The Buddhist Revival in Sri Lanka: Religious Tradition, Reinterpretation, and Response.* Columbia: University of South Carolina Press.

Bramadat, Paul, and David Seljak. 2009. *Religion and Ethnicity in Canada*. Toronto: University of Toronto Press.

Calhoun, Craig. 1997. *Nationalism*. Minneapolis: University of Minnesota Press.

Chalk, Peter. 1999. "Liberation Tigers of Tamil Eelam's (LTTE) International Organization and Operations – A Preliminary Analysis." Canadian Security and Intelligence Service, Commentary #77. https://www.csis-scrs.gc.ca/pblctns/cmmntr/cm77-eng.asp.

Chandler, Siobhan. 2011. "The Social Ethic of Religiously Unaffiliated Spirituality." PhD diss., Wilfrid Laurier University.

Cheran, R. 2009. "Pathways of Dissent: An Introduction to Tamil Nationalism in Sri Lanka." In *Pathways of Dissent: Tamil Nationalism in Sri Lanka*, ed. R. Cheran, xiii–xlvii. New Delhi: Sage Publications.

Demerath, N.J. III, and Terry Schmitt. 1998. "Transcending Sacred and Secular: Mutual Benefits in Analyzing Religious and Nonreligious Organization." In *Sacred Companies: Organizational Aspects of Religion and Religious Aspects of Organizations*, ed. N.J. Demerath III et al., 381–400. New York: Oxford University Press.

De Silva, Chandra R. 1978. "The Politics of University Admissions: A Review of Some Aspects of the Admissions Policy in Sri Lanka, 1971–1978." *Sri Lanka Journal of Social Science* 1 (2): 85–123.

– 1997. *Sri Lanka: A History*. New Delhi: Vikas Publishing House.

De Silva, K.M. 1998. *Reaping the Whirlwind: Ethnic Conflict, Ethnic Politics in Sri Lanka*. New Delhi: Penguin Press.

– 2005. *A History of Sri Lanka*. Colombo: Vijitha Yapa Publications.

DeVotta, Neil. 2002. "Illiberalism and Ethnic Conflict in Sri Lanka." *Journal of Democracy* 13 (1): 84–98.

– 2004. *Blowback: Linguistic Nationalism, Institutional Decay, and Ethnic Conflict in Sri Lanka*. Stanford, CA: Stanford University Press.

– 2005. "From Ethnic Outbidding to Ethnic Conflict: The Institutional Basis for Sri Lanka's Separatist War." *Nations and Nationalism* 11 (1): 141–59.

Ebaugh, Helen Rose, and Janet Saltzman Chafetz. 2000. *Religion and the New Immigrants*. Walnut Creek, CA: AltaMira Press.

– 2002. *Religion across Borders: Transnational Immigrant Networks*. Walnut Creek, CA: AltaMira Press.

Grant, Patrick. 2009. *Buddhism and Ethnic Conflict in Sri Lanka*. Albany: SUNY Press.

Guest, Kenneth J. 2004. "Liminal Youth among Fozhou Chinese Undocumented Workers." In *Asian American Religions: The Making and Remaking of Borders and Boundaries*, ed. Tony Carnes and Fenggang Yang, 55–75. New York: New York University Press.

Hannigan, John A. 1990. "Apples and Oranges or Varieties of the Same Fruit? The New Religious Movements and the New Social Movements Compared." *Review of Religious Research* 31: 246–58.
– 1991. "Social Movement Theory and the Sociology of Religion." *Sociological Analysis* 52: 311–31.
– 1993. "New Social Movement Theory and the Sociology of Religion." In *A Future for Religion?*, ed. William Swatos Jr., 1–18. Newbury Park, CA: Sage.
Haviland, Charles. 2011. "Sri Lanka Builds Army HQ on Tamil Tiger Cemetery." *BBC News South Asia*. http://www.bbc.co.uk/news/world-south-asia-12668613 (accessed 1 September 2011).
Hellmann-Rajanayagam, Dagmar. 1989. "Arumuka Navalar: Religious Reformer or National Leader of Eelam." *Indian Economic Social History Review* 26 (2): 235–57.
– 1994. *The Tamil Tigers: Armed Struggle for Identity*. Stuttgart: Franz Steiner Verlag.
– 2005. "And Heroes Die: Poetry of the Tamil Liberation Movement in Northern Sri Lanka." *South Asia: Journal of South Asian Studies* 28 (1): 112–53.
Hervieu-Leger, Danielle. 2000. *Religion as a Chain of Memory*. New Brunswick, NJ: Rutgers University Press.
Hoffman, Bruce, William Rosenau, Andrew J. Curiel, and Doron Zimmermann. 2007. *The Radicalization of Diasporas and Terrorism*. Santa Monica, CA: RAND Corporation.
Hoole, Rajan. 2001. *The Arrogance of Power: Myths, Decadence, and Murder*. Colombo: UTHR(J).
Horowitz, Donald. 1980. *Coup Theories and Officers' Motives: Sri Lanka in Comparative Perspective*. Princeton, NJ: Princeton University Press.
Indrapala, K. 2007. *The Evolution of an Ethnic Identity: The Tamils in Sri Lanka, c. 300 BCE to c. 1200 CE*. Colombo: Vijitha Yapa Publications.
Kearney, Robert. 1985. "Ethnic Conflict and the Tamil Separatist Movement in Sri Lanka." *Asian Survey* 2 (9): 898–917.
Keck, Margaret, and Kathryn Sikkink. 1998. *Activists beyond Borders: Advocacy Networks in International Politics*. Ithaca, NY: Cornell University Press.
Kemper, Steven. 1991. *The Presence of the Past: Chronicles, Politics, and Culture in Sinhala Life*. Ithaca, NY: Cornell University Press.
Kent, Daniel. 2008. "Shelter for You, Nirvana for Our Sons: Buddhist Belief and Practice in the Sri Lankan Army." PhD diss., University of Virginia.
Kurien, Prema. 1998. "Becoming American by Becoming Hindu: Indian Americans Take Their Place at the Multicultural Table." In *Gatherings in Diaspora: Religious Communities and the New Immigrants*, ed. R. Stephen Warner and Judith G. Wittner, 37–70. Philadelphia: Temple University Press.

Levitt, Peggy. 2008. "Religion as a Path to Civic Engagement." *Ethnic and Racial Studies* 31 (4): 766–91.

Little, David. 1994. *Sri Lanka: The Invention of Enmity*. Washington, DC: United States Institute of Peace Press.

Luckmann, Thomas. 1967. *The Invisible Religion: The Problem of Religion in Modern Society*. New York: Macmillan Publishing.

Lynch, Gordon. 2007. *The New Spirituality: An Introduction to Progressive Belief in the Twenty-first Century*. New York: I.B. Tauris.

McLellan, Janet. 1999. *Many Petals of the Lotus: Five Asian Buddhist Communities in Toronto*. Toronto: University of Toronto Press.

Min, Pyong Gap. 2010. *Preserving Ethnicity through Religion in America: Korean Protestants and Indian Hindus across Generations*. New York: New York University Press.

Park, Soyoung. 2004. "'Korean American Evangelical': A Resolution of Sociological Ambivalence among Korean American College Students." In *Asian American Religions: The Making and Remaking of Borders and Boundaries*, ed. Tony Carnes and Fenggang Yang, 182–204. New York: New York University Press.

Purdy, Margaret. 2003. "Targeting Diasporas: The Canadian Counter-Terrorism Experience." Armed Groups Project, Latin American Research Centre, Working Paper 2. http://www.armedgroups.org/.

Rahula, Walpola. 1974. *The Heritage of the Bhikku*. New York: Grove Press.

Richardson, John. 2005. *Paradise Poisoned: Learning about Conflict, Terrorism and Development from Sri Lanka's Civil Wars*. Kandy, Sri Lanka: International Center for Ethnic Studies.

Roberts, Michael. 1996. "Filial Devotion in Tamil Culture and the Tiger Cult of Martyrdom." *Contributions to Indian Sociology* 30 (2): 245–72.

Roberts, Michael. 2005a. "Tamil Tiger 'Martyrs': Regenerating Divine Potency?" *Studies in Conflict & Terrorism* 28 (6): 493–514.

– 2005b. "Saivite Symbols, Sacrifice, and Tamil Tiger Rites." *Social Analysis* 49 (1): 67–93.

Robertson, Roland. 1992. *Globalization: Social Theory and Global Culture*. London: Sage.

Roof, Wade Clark. 1999. *Spiritual Marketplace: Baby Boomers and the Remaking of American Religion*. Princeton, NJ: Princeton University Press.

Ross, Russell R., and Andrea M. Savada, eds. 1988. *Sri Lanka: A Country Study*. Washington, DC: GPO for the Library of Congress. http://www.countrystudies.us/sri-lanka/.

Schalk, Peter. 1997a. "Historisation of the Martial Ideology of the Liberation Tigers of Tamil Eelam (LTTE)." *South Asia: Journal of South Asian Studies* 20 (2): 35–72.

– 1997b. "The Revival of Martyr Cults among Ilavar." *Temenos* 33: 151–90.

Scholte, Jan Aart. 2005. *Globalization: A Critical Introduction*. Hampshire: Palgrave Macmillan.

Seneviratne, H.L. 1999. *The Work of Kings: The New Buddhism in Sri Lanka*. Chicago: University of Chicago Press.

Sheth, Manju. 1995. "Indian Americans." In *Asian Americans: Contemporary Trends and Issues*, ed. Pyong Gap Min, 169–98. Walnut Creek, CA: Sage.

Siriweera, W.I. 1980. "Recent Developments in Sinhala-Tamil Relations." *Asian Survey* 20 (9): 903–13.

Smith, Christian. 2009. *Souls in Transition: The Religious and Spiritual Lives of Emerging Adults*. Oxford: Oxford University Press.

Swamy, M.R. Narayan. 1994. *Tigers of Lanka: From Boys to Guerillas*. Colombo: Vijitha Yapa Publications.

Tweed, Thomas. 1997. *Our Lady of the Exile: Diasporic Religion at a Cuban Catholic Shrine in Miami*. New York: Oxford University Press.

Weiss, Gordon. 2011. *The Cage: The Fight for Sri Lanka and the Last Days of the Tamil Tigers*. London: The Bodley Head.

Williams, Raymond Brady. 1988. *Religions of Immigrants from India and Pakistan*. Cambridge: Cambridge University Press.

Wilson, A. Jeyaratnam. 1994. *S.J.V. Chelvanayakam and the Crisis of Sri Lankan Tamil Nationalism, 1947–1977*. Honolulu: University of Hawai'i Press.

– 2000. *Sri Lankan Tamil Nationalism*. Vancouver: UBC Press.

9 Religion, Reporting, and Radicalization: The Role of News Media in Securitized Discourses

JOYCE SMITH

A rabid new breed of so-called security experts hit the airwaves, talking in concise 15-second clips about the near and the far enemy that now, looking back, does not seem that different from the rhetoric Osama bin Laden spewed. I was part of the media machine that churned out these stories, which were heavy on drama and outrage, and light on analysis.

Michelle Shephard, *Toronto Star* security reporter (Shephard 2011b, 26)

It is difficult to imagine discussing religion, radicalization, and securitization in the current age without a serious discussion of the news media. Acting as the medium of communication for messages generated by religious groups, security officials, governments, and citizens as well as significantly influencing those messages themselves, news media of all forms are worthy of scrutiny. What follows is a consideration of the way in which journalists and the journalism they have produced with respect to stories involving terrorism may influence religious radicalization. A closely related part of this analysis must be a discussion of the role of journalism in the creation and distribution of what one might call securitization narratives. By examining both the processes and outputs of journalism available from Canadian news outlets, this chapter will suggest the ways in which reporting serves as a pivot point for domestic and foreign, radicalized and securitized, and religious and secular audiences. In so doing, it will also challenge traditional ideas of framing theory. I will begin by examining the constructs provided by beat reporting and how securitization both may be used and may produce frames for news coverage, and finally, I will suggest how framing itself is challenged in a global media and religious market.

Beats and Reporting in Canada

Gaye Tuchman's conception of the system of news collection as a net is very helpful when considering how institutional structures influence reporting on security issues. She describes stringers (or freelancers for various news organizations) as "intersecting fine mesh," reporters (full-time employees) as the "tensile strength" of the news net, and finally wire services (e.g., Reuters, Agence France-Press, and Canadian Press) as the steel links (Tuchman 1978, 22). She further categorizes the ways in which reporters can be assigned: by geographic territory, organizational specialty, and topical speciality. "Beat" reporting falls between the second and third of these options, with reporters dealing with politics, for example, often being based on Parliament Hill, while others, such as consumer, education, and sports reporters, are tied to a topic and not to a single organization or geographic marker.

The creation of a security beat after 9/11 fits what Stuart Allan identifies as the ability to "routinize the uncertainty of future happenings" (Allan 2010, 80). This means not only being prepared for breaking news events but guaranteeing a certain quantity (and, one hopes, quality) of reporting. It also suggests that stories will be told from a specific point of view.

A story about a new mosque (even one built at Ground Zero) could be covered as a zoning issue by the city hall reporter, as a new community story by the lifestyle reporter, or even as a profile of construction methods if given to the real estate reporter of a newspaper. Each of the journalists occupying one of these beats will have their own circle of contacts as well as hierarchies of trusted and official sources, which tends, as many critics suggest, to reaffirm "the iniquitous power relations underlying society's institutional order" (Allan 2010, 80).

There are fewer than ten journalists working a security beat in Canada, although many reporters without this official moniker routinely report on security stories. It is worth noting from the beginning that there are even fewer news outlets in Canada with a religion beat, so the arrival of a mosque in most communities is more likely to be covered either as a story where religious questions are secondary or by a reporter whose area of expertise is not religion. Most importantly for the analysis of reporting which may depict if not influence radicalization, reporters often will not have access to a specialist in religion in the newsroom, one who might be able to suggest sources for comment, as well as point out alternate or additional ways of telling or framing a story. This results in losses of opportunity for alternate stories to be told and also the potential for identifying and understanding the religious aspects of a story. The "tensile strength" of Tuchman's analogy is, therefore, considerably weakened.

Consider the following exchange between *National Post* reporter Stewart Bell and Mansour Jabarah, the father of convicted terrorist Mohammed Jabarah: "Mansour asks if I have ever written about Islam, and I tell him my writing concerns those who use religion to justify violence. 'Believe me,' he says, 'in Islam there are no terrorists'" (Bell 2005, 65). With such starting positions, the options for continuing a dialogue would seem limited. In Bell's retelling of this specific instance, he goes on to ask Jabarah about "those who invoke Islam to incite the killing of innocent people ... those who declare jihad by claiming that the West is at war with Islam." For his part, Bell reports that Jabarah points to North Korea and asks why (George W.) Bush didn't attack there. "Why, I ask, would the United States want to destroy an entire religion?" "'They are crazy,' he [Jabarah] says" (Bell 2005, 65). Without engaging in an informed discussion about the role of religion – on religion's terms – opportunities for further investigation are limited. If one of the prime motivators for radicalization is ideology – in these cases, religious ideology (Dawson 2010, 23) – it would seem even more important for reporters to have the skills at least to recognize and ideally to discuss religious symbols, words, and communities.

An analysis of the journalism produced after 9/11 suggests that while significant resources (in terms of time and travel) were put towards security beats immediately following the events, there has continued to be overlap between reporting done by security reporters and their colleagues. This has proven to be the case with reporters on foreign assignments as well as with crime and general assignment reporters.

Two of Canada's top security reporters admit to not having special training or education in religious or security affairs, although they do attend conferences and are "well-read" (Koring 2012). Another reporter, Michelle Shephard, recently wrote, "As a 29-year-old crime reporter for the *Star*, I knew more at that time about the Bloods and Crips than Osama bin Laden. On Sept. 10 [2001], I had written about a 16-year-old gun-toting purse snatcher and questioned why his elderly victim had not come forward. For the next decade, I went in search of the hows and whys, trying to define terrorism and understand its roots" (Shephard 2011a). Shephard had been on the crime beat for the *Toronto Star* and was one of the reporters involved in an award-winning series on racial profiling by Toronto police published in 2002. This series, she believes, helped her with networks in communities where radicalization takes place.

In previous research on national coverage of religion, I asked Canadian reporters whose bylines had appeared on stories with religious content to participate in a survey consisting of closed- and open-ended questions on religion and the coverage of religion (many of these same questions were also asked in a 2007 telephone survey of Canadians). Among the journalists was a person who was adamant that coverage of Canadian troops fighting against the Taliban shouldn't be included in a study of religion and journalism, as the Taliban had nothing to do with Islam (Smith 2010). Conversely, a reporter who covered the Roman Catholic World Youth Day events held in Toronto in 2002 said he thought the event wasn't really religious but rather a cultural event (Smith 2003). I continue to differ with these interpretations, but their comments remain very good reminders of the way in which some journalists define religion and, in so doing, influence their audience's definition of religion.

In addition to having a professional past, each journalist has his or her own personal history which, despite the desire and training to remain objective, can permeate reporting decisions. Despite theories which emphasize the corporate ownership of the media and the entrenched nature of hegemonic power structures in our society as determining coverage, I strongly believe that individual actors and their personal motivations must also be considered. Consider former *New York Times* executive editor and columnist Bill Keller's comments in a 9/11 anniversary essay: "my prudent punditry soon felt inadequate. I remember a mounting protective instinct, heightened by the birth of my second daughter almost exactly nine months after the attacks. Something dreadful was loose in the world, and the urge to stop it, to do something – to prove something – was overriding a career-long schooling in the virtues of caution and skepticism" (Keller 2011, 36). Objectivity and balance are not always easily maintained when journalists feel personally threatened.

It will be interesting to see if in the next decade, the security beat disappears as did labour and religion beats before it. Labour reporting featured in many news organizations during the years in which unions were perceived to be most powerful; today, while reporting on strikes and other labour actions is present, the labour beat itself is not (Ryan 2004, 492).

Religion reporting (particularly in American newspapers) surged following the Branch Davidian crisis in Waco (1993) and the first World Trade Center bombing (also 1993). The Religion Newswriters Association experienced a peak of membership and entries for their contests in the late 1990s, and the Lilly and Templeton Foundations' support of reporting initiatives also played an important role in giving the religion beat prominence and funding (Religion Newswriters Association 2012). The *Dallas Morning News*, which had been a beacon of American reporting with its full section devoted to religion since 1994, eliminated this initiative in 2007. In 2009 it reassigned the remaining religion reporters to covering schools (Pulliam 2009). Although Canada never had the same number or proportion of religion reporters, the religion beat and related pages have disappeared from most newspapers (evident, for example, in the cutting of the *Toronto Star*'s religion pages between 2005 and 2010). CBC radio's weekly show *Tapestry* is one of the few broadcasts on a non-denominational station to have survived.

But religion hasn't disappeared from public life any more than have labour issues. Research in Canada as well as in the United States and the Commonwealth has shown that newspapers, online news sites, and television and radio broadcasts are full of religion (e.g., an average edition of the *Globe and Mail* in 2007 contained over 40 stories with some religious content). Yet only a small number of Canadians (who self-identify either as religious or as atheists or agnostics) believe that religion receives more coverage than it should.[1]

The coverage of religiously linked terror – and it was clear during the tenth anniversary of 9/11 that the security beat is indeed thought of as the "terror beat" (English 2011) – has been handled in a way which is not always the case for other areas. With few reporters combining expertise in both religion and security issues, reporting rests with general assignment reporters or those with related interests or who are in the field (as with foreign reporters) at a given moment.

In his experience, the *Globe and Mail*'s Paul Koring (whose official title is "International Affairs and Security Correspondent") says that stories are covered based less on a title attached to a reporter's beat and more on who is available and who is both best situated and sited for a given story (Koring 2012). Once beginning a story (e.g., Koring's coverage of Abousfian Abdelrazik, a Canadian imprisoned and tortured in Sudan), reporters tend to follow the saga to the end when possible.

As Michelle Shephard recently noted, security reporting seeks contact with "spies and terrorists," neither known for their openness and transparency (Fatima 2012). Given the nature of these sources, getting the traditional comments and quotes from all parties is nearly impossible. Without official spokespersons representing all parties to a conflict, more often than not the voices included in security affairs reports are those of government, military, and security officials. The extent to which journalists on the beat rely on or feature the voices of such officials varies; I would argue that Stewart Bell of the *National Post*, for example, gives more frequent prominence to officials from CSIS and the RCMP than does Michelle Shephard. But without the existence of or access to spokespeople representing combatants, it is all but impossible for a journalist to cover all sides of the security story.

Even when it is possible to interview members of radical or violent groups, these stories are generally published or broadcast after reports featuring security and military voices. What Stuart Hall and others describe as the "primary definition" in the context of which all other discussions take place has already been set (Hall 1978). These definitions can delineate the discourse, deciding, for example, if an action is criminal or how best to describe otherwise a person's motivations. Journalists may unwittingly fall into this trap as they repeat key phrases and descriptions given to them by officials rather than exercise sufficient rhetorical independence (e.g., the identification of 9/11 attacks as an "act of war" versus a case of "mass murder" [Cunningham 2007, 36]). When reporting on stories where all stakeholders are willing to be interviewed, there is the opportunity for primary definitions to be challenged and given nuance; when this is not possible, there is less chance for the resulting reporting to be comprehensive, despite the best efforts of the journalist. The primary definition is not only the first to be heard; it is by default the most important, or at least it remains the central one. It also, however, remains the only one open to scrutiny and critique by the news audience.

In the context of this discussion, it is not surprising that the primary definition provided by the government and security officials may fit a securitization frame – in other words, they may naturally describe the actions of a perpetrator as indicative of a significant threat from a well-defined "enemy" of freedom and democracy. However, when such a definition is not only the primary but the sole definition, there are, I would suggest, consequences for radicalization as well. In order for journalism to succeed in one of its chief goals – the furtherance of democracy and civil society – stories must provide something to which citizens can react and respond. If members of radical groups are not interviewed or profiled, not only are their voices missing from the discourse but also missing is the ability for people to respond and react to them. The release of an audio or videotaped message from Osama bin Laden was always newsworthy not so much for what was said (which was often repetitive) but for the fact that people had the rare chance to see and hear him.

A journalist (and news consumer) can question what an official says and subject these statements to analysis and further reporting. Should they be able to find fault or suggest alternative interpretations, it is possible to see how some degree of opposition to the official security forces can ensue. But the silent parties in such a conflict can escape interrogation of their truth claims. This may make it easier for people to be drawn to groups which in some way are opposing those generating the sole and primary definitions of a conflict.

One notable exception to this state of reporting is the *Globe and Mail*'s award-winning "Talking to the Taliban" series (Smith et al. 2008). This series used go-betweens to allow men who identified themselves as Taliban members to record messages later featured on the website of the *Globe and Mail*. It is noteworthy that the chief journalist was not the paper's security reporter, Colin Freeze, but Graeme Smith, then the *Globe*'s foreign correspondent based since mid-2006 in Kandahar, Afghanistan. However, even Smith couldn't do the interviewing of the Taliban members himself: apart from the usual struggles of reporting in a war zone, as he notes in the "methodology" section of the "Talking to the Taliban" site, the kidnapping of journalists meant it became increasingly dangerous to attempt such reporting. (In the same year the series ran, Mellissa Fung, a reporter for CBC TV on her second posting in Kandahar, was kidnapped, stabbed, and held for 28 days before being released.)[2]

Another noteworthy development is the frequency with which reporters assigned to foreign coverage are "parachuted" into hot spots. This approach can make it much more difficult for a journalist to construct and maintain a good network of information and sources. But in considering the relationship of foreign and domestic news coverage with respect to radicalization, the commute may reinforce for journalists the real connections between "here" and "there." A recent panel featuring Michelle Shephard of the *Toronto Star*, Sonia Verma of the *Globe and Mail*, Gillian Findlay (now with the CBC's investigative television program *the fifth estate*), and Kathryn Blaze Carlson, then of the *National Post*, noted that the conjunction of the closing of permanent foreign bureaus with individual journalists establishing a family life based in Canada is

not necessarily all bad news (Reid 2011). Where once foreign correspon-
dents were posted for years in a foreign city, and so were to some extent
cut off from the tenor of day-to-day life in Canada, the parachuting correspondent, it could be argued, is more sensitive to how their reporting
connects with events at home. Shephard has said travel to a variety of
countries has helped her recognize the differences between regions, as
well as the "great divide" between "the Western cities, politicians and
public who would often determine the fate of those countries in tur-
moil" (Shephard 2011a).

In a world which now includes alternative sources for news, including the blogosphere and content created by citizen journalists, primary
definitions produced and repeated by the mainstream news media
are far from unassailable. But I would argue that until alternative outlets enjoy the same commercial and professional footing as that given
to established news organizations, their discourses too will be in the
shadow of primary definitions. Research has shown that social media
reporting continues to rely heavily on or at least react to the journalism produced by traditional news organizations (Pew Research Center's Project for Excellence in Journalism 2010). While the public does
not have undiluted trust in professional journalists, several high-profile
unveilings of social media sources who practised what Lisa Nakamura
has coined "identity tourism" (e.g., an American man living in Edinburgh blogging as a lesbian living in Syria) have put paid to utopian
faith in reporting by citizen journalists (Addley 2011).

Security Reporting and Securitization as a Framing Device

In Bramadat's introduction to this volume, securitization is defined
as "the way the state and society frame the individuals and groups
drawn to radical religious subcultures" and how to respond to them.
Also in this collection, Jamil notes in chapter 6 that securitization as
it has played out for Canadians affects not only specific radicals but
also all Muslims, who become "collectively … guilty by association."
While those who are specifically or "collaterally" the targets of securitized messages are most affected, I believe that this ripple effect goes
further. It is worth spending some time considering the influence on
all consumers of such messages, whose own response to securitization
may result in hypersensitivity and hyper-awareness of any seemingly
related stories.

To explain, a specific consideration of securitization and journalism
is appropriate. The theoretical strands which bear most relevance for

considering news are those that enable securitization to be seen both as an *effect* on an audience of reporting and as a *way* of reporting facts adopted (consciously or not) by at least some of those involved in the production of the news.[3] If at the core securitization is a means of convincing a public that an issue (in this case, terrorism) is a threat over and above the normal state of affairs, then the creation of security beats fits nicely. Whatever reporting had been done in the past by reporters covering crime, immigration, justice, politics, and foreign affairs, the post-9/11 situation was judged by news decision-makers as necessitating the creation of a new position. Scholars of journalism studies often turn to framing theory as a way of investigating coverage within a variety of beats. As Fred Vultee (2009, 11) summarizes, "frames organize the world in a way that makes sense to the people who produce the news as well as those who read it." For example, with regard to the religion beat, Mark Silk has identified tropes such as the "false prophet" used by reporters (Silk 1995), while other metaphors are used to make sense of reporting about groups of people or activities. Think, for example, of all the battle metaphors employed when reporting on sports matches.

Vultee has conducted studies on securitization and news reporting in the era of the "war on terror" in the United States. Using a group of undergraduate students of journalism who first were asked to identify the level of their support for the American government, he presented stories about immigration, border security, or political violence in the Philippines, Middle East, or Iraq, some of which included amplified emphasis on threat levels and thus were deemed to promote securitization. After reading such stories, students affirmed more trust in the government; this support was particularly strong among those who were already sympathetic to the government.

One of the most striking findings of Vultee's study is that "a sense of personal risk does not appear to be affected by securitization; rather, in line with the Copenhagen School's emphasis on the construction of threats to shared culture, securitization creates a sense of danger to 'us,' not to 'me'" (Vultee 2009, 22). This idea and sense of communal threat fits a traditional concept of news media as an important stand-in for the public square in contemporary society.

If one considers that in many ways, religious radicalization is the flip side of the securitization coin (cf. chapter 1 by Bramadat for more on this dialectical relationship), it is worth considering how we might understand the parallel effects of reporting on individuals and groups at risk.

The potential for simultaneous attraction and repulsion is at the heart of what Marcus Bullock describes as the media danger market. Nietzsche's recommendation to live dangerously is taken by Bullock as a powerful starting point for a discussion of the seductive power of fear at work in a securitized, post-9/11 America (Bullock 2006). There are individual attractions to fear (paying to see a horror film) as well as communal ones (the crowd gathering to see a train wreck). Bullock writes, "[T]o the extent that danger does circulate in our society as an object of fascination and desire, it does so because we choose it. This does not unmask such danger as necessarily unreal or only self-imposed. The dangers that offer the greatest challenge and the greatest thrill in meeting that challenge are the ones imposed on us" (Bullock 2006, 69).

Speaking specifically from a post-9/11, American stance, Bullock warns of the risks when a society fails to take into account the individual's response to danger: "The eagerness, one might almost say frenzied appetite, we have shown for the danger we imagine we are in reveals something about the security we have every reason to establish. Security is a value to us, but the sense of danger is a value as well. We have seized on the heightened state of alarm because this intensity of experience offers us a state of consciousness in which we can encounter ourselves in a heightened mode. The state of crisis manifests something that both attracts us and repels us. It figures as an internal part of our appointment with destiny" (Bullock 2006, 83). It is easy to hear echoes here of Bill Keller's remarks about the birth of his daughter affecting his post-9/11 sensibilities.

It would be folly, as well as a slap to truth-seeking, to suggest that news organizations should ignore threats. Threats exist, and wishing them away will not keep them from appearing. But it is also ridiculous to ignore the fact that as the coverage of danger shores up the need for belonging and safety among readers, it also results in sales of newspapers and media advertising, since the audience is drawn to the spectre of danger as well. Securitization methods and messages embedded in journalism not only "frame" those drawn to radical responses, they also help to prime the interest of non-radicals who are intrigued by potential threats. While journalists and news organizations adhere to goals of truth-telling, in most cases they do not do so as part of a non-profit endeavour. In the danger market, if a threat appears particularly strange, immediate, or easily described ("man bites dog"), it is easier for it to be sold.

Journalism and Radicalization

Sometimes it is hard not to picture terrorists holed up in caves, with AK-47s resting against the muddy walls and generators powering broadcasts of Fox News, around which they all huddle. Giggling. Rubbing their hands. "This is making our job too easy," one would exclaim. Gifts for al Qaeda recruiters: the Iraq war, the abuse of prisoners at Abu Ghraib, the burning of Qur'ans, the tortured death of an Afghan taxi driver in Bagram, waterboarding, misguided predator drones, faulty intelligence. (Shephard 2011b, 50)

It is easy to embrace Shephard's imaginary scene as reality, but do we in fact know if those radicalized have consumed news sources, particularly Canadian ones? Teotonio's reporting on the Toronto 18 for the *Toronto Star* suggests that many of the young men watched videos online of attacks against Westerners but doesn't include any information about mainstream news consumption (Teotonio et al. 2010). The same is true of Bell's description of Mohammed Mansour Jabarah's attraction to "jihadist" videos (Bell 2005, 37). In Shephard's discussions of Omar Khadr and other young men attracted to the struggle in Afghanistan, news reports don't figure (Shephard 2008), although jihadist videos do. So does reporting matter when it comes to reducing the risk of radicalization? I would strongly argue that it does and for a number of reasons.

Using examples bearing on radicalization involving Muslims, it is clear that reporting on conflict which involves Muslims and non-Muslims provides fodder for pro-terrorist propaganda. One need only think of the repeated stories of American pastor Terry Jones threatening to burn copies of the Qur'an and how these threats translated into protests and attacks. But there are ways of countering this ever-present possibility. First, while almost any reporting can be manipulated by propagandists, it is easier to refute this manipulation when the original report gets the details and context right. To continue with the Jones example, how many followers does he have? Only 30 showed up for a burning in March 2011. What percentage is this of all American evangelicals? Sometimes, journalists have the opportunity to directly challenge the twisting of facts. For example, after determining that a Somali girl stoned to death was in fact only 13 and not over 20 (as had been reported on numerous websites), Shephard writes, "[N]ot that her killing would have been justified had she been any age, but I took delight in debunking the jihadi websites" (2011b, 60). Second, apart from basic reporting accuracy, encouraging an open media marketplace for voices such as broadcaster Al Jazeera will add breadth to the point of view and interpretation of affairs. Third, reporting which includes Canadians identified as Muslims in stories that aren't centred on conflict can provide alternate verses to a chorus of universal oppression and strife. The same could be said of stories in which Sikhs figure prominently. In a recent appearance at a press freedom conference, Markham-based Sikh Canadian journalist Jagdish Grewal echoed this sentiment, noting that he and other well-known Sikhs are often at personal risk when quoted by mainstream news media. "We are often interviewed by them because we are the most visible faces of the community," he said. "The next day, you find that you have been quoted out of context, thus exposing you to a huge danger ... It's a good thing to cover the negative aspects as well, but there are a lot of positive things that are happening too ... Quote us in the positive stories where we can say, 'Yes, we're not only talking negatively about our community'" (Fatima 2012).

Better and more reporting will potentially benefit Canadians including those in the communities targeted by groups seeking to radicalize young people. But it won't directly touch those most at risk if they aren't engaged in mainstream media consumption. In this respect, the group most likely to be subjects of radicalization is of the age cohort least likely, for example, to consume traditional newspapers. There are many attempts at attracting young Canadians not only as audiences but as producers of news as well (Roy 2008).[4] But even if young people themselves don't follow, for example, stories about people being recruited to radical causes on campuses, if adults have the opportunity to see such reports, there is the chance that they may be more vigilant. Journalism studies in general are in their infancy, but it is possible to look at a few examples from scholars. Schatz reminds us of the media coverage of groups such as the Baader-Meinhof: "As the fight against terrorism in Germany in the 1970s and 1980s has shown, refuting the arguments of nonviolent 'sympathizers' at an intellectual level helps destroy the breeding ground for the extremists. Constantly repeating pictures of bearded suspects with a turban, however, only stirs up emotions" (Schatz 2003, xvi). (See chapter 3 by Dawson and chapter 11 by Norton and Upal for more on the role of argument and narrative as means of disabling radicalization.) Given Schatz's observations, having an opportunity to examine the religious nature of radicals would at least challenge the sway of an imagined identity and struggle.

At this point, I think it is worth considering the coverage of foreign and domestic news and how this might play into the creation of a sense of alienation and search for belonging. The dearth of religion beats and expertise is a challenge for tackling this kind of reporting at home. But it is not the only problem. The coverage of foreign events through Canadian eyes and ears – once a highly prized commodity for news outlets – has diminished in the age of shrinking budgets and shifting audience interests. This is not a situation unique to the Canadian media environment (Allan 2010), but because of our traditional healthy appetite for international news, it does have a particular effect when compared to other national news markets. In previous research, I have noted that an overwhelming amount of material about religion appearing in Canadian news sources originates somewhere other than Canada (Smith 1999). If Canadians are no longer the ones gathering this information, reporting done literally with a view to serving a Canadian audience by making clear the connections between abroad and at home – a long-held boast of the CBC – is no longer occurring, despite promises to the contrary (Taylor 2003).

The bridging of international and domestic news is crucial when considering issues of radicalization. Some have identified the persuasive power of al-Qaeda- and Taliban-style propaganda in linking the suffering of the ummah (rather than specific communities) to Western interference and influence (Bell 2005, 37). Appealing to Muslims by engaging a sense of membership in a global community diminishes national and local variations. The news environments of the United States and Canada present contrasting forms of resistance to this attempt by the radicals to cement the identification of Muslims with the plight of the broader ummah.

In discussing the reporting of terrorism from an American standpoint, Schatz writes, "Before the [9/11] attacks, foreign affairs were presented as irrelevant to anyone enjoying the 'American way of life.' Foreign conflicts and domestic security issues were rarely linked in the news. Accordingly, US foreign policies went largely unexamined, appearing as incontestable extensions of the best in cultural, political, and economic values" (Schatz 2003, xvii). To be an American, then, in this media sphere would seem to necessitate an embrace of an us/them approach to foreign affairs, even for Muslim Americans, which works against any tendency to identify with members of the global ummah.

Alternatively, the line-up of a nightly Canadian newscast seldom polarizes foreign and domestic issues to this extent, and in most cases, the goal is in fact to "localize" an international story, particularly in multicultural markets such as Toronto: "Many reporters like to poke fun at old-school *Star* editors who believe every foreign story needs a Toronto connection ... Earthquake in Pakistan? Find that injured guy who once lived in Toronto or has a cousin in Mississauga and suddenly your story is moving from A17 to the front page" (Shephard 2011b, 40). The effect of this localization strategy results in emphasizing that what happens to those outside Canadian borders often has a direct influence on those within. Security beats can further reinforce this bridging and in ways that suggest Canadians do care about what happens to others, Muslim or otherwise. But, of course, it also sometimes brings conflicts from abroad into the Canadian context.

Indeed, Canadian news outlets run stories about other countries' approach to controlling security and radicalization almost as often as Canada's own (cf. Goldman, Apuzzo, and Associated Press 2011). This isn't unreasonable, given the close relationship Canada has with the United States and the close links with other nations borne of its immigration histories. Nonetheless, in contrast to the coverage in other countries, this attention to the external is unusual. In fact, as Edna Keeble observes in chapter 10 of this book, our attention to foreign events and movements may influence the kind of Canadian dialogue that can happen around the Cross-Cultural Roundtable.

Time and the Front Lines of Reporting

One of the first questions asked of a journalism student is, what is news? News judgment is both art and science, but some basic criteria are used to evaluate information. How relevant is it to the reader/listener/viewer? How unusual is it? How recent is the event? Time elements drive much of the news decision-making in a 24-hour news cycle. Breaking news is among the most challenging types of reporting, and it is often where stories about terrorism and radicalization begin. In the Oklahoma and both World Trade Center bombings, as well as the more recent massacre in Norway, the importance of immediate attribution of blame by 24-hour broadcast and online news was both obvious and powerful. There are many pitfalls for news organizations in dealing with these situations, however, and both the absence and the overly hasty provision of news in cases of terrorism can have implications for the attitudes adopted towards radicalization and securitization. A foreign example involving immediate news decision-making will be explored here before turning to similar issues raised by Canadian examples.

An investigation of the reporting by one of Spain's major radio networks in the immediate wake of the March 2004 train bombings in Madrid (Rodero, Maíllo, and Tamarit 2009) illustrates very well the way in which officials may attempt to insert securitization messages in the heat of a breaking news event and how this can backfire. The reporting on the event went on long after the researchers' timeline for studying Cadena SER's coverage, but there is merit in considering the way in which breaking news is covered, given that this is when large audiences tune in and may be all they watch/listen/read and remember.

The study, conducted by Spanish scholars Emma Rodero, Aurora Pérez Maíllo, and Ana Tamarit, identified the frames used by Cadena SER in presenting the story of the Madrid bombings. They identify the most prominent one as the human interest frame (e.g., the suffering of the victims). This is followed closely by the responsibility frame, within which journalists reported suggestions, particularly those offered by government members of the Partido Popular, that the Basque separatist group ETA was responsible for the bombing. Other frames identified by the researchers include what they describe as the conflict (e.g., the identification of the damage), morality (e.g., condemnation of the attacks using moral terms), and mobilization frames (e.g., of citizens and politicians against the attacks). Finally, there is a frame dealing with the economic fallout of the event (Rodero, Maíllo, and Tamarit 2009, 88). During the first few hours of this event, attention on the Cadena SER broadcasts shifted between conveying the basic shock of destruction (variations of the human interest and conflict frames) and trying to ascertain who perpetrated this crime (the responsibility frame). The early theory advanced by the incumbent government centred on a non-religiously motivated, internal threat (the ETA), and the Partido Popular (PP) government continued to advance this claim long after Cadena SER and others began to report information suggesting the perpetrators were an al-Qaeda-influenced group of largely non-Spanish terrorists. The Partido Popular lost the national election which soon followed the bombing, and the Cadena SER reporting likely played a role in this turn of events. (Critics will point out that Cadena SER is traditionally an opponent of the PP.) Cadena SER encouraged people to defend democracy by going to the polls and voting in the election rather than remaining fearful and at home. This mobilization frame echoes Nossek's assertion that reporters assist citizens in taking back power from terrorists (Nossek 2008, 328). And the Partido Popular's election chances were almost certainly hampered by reporters who aired the government's ETA claims and then challenged their veracity as new evidence came to light. (Ironically, the victory of the opposition Partido Socialisto Obrera Español, or PSOE, satisfied one of the demands of the terrorists, since the new government immediately took steps to remove Spanish troops from the coalition of forces fighting in Iraq.)

Reporting on dramatic events in the first moments and hours of a breaking story often introduces into the public debate – consciously or otherwise – messages promoting the securitization of particular religious or political groups. But journalists also face challenges with stories which drag on over months and even years, with mixed implications once again for trends in radicalization and securitization in affected communities. Here I turn to Canadian examples of reporting.

In many cases, including that of the Toronto 18 (see Dawson's chapter 3 for more specific information), publication bans are often imposed by the courts, so it can be a long time before reporters are able to learn or publish important details. The vacuum of information during this time leaves the public and journalists grasping to know more. The first Toronto 18 arrests were made 2 June 2006, charges made public 5 June, and the publication ban on bail proceedings was put in place 12 June. The ban was broken almost four years later by the Quebec Superior Court on 17 February 2010 and the Supreme Court of Canada on 19 February 2010. Regardless of the reasons for the bans (multiple defendants, security concerns, publicity affecting jury selection), the effect of the lack of information is the same. In the immediate reaction to the arrests, reporters tended to focus on the potential of the threat, reinforcing the securitization frame. Then in the absence of other voices during the long period of the ban, the securitization frame was further emphasized, based on the information that was available from security officials. But for others the longer justice was delayed (or at least seemed to be on hold), the more it appeared to be denied, lending support to those who would advocate radical responses to the situation. There was considerable scepticism about the merits of the case against the accused young Muslims and some suspicion that they were the victims of Islamophobia. But it would be fair to say that in the Toronto 18 case, as more information about the admitted activities of some of those sentenced came to light, the public criticism of the security concerns of the authorities diminished significantly. Thus, the immediate securitization message which came with the arrests waxed and then waned in the vacuum of information during the publication ban, during which scepticism about the validity of the case gained in strength (also allowing for the adoption of more radical reactions to perceived crackdowns). As the cases came to court and information was entered into the public record, the news conveyed that there was a very real potential threat, although less than might have first been perceived.

But the delays associated with the case of the Toronto 18 are nothing compared with the Air India bombing saga (for more on the Sikh Canadian context, see chapter 7 by Jakobsh). The murder of 329 people aboard Air India Flight 182 took place on 22 June 1985, but primary suspects Ripudaman Singh Malik and Ajaib Singh Bagri weren't charged until 2000. They were eventually found not guilty in 2005, after the judge determined the evidence presented was inadequate for conviction. Inderjit Singh Reyat was only charged in 2001, and in October 2012 he appealed to the Supreme Court of Canada to overturn his related convictions for perjury. A federal public inquiry began in June 2006 and was finally completed four years later. There are few events, no matter how tragic, which can hold the public's attention for over 25 years.

The case of the 1985 Air India bombing (still the terrorist event responsible for killing the most Canadians in a single blow) is unique in that the factual "us" – the Canadians killed on board – were treated at the time by the government and some reports as "them" (witness then prime minister Mulroney's message of sympathy to the Indian government; Brethour 2010). And the fact that the plane exploded near Ireland, far from Canadian borders, further diminished the chance that the story could be identified as domestic in nature. Distance, religious and ethnic difference, complexity, and the long time span of the investigation and trials challenged reporters. Not many journalists want to or even can devote decades of their career to reporting such a case.

There are also the serious threats to the personal safety of journalists who have covered the story. *Indo-Canadian Times* publisher Tara Singh Hayer was shot and paralysed before being killed in 1998 for what many believe was his reporting and investigation into the Air India bombing. Kim Bolan of the *Vancouver Sun* worked on the story for decades, having to take on more and more security measures to protect herself and her family, a saga she recounts in her book *Loss of Faith: How the Air-India Bombers Got Away with Murder* (Bolan 2005). Terry Milewski, a journalist for CBC television and long-time reporter on the Air India attack and other national and international security issues, has also drawn the ire of Sikh groups, notably the World Sikh Organization, which has sued both Bolan and Milewski and their employers for libel.

In a 2009 speech to Regina journalism students, Milewski said, "[T]he purpose of such a suit is not to get at the truth but to harass you, to position the WSO as somehow entitled to speak for the Sikh community and to pressure your bosses into finding some other story for you to cover. For good measure, a toxic Facebook page supporting the lawsuit sprang up, on which more death threats were uttered. One said that we should 'find out where Milewski lives and put hiz [sic] head on a stick.' Such are the people who applaud the WSO's lawsuit against the CBC" (Milewski 2009).

Those who report on the Sikh Canadian community from within do not have the "luxury" of being an outsider like Bolan or Milewski. Jagdish Grewal, publisher of a variety of ethnic newspapers, including the *Canadian Punjabi Post*, recently spoke about the challenges and dangers of reporting on Sikh extremism.[5] He himself was attacked in the parking lot outside his newsroom in October 2009. The assailants have yet to be charged. Grewal said that "for ethnic media, there is nothing called freedom. All we know is that either you are on (the side of extremists) or you are facing them." He sees the ethnic press as a potential medium for the dissemination of radical views. "For hard cores, to reach out to the community, ethnic media is their tool" (Fatima 2012).

The final Canadian example is "live" as of the writing of this chapter. On 29 March 2011, a 25-year-old Canadian man named Mohamed Hersi was arrested at Toronto's Pearson International Airport. The trial began in late March 2014, with facts beginning to be provided in court three years after the arrest. Early reporting noted that he was arrested while awaiting a flight to Cairo. Police allege that this was but a first stop en route to Somalia, where he was to train with al-Shabaab. Since March 2010, al-Shabaab has been on the list of organizations recognized by the Canadian government as being associated with terrorism. The government's online listing describes the group as "an organized but shifting Islamist group dedicated to establishing a Somali caliphate, waging war against the enemies of Islam, and removing all foreign forces and Western influence from Somalia ... The group is believed to be closely linked with Al Qaida and recently formally pledged allegiance to Usama bin Laden and his terrorist network" (Public Safety Canada 2011).

The coverage of the arrest through his release on bail allows one to consider some of the ways in which Canadian journalists have reported on an alleged case of radicalization. As opposed to the more frequent case of trying to understand an individual's radicalization after the fact and often from overseas, this event (if the allegations are correct) would seem to offer us an opportunity to report on a person in the process of being radicalized. While all the details will not be available until the Hersi trial is completed, it would appear that he had yet to receive even the limited training and planning the Toronto 18 had undertaken before their arrests.

I examined broadcast transcripts, wire service texts, and stories from Canadian outlets dealing with Mohamed Hersi as catalogued by CBCA, Lexis-Nexis, and Factiva (Dow Jones) from 29 March (the day of his arrest) until September 2011. I found 36 stories, not including those which were for the most part reprints of the same narratives (e.g., a very similar story by the same reporter printed simultaneously in the *Ottawa Citizen*, the *Calgary Herald*, and the *National Post*).

There are marked differences in when and how much attention the case received: CTV, Global, and CBC television all covered the story on their flagship national evening newscasts on 30 March. But at least until the fall of 2011, Hersi's case hadn't been aired again. Also notable is the coverage by foreign wire services, Reuters and the Associated Press, which had stories out on 30 March but seemingly none again until September 2011. As many if not a majority of Canadians still get their daily news from television (in 2003, 67 per cent of Canadians watched a daily newscast on TV as compared to 42 per cent who read a newspaper daily; Canadian Media Research Consortium 2004), this initial reporting by broadcasters takes on added importance. And the lack of regular news about Canada showing up in foreign news outlets means that what does get reported often takes on exaggerated importance.

In examining the material, I quantified the following:

- How many stories specifically mention something religious? (64 per cent)
- How many make clear that he is a Canadian citizen? (100 per cent)
- How many include quotations from or references to his family? (11 per cent)
- How many name and explain al-Shabaab? (94 per cent)
- Is the reporter on an identified security beat? (28 per cent)
- How often are comments included from Somali Canadians? From authorities? (Both included, 47 per cent; only Somali Canadians, 5 per cent; only authorities (police, courts, experts), 33 per cent; none (narrative from reporter only), 15 per cent)

- How much follow-up is there after the initial news of the arrest? (64 per cent of stories came later)
- Do any of the reports suggest issues which may be involved in radicalization? (78 per cent)

Once past the basic figures, there are some interesting patterns and approaches which should be recognized. While the majority of stories (94 per cent) name and describe al-Shabaab, these descriptions vary. In some cases, there is mention of al-Qaeda but nothing more: "Authorities allege the suspect was planning to travel to Somalia to join al-Shabaab – an insurgent group with links to Al-Qa'ida" (Postmedia News 2011, A14). Yet others have a more elaborate description: "His flight to Cairo, police said, was only the first leg of a journey to Somalia, where he intended to join Al-Shabab, an al-Qaeda-linked armed Islamist extremist group that has been recruiting youths in the West" (Bell 2011b, A5).

It is also noteworthy that stories which only included comments from the Somali Canadian community were far fewer than those which featured authorities only. This fits an approach to reporting in which authority sources are privileged. While this might seem to perpetuate problematic notions of the "other," it is important to remember that in reporting short updates on legal cases, the legal and security authorities are the only sources of new information, and often during proceedings, family and community members either cannot or will not talk publicly. Hersi himself wasn't quoted until his release on bail: "Outside court, Mr. Hersi said he was happy to be out of jail, and thanked Justice of the Peace Hilda Weiss for granting bail last month. 'I'm not going to disappoint her,' he said" (O'Toole 2011, A11). However, even acknowledging the logistical challenges, the result is the same. Even if the journalist is not consciously promoting a securitization trope, the coverage can be identified as fitting such a frame because of the lack of alternative voices. As Vultee notes, "Journalists who decline to choose an ostensible frame, or who think the frame that looks most like 'news' is the only choice available under professional standards, are likely to end up with whatever the house is serving. However socially palatable that might seem at the time, it could produce consequences that run counter to the best professional intent of the practitioners" (2009, 24).

It is also important to reflect on comments on online sites, with all the attendant issues around the editorial moderation of postings. While these comments cannot be considered reporting, they do suggest the audience's reception of the information provided. And they are part of the means by which stories are judged to be most popular or most read, markers used to determine what kind of stories drive "hits" and advertising revenue, and therefore are more attractive for continued coverage. Following the package of material on the ctv.ca website dealing with the Hersi arrest were a number of reader-submitted comments which featured common themes: Hersi's citizenship, accolades for the police and CSIS, and concerns about an arrest made seemingly before any threatening actions occurred.

Glen in Ottawa said, This man should be tried and if convicted of being a terrorist sentenced accordingly. If he is not a Canadian citizen, he should then be deported to his homeland. Any persons subsequently supporting him finanacially [sic] should also face the same full force of the law. Canada must stop handing out citizenship like CrackerJack prizes to any one fotunate [sic] enough to set foot here, ten years to show your commitment, then you may apply to stay, and a one year limit to welfare during the ten first years.

Crusader said, Read the book Nomad by Ayaan Hirsi Ali and be on guard for her predictions. Also her new book a bestseller "Infidel" is now here.

Terry said, Thank you to Toronto police and RCMP. If guilty send him back to Somalia and dont [sic] let him back.

Anne said, Some of the posts here concern me – would you rather he be left to his own devices until a terrorist act is actually committed? Would that make you all feel better? Just think how different things would be if they had caught those responsible for 9/11 before it actually occurred. The rights of one criminal DO NOT override the rights of the majority of a society.

UNBLIND MAN said, The man was just going back home to visit family and unless there is uncertain evidence without doubt they cannot hold him, the immigration or CICI's [sic] must prove he was in the act while in Canada weather [sic] it maybe calling back home or plotting it in Toronto. This is just another case of Islamaphobia.

Public Speaker said, The family likely knew that this guy was up to no good. Through [sic] them all in jail! Good work RCMP keeping us safe.

Nick in Chatham said, [S]tories like this are fear mongering. They got a maybe-potential-sorta terrorist. Big deal. Know how many Canadian murderers and Canadian pedophiles are walking around right now? Way more than terrorists, I'll tell you that. (ctvtoronto.ca 2011)

Such comments illustrate clearly the links made by their authors between otherwise unrelated topics, certainly seeming to be influenced by securitization. Family members are implicated in the (unproved) actions of a single member, the theories and experiences of Ayaan Hirsi Ali and 9/11 terrorists are invoked, and security forces are thanked for keeping "us" safe. It is, however, noteworthy that some of those who added comments were sceptical of the charges and the real level of threat to the community. One can perceive in these comments how news reports occasion responses (originating from within radicalized, "collateral," or general audiences) which may be seen to react to a securitized frame. While not journalism, they in turn become part of the media response to a story.

While less than a third of the news stories on Hersi came from reporters on the security beat, those stories tended to be the longest, featured the most diversity of sources, and included religious elements. It isn't immediately evident why: are the stories longer because the news organization recognizes the need to give the security reporter space, or is the space larger because the reporter was able to file a longer, more compelling story? Again, in some ways it doesn't really matter: the correlation between the story length and depth and its filing by a reporter on the security beat is indisputable. With more space, there are better opportunities for more nuanced explorations of the issues, without having to resort to framed, shorthand explanations.

In coverage by the *National Post*'s Stewart Bell, the *Globe and Mail*'s Colin Freeze, and Isabel Teotonio in the *Toronto Star*, the more general topic of radicalization taking place among Somali Canadians is included. A number of follow-up articles made use of Hersi's arrest to uncover stories of other young people who had gone missing and were feared to have been radicalized, for example, "Somali Terrorists Lure City Women: Two Toronto Residents First Females Recruited" (Aulakh and Teotonio 2011, A1), "Missing City Woman Is Niece of Somali PM" (Aulakh 2011, A1), and "CSIS Investigating U of T Student Suspected of Ties to Somali Terrorist Group" (Freeze 2011). Hersi was also referred to in order to provide context for reports that Canadians had been killed in Somalia in June and August 2011 (e.g., Bell 2011c, A7). By linking the two, some indirect suggestions are made to the reader: first, that Hersi will be found guilty of the charges and, second, that his arrest saved him from a fate similar to "Abdurrahman the Canadian." The implicit result is that this case is an example of radicalization nipped in the bud. The follow-up stories suggest that young Somali Canadians are under threat of radicalization and so non–Somali Canadians are in turn threatened by those same young people.

Bell in particular has followed Canada's approach to radicalization, even across the border in the United States.

"This dangerous and constant anti-Western narrative is fed to them by radicals in our community who do not hesitate to use these vulnerable youth as gun fodder in their desire to establish a base for the al-Qaeda terrorist group in Somalia," Canadian Somali Congress president Ahmed Hussen testified in Washington last week.

Canada outlawed Al-Shabab last year due to concerns it was recruiting young Somali-Canadians. But Mr. Hussen criticized Ottawa for concentrating on detecting and arresting terror suspects while leaving their rhetoric unchallenged.

"The strategy of Canadian officials as they confront this phenomenon in my community has been to view this serious matter only through the prism of law enforcement," he said. "There has not been a parallel attempt to counter the toxic anti-Western narrative that creates a culture of victimhood in the minds of members of our community." (Bell 2011a, A6)

Closer to home, *Toronto Star* reporter Teotonio described the specific circumstances of Hersi's life in Toronto: "He was tired of living in a dilapidated public housing unit near Markham Rd. and Eglinton Ave. E. and of watching his mother, a widow who had raised four children alone, struggling to make ends meet. And as he told a cousin, Hersi wanted to go to Egypt to 'get the morals I've lost'" (Teotonio, Rush, and Mitchell 2011, A1).

Teotonio's observation echoes Dawson's earlier argument: "The grievances, affronts, or problems that precede their conversion, and sometimes are used as excuses for turning away from 'normal' society, are catalysts for change, but the real cause is an abiding sense of relative moral deprivation" (Dawson 2010, 9). Without going into great detail, Teotonio also included information about religious conversion and activities of those identified as the Toronto 18 in her report for the *Toronto Star* (Teotonio et al. 2010). This is also in keeping with Dawson's suggestion that "it is imperative to recognize and deal forthrightly with the 'religious' character of these groups and the process of radicalization (I suspect even in supposedly secular groups). In truth the individuals are seeking, and once they find it greatly prize, a 'sacralized' existence" (Dawson 2010, 8).

I believe it is fair to say that in most of the longer pieces of reporting, journalists do try to uncover some of the roots of radicalization, including religious ones. This is true of feature pieces or documentaries, or in books such as *Loss of Faith: How the Air-India Bombers Got Away with Murder* (Bolan 2005), *Guantanamo's Child: The Untold Story of Omar Khadr* (Shephard 2008), and *The Martyr's Oath: The Apprenticeship of a Homegrown Terrorist* (Bell 2005). Most religious processes, apart from Damascus-like conversion experiences, take time, and this can only be fully conveyed in a longer narrative, free of the strictures of space and time affecting daily journalism.

The Floating Frame

In conclusion, I would like to suggest a nuanced means of considering Canadian reporting on security issues and what this may mean for religious radicalization.

This begins by revisiting framing theory. The basic metaphor of a "frame" remains useful, but at least in the case of security reporting, it should evolve alongside tangible, real-world picture frames. A traditional frame surrounds an image, is mounted on a wall, and is viewed from a single side, giving preference and static solidity to one dimension. (Imagine if you will a "wanted" poster.) But today it's easy to find floating frames, in which an object is sandwiched between two panes of glass, allowing both sides to be viewed, especially if it is suspended from above rather than mounted on a wall. I would argue that it is this kind of frame which best represents the ideal approach to security reporting.

Facing the frame from one side may be analogous to standing in Rexdale, Ontario, reading a *Toronto Star* report about Mohamed Hersi. Moving to see the piece from the other side of the frame is to be living in Mogadishu, reading the same story online at thestar.com. Globalized, immediate, and simultaneous news dissemination demands that we no longer envision a story in one dimension, available in a single location and with little opportunity for the situation and all the people being discussed to also consume and critique the content. Once upon a time, "they" were the literal wallpaper providing background to a Canadian story reported by a foreign correspondent. Today this is seldom true. As Shephard notes, Somalia "was one of the countries in the world where the Toronto Star carried as much clout as the New York Times – and in some cases more. Many Somalia-born Canadians held positions of great influence in their birth country and had homes about a thirty-minute drive northwest of my newsroom" (Shephard 2011b, 33).

Geography is but one way of approaching the double-sided frame. Looking from one side could be a Somali Canadian worried about radicalization in his or her community. He or she may respond to a message of securitization suggesting a serious threat which requires special attention and action by alerting a journalist or security official to other missing Somali Canadian youth, as happened following the arrest of Hersi. On the other side one might find a younger Somali Canadian attracted to the idea of running away from his challenges in Canada to join al-Shabaab. On this side, the Hersi story will be read as the persecution of an individual who is trying to engage in a struggle of liberation; consequently, radicalization may find favour. As presented by journalists within the news media danger market, the same story can exert diametrically opposed attractions for two people from the same community, with totally different consequences for the surrounding society.

If the coverage is presented within a frame of two (or more) sides, there is at least the opportunity for the forces at work in the complex dialectic of radicalization and securitization to be critiqued and questioned. If all that is being consumed is propagandist Islamist websites, it is akin to staring at a picture in a frame screwed to a wall in a members-only gallery; the opposite but equally skewed effect can be witnessed if one were to attend only to anti-Islamic websites. In both cases, there is no opportunity to see, much less engage with, other perspectives, either by examining what is in the frame more closely or by discussing the presentations with a more diverse group of gallery-goers.

In a situation where terrorists seek to dominate a media frame, scholars such as Nossek seem to suggest that journalists should adopt an activist approach:

We should consider the terrorist event as an opportunity, at least for the media of the attacked country, to act independently to cope with the dilemma of how to cover the enemy, which essentially wishes to hijack the camera and microphone and use them for their purposes. In its response, the media takes back control of its social function by turning the tables on the terrorists' message. Instead of spreading a message of terror, dread, and alarm, the media sends its country messages of solidarity, partnership, and great endurance against the terrorist threat. (Nossek 2008, 328)

There were certainly echoes of this in the Cadena SER response to the Atocha train station bombings. But the risk is that journalists will adopt an "us versus them" stance, which, as discussed, results in less than professional coverage.

One example of this approach is exemplified in war reporting. The Canadian practice has wavered between cheerleading, practising strict policies of not identifying with the troops (e.g., using "the soldiers" rather than "our soldiers"), and a more recent return, by some reporters, to identifying explicitly with Canadian forces (Halton 2004). In an evaluation of media coverage of terrorism in Israel, the 9/11 attacks in the United States, and the Madrid bombing of 2004 as ritualized events, Nossek writes,

> [W]hen a foreign news item is defined as "ours," journalists' professional practices become subordinate to national loyalty, and when an item is "theirs," journalistic professionalism comes into its own ... In other words, the closer reporters and editors are to a given news event in terms of national interest, the further they are from applying professional news values. (Nossek 2008, 318)

But where Nossek can posit a master narrative which can be put into operation to rally Israelis (Zionism), it is more difficult to identify an obvious Canadian parallel, especially one that might be invoked by security officials or used by Canadian media in cases such as the Air India bombing or the Toronto 18 plot. It may be that Canadian news is particularly suited to embracing a form of coverage which avoids us/them, domestic/foreign, and radical/moderate dichotomies operating if not in one-dimensional, then two-dimensional forms.

Currently, the best we may do is to ask journalists to do a good job at reporting these issues within a multimedia platform, including user-generated content and comment, in an effort to create the infinitely sided floating frame. And when reporters enter the danger market to collect and offer their material, they must do their best to know who is selling securitization, who is buying radicalization, and vice versa.

NOTES

1 In a national telephone survey of Canadians conducted in 2007 for the author by the Survey Research Centre at the University of Waterloo, 32.7 per cent of those self-identifying as Catholic, 42.3 per cent of Protestants, and 35.6 per cent of those who were otherwise religious believed that

religion receives less coverage than it should in news media. Notably, only 13.1 per cent of those identifying as atheists or agnostic gave the same answer. At the other end of the spectrum, 20.9 per cent Catholics, 7.9 per cent of Protestants, 19.4 per cent of those claiming "other," and 28 per cent of atheists/agnostics believed that religion received more coverage than it should.

2 Fung has described how she coped by praying using her rosary and attempting to interview her captors to understand their motivations (Tremonti 2011). She has talked about how her Catholic faith sustained her but was challenged as she saw her captors also praying for success. In her subsequent memoir and interviews, she has described how, apart from the abuse she suffered, at least one of her kidnappers repeated that she had to become a Muslim, while another told her he saw her as his sister and would protect her. In any case, she doesn't think that her kidnappers recognized her religious devotion as being legitimate. While Fung wasn't at the time a security reporter or someone with specific professional expertise in religion or Islam, her attention to the religious aspects of her abduction in itself constitutes a recognition which is not common in reporting from Afghanistan. But clearly, being held and abused as a captive should not be the only means by which Canadian journalists can convey a picture of the religious motivations of combatants.

3 Here I am indebted to Fred Vultee's excellent summary and discussion (Vultee 2009).

4 Some media literacy and production projects have focused on visible minority groups and other Muslim youth (Centre for Faith and the Media 2009).

5 "Ethnic" is the word popularly used for media outlets serving distinct communities; in Canada, the umbrella group representing many such outlets is the National Ethnic Press and Media Council of Canada.

REFERENCES

Addley, Esther. 2011. "Syrian Lesbian Blogger Is Revealed Conclusively to Be a Married Man." *Guardian*, 12 June. http://www.theguardian.com/world/2011/jun/13/syrian-lesbian-blogger-tom-macmaster.

Allan, Stuart. 2010. *News Culture (Issues in Cultural and Media Studies)*. 3rd ed. Maidenhead, UK: McGraw-Hill/Open University Press.

Aulakh, Raveena. 2011. "Missing City Woman Is Niece of Somali PM." *Toronto Star*, 4 April, sec. NEWS.

Aulakh, Raveena, and Isabel Teotonio. 2011. "Somali Terrorists Lure City Women." *Toronto Star*, 1 April.

Bell, Stewart. 2005. *The Martyr's Oath: The Apprenticeship of a Homegrown Terrorist*. Mississauga, ON: J. Wiley and Sons Canada.

– 2011a. "Canadian Terrorism Recruit Killed in Somali Clash; Linked to al-Qaeda." *National Post*, 6 August.

– 2011b. "Man Arrested at Airport on Way to Join Terrorists, Police Say; Authorities Claim Case Highlights Risks of al-Qaida-style Radicalization in Canada." *Edmonton Journal*, 31 March.

– 2011c. "Canada-linked Militant Killed in Mogadishu; Al-Shabab Leader, 'Abdurrahman the Canadian' Reported Dead." *National Post*, 9 June, A7.

Bolan, Kim. 2005. *Loss of Faith: How the Air-India Bombers Got Away with Murder*. Toronto: McClelland and Stewart.

Brethour, Patrick. 2010. "Why Canada Chose to Unremember Air India and Disown Its Victims." *Globe and Mail*, 27 June.

Bullock, Marcus. 2006. "The Origins of the Danger Market." In *Rethinking Global Security: Media, Popular Culture, and the "War on Terror,"* ed. Andrew Martin, Patrice Petro, 67–84. New Brunswick, NJ: Rutgers University Press.

Canadian Media Research Consortium. 2004. "Report Card on Canadian News Media." http://www.cmrcccrm.ca/_OLDSITE/english/report card2004/01.html (site discontinued).

Centre for Faith and the Media. 2009. The Muslim Project. http://www.icfj. org/our-work/faith-media-improving-coverage-islam-and-other-religions (accessed 16 September 2011).

ctvtoronto.ca. 2011. "RCMP Allege Toronto Man was Joining Somali Terror Group." ctv.ca. http://toronto.ctvnews.ca/rcmp-allege-toronto-man-was-joining-somali-terror-group-1.625420 (accessed 12 September 2011).

Cunningham, Brent. 2007. "The Rhetoric Beat." *Columbia Journalism Review* 46: 36–9.

Dawson, Lorne L. 2010. "The Study of New Religious Movements and the Radicalization of Homegrown Terrorists: Opening a Dialogue." *Terrorism and Political Violence* 22 (1): 1–21.

English, Kathy. 2011. "Covering the Terror Beat." *Toronto Star*, 9 September, sec. Opinion.

Fatima, Sahar. 2012. "'There Is Nothing Called Freedom' for Journalists Working in Ethnic Media." *The Canadian Journalism Foundation*. http://j-source. ca/article/there-nothing-called-freedom-journalists-working-ethnic-media.

Freeze, Colin. 2011. "CSIS Investigating U of T Student Suspected of Ties to Somali Terrorist Group." *Globe and Mail*, 4 April.

Goldman, Adam, Matt Apuzzo, and Associated Press. 2011. "NYPD Urging Officers to Eavesdrop on Muslim Groups: Reports." *Toronto Star*, 31 August.

Hall, Stuart M. 1978. *Policing the Crisis: Mugging, the State, and Law and Order*. Critical Social Studies. London: Macmillan.

Halton, Matthew. 2004. "Return to Ortona." cbc.ca. http://www.cbc.ca/
archives/categories/war-conflict/second-world-war/reports-from-abroad-
matthew-halton/return-to-ortona.html.

Keller, Bill. 2011. "My Unfinished 9/11 Business." *New York Times Magazine*, 11
September.

Koring, Paul. 2012. Interview, 1 March.

Milewski, Terry. 2009. "The Unseen Muzzle – How Timidity, Self-censorship
and Libel Chill Work Their Magic." Paper presented at 29th Annual James
M. Minifie Lecture, University of Regina.

Nossek, Hillel. 2008. "'News Media'-Media Events: Terrorist Acts as Media
Events." *Communications: The European Journal of Communication Research* 33
(3): 313–30.

O'Toole, Megan. 2011. "Case Against Man Accused of Plotting to Join Terror
Group Delayed to June 30." *National Post*, 27 May.

Pew Research Center's Project for Excellence in Journalism. 2010. *How News
Happens*. Washington, DC: Pew Research Center.

Postmedia News. 2011. "Toronto Man Arrested on Terrorism Charges; On Way
to Cairo; No Direct Threat Faced by Canada, Police Say of Arrest." *Montreal
Gazette*, 31 March.

Public Safety Canada. 2011. "Currently Listed Entities." Government of Canada, 2011–2012. http://www.publicsafety.gc.ca/cnt/ntnl-scrt/cntr-trrrsm/
lstd-ntts/crrnt-lstd-ntts-eng.aspx.

Pulliam, Sarah. 2009. "Dallas Morning News Cuts Religion Beat." *Christianity
Today*, 30 April. http://www.christianitytoday.com/gleanings/2009/april/
dallas-morning-news-cuts-religion-beat.html.

Reid, Regan. 2011. "Women Reporters Face Extra Dangers in the Field." Ryerson Journalism Research Centre. http://ryejrnresearch.squarespace.com/
whats-new/2011/5/26/women-reporters-face-extra-dangers-in-the-field.
html.

Religion Newswriters Association. 2012. "Our History." http://www.rna.
org/?page=history.

Rodero, Emma, Aurora Pérez Maíllo, and Ana Tamarit. 2009. "El Atentado del
11 de Marzo de 2004 en la Cadena SER Desde la Teoría del Framing" [The
attacks of 11 March 2004 on Cadena SER as seen through framing theory].
Zer: Revista De Estudios De Comunicacion 14: 81–103.

Roy, Anindita Dutta. 2008. "Youth Journalism: Reporting the News for Global
Citizenship." *Youth Media Reporter* 2.

Ryan, Charlotte. 2004. "It Takes a Movement to Raise an Issue: Media Lessons
from the 1997 U.P.S. Strike." *Critical Sociology* 30 (2): 483–511.

Schatz, Roland. 2003. "Foreword." In *Media Wars: News at a Time of Terror*, ed.
Danny Schechter, xiii–xxiv. Lanham, MD: Rowman and Littlefield.

Shephard, Michelle. 2008. *Guantanamo's Child: The Untold Story of Omar Khadr*. Mississauga, ON: John Wiley and Sons Canada.

– 2011a. "Decade of Fear: Reporting from Terrorism's Grey Zone." *Toronto Star*, 9 September.

– 2011b. *Decade of Fear: Reporting from Terrorism's Grey Zone*. Vancouver: Douglas and McIntyre.

Silk, Mark. 1995. *Unsecular Media: Making News of Religion in America*. Urbana: University of Illinois Press.

Smith, Graeme, Jayson Taylor, Chris Manza, Alisa Mamak, Trish McAlaster, and Tonia Cowan. 2008. "Talking to the Taliban." Globeandmail.com. http://v1.theglobeandmail.com/talkingtothetaliban/.

Smith, Joyce. 1999. "Six Mediated Months in the Country – Religion as News in Canada." Rockefeller Seminar Series, Centre for the Study of Religion, University of Toronto.

– 2003. "Religion Beat or Dead Beat? Canadian Journalists Report on World Youth Day 2002." Conference presentation, Society for the Scientific Study of Religion, Norfolk, VA, 23–26 October.

– 2010. "Newsmakers, Newsbreakers and the Representation of Religion." Conference presentation, Society for the Scientific Study of Religion, Baltimore, 29–30 October.

Taylor, Carole. 2003. "The CBC Is Worth Fighting For." *Globe and Mail*, 22 October 2003, A17.

Teotonio, Isabel, Noor Javed, Kevin Scanlon, Scott Simmie, Bernard Weil, Randy Risling, Chris So, and James Ma. 2010. "Toronto 18." *Toronto Star*. http://www3.thestar.com/static/toronto18/index.html.

Teotonio, Isabel, Curtis Rush, and Bob Mitchell. 2011. "Arrest Alarms Toronto Somalis: Terror Charges Against U of T Graduate Spark Fears al Qaeda-inspired Group Is Recruiting from Abroad." *Toronto Star*, 31 March, sec. Front.

Tremonti, Anna Maria. 2011. *A Memoir of Captivity: Mellissa Fung*. Toronto: CBC Radio, The Current.

Tuchman, Gaye. 1978. *Making News: A Study in the Construction of Reality*. New York: Free Press.

Vultee, Fred. 2009. "Securitization as a News Frame: Effects on Attitudes and Story Processing when the Media 'Speak Security.'" *Conference Papers – International Studies Association* (2009): 1–28.

10 The Cross-Cultural Roundtable on Security as a Response to Radicalization: Personal Experiences and Academic Reflections

EDNA KEEBLE

Introduction

The dialectical relationship between securitization and radicalization in the post-9/11 environment, as framed by Bramadat in the introductory chapter, is expressed distinctively in the Canadian context. Some of the features of the Canadian setting have included the way religious differences have been articulated against the backdrop of the Palestinian-Israeli conflict as well as related sentiments and public discourses around Islamophobia and anti-Semitism. Understanding the term "securitization" as a reference to "the way the state and society frame the individuals and groups drawn to radical religious subcultures" (Bramadat's chapter in this volume) would appear to focus the discussion narrowly on "members of religious groups under scrutiny." Although this volume brings out the extent to which Sikhs, Hindus, Buddhists, and Christians have been subject to securitization in various ways, the religious identities of the 9/11 terrorists have placed Muslims front and centre in the current security environment. In the argument presented here, I contend that we need to broaden our understanding of securitization to include not only individuals or groups who are radicalized but also individuals or groups who respond to the radicalization. In particular, members of the Jewish tradition also merit attention by those exploring the linkages between religion and radicalization. This broader frame of reference is instructive for analysing governmental initiatives to reach out to affected communities, in particular the Cross-Cultural Roundtable on Security (hereafter referred to as the Roundtable), a 15-member advisory body to the Ministers of Public Safety and Justice created under the auspices of the National Security Policy

(Government of Canada 2004, 2) and supported by a secretariat in Public Safety Canada.

I was a member of the Roundtable from its inaugural meeting in March 2005 until June 2008. After the Liberal government released its policy in 2004, Public Safety Canada initiated an open nomination process for membership which resulted in 238 nominations received by the department.[1] The final decision on appointing the 15 members would rest with the Public Safety Minister, who at the time was Anne McLellan, as well as the Justice Minister, a position then held by Irwin Cotler. Governments change; so, too, do memberships in advisory councils, boards, agencies, and other bodies that are subject to appointments by the government of the day. According to the original guidelines governing the Roundtable, members are appointed for one-year terms, renewable for a maximum of three years. Although there were some fears among Roundtable members that the new Conservative government elected in January 2006 would use the opportunity of the one-year term to begin immediately replacing members, then Public Safety Minister Stockwell Day and Justice Minister Rob Nicholson did not act until March 2008, when they replaced five members, including the chair of the Roundtable.[2] Although I had stepped down after the June 2008 meeting, it was not until March 2011 that five additional new members were appointed to the Roundtable, leaving at that point five from the original membership.[3] The Roundtable significantly changed membership in 2012 and 2013, and it continues to meet about three or four times annually.

There are short summaries of Roundtable meetings posted on Public Safety Canada's website, but meetings are held in camera. Although this would rightly prevent me from attributing statements or comments to specific members, my three-year experience as a member of the Roundtable has given me insight into the challenges of a government-led initiative that invites and supports community voices, the significance of religious identities in a "cross-cultural" advisory body that is meant to be reflective of Canadian diversity, and the questions that arise when the focus is less on the impacts of security measures on communities and more on the impacts of communities on Canada's security. Woven throughout the discussion of my personal experiences on the Roundtable are broader academic reflections about being part of the "globalized elite culture," as Peter Berger (1999) pointed out over a decade ago, schooled in the humanities and social sciences; becoming a "principal 'carrier' of progressive, Enlightened beliefs and values" (10); and (once) uncritically accepting the idea of Canada as a secular state. The reflections that I present here stem largely from the time that I was on the Roundtable. I was invited to participate in the Roundtable because I am an academic, and since my expertise in security studies and political science frame my experiences in this group, Dawson and Bramadat thought I could contribute something interesting to this book; however, the main objective of this chapter is to offer personal rather than scholarly assessments.

I make two central observations in this chapter: one rests on the negative perception of government actions and the other on the positive perception of community outreach and consultations. First, academic and activist critiques of government-led initiatives, like the Roundtable, are underpinned too often by a fundamental distrust of anything that the government does. Governments are usually regarded as monolithic entities, treating the current governing Conservative Party, Public Safety Canada, the RCMP, CSIS, and the Canada Border Services Agency (CBSA) as if they were one coherent and consistent body and perceiving politicians, civil servants, police officers, intelligence officials, and border agents not as individuals who are themselves products and members of the Canadian society but as mere agents of this abstracted unitary entity called "the government." Of course, a significant cohort within the academic community is deeply suspicious of the government (the Conservative one as well as the previous Liberal one). This normative judgment comes not only from left-critical voices who point to the specific targeting by the government of individuals and communities in the post-9/11 era because of race, religion, or ethnic origin – thus creating a climate of fear (Abu-Laban 2002; Byrne 2010) – but also from right-leaning commentators who argue that policies on multiculturalism and immigration made by the government are partly or wholly responsible for ethnic enclaves, unreasonable accommodations, and hidden dangers within communities, thus fostering the threat from within (Moens and Collacott 2007). So, for the left, an initiative like the Roundtable might be thought of as an advisory body composed of community members co-opted by the government, serving to legitimize problematic anti-terrorism policies and practices; and for the right, the Roundtable might be interpreted as another example of political correctness run amok, undermining security because police, intelligence, and border agencies have become too preoccupied with the sensitivities of certain communities.

I would contend that an initiative such as the Roundtable is perhaps too easily promoted by the government as a significant course of action in reaching out to affected communities in the post-9/11 environment.

This promotion by the government is widespread in both domestic and international circles; indeed, it is now part of Canada's "brand." The Roundtable has been identified as a "best practice" in multiculturalism in the federal government (Canadian Heritage 2006, 43); it has been described as one of the "concrete steps [that] have been taken to develop a dialogue with Canada's diverse communities to foster understanding, trust, and cooperation between those communities and law enforcement, border and security agencies" (Government of Canada 2007); and it has been regularly cited in Public Safety Canada's annual Departmental Performance Reports to the Treasury Board Secretariat since 2004–5 as evidence of the department meeting its responsibility for national security. Indeed, in the 2006–7 Departmental Performance Report submitted under then Public Safety Minister Day, the Roundtable is discussed in the "overview" section as the specific body tasked with assisting the minister "in relation to emerging developments in national security matters and their impact on Canada's diverse and pluralistic society." More recently, the Roundtable is cited as part of the government's efforts "to prevent individuals from engaging in terrorism," one of the four-prong elements (prevent, detect, deny, respond) of the government's first official Counter-terrorism Strategy, released in February 2012 (Government of Canada 2011). The government also promotes the Roundtable in international circles. It was identified by the UN Committee on the Elimination of Racial Discrimination in 2007 as a positive step by the Canadian government in dealing with national security issues, but more importantly, as it has become de rigueur to bring in affected communities as part of a country's counter-radicalization efforts, the American government has recognized the Roundtable in its *Country Reports on Terrorism*, specifically mentioning it in the 2007, 2008, 2010, 2011, and 2012 *Country Reports* on Canada. In the "Countering Radicalization and Violent Extremism" section of the 2010 *Country Report*, the US government states, "The [Canadian] government worked with non-governmental partners and concerned Canadian communities to deter violent extremism through preventative programming and community outreach … The Cross-Cultural Roundtable on Security fostered dialogue on national security issues between the government and community leaders."[4] Interestingly, in the same section of the latest 2012 *Country Report*, the wording changes to this: "The Department of Public Safety's (DPS) Cross-Cultural Roundtable on Security fostered dialogue on national security issues between the government and community leaders," making more explicit not only that the role of the Roundtable is to "foster dialogue" with (i.e., reach out to) communities but also that it was initiated, and is supported, by the government.

The Roundtable *is* an important initiative by the Canadian government, but in assessing it as a response to radicalization, we need to consider three factors: first, it is composed of 15 individuals who were originally reflective, but not representative, of Canada's ethnocultural and religious communities; second, it propagates the view of a pan-Canadian identity of cross-cultural diversity despite differences based on religious identities; and third, it remains primarily a body that provides input at the policy level, not at the community level, despite many attempts to develop an outreach strategy. I explore each of these factors in this chapter, recognizing that I do so both as a sort of participant observer during the three years that I was a member of the Roundtable (2005–8) and as a more removed, but very interested, observer in the five years that have passed since. I end with some reflections about my academic training as a political scientist and my (once) uncritical acceptance of the relegation of religion to the private sphere.

Co-optation or Dialogue?

Canada is a liberal democratic state. This apparently empirical fact, unproblematic to many of the public and those holding elected and bureaucratic positions in the government, is problematized by scholars informed by post-Marxism, critical feminism, and postcolonialism and those who argue that we see in Canada what we see in other liberal democracies: a great many contradictions between the universal ideals of equality, freedom, and justice and the actual material conditions of individuals and groups living in the country (see Edkins and Vaughan-Williams 2009). To be clear, some critics suggest, Canada is actually a liberal democratic capitalist state. For that reason, given the differential conditions which perpetuate inequalities (privileging some and oppressing others) for some members of our society, the Canadian state is an entity that perpetuates classism, sexism, racism, heterosexism, ableism, and neo-imperialism. Such understandings of the state stemming from this line of scholarship lead not only to a questioning of the state itself as a way of organizing relations between people, but also to a suspicion of those who work with or within it. Against this sort of ideological backdrop, these critical scholars fear co-optation by the state and are wary of those who may find value in working with the government.

Discussions at the first Roundtable meeting in Ottawa in March 2005[5] focused in part on the issue of co-optation, not least because our secretariat was located in Public Safety. No one, as expressed at the meeting, wanted to be a "mouthpiece" of "the government." We wanted to make a difference, and we all believed that being on the Roundtable was an opportunity to do so. Many of us were impressed by the high rank of the officials who presented to us at the first meeting (e.g., the Deputy Ministers of PSEPC,[6] Justice, and Heritage; the National Security Advisor; the director of CSIS; the commissioner of the RCMP; and the executive vice president of CBSA) and by the hands-on attitude of the Minister of PSEPC and the Minister of Justice as well as the Minister of State for Multiculturalism, who all explicitly asked us for our views on the impacts of Canada's anti-terrorism legislation and measures on the communities from which each of us had emerged.[7] The Roundtable was established because the government recognized that it needed "to reach out to communities in Canada that may be caught in the 'front lines' of the struggle against terrorism" and because it wanted to "engage in a long-term dialogue to improve understanding on how to manage security interests in a diverse society." The Roundtable was asked "to provide advice to promote the protection of civil order, mutual respect and common understanding" (Government of Canada 2004, 2). It was apparent from that first meeting that this would be a high-level dialogue, giving many of us on the Roundtable a sense that our voices would be heard and policies could be changed.

However, the Roundtable quickly came under criticism. The Anti-Terrorism Act, passed in December 2001, mandated a parliamentary review of the legislation after three years, and in the course of testimonies by community, human rights, refugee advocacy, and legal-based organizations to the Special Senate Committee on the Anti-Terrorism Act and the House of Commons Subcommittee on Public Safety and National Security from May to October 2005, the Roundtable was not only misperceived as a body dedicated solely to outreach to Muslim communities but also criticized for being unrepresentative, particularly of Canada's large Muslim communities in Toronto and Montreal (the testimonies were read and discussed by the Roundtable, and the chair along with the Assistant Deputy Minister, Portfolio Relations and Public Affairs Branch, from Public Safety testified in front of the Special Senate Committee on 24 October 2005; but see also Roach 2006, 410–13). Conceived as a cross-cultural body reflecting the diversity of Canadian communities, the Roundtable is not the equivalent of the Muslim

Council of Britain (which was established in 1997) or the French Council for the Muslim Faith (which was established in 2003); nor were members appointed to act as representatives for various communities.

Roundtable members differed, however, in how to deal with these misperceptions and criticisms. Some pointed out that representation was never the intent of the government in establishing the Roundtable and that we were selected to advise the government about the impacts of Canada's anti-terrorism measures based on our specific experiences as individuals. We were part of our communities through volunteer activities, community networking, and ongoing work,[8] and we would obviously draw from our community experiences, but we were on the Roundtable as individuals. The dialogue was primarily between us and the government. As a quote from a redacted[9] source in the 2008 evaluation of the Roundtable undertaken for Public Safety Canada points out, "Unlike the Advisory Council on National Security [the other advisory body established by the 2004 National Security Policy], whose mandate is to provide *expert* advice on national security, the CCRS is meant to provide *community* advice related to how security measures might impact those communities" (Public Safety Canada 2008, 7).

Others argued that although representation was never the intent of the government, many community organizations expected the Roundtable to be representative of or, at the minimum, receptive to their concerns so that the dialogue was not only between us and the government, but also between the government and ethnocultural communities in a broader context. Moreover, some members expressed discomfort that as individuals we could do anything but speak from our own experiences so that, for example, just because a member was Muslim did not mean that s/he spoke for – or was even exclusively interested in speaking about – the Muslim community. That is why from the outset, even before the parliamentary testimonies criticizing the Roundtable, community outreach was an agenda item. I was tasked with chairing a subcommittee on developing an outreach strategy for the Roundtable and reporting at our second meeting in May 2005. The secretariat hired a consultant to aid this committee with developing the strategy; the process highlighted three primary challenges that would continue to plague any viable strategy for the Roundtable. First, there was the question of *how much* time and resources would be needed. Roundtable members are volunteers who have very busy professional and personal lives, and although the body is supported by Public Safety, the secretariat has limited funds to help organize, support, and run outreach activities. With hundreds of ethnocultural communities of interest throughout Canada, any outreach would necessarily be limited. Would members be able to play a role significant enough to enhance rather than undermine the credibility of the Roundtable, and could outreach activities be properly executed and received so that they would not become mere public relations exercises?

Second, there was the question of *which* communities would be invited to participate. Would there be a focus on Muslim communities given the apparent disproportionate impacts of security measures on them since 9/11, or would it be important to invite a wide array of communities in order not to perpetuate inadvertently the view of an Islamic threat? In addition, given the diversity, for example, of Canada's Muslim communities, the groups or organizations that could be invited included organizations such as the Canadian Council of Muslim Women, the Canadian Council on American-Islamic Relations (CAIR-CAN), the Canadian Islamic Congress, or the Muslim Canadian Congress, as well as larger (and not exclusively Muslim) umbrella organizations, such as the Canadian Arab Federation. However, these organizations were already well established and their views were well known, so would it be more appropriate to find voices in the broader Muslim population who may or may not be represented in these organizations?

Third, there was the question of *what* the purpose of the outreach sessions would be, specifically in terms of which government representative would speak, who would respond to concerns raised in the sessions, and whether there would be any follow-up. Although it may be obvious that representatives from Canada's national security agencies, such as the RCMP, CSIS, and CBSA, should be visible at these sessions and speak on their activities, would they really be committed to hearing community voices, in essence bringing concerns in as opposed to pushing information or ideas out? Government bureaucracies would have their own interests to protect, so just because a branch of the government would have identified that community voices were important, this would not necessarily translate to a buy-in by all departments and agencies. That is why the active involvement at the highest level, namely by the Ministers of Public Safety and Justice, would set the tone that this was a priority. Conversely, ministerial disinterest or indifference would also be telling.[10]

Although a few Roundtable members organized and held outreach sessions in the first part of 2006, more systematic efforts came in the later part of the year. Roundtable members, however, did not plan and organize these events. Through a consulting firm hired by the secretariat to organize and run four day-long outreach sessions between October 2006 and March 2007 in Montreal, Vancouver, Calgary, and Toronto, individual Roundtable members participated in broader discussions by being invited to one of the four sessions. The results of these activities, however, were not altogether fruitful, and when a "Draft Final Report" submitted by the consulting firm was circulated to members in April 2007, some of us were critical not only of how the sessions were conducted but also of why outreach events were being contracted out to an outside consulting firm.[11] I attended the 17 February 2007 session in Toronto, which was secretly taped and leaked to *National Post* reporter Stewart Bell, who wrote that "the meeting digressed into a shouting match between rival Muslim factions," observing that "RCMP and CSIS officers have been spending their days off sitting through meetings like [that] event, listening to a barrage of complaints and trying to clear up misconceptions about what they do and why they do it" (Bell 2007). Bell's latter observation gets at the crux of the purpose of the outreach sessions and indeed the purpose of the Roundtable.

Some of my colleagues described our meetings as "government show-and-tell" in large part because most of our meeting times were filled with presentations by various government agencies and departments. Government officials, it would appear, were educating us about Canada's national security framework, as if underpinning their presentations was the assumption that criticisms of Canada's national security policies must be due to a lack of knowledge or understanding as opposed to what some of us saw as legitimate questions raised about the security-rights balance in the current context. On the one hand, the government's approach made sense because Roundtable members were not experts in security matters. On the other hand, some of us assessed that the government did not have the balance right with certain policies. For example, I and others specifically questioned it with regard to the security certificate regime. These certificates allowed the Ministers of Public Safety and of Citizenship and Immigration to declare landed immigrants and refugee claimants national security threats, leading to their immediate arrest, denying them and their lawyers the right to see the evidence against them which had led to the issuance of the security certificates and deportation orders, and causing them to be detained indefinitely if deportation to their countries of origin could lead to torture (see Bell 2006). Having raised the issue of the certificates from the very first meeting in March 2005, we argued that we were advocating not for their elimination but rather for the necessity to amend the legislation to address the secrecy around the proceedings.

The security certificate issue in the Roundtable is an interesting case with which to consider, in retrospect, whether an advisory body to the government with access to the ministerial level can make a difference. For a number of us, the disproportionate impact of this measure on Canada's Muslim communities was obvious, but the secrecy inherent in the process made it more troubling, not only because some of us felt the rights of five men – Hassan Almrei, Adil Charkaoui, Mohamed Harkat, Mahmoud Jaballah, and Mohammad Mahjoub – were being violated, but also because this kind of secrecy was undermining public trust. An issue that mobilized many in the public beyond Muslim groups, including many legal and community organizations, it found a champion in Alexandre Trudeau, the son of the late prime minister, who testified in a Federal Court hearing in June 2005 to support Almrei, one of the men detained, and also subsequently produced a 2006 documentary film to raise public awareness about the injustices of the certificate process. As it became commonplace to hear journalists, activists, and members of various ethnocultural communities and the general public alike refer to the men as the "Secret Trial Five" and to the Kingston Immigration Holding Centre where four of the five men were imprisoned at one point as "Guantanamo North," some of us saw the security certificate issue as a straightforward case where, in voicing our concerns and opposition, we could make a difference and the government would respond by changing the legislation. However, during a number of meetings in 2005 and 2006 that spanned both the Liberal and Conservative governments, we were told by government bureaucrats that security certificates were reasonable measures that had been part of Canada's immigration law since 1978 and were rarely used. More significantly, Public Safety officials also shared public opinion surveys commissioned by the department which showed Canadians were generally supportive of the country's security measures, including the security certificate regime. Faced with what some Roundtable members perceived as bureaucratic resistance and not merely an attempt by officials to provide information, a number of us addressed these concerns directly with both Liberal and Conservative Ministers when they met with us, and it was a prominent issue of discussion with Public Safety Minister Day in June 2006. In the end, the government did respond, but the response was necessitated by the Supreme Court handing down its decision in *Charkaoui v. Canada* in February 2007, declaring the security certificate process unconstitutional and giving the government one year to amend the legislation.

Religious Identity-Based Understandings

The security certificate issue would, at first glance, be prime evidence that the dialogue between the Roundtable and the government was primarily one-sided and that even having access to the highest levels, namely to the ministers themselves, could not lead to change. However, during our meetings a number of Roundtable members were equally vocal in their support for the certificate regime, so it was clearly not the case that the Roundtable was uniformly in opposition to the government. The division was between those like me who wanted the process changed because the evidence was kept secret from the accused and others who saw the process as acceptable. Unlike in debates outside of the Roundtable, the division was not about CSIS and the fact that it works in secrecy, because as long as there were appropriate oversight and review mechanisms, we all could see the need for an intelligence agency to operate in secrecy to some degree. Those who supported the security certificate regime argued that it was a reasonable measure, applied to such a small handful of Arab Muslim men who were not Canadian citizens. From my perspective, the framing of the issue primarily in terms of the religious identity of the men, as opposed to the secrecy of the process, hindered efforts to find a common ground within the Roundtable. Indeed, when I had indicated in earlier meetings in 2007 that I was willing to step down for the purpose of membership renewal, one colleague in particular convinced me to stay. He argued that my advocacy of certain issues that had become associated with "a Muslim cause," such as the security certificate complaints, actually had more credence because I was *not* a Muslim.

Any analysis of the Roundtable must take into consideration the extent to which religious identities informed the contributions and positions of members. Two principal forces animated our discussions: Islamophobia and anti-Semitism. Both concerns stemmed primarily from the community experiences of Muslim and Jewish members, respectively, and more broadly shaped the responses each had to the other in our meetings. Essentially, our discussions were operating at two levels. On one level, the focus was on the government. Officials from Public Safety, Justice, Canadian Heritage, the RCMP, and CSIS were regular participants at our meetings, and at various points we also heard from CBSA, Foreign Affairs and International Trade, National Defence, Transport Canada, and Statistics Canada. We were specifically consulted on Justice O'Connor's recommendations in the Arar inquiry report, the government's response to the parliamentary review of the Anti-Terrorism Act, the CBSA's complaints procedure, and Transport Canada's Passenger Protect program. A Roundtable subcommittee also helped to develop the RCMP's Bias-Free Policing Policy. According to the 2008 evaluation, the Roundtable affected the "government's understanding and sensitivity to community needs"; the evaluation highlighted that the government has a "more effective and culturally sensitive approach to border security, law enforcement and security intelligence activities," specifically citing "a new approach to preparations to press releases in arrests of 17 [later 18] alleged terrorists in Toronto in June 2006 that involved pre-briefings of select community leaders, and a new lexicon for these communications that was more specific to the threat" (Public Safety Canada 2008, 19, 22). However, in terms of the Roundtable contributing to better community understanding of national security policies, evident in the sorts of outreach efforts discussed earlier, the evaluation stated that there was "limited evidence" (22).

On another level, the focus was on the community. Although a number of our discussions centred on Muslim Canadians being singled out in the post-9/11 environment, Roundtable members contended that many of Canada's ethnocultural communities had been targeted in the past and continue to face discrimination. Reflecting the diversity of Roundtable members, the experiences of the Indo-Canadian, Chinese Canadian, Sikh Canadian, Tamil Canadian, black Canadian, and Jewish Canadian communities in facing xenophobia, racism, and discrimination were discussed. Indeed, in these discussions we also recognized the discrimination faced by Canada's aboriginal peoples even though their community was not reflected in the original composition of the Roundtable. What we all had in common became clear, and the faces of colour, strong accents, and traditional ethnic dress around the room vividly illustrated some of the racialized realities of Canada's multicultural society, but instead of these bringing us together, there emerged within the Roundtable a divide along Muslim-Jewish lines. As particularly evident in the different responses to the use of security certificate measures, the divide became such a prominent component of the Roundtable's work that it resulted either in underlying resentment by some members who, being non-Muslim and non-Jewish, believed that their concerns were being unfairly overlooked or in the apparent endorsement of one side or the other, as in my case, when I became associated with "a Muslim cause."

The Muslim-Jewish divide in the Roundtable was a manifestation of larger issues that go beyond Canada's borders and were significant points of tension well before 9/11. It was clear from the very beginning that it would be difficult to isolate ourselves from the global context. During our November 2005 meeting, officials from the Department of Foreign Affairs and International Trade presented on Canada's international security policy and, in so doing, precipitated a discussion about the Palestinian-Israeli conflict. Those who sympathized with the plight of the Palestinian people found themselves at odds with those who prioritized the security of the Israeli state; and because this was a religiously defined conflict, the divide became apparent. When, after the meeting, one member shared short articles by email that highlighted Palestinian suffering, another responded by posting articles that brought out the terror faced by the Israeli people. In other meetings when government officials or academic experts would bring out (even tangentially) that an apparent motivation for terrorist acts was the identification with Palestinian suffering, Roundtable members would again find themselves in disagreement, not about the motivation but about the contention that the Palestinian people were "suffering." In the end, we decided that there were certain topics that the Roundtable would (or should) not consider, leading to an agreement that the mandate of the Roundtable was to focus on matters *internal* to Canada, precluding us from discussing external issues, such as the Palestinian-Israeli conflict. In other words, the Roundtable was an advisory body on domestic policy matters and not ones in foreign policy.

The possibility that we could build a firewall around the deliberations of the Roundtable, insulating us from the global and globalized realities of religiously defined conflicts, stemmed from an expressed desire to build a consensus around the idea that we were all "Canadian," and despite the multiplicity of identities that defined all of us, we had one national identity. In that way, we embraced the government's intent of creating a "cross-cultural" body that exemplified Canada's multicultural identity. There was a sense that we could overcome differences, particularly as we were getting to know each other during our many meetings, building trust and realizing that the dialogue was not simply between us and the government but also among ourselves. Part of the concern around the Conservative Party taking power in 2006 and possibly changing the Roundtable membership derived from a belief that after a year we had moved forward and we were "gelling," as one of my colleagues liked to explain it.

New Challenges to the Roundtable?

The Conservative government did not change the membership for another two years, and by then I was no longer on the Roundtable. What was interesting about the changes in membership announced in 2008 and in 2011 was the appointment of high-level representatives from ethnocultural or religious organizations, namely B'nai Brith Canada, the National Association of Friendship Centres, the Canadian Muslim Lawyers Association, and the Canadian Somali Congress. Although not all the new appointees on the Roundtable were representatives of groups, I began to question the accuracy of my observation that the Roundtable was simply a reflection of Canada's diverse communities. There were now high-level individuals who could speak for their group or community, although it is not entirely clear that they would (or did) in the Roundtable. However, in cases when an individual was associated with a specific group or community in the public eye, such as the public statements of Roundtable members who would have represented B'nai Brith Canada, the Canadian Muslim Lawyers Association, and the Canadian Somali Congress (e.g., see Hussen 2011), questions could arise about whether they would be speaking at meetings simply as "individuals." Interestingly, the most recent changes in membership in 2012 and 2013 seem to point to less high-level representation of well-known groups.

Moreover, in its first three years the Roundtable believed it could overcome a religious divide fuelled by differences over the Palestinian-Israeli conflict by emphasizing the idea of a multicultural identity. The Roundtable is a government body which provides advice at the ministerial (political) level. However, in recent years, the Conservative government's priorities in both combating anti-Semitism and advocating a pro-Israeli stance have become determinative factors in Canada's multiculturalism and foreign policies. For example, the *Annual Report on the Operation of the Canadian Multiculturalism Act 2009–2010* (Citizenship and Immigration Canada 2011) has an opening section dedicated to the government's actions to address anti-Semitism in Canada and abroad. Quoting Prime Minister Stephen Harper, this section of the report states that anti-Semitism is "a pernicious evil ... an evil so profound ... that it is ultimately a threat to us all." The section clearly outlines the government's rejection of the Durban process (the first World Conference against Racism was held in Durban, South Africa, in 2001), which, according to the government, has become a platform for anti-Semitism in singling out Israel as a racist regime. Canada boycotted the UN Durban Review Conference in 2009 (also known as Durban II) and made the decision not to participate in the tenth anniversary commemoration of the Durban Declaration and Program of Action in 2011 (also known as Durban III). Indeed, Jason Kenney, the Minister of Citizenship, Immigration, and Multiculturalism, spoke at a "counter-conference" to Durban III on 22 September 2011, which was held at the same time in New York as the UN General Assembly meeting on Durban III. Entitled "The Perils of Global Intolerance," the conference attracted well-known pro-Israeli speakers, including John Bolton, Mike Huckabee, and Alan Dershowitz.

In addition, the *Annual Report on the Operation of the Canadian Multiculturalism Act 2009–2010* discusses the government's support of the Inter-parliamentary Coalition for Combating Antisemitism. This group, which held its second conference in Ottawa in November 2010, had given birth earlier to the Canadian Parliamentary Coalition to Combat Antisemitism (CPCCA) in March 2009 after the first conference in London that February. The coalition is not a committee of Parliament, but it nevertheless held hearings to examine the phenomenon of anti-Semitism in Canada and make recommendations to the government. Composed of members from all four political parties, at least until the Bloc Québécois withdrew in March 2010 citing a lack of balance by the witnesses called to testify, the coalition released its report in July 2011. The 92-page report makes 24 recommendations, and although many parts of the report merit comment, I want to focus on its analysis of the new anti-Semitism and its sources because it calls into question not only whether the Roundtable can set aside the Palestinian-Israeli conflict in its deliberations, but also whether the focus on anti-Semitism represents or refers only to radical forms of Islam.

The new anti-Semitism, according to the report (Canadian Parliamentary Coalition to Combat Antisemitism 2011), is a pernicious phenomenon that conflates Jews/Zionists/Israelis and shrouds anti-Semitism in anti-Zionist and anti-Israeli political discourse. As explained to the inquiry by Ruth Klein, the national director of the League for Human Rights of B'nai Brith Canada, "In Canada, these dual themes of anti-Semitism and anti-Zionism run parallel and are used interchangeably ... The extreme left will borrow Holocaust imagery and age-old Jewish stereotypes to attack Israel … So whereas before the talk was of Jewish control of the media and Jewish control of the government and the financial world, the terminology now has changed. It's Israeli control. It's Zionist control" (ibid., 15). The sources of this new anti-Semitism are not only the radical left on many of Canada's university campuses but also radical Islam or Islamism which "views Jews in 'conspiratorial terms' as enemies of Islam" (19). The radical left increasingly sees "the Palestinian struggle as 'the most legitimate and noble struggle of the underdog'" (17) but crosses over into anti-Semitism when it uses anti-Semitic symbols and targets Jewish students. Radical Islamists hold views that are "antithetical to Canadian values, advocating not only hatred for Jews, but also the subjugation of women, and the justification of the killing of gay people," and also reject the existence of any non-Muslim state in the Middle East (20). Combating the new anti-Semitism and defending Israel would necessarily go hand-in-hand because anti-Semitism/anti-Zionism/anti-Israel have become one in the minds of the radical left and radical Islam. The Canadian government has become one of the staunchest supporters of Israel internationally, accounting in part for Canada's loss in the October 2010 election for a non-permanent seat in the UN Security Council, the first loss for the country since the founding of the United Nations in 1945.

Given the government's priorities and its strong support of Israel, questions would likely arise for members of the Roundtable, who take either a proactive position on the predicament of the Palestinian people or even a more nuanced approach to Israel. Would the government listen to their advice? The governing Conservative Party won a majority in the 2 May 2011 election in part because of the support of specific ethnocultural and religious communities, cultivated through the years under the leadership in particular of Jason Kenney, and the party's pro-Israeli position was crucial although not necessarily decisive in many constituencies with large numbers of Jewish voters. Even former Liberal Justice Minister Irwin Cotler, who is a co-founder of the Interparliamentary Coalition for Combating Antisemitism and a prominent voice in the CPCCA, saw his support decline in the Jewish community in his riding (Arnold 2011). With radical Islam being the focal point of the Conservative government's anti-discrimination agenda, as stated in the CPCCA report, Muslim communities would inevitably remain under scrutiny.

At the same time, the government is not a unitary entity. To what extent do police, intelligence, and border officials in their day-to-day work focus on radical Islam as a form of anti-Semitism? The Round-table is a diverse body, with Muslim as well as Jewish voices, allowing government officials to tap into differing community experiences as the government creates policies to address radicalization. Roundtable members are not experts in radicalization; they receive materials from different governmental bodies and agencies and provide feedback from a community perspective. In that way, there is arguably space for dialogue regardless of the party in power. Ministers may be less inclined to heed advice, but that is not the case for all government officials. As one Roundtable colleague has stated, there is value if even one government official is affected by his contributions, leading to changes in policy directions, strategies, or even individual behaviour.

The point is that the Roundtable is a body that provides advice on, rather than acts in, countering radicalization and violent extremism in communities. The input is primarily at the policy level, not at the community level. Although there were further discussions about an outreach strategy, including the introduction by the secretariat of a more formalized process at the last meeting that I attended in June 2008, Roundtable activities have been virtually non-existent in terms of outreach or community consultations, and that is part of the problem with the government overstating or promoting the Roundtable as a major initiative in international circles. The Roundtable has been more of a sounding board for the government than a body that can facilitate dialogue between it and communities more broadly. Thus, whether the consultation with Roundtable members is about security measures generally, or the Anti-Terrorism Act review, or counter-radicalization, the dialogue is between the government and the Roundtable. The focus or topic of the consultation has changed, not the process of consultation. The only recent exception was in February 2011 when CBC News reported that the Roundtable organized a meeting of representatives from the RCMP, CSIS, CBSA, and the Justice Department with the Somali community in Ottawa. Interestingly, these were the sorts of outreach efforts undertaken by the Roundtable in its early years.

Academic Reflections

The very existence of the Cross-Cultural Roundtable on Security is arguably a response to radicalization because the principal framing of the terrorist threat in the post-9/11 environment has been one of radicals. The question is whether they are necessarily Islamic radicals. As we approached the tenth anniversary of 9/11, Prime Minister Harper identified "Islamicism" [sic] as the threat to Canadian security and, in so doing, evoked vocal opposition immediately from the leaders of the other political parties for targeting Islam and thus (as the other leaders argued) fuelling Islamophobia (Taber 2011). My first reaction to the story was to wonder why the Canadian prime minister would continue to propagate a religious label for violent extremism when over a year ago even the American president had decreed that the word "Islam" would be banned from White House policy statements describing terrorist enemies. Why would Canada continue to focus so much on religion as a cause of terrorism when even the American president had instituted this kind of informal policy restriction?

I realized through my interactions with the editors and authors in this book that my immediate reaction stemmed from an academic training that tends to treat religion in two rather contradictory and naive ways. On the one hand, it is common to see religion as something that is, in essence, good and peaceful. On the other hand, religion is something that is or ought to be private because it only creates troubles when it is allowed into the public arena. As the former Public Safety Minister Stockwell Day learned the hard way when he was campaigning as the leader of the Canadian Alliance party in the 2000 election, the public expression of one's religious beliefs (in his case, conservative Protestant and creationist) can amount to a death knell in Canadian politics. Yet we cling to the naive notion that religion is still somehow essentially good. The peaceful essence of religion is thoroughly problematized, however, by Bramadat, Reader, and Dawson in this book (see also Bramadat and Koenig 2009).

The political motivations for separating religion from the political and, later, public spheres in some societies can be found in the 1648 Treaty of Westphalia, which codified the "jettisoning of religion from the political space" (Hatzopoulos and Petito 2003b, 12). That famous treaty signalled "the end of an era in which international relations and wars had been about religion" (Laustsen and Wæver 2003, 148). The nearly 100-year-long European wars of religion in the sixteenth and seventeenth centuries taught international relations scholars that "when religion is brought into international public life, it causes intolerance, war, devastation, political upheaval and even the collapse of the international order ... [That is why] the modern state, the privatization of religion, and the secularization of politics arose to limit religion's domestic influence, minimize the effect of religious disagreement, and end the bloody and destructive role of religion in international relations" (Thomas 2003, 24).

This "political myth," however, has been exposed and problematized by some international relations scholars in their interrogations of the liberal democratic state (Hatzopoulos and Petito 2003a; Hurd 2008). In addition to classism, sexism, racism, heterosexism, ableism, and neo-imperialism being perpetuated by states such as Canada, some scholars would add (righteous) secularism,[12] where nominal Christianity is subtly propagated as the norm and Islam, in particular, as its contradistinction, or the "other." Notably, political scientist Elizabeth Hurd (2008) has argued that secularism, virtually unacknowledged in political science, is "a form of political authority in its own right, and its consequences [need to be] evaluated for international relations" (1). She suggests that there are two variants of political secularism which have been influential in international relations. The first variant, laicism, which has its origins in the French term laïcité, stems from a "separationist" narrative in which religion is outside of politics, "rul[ing] out in advance the linkages between religion and spheres of power and authority such as law, science, and politics within states." Within this framework the state "posit[s] itself as public, neutral, and value-free, while assigning religion the role of its private, affective, and value-laden counterpart" (36–7). The second variant, which she calls Judeo-Christian secularism, stems from a more "accommodationist" perspective where the Judeo-Christian tradition is seen as the root of Western political order and democratic political institutions. Whereas "[i]n the laicist account of secularization, the [Judeo-]Christian identity of the West was superseded, radically transformed, and for all practical purposes rendered irrelevant," in this second type the religio-cultural heritage of the West is seen as central to the emergence of the modern liberal democratic, secular state (39–40). Both of these variants have contributed to the "consolidation of modern national identities as secular and democratic," and particularly in the case of French and American national identities, Hurd argues that the consolidation has been in opposition to Islam. She goes further in pointing out that "laicist assumptions contribute to depictions of Islam as a surmountable though formidable stumbling block to the rationalization and democratization of societies, whereas Judeo-Christian secularist assumptions lead to more ominous conclusions in which Islam is portrayed as a potential threat to the cultural, moral, and religious foundations of Western civilization that must be successfully defused" (47).

Although one would want to add to Hurd's arguments by pointing out that Roman Catholics and Jews have only recently achieved proper accommodations in liberal democratic societies and Hindus,

Buddhists, Sikhs, aboriginal spiritualities, and other minority Christian sects – such as the Mormons and the Doukhobors – continue to be marginalized, her focus on Judeo-Christianity (qua national self or antecedent) and Islam (qua national other) found resonance in international relations literature after 9/11. Hurd's premises are found in many critiques of security measures undertaken by Canada, the United States, and many European states because these ideas help to explain not only the popularity of the "clash of civilizations" world view but also the "Muslim-man-as-terrorist" and the "Muslim-woman-as-oppressed" constructions so prevalent in Western public discourse (Byrne 2010). In order to address and modify these problematic understandings, Hurd offers a solution of "agonistic secular democracy" where, she argues, "public expression of contending views of religion and its relationship to the political" would be elicited and sought out, "encourag[ing] contestation and shun[ning] final settlements" (2008, 147). This approach would expose the construction of Judeo-Christianity as the norm and allow for contending perspectives, both theistic and nontheistic, to flourish nationally and internationally. Religion would be incorporated "on and into politics," and states (and the world) would be better for it.

Drawing from Hurd's insights, Prime Minister Harper's statement about "Islamicism" at least reminds us that in Canada, religion is front and centre in discussions about security and that serious consideration must be given to religiously motivated violence. President Barack Obama, in keeping with his outreach to Muslim-majority countries as well as to Muslim American communities, had banned references to Islam in connection with government claims about terrorist acts. In that way, the US president refused to deal with whether Islamic ideas led to a particular violent movement or act, electing instead to propagate the view that Islam was a religion of peace. Yet, when the story of Obama's White House policy broke in July 2010, it was in the context of the US Army's counter-insurgency manual specifically referring to "Islamic insurgents," "Islamic extremists," and "Islamic subversives" and detailing ties between Muslim support groups and terrorists. General David Petraeus, whom President Obama had appointed to be the top military commander in Afghanistan (and more significantly became the head of the Central Intelligence Agency until his resignation in November 2012 as a result of an extramarital affair), was the one who led the production of the manual (Scarborough 2010). The White House may have banned the use of "Islam" to describe terrorist enemies, but the US national security structure has not fully accepted the practice.

At the same time, as Bramadat, Dawson, Jamil, and Smith show in this volume, placing Islam at the forefront of the current security environment profoundly affects Muslims in their day-to-day lives. The government created the Roundtable in the post-9/11 era arguably as a way to take the focus away from Islam, but one of the unintended consequences was the emergence of a Muslim-Jewish divide. Members of the Roundtable were expected (at least initially) to speak only for themselves, and their community experiences were meant to inform their contributions, but individuals cannot check their identities at the door. It is one thing to say that the Roundtable was "reflective" of Canada's diverse communities and therefore as individuals we were not speaking for any one group or community. It is quite another thing, however, for that to happen in practice. When some of my colleagues were faced with troubling characterizations of their positions, such as support for "Muslim suicide bombers" or for "Jewish state aggression" and such characterizations were made by a Jewish or a Muslim member, it became difficult not to represent and speak for one's community against that of the other.

In addition, neither my Muslim nor my Jewish colleagues would deny that extreme violence could indeed be religiously motivated. The problem is whether Islam stands alone as the source of extreme violence. Reader argues in chapter 2 of this volume that all religions are violent, but that is not the starting point in many security discussions and that certainly was not the starting point in the Roundtable. As one colleague shared with me, he became even more entrenched in his Muslim identity because he felt that he, as an Arab Muslim man, was the one under attack as others propagated the view of who in the post-9/11 world would be motivated by religion to become violent. The problem with Harper's statement on "Islamicism" is not that he draws attention to religiously motivated violence, including violence motivated by Islamic ideas, but rather that he does not go far enough in recognizing the religious context in which he lives in Canada. It is not that religion has to be brought into politics, or that 9/11 or the Toronto 18 necessitate that we must bring religion into the public arena; rather, it has never left. In the post-9/11 world, international relations scholars have been asking the wrong question. Scholars should not be asking, "What is religion and how does it relate to politics, specifically security?" Instead, drawing from Hurd's work, they should ask, "How do institutions and states come to be understood as religious versus political, or religious versus secular?" Arguably, the prime minister is blinded to the extent to which political secularism, with its laicist and Judeo-Christian secularist variants, is characteristic of virtually every liberal democratic state, including Canada. Harper, however, is not alone. Many government officials, journalists, and academics, including myself, have been guilty of this blindness, too.

NOTES

1 Ministers McLellan and Cotler wrote a letter of response on 17 October 2005 to Senator Joyce Fairburn, who, as chair of the Special Senate Committee on the Anti-Terrorism Act, asked for a description of the nomination process for the Roundtable. The ministers stated the following in their letter:

> "The nomination process for the Roundtable was open, transparent and inclusive. We wrote to all Parliamentarians and 290 non-governmental organizations to inform our colleagues and various communities of interest in Canada about the nomination process. The nomination period was also extended for another three weeks to ensure broadness and diversity with regard to the applications to be received. PSEP officials further contacted various ethnic media outlets about the proposed establishment of the Roundtable and provided information about how communities could nominate their members. The process encouraged individuals from all backgrounds and communities to submit their applications as demonstrated by the 238 applications received. The need to consider regional, gender, and linguistic representation was also identified publicly.
>
> The selection process was based on four advertised criteria:
>
> – Awareness of security matters as they relate to the community and relevant community dynamics;
> – Knowledge and experience in engaging diverse and pluralistic communities;
> – Ability to facilitate the exchange of information with communities; and
> – Commitment to building community capacity and safer communities.
>
> The selection of the fifteen members from across Canada was based on their demonstrated understanding of national security issues in a multicultural community, and a demonstrated commitment to inter-cultural dialogue and healthy, safe, pluralistic communities."

2 The former chair of the Roundtable, Dr Zaheer Lakhani, was appointed to the Advisory Council on National Security in May 2010. This is a positive action by the Conservative government (as was the appointment of Anju Virmani to both the Roundtable and the Advisory Council in 2008; Virmani

is no longer on the Advisory Council but remains on the Roundtable). The 2004 National Security Policy established two advisory bodies: the Cross-Cultural Roundtable on Security and the Advisory Council on National Security. The government established two bodies because the Roundtable was to provide "community" advice on the impacts of security measures on communities, and the Advisory Council was to provide "expert" advice on security issues. There are no strictly "technical" security issues that should not have community input, and the Liberal government should have linked the work of these two bodies from the very beginning (see Crocker et al. 2007; this was the collaborative research and public education project of which I was a part that led to me being nominated for the Roundtable in October 2004 by my academic and community partners on the project).

3 Until 2011, the Roundtable only had 13 members. The current 15 members of the Roundtable along with their year of appointment are Dr Myrna Lashley (chair; appointed 2005); Mr Leo Adler (2005); Mr Riazuddin Ahmed (2005); Dr David Bensoussan (2005); Mr Hussein Hamdani (2005); Dr Frank Dimant (2008); Mr Peter Dinsdale (2008); Ms Bronwyn Shoush (2008); Mr Sukhvinder Sing Badh (2008); Ms Anju Virmani (2008); Ms Rita Giang (2011); Mr Ahmed Hussen (2011); Mr Soon Kim (2011); Ms Sharon Ross (2011); and Ms Yusra Siddiquee (2011).

4 As required by law, the US State Department issues *Country Reports on Terrorism* on an annual basis. Until 2004, it was referred to as *Patterns of Global Terrorism*. See http://www.state.gov/j/ct/rls/crt/.

5 The Roundtable's inaugural meeting took place in Ottawa in 2005, one year after the Martin government's National Security Policy called for its creation. Public Safety called for nominations in the summer of 2004 with a closing date of 4 October 2004. I was notified in January 2005 that I was chosen as a member of the Roundtable.

6 When it was first established in 2003, the department was called Public Safety and Emergency Preparedness Canada (PSEPC). It is now simply Public Safety Canada.

7 From the very beginning, I asked myself, what exactly was my community? As I stated in note 2, my academic and community partners on a collaborative project looking at immigration and security issues in Atlantic Canada nominated me to the Roundtable because one of the objectives of our project was to inform policymakers about our research findings. At the same time, as a visibly racialized, female Nova Scotian who was born in the Philippines, I arguably reflected a number of communities (non-white, female, Atlantic-Canadian, immigrant) that the government would find appealing in a national body like the Roundtable.

8 In my case, because of the collaborative research and public education project of which I was a part, working with communities was an aspect of my academic work.

9 Redacted sources are usually indicative of sensitive government material. Because the Roundtable deals with security matters, it is probably not surprising that these types of sources were consulted in the 2008 evaluation of the Roundtable.

10 The Roundtable was established under the Martin government to advise specifically the Ministers of Public Safety and Justice, and the interest of the Liberal ministers (as I noted earlier in the text) was palpable. Once the Conservatives took power in 2006, ministerial interest was also evident with Public Safety Minister Stockwell Day and, later, with Justice Minister Rob Nicholson. Vic Toews, who is the current Public Safety Minister, did not have the opportunity to meet with the Roundtable when he was Justice Minister.

11 It was not altogether clear to some of the Roundtable members how the decision came about to use a consulting firm as opposed to members themselves organizing outreach sessions. Likely, the busy lives of members precluded systematic efforts to organize such sessions.

12 I use the term "righteous secularism" because, as Hurd (2008, 34–5) argues, both variants can be located on the spectrum of theological discourse, Judeo-Christian secularism more overtly, but also laicism.

REFERENCES

Abu-Laban, Yasmeen. 2002. "Liberalism, Multiculturalism and the Problem of Essentialism." *Citizenship Studies* 6 (4): 459–82.

Arnold, Janice. 2011. "Most Jews in Riding Voted Tory, Cotler Concedes." *Canadian Jewish News*, 12 May. http://cjnews.com/node/87715.

Bell, Colleen. 2006. "Subject to Exception: Security Certificates, National Security and Canada's Role in the 'War on Terror.'" *Canadian Journal of Law and Society* 21 (1): 63–83.

Bell, Stewart. 2007. "The Sound and Fury of Ethnic Outreach." *National Post*, 17 February. http://www.nationalpost.com/news/story.html?id=72ce20cc-b4fe-426b-8d7a-dd428fe2dab4.

Berger, Peter L., ed. 1999. *The Desecularization of the World*. Washington, DC: Ethics and Public Policy Center.

Bramadat, Paul, and Matthias Koenig, eds. 2009. *International Migration and the Governance of Religious Diversity*. Montreal: McGill-Queen's University Press.

Byrne, Siobhan. 2010. "Framing Post-9/11 Security: Tales of Securitization of the State and of the Experiences of Muslim Communities." In *Locating Global Order: American Power and Canadian Security after 9/11*, ed. Bruno Charbonneau and Wayne S. Cox, 167–82. Vancouver: UBC Press.

Canadian Heritage. 2006. *Annual Report on the Operation of the Canadian Multiculturalism Act 2004–2005*. Ottawa: Minister of Public Works and Government Services Canada.

Canadian Parliamentary Coalition to Combat Antisemitism. 2011. *Report of the Inquiry Panel*. http://www.jewishvirtuallibrary.org/jsource/anti-semitism/canadareport2011.pdf.

Citizenship and Immigration Canada. 2011. *Annual Report on the Operation of the Canadian Multiculturalism Act 2009–2010*. Minister of Public Works and Government Services Canada. http://www.cic.gc.ca/english/resources/publications/multi-report2010/index.asp.

Crocker, D., A. Dobrowolsky, E. Keeble, C.C. Moncayo, and E. Tastsoglou. 2007. *Security and Immigration: Changes and Challenges: Immigrant and Ethnic Communities in Atlantic Canada, Presumed Guilty?* Ottawa: Status of Women Canada and Canadian Heritage.

Edkins, Jenny, and Nick Vaughan-Williams, eds. 2009. *Critical Theorists and International Relations*. Florence, KY: Routledge.

"Federal Security Officials Meet Local Somali-Canadians." 2011. *CBC News*, 25 February. http://www.cbc.ca/news/canada/ottawa/federal-security-officials-meet-local-somali-canadians-1.1004678.

Government of Canada, Privy Council Office. 2004. *Securing an Open Society: Canada's National Security Policy*. Her Majesty the Queen in Right of Canada. http://publications.gc.ca/collections/Collection/CP22-77-2004E.pdf.

– 2007. "Response to the Seventh Report of the House of Commons Standing Committee on Public Safety and National Security: Rights, Limits, Security: A Comprehensive Review of the Anti-Terrorism Act and Related Issues." http://www.parl.gc.ca/HousePublications/Publication.aspx?DocId=3066235&Language=E&Mode=1&Parl=39&Ses=1#A.

– 2011. *Building Resilience Against Terrorism: Canada's Counter-Terrorism Strategy*. Her Majesty the Queen in Right of Canada. http://www.publicsafety.gc.ca/cnt/rsrcs/pblctns/rslnc-gnst-trrrsm/rslnc-gnst-trrrsm-eng.pdf.

Hatzopoulos, Pavlos, and Fabio Petito, eds. 2003a. *Religion in International Relations: The Return from Exile*. New York: Palgrave Macmillan.

– 2003b. "The Return from Exile." In *Religion in International Relations: The Return from Exile*, ed. Pavlos Hatzopoulos and Fabio Petito, 1–20. New York: Palgrave Macmillan.

Hurd, Elizabeth. 2008. *The Politics of Secularism in International Relations*. Princeton, NJ: Princeton University Press.

Hussen, Ahmed. 2011. "Al Shabaab: Recruitment and Radicalization within the Canadian Somali Community and that Community's Response." Testimony to the US House Committee on Homeland Security Third Hearing on Islamic Radicalization, 27 July. http://homeland.house.gov/sites/home land.house.gov/files/Testimony%20Hussen.pdf.

Laustsen, Carsten Bagge, and Ole Wæver. 2003. "In Defense of Religion: Sacred Referent Objects for Securitization." In *Religion in International Relations: The Return from Exile*, ed. Pavlos Hatzopoulos and Fabio Petito, 147–80. New York: Palgrave Macmillan.

Moens, Alexandra, and Martin Collacott, eds. 2007. *Immigration Policy and the Terrorist Threat in Canada and the United States*. Vancouver: Fraser Institute.

Public Safety Canada. 2007. *2006–2007 Departmental Performance Report*. http://www.tbs-sct.gc.ca/dpr-rmr/2006-2007/inst/psp/psp00-eng.asp.

– 2008. "2008–09 Targeted Evaluation of the Cross-Cultural Roundtable on Security." Prepared by Government Consulting Services. Project no. 570–2712, March. http://www.publicsafety.gc.ca/cnt/rsrcs/pblctns/archive-vltn-crss-cltrl-2008-09/archive-ccrs-trts-eng.pdf.

Roach, Kent. 2006. "National Security, Multiculturalism and Muslim Minorities." *Singapore Journal of Legal Studies*, December: 405–38.

Scarborough, Rowan. 2010. "Obama at Odds with Petraeus Doctrine on 'Islam.'" *Washington Times*, 11 July. http://www.washingtontimes.com/news/2010/jul/11/obama-at-odds-with-petraeus-doctrine-on-islam/.

Supreme Court of Canada. 2007. *Charkaoui v. Canada (Citizenship and Immigration)*, 1 S.C.R. 350, 2007 SCC 9. http://scc-csc.lexum.com/scc-csc/scc-csc/en/item/2345/index.do.

Taber, Jane. 2011. "Harper's 'Islamicism' Remark Draws Heavy Opposition Fire." *Globe and Mail*, 8 September. http://www.theglobeandmail.com/news/politics/ottawa-notebook/harpers-islamicism-remark-draws-heavy-opposition-fire/article2156458/

Thomas, Scott. 2003. "Taking Religious and Cultural Pluralism Seriously." In *Religion in International Relations: The Return from Exile*, ed. Pavlos Hatzopoulos and Fabio Petito, 21–53. New York: Palgrave Macmillan.

11 Narratives, Identity, and Terrorism

SEAN NORTON AND AFZAL UPAL

Introduction

Following the July 2005 attacks in London, former CIA operative Robert Baer (2005) warned, "[T]here is a new plague on the streets of London, the pathological virus of the cult of suicide bombing." It is "[a]n enemy that springs up like a virus from nowhere," says Baer (2005). The highly communicable disease to which Baer refers is the ideology that supports suicide terrorism. Hence, what is most thought-provoking is not what Baer says or his manner of speech – his use of provocative language and imagery – but what his words suggest. If terrorist ideology is to be viewed as a highly infectious virus, in the language of epidemiology, there must be a disease vector that transmits the infection from one person to another.

As government researchers working on security-related issues, we frequently encounter the term "narratives" to refer to the discourse that al-Qaeda purportedly uses to "infect" people's thinking and excite their tendencies towards violence. The belief that the West is at war with Islam is widely viewed by security analysts as the "master-narrative" (Halverson, Goodall, and Corman 2011) or central basis of the conflict. Indeed, Burke (2004, 18) refers to al-Qaeda's world view as "*al-Qaedaism*," the anti-Western, anti-Zionist, and anti-Semitic ideology that motivates terrorist activity. Believing that it is really just words and ideas that lead people to radicalize towards terrorist violence, some Western governments have sought to attack the veracity of al-Qaedaism by developing their own counter-narratives. They hope to "vaccinate" those who are receptive or vulnerable through such means. However, there are limitations common to how governments approach "narratives" and the efforts to counter them. Narratives tend to be implicitly and mistakenly viewed narrowly in terms of language and ideas, as conduits for stories that convey self-evident truths or lies. Ideas are commonly viewed as entities that have a public, objective existence that is independent of the thinker (Lakoff and Johnson 1999, 244). Ideas are often understood as objects that can be perceived, grasped, shared, and even attacked. Based on these philosophical views, governments have often viewed the war of terrorism as being in part a mere conflict between sets of ideas.

This chapter has two objectives. On the surface, our chapter is essentially a plea to treat narratives differently. However, it provides in addition a window into the kinds of debates that occur among at least some of our colleagues in the defence and security communities. While we approach narratives and counter-narratives from a vantage point that differs from those of the academics in this book, the questions we pose are closely related to those addressed by these scholars. We hope, therefore, that this chapter might illustrate the overlapping interests of academics and activists on the one hand and those of us involved in defence and security policy research and analysis on the other hand.

A "war of ideas" is not a new concept. After all, this term captures well what took place during the Cold War. Historically, other terms have been used, such as psychological operations, counter-ideological or propaganda campaigns, information warfare, strategic influence, or influence operations. While these campaigns vary, they appear to share the common goal of using literary and oral devices to disseminate ostensible or alleged truths, oftentimes with the goal of maligning and discrediting a person, group, or cause.

In this chapter we argue against the assumption – common among security officials and laypeople alike – that narratives are just stories and ideas that people readily accept and are thus equally willing to dismiss. Believing narration to be a discursive activity is correct, to a point. However, we need to acknowledge the relationship between narration and identity. A narrative is not merely "communicative" but "constitutive" of identities and communities. Through narrating, people actively construct, negotiate, and experience identity. With this view, attacking a person's stories and ideas is the same as attacking their sense of self, both personally and in terms of the groups with which they identify. The realization of this has significant implications for policies such as the recent US "war of ideas."

Security Discourse

Even though the US government no longer argues that it is engaged in a "war of ideas," a recent White House document entitled *Empowering Local Partners to Prevent Violent Extremism in the United States* (United States 2011) suggests otherwise. This document pits US "ideals" against violent extremist "propaganda." US ideals are tacitly assumed to be right and good, whereas the members of al-Qaeda are discredited as "violent extremists" who "twist facts" and "distort religious principles" (United States 2011). Al-Qaeda is said to use "narratives and ideologies that feed on grievances, assign blame and legitimize the use of violence against those deemed responsible" (6). The conflict is not one of ideals. Nor, apparently, is it an "issue-oriented conflict" (Rapoport 1974). As Rapoport explains, a conflict that is based on underlying issues is resolved when the issues are resolved. By discrediting the members of al-Qaeda as "violent extremists" and by referring to their narratives as mere "propaganda," people are, in effect, prevented from even discussing the political and social issues invoked by these narratives.

The White House document seeks to repudiate, rather than refute, the views of al-Qaeda. According to the document, the Americans "live [*sic*] what al-Qaeda violently rejects – religious freedom and pluralism" (United States 2011, 7). By contrast, al-Qaeda is said to have a "destructive and bankrupt ideology" composed of "false narratives" (7). There is no need to debate issues when the opponent's views are patently false. In any case, there are no real issues to resolve – or so we are told.

The White House document appears to be little more than the propaganda it is meant to discredit. It may be that this document was not intended to be an official "counter-narrative," but it is a narrative all the same. However, it is not going to change the minds of their opponents who surely are convinced of their own moral superiority and the veracity of their truth claims. "The literature on non-conformity and deviance in group contexts indicates that … group members are not particularly receptive to criticisms of their group" (Upal, Parker, et al. 2011, 1). Indeed, in general, when people are criticized they tend to reject the criticism and malign the critics (Upal, Parker, et al. 2011, 1). Whatever the intent, it should be obvious that derogating groups, however objectionable they might be, is not an effective counter-narrative.

An expert meeting on countering violent extremist narratives, hosted in 2009 by the National Coordinator for Counterterrorism in the

Netherlands, led to a compilation of articles by specialists in the field (Kessels 2010). Many contributions include rhetoric related to truth and fiction, language and argument. One author appeals to democratic governments to shatter terrorist myths and half-truths (de Graaff 2010b, 18), whereas another believes "al-Qaeda's single narrative is based on weak argumentation, half-truth and downright lies" (Schmid 2010, 54). Terrorist "propaganda" is commonly cited, and several contributors refer to "believers" as "vulnerable" (Schmid 2010; Akerboom 2010; Jacobson 2010; Quiggin 2010), even "ignorant and semi-educated" (Schmid 2010, 49). One author hopes Western governments will become better listeners (de Graaff 2010a, 43). "It's not about telling our story," he says, but then later, this same author remarks, somewhat contradictorily, "western information campaigns should stress that jihadists champion a culture of death and destruction – after all, terrorism kills" (43). It is not clear what it means to be a better listener when one's views are already decided. Interestingly, the same rhetoric of truth is evident among Muslim extremists, too. For example, Sayf Muhammad writes in *Sada al-Malahim* (The echo of epic battles), an e-magazine published by al-Qaeda in the Arabian Peninsula (AQAP), "The jihadi media has earned the trust of those who are seeking the *truth* … We assure everyone that *the mujahidin media will broadcast the truth* as it is" (Page, Challita, and Harris 2011, 151; emphasis added).

Conceptual Territory

[N]arrative is not merely story-telling, or even simply linguistic, but is a structuring principle that precedes language, even gives it birth. (Kubiak 2004, 295)

While stories and their impact on people have been studied by literary theorists, historians, and other social influence researchers (DeFina 2003; van Dijk 1993; Green, Strange, and Brock 2002), such research has not always been widely favoured. In the past, some researchers argued that narrative research could produce general laws capable of explaining history (e.g., Hempel [1942] 1959, [1962] 1966). However, there were many others who rejected the emphasis on narratives, arguing that this avenue of research does not lend itself to the development of theories or explanations (Somers 1992). In the last two decades, however, the study of narratives has seen a revival among social scientists. Recently, there has also been a surge of interest in narratives by those in the military and international security domain (e.g., Kessels 2010; Halverson, Goodall, and Corman 2011; Larson 2011; Leuprecht et al. 2010). Notwithstanding the renewed popularity of this intellectual and political sub-field, there is no apparent agreement among the interested parties about what constitutes a narrative.

The concept of "narrative" has radically changed in the last 20 years. Although narratives are still regarded by some to be or to contain a set of disembodied ideas and claims, they are increasingly viewed as a constitutive feature of social life and human cognition (Somers 1992, 1996). Our lives are inherently "storied" (Somers 1992, 1996; Carr 1986; Sarbin 1986).

Narratives and the act of narrating are what make life intelligible and understandable. While security experts tend to be concerned with the *content* of narrative discourses, as Bamberg (2007, 221) explains, the content is merely a means for understanding the *context* of the way the speaker's identity is constructed. In this view, narratives are not just rhetorical devices for making truth claims but, more profoundly, are ways of creating and sharing our personal life story (Bamberg 2011). According to Somers, people "adjust stories to fit their own personal and social 'identities,' and conversely, they tailor 'reality' to fit their stories" (1992, 604). However, they do not create narratives ex nihilo. A repertoire of narratives always already exists in cultural and relational settings that can be traced over time and space and that people draw on to construct a sense of identity. It is through narrating that people are able to sort out who they are in their everyday interactions; to resolve ambiguities; to derive a coherent view of themselves by bringing "connectivity" and meaning to otherwise independent experiences over time; and to position themselves as being similar to but also different from others (Bamberg 2011). While ultimately, each personal story is unique, Baumeister and Leary (1995, 522) remind us that people are "fundamentally and pervasively motivated by a need to belong, that is, by a strong desire to form and maintain enduring interpersonal attachments" (cf. Bamberg 2011).

By revealing the patterned and contested network of relationships that exist between people and groups, narratives also have an "explanatory dimension" (Somers 1992, 602) that is easily overlooked. Indeed, people's need to understand events in their lives means that narratives also have an evaluative dimension. "Evaluation enables us to make qualitative and lexical distinctions among the infinite variety of events, experiences, characters, institutional promises, and social factors that impinge on our lives" (Somers 1996, 602). For instance, when Muslims "story" themselves as victims of the Western "war against Islam," this master narrative greatly influences the way some adherents characterize the otherwise isolated and disparate events in their lives. A "war against Islam" has been called an "enabling interpretation" (Sageman 2008, 75) and a "sense-making" explanation (Post 2005, 622). It permits those who have experienced, for example, discrimination, exclusion, or alienation to make sense of that experience from the "bottom up," according to Sageman, or from the top down by a "hate-mongering leader" who will use that narrative to nurture a "collective identity" among the "discontented and aggrieved" (Sageman 2008, 75). When narratives involve religious identification, which a Western "war against Islam" clearly does, they are likely to have an even tighter grip over a person or group's self-concept. After all, as Reader (chapter 2 in this volume) demonstrates, religious narratives, oriented towards their own ultimate veracity, seem to be more effective than political or social narratives at motivating individuals to sacrifice themselves or kill others.

"Al-Qaedaism"

The modern nuanced understanding of narratives allows us to analyse what has been referred to as the "master narrative for al-Qaeda," which depicts the ummah (the "Muslim community") as a decontextualized and undifferentiated global community of Muslims who are suffering violence and injustice at the hands of a Western Zionist-Crusader alliance. The West is often referred to as a similarly homogeneous and undifferentiated enemy. By using metaphors as well as historical and contemporary analogies that objectify, stereotype, demonize, and blame Western governments and their citizenry, the narrative sets the stage for a high-level conflict between these groups. Despite there being significant heterogeneity within and across different Muslim populations across the globe, the al-Qaeda narrative relies, first and foremost, on the singular, unifying categorization of Muslims as a superordinate categorical identity and a perfect example of Anderson's "imagined community" (Anderson 1983). The generalized concept of ummah additionally functions to greatly emphasize the religious dimensions of individual and group identity over competing social, political, professional, and regional dimensions of identities (e.g., Ysseldyk, Matheson, and Anisman 2010; Kinnvall 2004; Verkuyten and Yildiz 2007). As is the case with other group identities, what it means to be a "Muslim" is being constantly debated. Such internal conversations about identity, belonging, and boundaries are normal features of all imagined communities – especially those that include hundreds of millions of "members" (e.g., Muslims, Russians, Chinese, Christians). Charismatic leaders continuously and selectively construct, appropriate, and advance cultural, historical, and religious narratives that lend meaning and coherence to the everyday experience and identity of individual group members.

Since there are usually many different "stories" that allow individuals to make sense of their lives, multiple narratives interact in a contested political space, and some become more or less dominant than others. Scholars such as Roy (2008, 3) have argued that Osama bin Laden's success "is not to have established a modern and efficient Islamist political organization, but to have invented a narrative that could allow rebels without a cause to connect with a cause." It is highly speculative to suggest that bin Laden invented the identity of Muslims as victims of a ruthless Western colonialism and aggression and the associated narratives, but bin Laden was one of its most vocal champions in the early twenty-first century.

Whatever else bin Laden was, he was a *social identity entrepreneur* (Postmes et al. 2006; Haslam and Reicher 2007; Upal 2005, 2011a). His triumph lay in appropriating existing historical and cultural themes, then arranging and connecting them to actual events to construct a coherent "plot" that renders a meaningful identity to twenty-first-century Muslims worldwide. *Al-Qaedaism* is a "narrative identity" – to use Somers's phrase (1992) – that has reignited the perception that the West is at war with Islam, thereby helping to mobilize Muslims to act in defence of their religion. It is a narrative that has assuaged those with an appetite for meaning and defined a way for Muslims to establish identities as righteous defenders of Islam.

Further research is needed to better understand why some stories find greater acceptance than others (see Upal, Gonce, et al. 2007, for preliminary research on this topic; Heath and Heath 2007; Upal 2011b). Maybe there are personality characteristics that make the adoption of certain stories more likely. For instance, Roy may be correct in assuming that the al-Qaeda narrative more readily seduces rebels in search of a cause. However, stories can also find resonance for reasons that are unique to the social, cultural, or religious contexts in which people live. In the case of Aum Shinrikyō, Reader (in chapter 2) described how the movement's guru, Asahara, plucked teachings from the world's religions that justified killing out of compassion. Some of these teachings were already quite influential in Japan, which is probably a key reason why Asahara's disciples were more willing to accept his world view that killing is a spiritually virtuous and legitimate act when done to purify the world.

Here it is important to note the various roots of the tree of al-Qaedaism. In particular, there are many Muslims around the world who blame Western governments for the socio-economic and other problems they face. Where local regimes are seen as corrupt and incompetent they contend that this situation is a result of political control and exploitation by the West, in particular the United States, Israel, and Europe (Page, Challita, and Harris 2011, 156). In recent issues of *Sada al-Malahim*, the popular online Arabic magazine published by AQAP, Muslims are said to be experiencing "excruciating suffering," to be "suffering injustice," to be faced with corrupt governments and oppression, to have had their lands dominated and their dignity shattered (Page, Challita, and Harris 2011). Public officials are accused of being dishonourable and of having permitted moral degradation to flourish.

Al-Qaedaism has not developed only in response to oppression, however. Al-Qaeda has been vocal in its condemnation of Western materialism and moral decay. In the writings of AQAP, in particular (though also in the discourse of many others in the Arab and Islamic world), the West is widely associated with the spread of "immorality and promiscuity such as alcohol and drugs, prostitution, homosexuality, and lesbianism among [their] communities" (Page, Challita, and Harris 2011, 157). The West is also the source of "the forces of mendacity, apostasy, oppression, and blasphemy" that must be combated (ibid., 159). These are the repeated justifications for waging a defensive war against the West and overthrowing corrupt Muslim regimes.

We have found that security officials often discount the role of cultural milieu, in particular religion, in al-Qaeda-inspired terrorism, particularly among "home-grown" terrorists. Many favour a political view of terrorist violence. Reader, Dawson, and Bramadat (in this book, chapters 2, 3, and 1, respectively) have each observed what they believe is a general tendency among politicians and academics, in Western liberal democracies, to dismiss any deep connection between religion and violence. Reader's research on Aum Shinrikyō is just one example in which religious ideas and movements played decisive roles in the development of this small, but deadly, religious group. While motivations for al-Qaeda-inspired terrorism are surely complex and various, there is no denying al-Qaedaism's explicit religious character. As Dawson explains, the "consistent use of religious rhetoric may well be indicative of the dominance of religious over political objectives." As well, Bramadat points out that the Nigerian Islamic group Boko Haram would be puzzled by the Western media's sharp distinction between their religious and political-economic motivations. For this Nigerian group – and for many "fundamentalist" groups around the world – the distinction between religious, material, and political concerns is indicative of our corrupt society (or even civilization). Similarly, al-Qaedaism has not arisen merely out of a narrowly "political" concern for injustice. "The primary goal of ... [al-Qaedaism] is and always has been the destruction of the atheist political and social order ... and its replacement with authentic Islamic states" (Gerges 2007, 3–4).

The Counter-narrative – A Real Possibility or False Hope

There is a great emphasis within global security and intelligence circles on the need for a narrative to counter what we are calling al-Qaedaism. Fishman calls for "a strategic message built around al Qaeda's hypocrisy and its failures" (2008, 51). A tremendous amount of energy is expended in developing literary and oral devices to discredit al-Qaeda's ideological failings. When narratives are interpreted as purely discursive activities – something akin to rhetoric – then forms of communication are seen as the best means to invalidate opposing beliefs and attitudes and influence the adoption of new ones. By relegating narrative to the realm of mere language, an even greater issue arises – one that should be obvious but, regrettably, does not appear to be. Governments are complex social systems, and very often, there is a disconnection between the working-level folks who are tasked with strategic communications or who influence operations, for instance, and politicians who must account for a whole series of factors, most notably public opinion, when enacting policies or senior military officers who command an entire battle space. In situations such as these, those involved in policy analysis and influence operations lack any real authority to ensure coherence between *what they say* and *what others do*. A classic example is when former US president George W. Bush stated in unscripted remarks on 16 September 2001, "This *crusade*, this war on terrorism is going to take a while" (Bush 2001b). Unwittingly he invoked a narrative tied to a history of antagonism between Christians and Muslims. Even though Bush later referred to the enemy as a "radical network of terrorists" (Bush 2001a), his initial reaction stuck in people's minds, for it breathed life into a centuries-old story about the incommensurability of Islam and Christianity, a claim that is an important part of militant Muslim groups' perception of the West's hostility.

Any situation in which one side appears to violate its cherished values and ideals will expose governments to accusations of hypocrisy. Much harm can follow from merely the perception of hypocrisy, but when there is actual wrongdoing (e.g., the Abu Ghraib prison scandal, burning of the Qur'an), it can be easily used to make narratives, such as a Western war against Islam, seem credible. The same can be said for groups, such as al-Qaeda. When al-Qaeda in Iraq targeted fellow Muslims and engaged in gratuitous violence with on-camera beheadings of kidnapped civilians, it undercut its message of engaging in a purely defensive war to save the Muslim homelands from foreign invaders. When developing narratives, it is not enough to tout one's cherished values if ready examples of situations exist in which those values were violated.

An inquiry led by the UK government on their foreign policy approach to Afghanistan provides a case in point. As one witness remarked, the Taliban have propagated a "well-rehearsed narrative on the notion that the British army is in Afghanistan to seek revenge for 19th century defeats" (United Kingdom 2011, 85). In contrast to the simply rhetorical counter-narrative campaign adopted by the International Security Assistance Force (ISAF), the Taliban invoked a compelling historical narrative that construed involvement by international forces in Afghanistan in highly negative terms. It appears international forces failed to identify and invoke a narrative that was culturally and historically meaningful to the Afghan people, one that would cast their involvement in more favourable (or less negative) terms. A witness to the UK inquiry conceded, "[W]e have a fundamental problem in the narrative of what all these countries are doing in Afghanistan" (United Kingdom 2011, 84). As a result, the UK committee recommended that the government "greatly improve the quality and coherence of its public messaging efforts," even though others were "not convinced that ISAF's message is resonating with ordinary Afghans" (84–5). For the United Kingdom, the answer was still "communicating the case" more effectively for fear the United Kingdom might lose the "war of information" (84–5). The UK Foreign Secretary called for "better ... strategic communication of what our objectives are, how we are achieving them and how the nations of ISAF – and indeed the Afghan Government – are working together" (United Kingdom 2011, 138).

When public messaging, strategic communications, or a war of information – whichever phrase one prefers – fails to resonate with an intended audience, there is a tendency, as the UK example clearly illustrates, to view this as a public messaging failure. However, this lack of resonance may have something to do with the inherent inadequacy of these so-called counter-narrative campaigns to change the way people see the world. We argue that these flaws reflect deeper problems with rather naive and limited views of narrative itself.

Having greater awareness of various cultural and historical repertoires will aid understanding of how words and deeds are likely to be interpreted. Narratives are the cultural, religious, and historical lens through which people, implicitly at times, characterize and evaluate people, relationships, and events. The events in question need not be actually related in time or space. The way they are interpreted is what links them together. Segments of the Afghan public more readily adopted the Taliban's narrative of why international forces were in Afghanistan because it felt true given their views of the past. "Narrative structures exert their persuasive power through a heuristic route, involving intuitive or low effort thought processes" (Upal, Parker, et al. 2011, iii). Since the messages conveyed by international forces did not fit as easily into existing storylines, they were more easily rejected.

If governments hope to develop counter-narratives that will change how people think, and how they see themselves or their group in relation to others, they may be underestimating the difficulty of the endeavour. Designing effective influence campaigns requires a thorough understanding of the sociocultural, historical, and religious beliefs of the target population. Also required is credibility in the eyes of the target population, which can be achieved, in part, by adhering to cherished values and minimizing the gap between what is said and what is done.

Conclusion

Contrary to the prevalent view within governments, narratives are not merely a form of communication, a set of descriptive facts, or a series of statements that support an argument. Nor are they a set of disembodied ideas that can be attacked and changed through the force of reason. Narratives are not fictional stories or rhetoric that people casually believe and are equally willing to dismiss. Rather, as we have argued, narratives develop over time and space as repertoires that render the events in people's lives and their relationships meaningful. Narratives are often deeply rooted in history, culture, religion, and relational settings, and the act of narrating is profoundly related to the development of a sense of self. As Bamberg (2007, 223) explains, "narratives, irrespective of whether they deal with one's life or an episode or event in the life of someone else, always reveal the speaker's identity."

Whatever their role in developing counter-narratives, government officials have fairly rudimentary things they can do to reduce the likelihood of alienating particular groups and adding fuel to the fire of opposing narratives. Governments need to be especially cautious in the way their activities are framed. For instance, when counter-narrative activities are viewed as part of a "war" to discredit, disparage, and change the way some Muslims understand themselves, their relationships, communities, and experience, they may inadvertently feed the perception that Western societies are at war with Islam – the very notion that governments have actively sought to refute. As well, governments can always do better at managing the relationship between *what they say* and *what they do*. Their credibility demands as much.

One question government officials and members of security organizations may wish to consider is this: is it reasonable to think that Canada, the United Kingdom, the United States, or any government can discredit and delegitimize al-Qaedaism or other extremist "propaganda" through the use of oral devices and "counter-narratives" without also reflecting on the ways in which they are implicated in opposing narratives? Choosing to derogate and blame does shift attention away from and obviate the need to think carefully about one's own actions as a source of grievance. Trying instead to understand how one's actions are being framed by an opponent's narrative or to seek to uncover and resolve the issues underlying a conflict is obviously much more difficult. Yet this is precisely what governments must do in our view. They must be willing to explore the real and perceived "root causes" of extremist violence and to realize that doing so does not in any way lend legitimacy to violence.

Al-Qaeda has effectively leveraged a global Muslim identity using a master narrative, in effect creating an ideology that has outlived many of its core members. However, further research is needed to better understand how different narratives interact, including the ways different people come to see themselves and others in the stories that are promulgated. Fruitful avenues of research would aim to better comprehend how Muslims in the West and elsewhere understand themselves in relation to the different narratives that are available to them. For instance, what is it that leads people to adopt narratives that are less socially predominant? It may be that there is a strategic logic to how and when certain identities are upheld, or it may be that there are iden- tifiable factors and conditions that make the adoption of certain narra- tive identities more likely. One thing is clear: if the adoption of a global al-Qaeda narrative is what galvanizes ideological support for al-Qaeda and motivates terrorist involvement, then perspectives that limit *narra- tive* to the realm of language and argument are not likely to have much influence, particularly when that narrative identity involves religion. It is time to treat narratives more seriously. Furthermore, it is incumbent on governments to ensure their words and deeds better enable people to resist the attack of an infectious and violent ideology and do not sim- ply become vectors for transmitting the disease. Clearly, there are many ways in which the argument presented here overlaps with the claims made by the other authors in this book. The common interests shared by us – as government employees involved in security studies – and these authors suggest that political and academic perspectives might both contribute to more informed approaches to narratives of religious violence.

REFERENCES

Akerboom, Erik. 2010. "Preface." In *Countering Violent Extremist Narratives*, ed. Eelco J.A.M. Kessels, 5. The Hague: National Coordinator for Counterterror- ism (NCTb).

Anderson, Benedict. 1983. *Imagined Communities: Reflections on the Origin and Spread of Nationalism*. London: Verso.

Baer, Robert. 2005. "This Deadly Virus." *Observer*, 7 August.

Bamberg, M. 2007. "Narrative, Discourse and Identities." In *Narratology beyond Literary Criticism: Mediality, Disciplinarity*, ed. Jan Christoph Meis- ter, Tom Kindt, and Wilhelm Schernus, 213–37. Berlin: Walter de Gruyter GmbH & Co.

– 2011. "Who Am I? Narration and Its Contribution to Self and Identity." *Theory & Psychology* 21 (1): 3–24. doi:10.1177/0959354309355852.

Baumeister, R.F., and M.R. Leary. 1995. "The Need to Belong: Desire for Inter- personal Attachments as a Fundamental Human Motivation." *Psychological Bulletin* 117: 497–529.

Burke, Jason. 2004. "Al Qaeda." *Foreign Policy* 142: 18–26.

Bush, President George W. 2001a. "Address to a Joint Session of Congress and the American People." Press release. Joint Session of Congress. Washington, DC: Office of the Press Secretary, the White House.

– 2001b. "Remarks by the President upon Arrival." Press release. Washington, DC: Office of the Press Secretary, the White House.

Carr, David. 1986. "Narrative and the Real World." *History and Theory* 25 (2): 117–31.

DeFina, Anna. 2003. *Identity in Narrative: A Study of Immigrant Discourse*. Amsterdam: John Benjamins.

de Graaff, Bob. 2010a. "Redefining 'Us' and 'Them.'" In *Countering Violent Extremist Narratives*, ed. Eelco J.A.M. Kessels, 36–45. The Hague: National Coordinator for Counterterrorism (NCTb).

– 2010b. "Counter-narratives and the Unintentional Messages Counterterrorism Policies Unwittingly Produce: The Case of West-Germany." In *Countering Violent Extremist Narratives*, ed. Eelco J.A.M. Kessels, 12–19. The Hague: National Coordinator for Counterterrorism (NCTb).

Fishman, B. 2008. "Using the Mistakes of al Qaeda's Franchises to Undermine Its Strategies." *ANNALS of the American Academy of Political and Social Science* 618 (1): 46–54. doi:10.1177/0002716208316650.

Gerges, Fawaz A. 2007. *Journey of the Jihadist: Inside Muslim Militancy*. Orlando, FL: Harcourt Books.

Green, M.C., J.J. Strange, and T.C. Brock. 2002. *Narrative Impact: Social and Cognitive Foundations*. Mahwah, NJ: Lawrence Erlbaum Associates.

Halverson, J.R., R.L. Goodall, and S.R. Corman. 2011. *Master Narratives of Islamist Extremism*. New York: Palgrave Macmillan.

Haslam, S. Alexander, and Stephen Reicher. 2007. "Identity Entrepreneurship and the Consequences of Identity Failure: The Dynamics of Leadership in the BBC Prison Study." *Social Psychology Quarterly* 70 (2): 125–47.

Heath, Chip, and Dan Heath. 2007. *Made to Stick*. New York: Random House.

Hempel, Carl G. (1942) 1959. "The Function of General Laws in History." In *Theories of History*, ed. Patrick Gardiner, 344–56. New York: Free Press of Glencoe.

– (1962) 1966. "Explanation in Science and History." In *Philosophical Analysis and History*, ed. William H. Dray, 95–126. New York: Harper and Row.

Jacobson, Michael J. 2010. "Learning Counter-narrative Lessons from Cases of Terrorist Dropouts." In *Countering Violent Extremist Narratives*, ed. Eelco J.A.M. Kessels, 72–83. The Hague: National Coordinator for Counterterrorism (NCTb).

Kessels, Eelco J.A.M. 2010. *Countering Violent Extremist Narratives*. The Hague: National Coordinator for Counterterrorism (NCTb).

Kinnvall, C. 2004. "Globalization and Religious Nationalism: Self, Identity, and the Search for Ontological Security." *Political Psychology* 25: 741–67.

Kubiak, Anthony. 2004. "Spelling It Out: Narrative Typologies of Terror." *Studies in the Novel* 36 (3): 294–301.

Lakoff, George, and Mark Johnson. 1999. *Philosophy in the Flesh: The Embodied Mind and Its Challenge to Western Thought.* New York: Basic Books.

Larson, Eric V. 2011. "A Diplomatic Strategy to Counter al Qaeda's Narrative." *Rand Review* 35 (2): 21–3.

Leuprecht, Christian, Todd Hataley, Sophia Moskalenko, and Clark McCauley. 2010. "Narratives and Counter-narratives for Global Jihad Opinion versus Action." In *Countering Violent Extremist Narratives*, ed. Eelco J.A.M. Kessels, 58–70. The Hague: National Coordinator for Counterterrorism (NCTb).

Page, Michael, Lara Challita, and Alistair Harris. 2011. "Al Qaeda in the Arabian Peninsula: Framing Narratives and Prescriptions." *Terrorism and Political Violence* 23 (2): 150–72. doi:10.1080/09546553.2010.526039.

Post, Jerrold M. 2005. "When Hatred Is Bred in the Bond: Psycho-cultural Foundations of Contemporary Terrorism." *Political Psychology* 26 (4): 615–36.

Postmes, T., G. Baray, S.A. Haslam, T. Morton, and R.I. Swaab. 2006. "The Dynamics of Personal and Social Identity Formation." In *Individuality and the Group: Advances in Social Identity*, ed. T. Postmes and J. Jetten, 1–37. Thousand Oaks, CA: Sage.

Quiggin, Tom. 2010. "Contemporary Jihadist Narratives: The Case of Momin Khawaja." In *Countering Violent Extremist Narratives*, ed. Eelco J.A.M. Kessels, 84–93. The Hague: National Coordinator for Counterterrorism (NCTb).

Rapoport, Anatol. 1974. *Conflict in Man-made Environments.* Baltimore: Pelican Books.

Roy, Oliver. 2008. "Al Qaeda in the West as a Youth Movement: The Power of a Narrative." *MICROCON Policy Working Paper 2.* Brighton: MICROCON.

Sageman, Marc. 2008. *Leaderless Jihad: Terror Networks in the Twenty-first Century.* Philadelphia: University of Pennsylvania Press.

Sarbin, Theodore R., ed. 1986. *Narrative Psychology: The Storied Nature of Human Conduct.* New York: Praeger.

Schmid, Alex P. 2010. "The Importance of Countering Al-Qaeda's 'Single Narrative.'" In *Countering Violent Extremist Narratives*, ed. Eelco J.A.M. Kessels, 46–57. The Hague: National Coordinator for Counterterrorism (NCTb).

Somers, Margaret R. 1992. "Narrativity, Narrative Identity, and Social Action: Rethinking English Working-class Formation." *Social Science History* 16 (4): 591–630.

– 1996. "The Narrative Constitution of Identity: A Relational and Network Approach." *Theory and Society* 23 (5): 605–49.

United Kingdom. 2011. *The UK's Foreign Policy Approach to Afghanistan and Pakistan.* Fourth Report of Session 2010–11. London: House of Commons Foreign Affairs Committee.

United States. 2011. *Empowering Local Partners to Prevent Violent Extremism in the United States*. Washington, DC: White House.

Upal, M. Afzal. 2005. "Towards a Cognitive Science of New Religious Movements." *Cognition and Culture* 5 (2): 214–39.

– 2011a. "From Individual to Social Counterintuitiveness: How Layers of Innovation Weave Together to Form Multilayered Tapestries of Human Cultures." *Mind and Society* 10 (1): 79–96. doi:10.1007/s11299-011-0083-8.

– 2011b. "Memory, Mystery, and Coherence: Does the Presence of 2–3 Counterintuitive Concepts Predict Cultural Success of a Narrative?" *Cognition and Culture* 11 (1–2): 23–48.

Upal, M. Afzal, Lauren Gonce, Ryan Tweney, and D. Jason Slone. 2007. "Contextualizing Counterintuitiveness: How Context Affects Comprehension and Memorability of Counterintuitive Concepts." *Cognitive Science* 31 (3): 415–39.

Upal, M. Afzal, D. Parker, G. Moskowitz, and M. Kugler. 2011. "Investigating the Dynamics of Identity Formation, and Narrative Information Comprehension: Final Report." Technical Report 2011–061. Toronto: Defence R&D Canada.

van Dijk, Teun. 1993. "Stories and Racism." In *Narratives and Social Control*, ed. D. Mumby, 121–42. Newbury Park, CA: Sage.

Verkuyten, M., and A.A. Yildiz. 2007. "National (Dis)identification and Ethnic and Religious Identity: A Study among Turkish-Dutch Muslims." *Personality and Social Psychology Bulletin* 33: 1448–62.

Ysseldyk, R., K. Matheson, and H. Anisman. 2010. "Religiosity as Identity: Toward an Understanding of Religion from a Social Identity Perspective." *Personality and Social Psychology Review* 14 (1): 60–71. doi:10.1177/1088868309349693.

12 Conclusion

PAUL BRAMADAT AND LORNE DAWSON

In this book a group of scholars and policymakers, trained in a variety of methods and embedded in a variety of professional, social, and religious contexts, risked subjecting their own research to criticism from people situated well outside of their conventional circle of peers. This sort of scrutiny often makes people uncomfortable, but the responses it elicits can yield fascinating insights. It is a rare accomplishment to draw anthropologists, sociologists, historians, political scientists, security analysts, and religious studies experts, as well as religious insiders and outsiders and government employees and government critics, into one common and respectful conversation. Indeed, it was the numerous face-to-face dimensions of the conversation we have had during this project that have most dramatically challenged and strengthened these chapters and have spawned friendships and a research network that will outlast this engagement.

In this final chapter we reflect on the key empirical and theoretical contributions the book's authors have made to this broader discussion, as well as the outstanding political and academic questions that now more clearly demand attention.

Micro and Macro Orientations to Religious Radicalization and Securitization

When scholars, policymakers, journalists, and others discuss radicalization and securitization, what we might call macro-political themes tend to attract the vast majority of attention. That is, for many of us, it is intuitively obvious that what matters when discussing religiously linked terrorism are major political forces and facts such as large-scale discourses about religious others; national revolutionary movements; tensions between superpowers, their proxies, and subaltern groups; the rise and fall of despotic regimes; colonial and postcolonial political formations; competition for scarce natural resources; changes in immigration and refugee policies; and global communications technologies that facilitate new forms of radical activities, personal identity, and social movements.

While these large-scale forces are certainly important factors in the development of most radical movements, and while they establish many of the analytical guideposts in this book, one's views of others take shape in very particular places and times: in this year, in this city, on that sidewalk, in that school hallway, in this restaurant, in that intimate relationship, in this taxi. Amiraux and Araya-Morena argue that more attention is needed to what one might call the micro-politics of everyday life, the ways in which our daily interactions with others in pluralistic milieux do not simply reflect but also enforce – or even undermine – those macro-political forces we normally think of as being determinative. This emphasis on the power of one's particular social location to condition one's experience of and thoughts about religious and ethnic diversity and political communities is most clearly elaborated in their chapter. However, the interview data discussed in Beyer's and Jamil's chapters also illustrate the power of both local forces and personal relationships between people of dominant and minority communities to shape the ways members of minority communities come to understand those with whom they live in pluralistic societies.

In fact, while Dawson underlines the complexity of trying to determine why members of the Toronto 18 were attracted to a radical form of Islam, it is important to remember that these men were, after all, individuals, residents of neighbourhoods, students in particular schools, employees in particular businesses, children of particular families, and so on. As such, to understand these would-be "home-grown" terrorists we need to pay close attention to their interactions with members of the dominant society, as this will provide clues about how this small group of young men came to view the non-Muslim world as hostile to their deepest values. A concern for these micro-political forces certainly complements the more conventional approaches. Although these relatively novel analyses may not translate easily into specific policy initiatives, they might help us to understand the relationship between what Amiraux and Araya-Moreno describe as local "troubles" and broader political "issues."

Distinctive Perspectives on the Media, Military, and Government

Another feature of this book that most clearly distinguishes it from others is the window it opens up to the influential spheres of media, government, and the military. Smith's account of the way journalists cover stories related to radicalization is an excellent illustration of how securitization discourses emerge and are circulated within the public arena. As well, from this chapter we learn about the unique pressures facing journalists when they are asked to tell stories in which religion and radicalization are combined. Often the writers assigned to these stories are ill-prepared to understand the specifically religious dimensions of their subjects, and even when they are familiar with these, they must nevertheless ensure that they write something appropriate for a particular "beat" in a particular television program, newspaper, website, or magazine. These specific venues and the considerable time pressure facing journalists often shape the final product more than people outside of the profession can appreciate.

Just as Smith provides us with a unique vantage point for understanding the media, Norton and Afzal take readers into the world of military and security studies, social contexts that will be completely foreign to many. While the professional settings in which security analysts work are characterized by their own distinctive political pressures, we suspect many readers will be relieved – perhaps even surprised – to read that the kinds of issues that concern anthropologists, sociologists, and even minority group advocates also concern government employees such as Norton and Afzal. Indeed, although these authors work in a military setting, their approach to narratives and counter-narratives is as critical as the approach adopted by the authors of the other chapters in this book.

Keeble's chapter on the Cross-Cultural Roundtable presents a personal analysis of a distinctive feature of the Canadian approach to security. Although efforts were made to ensure that the Roundtable was not shrouded in mystery, soon after it was launched scholars and advocates interested in diversity, discrimination, security, and religion began to wonder about the relationship between the interests of Public Safety (which initiated the Roundtable) and those groups and individuals drawn into the discussion. Keeble's frank description of her experiences and her analysis of the many personal and political forces at work among her fellow Roundtable members will no doubt fascinate many readers.

These three chapters demonstrate the extremely problematic nature of the stereotypes one typically finds about the media, the government, and the military, not just in public but also in academic discourse. Too often, scholars make unfounded claims about the inner logic(s) of these three settings. If we wish to foster a more subtle and honest discussion about religion, radicalization, and securitization in our society, we will need to move past these monolithic preconceptions to grapple with the complex (and often surprising) forces at work in these contexts.

Taking the Link between Religion and Violent Extremism Seriously

In the Canadian context the forms of terrorism that have been most consequential are religious. In the Air India bombing of 1985 and the Toronto 18 arrests in 2006, and in the many other recent situations in which Canadians or those living in Canada have been convicted on terrorism-related charges (e.g., Inderjit Singh Reyat in 1991, Ahmed Ressam in 2001, Mohammad Momin Khawaja in 2009, Said Namouh in 2009), we are dealing with what appear on the surface to be clearly political acts, grounded in political grievances and with political objectives. But the relevant identity of the perpetrators in most cases, and the manner in which they chose to frame the nature and justification of their actions, is religious, and that matters. In these situations, the men in question believe they are defending inviolable and religiously defined collective identities that they believe to be under siege; they believe that their violent defence of those identities is legitimate because they are acting in accord with a set of religious values and obligations that transcend the dictates of civil society and law in Canada and elsewhere. As Reader demonstrates in his chapter, from their perspective there are no "innocents," and hence the (real or potential) death of civilians at their hands is not an act of terrorism per se. Moreover, as Dawson argues, the political aspects of their actions are subsumed under a broader and largely symbolic preoccupation with the fulfilment of religious purposes. Even though their acts might be strategically unsuccessful in the sense that they do not bring about real or immediate political change, these actors understand themselves as the instruments of God, and as such, their actions are designed to demonstrate the virtue of their cause and by their example help initiate a larger divine plan for humanity. The bombing of skyscrapers, government offices, churches, airplanes, or pornography shops by religious extremists, whether Christian, Hindu, Sikh, or Muslim, is consequential because such acts are symbolic enactments of their faith in and commitment to this transcendent vision. Their unusual, and yet internally coherent, reasoning needs to be taken into account in seeking to understand and effectively counter this threat.

Curiously, as Bramadat, Reader, and Dawson demonstrate, there has been a consistent tendency in the research literature on terrorism to discount the significance of religion as a primary motivator of the acts. There is evidence of a profound ambivalence in the way scholars, policymakers, and security experts treat religion when it comes to terrorism and counterterrorism. Most contemporary Western researchers and government officials follow a set of assumptions and prejudices rooted in the Enlightenment tradition, according to which the political explanations for terrorist acts are prima facia legitimate, if objectionable, while the religious explanations beg further explication in terms of some other more fundamental set of latent functions and motivations. This is the natural attitude of people raised and conditioned to a largely secular social existence, but it introduces into the assessment of radical forms of religion unexamined interpretative inclinations that widen the "explanatory gap" that Dawson highlights as one of the primary methodological hurdles faced by terrorism studies.

In particular, if so many individuals are affected by the issues normally associated with terrorism – geopolitical conflicts, economic deprivation, or social and personal identity struggles – then why do so few people actually become terrorists? Isolating the key variables that explain the (exceedingly rare) radicalization of particular individuals and groups is the abiding concern of contemporary research on terrorism, both academic and applied. In this regard, being religious, let alone simply being Muslim or even a Muslim immigrant living in a non-Islamic or even somewhat anti-Islamic context, is obviously an insufficient causal explanation of terrorism, given that it applies to large (and increasing) numbers of people in the West, the overwhelming majority of whom never turn to violence. Beyer's study of young Muslim men in Canada is indicative of this state of affairs. Obviously the careless general linkage of Islam or Sikhism (to use the two most relevant Canadian referents) with terrorism is wildly unfair and injurious to these communities. Government officials and research scholars are keenly aware of this liability and strive to avoid promoting Islamophobia or other forms of prejudicial treatment of minority religious communities in Canada (though inadvertently some policies may have this effect). But this does not mean that religious convictions have no role to play in violent forms of extremism. Certain extreme expressions of these religions are absolutely instrumental to the emergence of violent radicalization, as Reader and Dawson both argue, and we can learn to be more precise in identifying the problematic aspects of those forms of religiosity. Efforts to do so are blocked, though, by a number of overlapping and sometimes conflicting arguments which arise in various forms in discussions of terrorism.

In the research literature on terrorism one can identify five different yet overlapping arguments invoked to discount the apparent role of religion in the instigation of violence. The first three arguments are conceptual in nature and reflect a more scholarly approach to the issue. The final two arguments are more substantive in nature and less reflective. But they are also more pervasive in both the scholarly and media accounts of terrorism, especially so-called jihadist terrorism.

First there is what we might call the naive essentialist argument discussed by Bramadat in the introduction to this book. When religion is identified exclusively with love, charity, and compassion, those who perpetrate acts of terrorism in the name of religion must, by definition, be intentionally misappropriating religious symbols and identities for political reasons; or, indeed, the perpetrators of such violence may be framed as the victims of profound ignorance of the religious tradition in whose name they wreak havoc. Those who promote this essentialist account of religion usually mean well, but they unwittingly perpetuate understandings of religion that are wildly inconsistent with what ordinary observers report.

A second argument discounts the role of religion more indirectly, arguing that terrorism is first and foremost a strategy used by relatively weak political groups, under certain specific conditions (e.g., foreign occupation or control), to subvert the power of a much stronger opponent. It is a form of asymmetric warfare that is intrinsically rational in the sense that it is a strategic and intentional use of one of the few options available to an oppressed group. In this second argument, while a religious justification may be used by some cunning leaders to dupe less informed people into supporting or even participating in terrorism, the essential irrationality of religion is incompatible with the cold instrumental reasoning at the heart of many terrorist organizations (e.g., Pape 2005). As such, religion per se is not a significant factor in explaining either the real origins or the perpetuation of terrorist violence; it is a mere rationalization for violence exploited by politically motivated leaders.

The third argument, as reviewed and criticized by Reader in his chapter, takes an even more indirect and complicated approach. The proponents of this argument (e.g., Cavanaugh 2009) start with the postcolonial theoretical assertion that the very category of "religion" is a Western construct that has been inappropriately imposed on other cultures in the world. They then argue that Western scholars, security analysts, and government officials use this ethnocentric conception of religion to stigmatize and dismiss forms of political protest to which they are opposed by identifying the acts of resistance to Western oppression perpetrated by their opponents as instances of "religious violence." This designation works to stigmatize and belittle the validity of the violent actions undertaken by the terrorists because the conception of religion called on evokes the culturally engrained revulsion of Western elites to the excesses of the post-Reformation wars of religion that ravaged Europe. Operating with this ethnocentric conceptual framework, all acts of terror designated as "religious" are deemed to be inherently irrational and subject to the most severe sanctions, while the violence the Western states use to defeat the "religious terrorists" is framed as nothing more than the rational and morally justified defence of the civil liberties of the citizens of the Western states. In other words, the scholars who propose this argument are asserting two things: on the one hand, the use of the label "religious terrorism" is political, in the sense that it is designed to divert attention away from any consideration of the reasonableness or legitimacy of the causes for which the terrorists are fighting; on the other hand, this understanding of "religious terrorism" is being used to galvanize unthinking support for the violent suppression of terrorists, despite the collateral damage that may ensue.

The fourth and fifth arguments against the primacy of a religious motivation for terrorism are simpler and also more pervasive. The fourth one entails assuming that religion could only be a post hoc rationalization for terrorism, because religion is assumed to be little more than a secondary social manifestation of other, more primary and universal human needs. As Dawson demonstrates in his chapter and has elaborated elsewhere (e.g., Dawson 2012), the scholars who make this argument offer little in the way of actual evidence or even argumentation in support of this claim when it appears, explicitly and implicitly, in discussions of terrorism (e.g., Silke 2008, 110–11; McCauley and Moskalenko 2011, 219–21). They seem to be relying on the unspoken and unexamined bias of most social scientists in the West, who have a decidedly secular approach to the world.

Fifth and lastly, as Dawson begins to address in his chapter, it is assumed that the religion of home-grown terrorists in particular is superficial, and hence not a prime motivator, because terrorists either lacked a religious upbringing, are recent converts, or do not have a particularly sophisticated understanding of their religion. Dawson argues that this interpretive tendency displays a naive grasp of the nature of "religiosity," one biased towards the norms of conventional, official, and elite forms of religion dominant in Western societies. All new religious convictions, by this reasoning, are somehow less intrinsically religious, yet there are no feasible criteria for logically holding such a view.

While there is some merit to each of these arguments and the points they raise warrant further serious debate, more often than not they are used in various mixed and conflated ways to sideline serious consideration of the instrumental role of religious ideas and emotions in fomenting terrorist violence. For largely non-religious Western societies the consequences of serious religious commitments are inconvenient and troublesome, since they fall beyond the scope of what is most naturally understood. There is a marked preference for us to assume that terrorists are either essentially rational (and just using religion as a diversion) or simply insane (and incapable of or hostile to rational engagement). More often than not, neither is the case.

New Directions

The chapters in this volume call our attention to a number of other issues that demand more sustained critical attention than we have been able to provide. What follows is an account of some promising new questions.

Broadening the Focus

While critical assessments of the current state of radicalization and securitization related to Jewish, Christian, indigenous, and other forms of religion are conspicuous in their absence from this book, the authors and editors do not believe that only Muslim, Sikh, Buddhist, and Hindu forms of radicalization are noteworthy or troubling. At the first meeting of all of the authors, editors, government colleagues, and funders, this issue was discussed at great length. We all realized that no single book could cover all forms of a now quite multifarious social and political phenomenon. Nonetheless, we needed to be guided in our deliberations by some kind of overarching principle – and ultimately we agreed to address those communities on which the vast majority of public and political attention has been focused for the past decade. While we stand by this decision, we also recognize the problems associated with attending almost exclusively – as politicians, journalists, and so many in the general public also do – to those forms of religion associated with non-white, non-European (relative) newcomers. In response, thoroughly addressing those traditions not covered here might give these movements the attention they deserve.

Enhancing Our Understanding of Radicalization and the Impact of Securitization in Immigrant Communities

In comparison with the United States, Britain, and many European nations,[1] relatively little work has been done in Canada on three interrelated issues bearing on the study of Muslims and other securitized communities: (1) studies of specifically how and to what extent extremist views are present in those communities; (2) studies of what the leadership in these communities, both secular and religious, is thinking about the issue of radicalization and its prevention; and (3) studies, like Jamil's chapter, of the impact of securitization on daily life and attitudes of people in the most affected newcomer communities. We need both survey-based studies and those that employ interviews and ethnography to capture the broad attitudes and trends, as well as those forms of research that assess the micro-level consequences, which Amiraux and Araya-Morena highlight in their chapter. We need to develop a more subtle sense of the ways these communities are interpreting radicalization and securitization, especially the extent to which the new securitized environment has bred resentment and, if so, among whom and to what effect. Some work of this kind is in hand, but it is limited and just a beginning (e.g., Bartlett and Birdwell 2010; McCauley et al. 2011). New research into these kinds of issues is being supported by the Canadian Network for Research on Terrorism, Security, and Society (www.tsas.ca), which was launched in the spring of 2012.

International Dimensions of Radicalization and Securitization

In the case of terrorism we live, as Crelinsten (2009, 26) observes, "in a world of de-territorialized threats." It is worth noting that while many of the chapters in this book focus on the Canadian context, authors have been mindful of the ways radicalization and securitization in any nation are always ineluctably linked with analogous phenomena in other settings. The reflections in this book on the Indian, Japanese,

Nigerian, Sri Lankan, Pakistani, Egyptian, American, British, Somali, French, Dutch, and Swiss contexts underline clearly the international dimensions of the dialectical relationship between religious radicalization and state and societal securitization. Of course, the challenge this poses for scholars is significant, since there is no uniformity among the ways states manage religion (or religions), not to mention securitization; nor is there much evidence that states are moving in a single direction. Each society is characterized by distinctive (past and present) relations between "church" (or mosque, or temple) and "state" (Bramadat and Koenig 2009). This heterogeneity is not just evident when one compares, say, Canada with Egypt, China, or Switzerland, but even when one compares Canada to its more obvious national cousins: the United Kingdom, the United States, and France. While we have sought to illustrate that no society develops norms and policies – and no religious movements exist – in a vacuum, we would all benefit from even more comprehensive assessments of the global interdependence of both contemporary states and radical religious organizations, among themselves on this issue and between the specific states and various forms of religious radicalism.

Final Remarks

In an effort to protect religious minorities from discrimination, to be judicious in the treatment of religion as a cause of terrorism, or simply because many are ignorant about the nature of religious commitments, policymakers, journalists, and scholars often miss the opportunity to more precisely identify the common denominator of forms of terrorism characterized by an overt clash of competing religious, or religious and non-religious, values and identities. It is neither religion per se that is problematic nor one specific religious tradition. It is, rather, a clearly discernible form of religious extremism, which postulates an absolute vision of the final order and purpose of this world, that is problematic. Forms of millennialism and apocalyptic belief systems pose the real danger. Of course, since the vast majority of people holding millennialist views are non-violent, it is important to bear in mind that they too are only dangerous under specific conditions that scholars have researched (e.g., Reader 2000; Bromley and Melton 2002). Proponents of violent religious world views, as Reader's and Jakobsh's chapters remind us, display strong tendencies towards antinomianism, the demonization of enemies, and a radical dualism. Each of these tendencies puts them into sharp conflict with those who disagree with them, and with the prompting of fanatical leaders it is relatively easy for their mounting hostility to be converted to acts of violence in defence of the "truth" (cf. Dawson 2006, 150–2; Dawson 2010). As many commentators have argued (e.g., Neumann 2009), and as Peter Henne (2012, 52) recently demonstrated through a quantitative analysis of suicide terrorist attacks over the past three decades, "[g]roups with religious ideologies cause more deaths ... than nationalist and leftist groups. This relationship holds in conditions of varying political freedom, economic development, ethnic fractionalization, and military occupation."

Of course the debate over the relative significance of and the relationship between the social, political, and religious motivations for terrorism is far too complex to survey in this conclusion (e.g., Pape 2005; Moghadam 2006; Juergensmeyer 2006; Jones 2008; Hegghammer 2009). The chapters in this book addressing these issues highlight the relevance of religion as a factor in the Canadian context, but they are preliminary. We need further detailed case studies of the Air India, Toronto 18, and other controversial individual cases (e.g., Mohammad Momin Khawaja) that specifically explore the role of religion. In other words, we need to test the fit of theory and data with regard to specifically Canadian groups, contexts, and individuals. This would help to advance the general debate on these matters, highlight the connection between Canadian cases and the international debate, and underline the significance of the larger discussion to Canadian policymakers and security analysts. Such research would also help to cultivate a new generation of scholars focused on the issues of terrorism and the processes of radicalization in Canada, since currently there are only a handful of scattered and rather disconnected Canadian scholars exploring these and other fundamental issues in the study of terrorism. We lag well behind our colleagues in the United States, Britain, and many other countries (e.g., the Netherlands, Denmark, Sweden, and Norway). We need to be involved in the attempt to understand the roots and nature of the process of radicalization; and, when there are any distinctively Canadian aspects or factors which either aggravate or hinder the process, counter and preventive measures need to be developed and implemented effectively. The book in your hands and the network of scholars and policymakers out of which it emerged represent preliminary yet productive efforts to improve both public safety and, more broadly, public life. Since there is a growing awareness of the issues at stake and plenty of goodwill within religious, political, and academic communities in Canada, we have reason to believe that these efforts will bear fruit in the near future.

NOTE

1 See, for example, Slootman and Tillie 2006; Change Institute 2008; McCauley and Stellar 2009; Schanzer, Kurzman, and Moosa 2010; Kühle and Lindekilde 2010; Quilliam 2010; Sobolewska 2010; and Githens-Mazer 2010.

REFERENCES

Bartlett, Jamie, and Jonathan Birdwell. 2010. *The Edge of Violence*. London: Demos. http://www.demos.co.uk/publications/theedgeofviolencefullreport.

Bramadat, Paul, and Matthias Koenig, eds. 2009. *International Migration and the Governance of Religious Diversity*. Montreal: McGill-Queen's University Press.

Bromley, David G., and J. Gordon Melton, eds. 2002. *Cults, Religion and Violence*. Cambridge: Cambridge University Press.

Cavanaugh, William T. 2009. *The Myth of Religious Violence*. New York: Oxford University Press.

Change Institute. 2008. *Studies into Violent Radicalisation: The Beliefs, Ideologies and Narratives*. European Commission (Directorate General Justice, Freedom and Security). http://changeinstitute.co.uk/images/publications/changeinstitute_beliefsideologiesnarratives.pdf.

Crelinsten, Ronald. 2009. *Counterterrorism*. Cambridge: Polity Press.

Dawson, Lorne L. 2006. *Comprehending Cults: The Sociology of New Religious Movements*. 2nd ed. Toronto: Oxford University Press.

– 2010. "Religion and Violent Extremism." Presented to joint meeting of Public Safety Canada and Homeland Security, Ottawa, 27 September.

– 2012. "The Missing Link: Religion and the Social Ecology of Terrorist Radicalization." Presented to the Social Conditions and Processes of Radicalization workshop of the Canadian Network for Research on Terrorism, Security, and Society, Ottawa, 10 November.

Githens-Mazer, Jonathan. 2010. "Mobilization, Recruitment, Violence and the Street: Radical Violent Takfiri Islamism in Early Twenty-first-century Britain." In *The New Extremism in 21st Century Britain*, ed. Roger Eatwell and Matthew J. Goodwin, 47–66. London: Routledge.

Hegghammer, Thomas. 2009. "Jihadi-Salafis or Revolutionaries? On Religion and Politics in the Study of Militant Islam." In *Global Salafism: Islam's New Religious Movement*, ed. R. Meijer, 244–66. New York: Columbia University Press.

Henne, Peter S. 2012. "The Ancient Fire: Religion and Suicide Terrorism." *Terrorism and Political Violence* 24: 38–60.

Jones, James W. 2008. *Blood That Cries Out from the Earth: The Psychology of Religious Terrorism*. New York: Oxford University Press.

Juergensmeyer, Mark. 2006. "Religion as a Cause of Terrorism." In *The Roots of Terrorism*, ed. Louise Richardson, 133–44. New York: Routledge.

Kühle, Lene, and Lasse Lindekilde. 2010. *Radicalization among Young Muslims in Aarhus*. Centre for Studies in Islamism and Radicalization, Department of Political Science, Aarhus University. http://cir.au.dk/fileadmin/site_files/filer_statskundskab/subsites/cir/radicalization_aarhus_FINAL.pdf.

McCauley, Clark, Christian Leuprecht, Todd Hataley, Conrad Winn, and Bidisha Biswas. 2011. "Tracking the War of Ideas: A Poll of Ottawa Muslims." *Terrorism and Political Violence* 23 (5): 804–19.

McCauley, Clark, and Sophia Moskalenko. 2011. *Friction: How Radicalization Happens to Them and Us*. New York: Oxford University Press.

McCauley, Clark, and Jennifer Stellar. 2009. *Living in America as a Muslim after 9/11: Poll Trends 2001–2007*. College Park, MD: START. http://www.start.umd.edu/start/.

Moghadam, Assaf. 2006. "Suicide Terrorism, Occupation, and the Globalization of Martyrdom: A Critique of 'Dying to Win.'" *Studies in Conflict and Terrorism* 29 (8): 707–29.

Neumann, Peter R. 2009. *Old and New Terrorism*. Cambridge: Polity Press.

Pape, Robert. 2005. *Dying to Win: The Strategic Logic of Suicide Terrorism*. New York: Random House.

Quilliam. 2010. "Radicalisation on British University Campuses: A Case Study." http://www.quilliamfoundation.org/radicalisation-on-british-university-campuses-a-case-study/.

Reader, Ian. 2000. *Religious Violence in Contemporary Japan: The Case of Aum Shinrikyō*. Honolulu: University of Hawai'i Press.

Schanzer, David, Charles Kurzman, and Ebrahim Moosa. 2010. *Anti-terror Lessons of Muslim-Americans*. National Institute of Justice, U.S. Department of Justice. https://www.ncjrs.gov/pdffiles1/nij/grants/229868.pdf.

Silke, Andrew. 2008. "Holy Warriors: Exploring the Psychological Processes of Jihadi Radicalization." *European Journal of Criminology* 5 (1): 99–123.

Slootman, Marieke, and Jean Tillie. 2006. *Processes of Radicalisation: Why Some Amsterdam Muslims Become Radicals*. Amsterdam: Institute for Migration and Ethnic Studies, Universiteit van Amsterdam. http://dare.uva.nl/document/337314.

Sobolewska, Maria. 2010. "Religious Extremism in Britain and British Muslims: Threatened Citizenship and the Role of Religion." In *The New Extremism in 21st Century Britain*, ed. Roger Eatwell and Matthew J. Goodwin, 23–46. London: Routledge.

Contributors

Amarnath Amarasingam is a Social Science and Humanities Research Council of Canada (SSHRC) Post-Doctoral Fellow in the Resilience Research Centre at Dalhousie University and also teaches at Wilfrid Laurier University and the University of Waterloo. He is the author of *Pain, Pride, and Politics: Sri Lankan Tamil Activism in Canada* (under contract with the University of Georgia Press). His research interests are in diaspora politics, post-war reconstruction, social movements, radicalization and terrorism, media studies, and the sociology of religion. He is the editor of *The Stewart/Colbert Effect: Essays on the Real Impacts of Fake News* (2011) and *Religion and the New Atheism: A Critical Appraisal* (2010). He is also the author of several peer-reviewed articles and book chapters, has presented papers at over 40 national and international conferences, and has contributed op-ed pieces to *Al-Jazeera English*, *The Daily Beast*, *The Toronto Star*, *The Huffington Post*, and *Groundviews*.

Valérie Amiraux is full professor of sociology at the University of Montreal, where she has held the Canada Research Chair for the Study of Religious Pluralism (CRSH) since 2007. She is on leave from her position as permanent research fellow at the National Center for Scientific Research in France (CNRS/CURAPP). Her main fields of research are sociology of religion, comparative politics, Muslim minorities, and discrimination. Current projects focus on the articulation between pluralism and radicalization, with a special emphasis on the interaction between majority societies, Jews, and Muslims in Europe and in Quebec. Another project looks at the legal controversies around religious signs in four EU member states.

Javiera Araya-Moreno holds a master's in sociology at the University of Montreal. She is the coordinator of the Canada Research Chair for the Study of Religious Pluralism and in particular the research team "Pluralism and Religious Radicalization in a Minority Context" (PLURADICAL), led by Valérie Amiraux. Her research interests include ethnographic and interaction-centred approaches. Her master's project focuses on the relationship between the state and non-citizen populations through an analysis of immigrant selection by the Canadian government.

Peter Beyer is professor of religious studies at the University of Ottawa, Canada. His work has focused primarily on religion in Canada and on developing sociological theory concerning religion and globalization. His publications include *Religion and Globalization* (Sage, 1994); *Religions in Global Society* (Routledge, 2006); *Religion, Globalization, and Culture* (edited with L. Beaman, Brill, 2007); and *Religious Diversity in Canada* (edited with L. Beaman, Brill, 2008). Since 2001 he has been conducting research on religious diversity in Canada and specifically on the religious expression of second-generation immigrant young adults in that country. From this research, he is principal author and editor, along with Rubina Ramji, of *Growing Up Canadian: Muslims, Hindus, Buddhists* (McGill-Queen's University Press, 2013).

Paul Bramadat is associate professor of religious studies and history, and director of the Centre for Studies in Religion and Society at the University of Victoria. He has published broadly on issues related to religious and ethnic diversity in Canada. He is the author of *The Church on the World's Turf: An Evangelical Christian Group at a Secular University* (Oxford, 2000) and editor of *International Migration and the Governance of Religious Diversity* (McGill-Queen's University Press, 2009, with Matthias Koenig), *Religion and Ethnicity in Canada* (Pearson, 2005, with David Seljak), and *Christianity and Ethnicity in Canada* (University of Toronto Press, 2008, with David Seljak). He is currently at work on several new initiatives including a project examining religious and cultural roots of vaccine refusal.

Lorne L. Dawson is a professor of sociology and religious studies at the University of Waterloo. He is currently chair of the Department of Sociology and Legal Studies and a past chair of the Department of Religious Studies. His research on millennialist movements and violent new religious movements led to numerous projects and publications on home-grown terrorist radicalization, including the 2010 article "The Study of New Religious Movements and the Radicalization of Home-grown Terrorists: Opening a Dialogue," in *Terrorism and Political Violence* 22. He has made many presentations on this subject to academic and government organizations in Canada, the United States, and Europe.

Doris R. Jakobsh, who holds degrees from the University of Waterloo, Harvard University, and the University of British Columbia, is associate professor in the Department of Religious Studies and is currently Acting Director of Women's Studies at the University of Waterloo. She has authored a number of articles and books including *Relocating Gender in Sikh History: Transformation, Meaning and Identity* (Oxford University Press, 2003) and *Sikhism* (University of Hawai'i Press, 2011) and is editor of *Women in Sikhism: History, Texts and Experience* (Oxford University Press, 2010) and *World Religions: Canadian Perspectives, Eastern and Western Traditions* (Nelson, Toronto, 2013), two volumes. Professor Jakobsh has served on the steering committee of the Sikh Consultation of the American Academy of Religion as well as numerous local and international editorial boards as well as advisory committees associated with the study of religion and Sikh studies.

Uzma Jamil is a research fellow at the International Centre for Muslim and Non-Muslim Understanding at the University of South Australia. Her research focuses on the social and political relations of Muslim minorities with non-Muslim majorities in Quebec and Canada. As a member of the McGill Transcultural Research and Intervention team, she has worked on several projects on the impact of the war-on-terror context for local Muslim families and communities. In addition to her publications on this topic, she has also published on the securitization of Muslims in the war on terror and the construction of Muslim subjectivities.

Edna Keeble is professor and chair of the Department of Political Science at Saint Mary's University in Halifax. Her work has focused on security and has broadly covered the themes of national security, feminist definitions of security, and human security. She is a recipient of three teaching awards and was the Saint Mary's 2008–9 Teaching Scholar. She has served in an advisory role to the Canadian government in several capacities, including membership on the advisory board for Canada's Foreign Affairs Minister Lloyd Axworthy (1997–2000), the Canada Border Services Advisory Committee (2007–10), and the federal government's Cross-Cultural Roundtable on Security (2005–8), which advises the Public Safety and Justice Ministers.

Sean Norton is a defence scientist who conducts multidisciplinary, policy-relevant research on issues related to public safety and national security on behalf of Defence Research and Development Canada (DRDC). His current areas of research explore domestic violent extremism with particular emphasis on the social features of home-grown violent extremists, processes governing involvement in extremist organizations, and risk assessment methodologies. Other research domains combine quantitative and qualitative approaches to research on disaster response, security operations, and military human resource issues. Mr Norton holds postgraduate degrees in sociology and international development studies in addition to training in anthropological theory and methods and earning a degree in economics.

Ian Reader is currently professor of religious studies at Lancaster University. He previously was professor of Japanese studies at the University of Manchester and has also held academic positions at the University of Stirling, the University of Hawai'i, the Nordic Institute for Asian Studies in Denmark, and various universities in Japan. He is author of several books, including *Pilgrimage in the Marketplace* (Routledge, 2014), *Making Pilgrimages: Meaning and Practice in Shikoku* (University of Hawai'i Press, 2005), and *Religious Violence in Contemporary Japan: The Case of Aum Shinrikyō* (University of Hawai'i Press, 2000), and numerous journal articles and book chapters on topics including religion in Japan, religion and violence, and pilgrimage in comparative contexts. His current research interests focus on religion, violence, and terrorism in global contexts and on the production and consumption of pilgrimage in the modern world.

Joyce Smith is an associate professor in the School of Journalism at Ryerson University, where she has directed the graduate program. Prior to her arrival in 2001 as the first faculty member specializing in online journalism, she was the features editor for globeandmail.com. A graduate of the University of Toronto, the University of Western Ontario, and the University of Natal (where she was a Rotary International Ambassadorial Scholar), Joyce has conducted research into religion and journalism as practised in South Africa, the United States, and Canada, including as a Rockefeller Foundation Fellow.

M. Afzal Upal is leader of the Effects and Influence Research Group at Defence Research and Development Canada's Socio-cognitive Systems Section. Prior to joining DRDC, Dr Upal worked as professor of cognitive science at Occidental College in Los Angeles. In the last ten years, he has published 65 peer-reviewed research articles in the areas of cognitive science of religion, cognition and culture, and concept learning. He was chair of the 14th Annual Meeting of the North American Association for Computational Social and Organizational Sciences, the Cognitive Science Society Workshop on Cognition and Culture, and the AAAI Workshop on Cognitive Modelling and Agent-based Simulation.

Index